# Applied Social Care

## An Introduction for Irish Students

*Edited by*

PERRY SHARE & NIALL McELWEE

GILL & MACMILLAN

Gill & Macmillan
Hume Avenue
Park West
Dublin 12
with associated companies throughout the world
www.gillmacmillan.ie

0 7171 3839 9

Index compiled by Cover to Cover
Print origination in Ireland by Carrigboy Typesetting Services, Co. Cork


The paper used in this book is made from the wood pulp of managed forests. For every
tree felled, at least one is planted, thereby renewing natural resources.

A catalogue record is available for this book from the British Library.

# Contents

# Contributors

**Teresa Brown**
Has extensive front-line experience in residential childcare, project work and community childcare. Has presented at national level and currently sits on the practicum subcommittee of the Irish Association of Social Care Educators [IASCE]. Has particular interests in student placements and in Romanian child and youth care systems.

**John Byrne**
Lecturer in applied social studies, advanced childcare and professional and personal development at Waterford Institute of Technology and St Patrick's College, Carlow. Coordinator of the Irish Association of Social Care Workers [IASCW] and manager of a residential children's home with Community Children's Centres in Co. Wicklow.

**Dr Grant Charles**
Assistant Professor at the University of British Columbia, Canada. Has worked in a variety of mental health, special education and child welfare settings. He has been the director of a number of specialised community and residential treatment programmes working with such diverse client groups as adolescent sexual offenders, aboriginal adolescent solvent abusers and other hard-to-serve young people and their families.

**Dr Sinéad Conneely**
Lecturer in law at Waterford Institute of Technology. Her research interests are in the areas of family and child law, particularly the area of family mediation. She is a member of the Centre for Social and Family Research at the Institute.

**Damien Cussen**
Lectures on the philosophy of science and communications in the Department of Social and General Studies at Cork Institute of Technology. Founder member of the college's interdisciplinary journal, *Tableau*; its fourth edition on the subject of ethics is due for publication in October 2005.

**Dr Áine de Róiste**
Lecturer in psychology at the Cork Institute of Technology and coordinator of the BA(Hons) full-time course in social care. Has worked as a psychologist with

infants at-risk and has a wide range of publications in child and adolescent psychology. Currently undertaking research commissioned by the National Children's Office into adolescent recreation and leisure.

### Rose Doolan
Lecturer and course coordinator for applied social studies at the Blanchardstown Institute of Technology. Has worked as a social care practitioner since 1994, with experience of working with service user groups from a variety of different social care environments nationally and internationally.

### Judy Doyle
Lecturer in the Department of Social Science and Legal Studies, Dublin Institute of Technology. Has worked as a social care practitioner and manager in residential childcare for sixteen years, and has been involved in team facilitation, consultancy, and supervision with social care practitioners and managers. Currently working on her PhD with the Department of Equality Studies, University College Dublin.

### Karen Finnerty
Director of the Open Training College. Has fifteen years' experience of working in the disability sector in Ireland encompassing first-line, management, training, education and consultancy positions. Areas of interest include disability service management, strategic management, leadership and quality. Former editor of *Frontline* magazine and has extensive experience of developing open learning materials in the area of disability.

### Cormac Forkan
Lecturer in the Department of Political Science and Sociology at NUI, Galway, based at St Angela's College, Sligo. Formerly course leader for the National Diploma in Applied Social Studies at Waterford IT. Research centres on family systems and support, independent-living facilities for the elderly and the participation and attainment of Travellers in Education. The concept of Irish national identity is the focus for his doctorate.

### Carmel Gallagher
Lecturer in sociology at the Dublin Institute of Technology. Completing a PhD on the participation of older people in their communities and was awarded a Government of Ireland Senior Research Scholarship for this work in 2002. Has presented papers at conferences both in Ireland and abroad and has a number of publications.

### Dr Thom Garfat
Has been working in child and youth care for over thirty years as a front-line practitioner, supervisor and director in residential and non-residential programmes, an instructor for colleges and universities and has participated in numerous

conferences and training events around the world. Co-founder and co-editor of *CYC-Net* and an International Fellow of the Centre for Child & Youth Care Learning.

### Pelle Hallstedt
Lecturer in social work in the Department of Social Work, Malmö University, Sweden. His research area is in the Sociology of Education. With Mats Högström he is involved in a project that compares three Social Care educational programmes in the Netherlands, Ireland, and Norway.

### Mats Högström
Lecturer in social work in the Department of Social Work, Malmö University, Sweden. His research area is in the Sociology of Education. With Pelle Hallstedt he is involved in a project that compares three Social Care educational programmes in the Netherlands, Ireland, and Norway.

### Ashling Jackson
Lecturer in sociology and community development in the Department of Humanities, Athlone Institute of Technology. Formerly public health research officer with the Midland Health Board. Has published nationally and internationally in the area of health and social care. Currently completing a PhD in the sociology of the family.

### Dr Kevin Lalor
Head of Department of Social Sciences at the Dublin Institute of Technology. Has extensive experience as a tutor to social care students and has conducted hundreds of site visits to social care agencies throughout the country. Current research interests include the needs/views of young people towards delivery of services and the role of child sexual abuse in HIV transmission in sub-Saharan Africa.

### Dr Celesta McCann James
President of the Irish Association of Social Care Educators (IASCE) and Head of Department of Humanities at the Institute of Technology, Blanchardstown. Originally from California, worked in a long-term secure residential unit for juveniles in Orange County before moving to Dublin. Her research relates to oppression and the social world of women in prison. She has also researched and published on social policies regarding paid work and family initiatives; women returning to formal education; and ethical issues related to cultural diversity and the professional provision of social care.

### Dr Niall McElwee
Author of several books and national reports in the area of child and youth care. Founding editor of the *Irish Journal of Applied Social Studies* and past President of

the Irish Association of Social Care Educators [IASCE]. Director of the Centre for Child and Youth Care Learning at Athlone IT and a regular visitor to North America where he lectures and consults.

### Patrick McGarty
Head of Department of Business and Humanities at the Institute of Technology, Tralee. Has extensive experience of the development of social care education programmes at Athlone, Blanchardstown and Tralee ITs. A founder of the Irish Association of Social Care Educators [IASCE]. Research interests include the management of change and the development of leadership and teamwork in organisations.

### John McHugh
Coordinator of social studies at St. Patrick's College, Carlow. Previously worked as placement co-ordinator and compiled the *Working Models* placement guidelines booklets published by IASCE in 2000 and subsequently. Has extensive experience in social care practice in residential and community-based projects.

### Susan McKenna
Has lectured with both the Athlone and Waterford Institutes of Technology social care programmes and has extensive front-line and management experience of caring environments and in therapeutic community childcare. A consultant practitioner with the *Irish Journal of Applied Social Studies* and currently works in management.

### Danny Meenan
Seconded from Health Services Executive, North West Area as coordinator of the IT Sligo work-based BA in Applied Social Studies. Lectures in professional practice, social administration and management. Has worked as a social care practitioner and manager for over sixteen years in residential childcare in both Northern Ireland and the Republic of Ireland. Completed the MBA in Health Services Management in 2002.

### Eileen O Neill
Independent trainer and consultant with broad experience in social care, having worked extensively in both community and residential services. Now provides training, consultancy, professional development and team development programmes in the social care and healthcare sectors. Has a particular interest in and experience of professional supervision and has published and presented extensively at conferences on this topic. Is currently working on a practice-based model to evaluate professional supervision. Her book, *Professional Supervision: Myths, Culture and Structure*, was published by the RMA in 2004.

**Dr Colm O'Doherty**
Lecturer in applied social studies at the Institute of Technology, Tralee. Has held major responsibilities as a social worker in England, Wales and Ireland. Left social work to take on a pivotal role in social work, youth work and community work education at University College Cork. Then moved to IT Tralee to develop a range of courses in the social studies field. Completed his PhD in 2004. His research interests are in the possibility of developing family support practices that draw on the concept of social capital.

**Jacqueline O'Toole**
Lecturer in the Department of Humanities at the Institute of Technology, Sligo with teaching interests in social research, qualitative methodology, gender and sexuality and women's studies. Currently engaged in funded research into the development of a cross-border access programme for women. Her PhD research explores women's perspectives on and experiences of their bodies.

**Dr Perry Share**
Head of Department of Humanities and lecturer in sociology at the Institute of Technology, Sligo. Co-author of *A Sociology of Ireland* (2 editions, Gill and Macmillan, 2003) and maintains the Irish Social Care Gateway on behalf of the Irish Association of Social Care Educators [IASCE]. Research interests are in the fields of education, social policy and the sociology of food and eating.

# Part I

## The Field of Social Care

1

# What is Social Care?

Perry Share & Niall McElwee

## OVERVIEW OF THE CHAPTER AND THE BOOK

There's a good chance you are reading this book because you are thinking about becoming, or planning to be, or already are, a social care practitioner. Yet for many people in Irish society, even those entering the field themselves, the meaning of the term 'social care' is not self-evident. A common question directed at social care students and professionals alike is, 'What do you do?' Misconceptions abound, and in many cases practitioners are not accorded the respect or status they deserve, at least in part as a consequence of a limited understanding of what the term means.

Part of the blame for this situation lies with the educators in the field. Though the first social care training course (in residential child care) was established in Kilkenny as far back as 1970, there has been a dearth of authoritative written material related to the area. As we indicate in Chapter 4, social care syllabi have been forced to draw on fragments of knowledge from social work, sociology, social policy, psychology and a broad range of other disciplines. Most of this knowledge was obtained from outside the country, largely from Britain. This text represents the first integrated attempt by the educators and practitioners in the social care field in Ireland to define and describe the practice of social care. We hope that it will stimulate much debate and further research and writing by students, practitioners, academics and service users. We hope that if this book were to be reissued in 2015, nobody would need to ask the question, 'What is social care?'

This opening chapter briefly explores the notion of social care itself. It opens with an examination of some definitions, taking these apart phrase by phrase to see what is involved. Then it provides a very short history of social care in Ireland, placing the current set of institutions and practices in a historical context. The bulk of the chapter describes aspects of social care practice itself: what qualities do practitioners possess, what sort of work is involved, what do practitioners do — and where do they do it? How much do they get paid and what is the difference between a social care practitioner and a social worker? It is hoped that this opening chapter will answer some of those basic questions voiced by students, practitioners and others.

The chapters of the book fall into four sections. In Part 1 (Chapters 1–4), we attempt to sketch out the parameters of the field, drawing on experience in Ireland, Europe and North America. It will become clear that the practice of social care, while common across contemporary developed societies, has different nuances and emphases. These very much reflect the different political and social systems experienced across the world. You are encouraged to view social care practice in this international context; it is always desirable to see what is happening elsewhere, in particular to draw upon international best practice, but also to be aware of national traditions, histories and particularities. The section closes with a discussion of the issue of professionalism in social care — a very important theme that you will no doubt encounter at every stage of studying in this field.

Part 2 of the book (Chapters 5–8) identifies some of the theoretical bases on which social care practice is based. These include ideas drawn from psychology, sociology, philosophy and ethics. The theory base of social care practice is an evolving one, and the years to come will see the emergence in Ireland of an ever more distinctive body of knowledge and thought. This will be inextricably linked to the development of professionalism.

Part 3 (Chapters 9–17) focuses on practice issues. These range from the key role of the law, to work-based practices such as student placement and workplace supervision, to specific aspects of practice such as teamwork and aftercare. This is an eclectic section, the aim of which is to provide some knowledge about and insight into the realities of social care practice, as well as linking that practice to theory.

Part 4 (Chapters 18–23) examines social care work with particular social groups, from older people to communities. You will see that there are common themes that span social care practice — respect for those with whom social care practitioners work; a close relationship to the life-worlds of others — but also very particular skills and approaches associated with working with people within specific social structures and circumstances. Social care is becoming an ever more complex mosaic, and this section tries to illuminate some of the pieces that help to make it up.

## DEFINITIONS

The literature often refers to social care as a *form of practice*. At various times, writers have described the uniqueness of the field and even its 'magic' (Garfat, 1988). But what is social care? For a number of reasons it is quite difficult to define. Undeniably it has suited governments and some agencies *not* to have a standard definition: as a consequence, salary and career structures have remained vague for some time. A further, and linked, problem is the contested notion of social care as a profession. There is something of a chicken-and-egg situation here: it is hard to define social care because of the lack of a clear professional grouping to whom we can point as 'doing social care'; this in turn makes it hard to pin down what social care might be.

We hope that by the time you have read this book, and certainly by the time you qualify as a social care practitioner, you will have formed a clearer idea of what social care means. Inevitably, though, this understanding will be complex: you will have become aware of social care's flexible nature; its contested position vis-à-vis other practices and occupations (such as nursing, social work, counselling, occupational therapy and so on); and, above all, its dynamism. Social care is a rapidly changing and developing field, in Ireland as elsewhere. We hope that you will pick up something of this dynamism from this book, from your studies, and from your own practical experience.

Below we offer a variety of definitions/descriptions of social care. These have emerged from attempts by a number of key bodies in the field to clarify what social care is. These attempts at clarification have largely emerged for pragmatic reasons: the bodies concerned are closely involved in the provision of, management of, or funding of social care, or in the education and training of its practitioners — they have a strong stake in attempting to define it. As a possible future — or current — practitioner, you will also have a strong interest in how to define the field you are entering.

A basic definition agreed by the Irish Association of Social Care Educators [IASCE], the body that represents the educators in the field, runs as follows:

> [social care is] a profession committed to the planning and delivery of quality care and other support services for individuals and groups with identified needs.

We can see some key terms here that help to mark out the territory of social care practice. These include:

- *a profession*
  This implies that social care is not just an ordinary job, nor is it something that is done on a voluntary or amateur basis. This distinguishes it from the vast bulk of (equally valuable) care that is carried out informally in our society by family and community members. The notion of 'professionalism' also implies that this is an occupation with some status and one that requires access to a specific body of skills and knowledge. The complex issue of professionalism is discussed in detail in Chapter 4.

- *planning and delivery*
  Social care is not just about providing services, but also about devising and planning them. It thus requires at least two types of skill and understanding: the ability to provide 'hands-on' care and support to people, but also the ability to identify what people require and to be able to plan accordingly. This dual role makes social care practice difficult and challenging, yet also rewarding.

- *quality care and other support services*
  Social care is indeed about care, and it requires qualities of compassion, empathy, patience and resilience. But it is also about providing other supports,

which may include advocating on behalf of another, turning up in court to speak before a judge, or knowing where to refer a person who has particular problems.

- *individuals and groups*
  Social care can be, and often is, provided in a one-to-one situation, but it can also mean working with small or large groups of people, As a result, both interpersonal communication skills and a knowledge of group dynamics are required.

- *with identified needs*
  The traditional 'client group' of social care practitioners in Ireland (and many other countries) has been children in the care of state or voluntary organisations. While caring for this group remains an important task, social care practitioners may now find work with a broad range of groups that have had special 'needs' identified. The needs and the groups are various, as we will see. Of course, there may be people whose needs have *not* previously been identified, or have been identified only recently — for example, survivors of clerical sexual abuse, or children with hyperactivity disorders. Our society has only recently recognised and identified the needs that such people have, and sought to respond to them. This helps to explain why social care is a constantly changing field of practice.

We can see that even a single sentence can constitute quite a complex definition. Two further definitions cast a little extra light on what social care might be, and what social care practitioners might do.

The following definition comes from the IASCE brochure 'What is Social Care?' which is distributed to guidance teachers and other members of the public. It defines social care thus:

> Social care is an (emerging) profession characterised by working in partnership with people who experience marginalisation or disadvantage or who have 'special needs'. Social care practitioners may work, for example, with children and adolescents in residential care; people with learning or physical disabilities; people who are homeless; people with alcohol/drug dependency; families in the community; older people; recent immigrants to Ireland; and others. Typically, although not always, social care practitioners work with children, youth and their families.

There are some additional terms here that are significant:

- *working in partnership*
  The notion of partnership is important. Social care aims to be not a 'top down' practice, but one that respects the position of the 'client' or 'service user'. In other

words, all are equal, working together to find solutions to various challenges. In practice, this aim may not be attained, and the extent to which it is provides much debate in social care.

- *marginalisation or disadvantage*
These terms draw attention to the 'social' aspect of social care. They refer to the structures of society that help to create the problems that people face. This is a rejection of the 'blame the victim' approach; it seeks answers to problems, at least partially, in the unequal and discriminatory areas of our society, such as poverty, racism, sexism or violence.

- *people with learning or physical disabilities; people who are homeless; people with alcohol/drug dependency; families in the community; older people; recent immigrants to Ireland*
This list illustrates some of the people with whom social care practitioners work. Generally what they have in common is that they are less powerful in Irish society, experience various forms of disadvantage, and often suffer through discrimination. It is not an exhaustive list, as will become clear in the course of this book.

- *children, youth and their families*
This draws attention to the *holistic* nature of social care practice. Often it involves working not just with an individual, but with a network of people, whether a couple, a family or a group. This is another way of emphasising the 'social' in social care.

A third definition of social care is offered by the Joint Committee on Social Care Professionals. This committee was set up in 2001 in the wake of a number of Labour Court recommendations. These followed a period of industrial unrest in the social care sector. Part of the task of the Joint Committee was to agree a definition of a social care practitioner, so that government and employers would be better able to decide on what they did, what their status was vis-à-vis other occupations and, ultimately, how much to pay them. The Joint Committee defined social care as:

> the professional provision of care, protection, support, welfare and advocacy for vulnerable or dependent clients, individually or in groups. This is achieved through the planning and evaluation of individualised and group programmes of care, which are based on needs, identified where possible in consultation with the client and delivered through day-to-day shared life experiences. All interventions are based on established best practice and in-depth knowledge of life-span development. (JCSCP, n.d.: 13)

We can see that many of the terms used here are similar to those in the other definitions, but there are some extra important features:

- *day-to-day shared life experiences*
  This refers to an important aspect of social care work. It is an aspect that for many practitioners is a key defining element of their work: that they interact with those with whom they are working in a relatively informal, extended and intimate way. This can be contrasted, for example, with a doctor who may see a patient for just as long as it takes to provide a diagnosis or carry out a procedure. Social care practitioners sometimes (not always) live for a period of time in the same space as those with whom they work, interact with them in normal daily activities, and get to know them on a much deeper level. A number of chapters of this book (such as Chapters 8 and 16) draw attention to this crucial dimension of social care practice.

- *established best practice*
  Social care practice is not dreamed up in response to a given problem. Rather it should draw on established models and knowledge about how to work in given situations. Much of the education of social care practitioners concentrates on helping them to develop their knowledge and expertise regarding what to do in given situations; this is learned at both a theoretical and a practical level. Both are vital.

- *in-depth knowledge of life-span development*
  Much of the expertise of social care is in knowing how people change and develop over time, and how that development is interlinked with the actions and attitudes of others, particularly families and communities. This knowledge has psychological, sociological, physiological and philosophical dimensions.

At this stage, we have discussed several elements that you could assemble to create a 'perfect' definition of social care. To some extent, this will help you to understand what social care is. But it is also the case that the reality of social care practice does not always adhere tightly to the definition. Sometimes the elements outlined above are ideals that may never be attained in practice. Often, particular elements are favoured in specific situations. There are also quite political debates and disagreements over what social care *should* be (some of these are explored in Chapter 2). So, we suggest that you make use of these ideas to examine carefully and think about any examples of social care practice that you encounter, either directly or through reading and research. Ask yourself which aspects are brought to the foreground. How could things be done differently? How could they be done better?

In the broader European context, social care work is usually referred to as *social pedagogy* and social care practitioners as *social pedagogues*. In the United States and Canada, the term 'child and youth care' (abbreviated as CYC) is commonly used with the derivation child and youth care worker. The social care contexts of Europe and North America are explored in some detail in the next two chapters.

## A BRIEF HISTORY OF SOCIAL CARE IN IRELAND

In order to understand what social care *is*, it is important to understand where it has *come* from. Modern social care in Ireland was born out of 'serious deficiencies in the running of children's centres . . . and the recognition of the need for professionally trained staff' (Kennedy and Gallagher, 1997). Social care was historically provided by the Catholic Church and was unregulated until very recently. For example, pre-school regulations were introduced only in 1996, after decades of both public and private provision. The 1908 Children's Act provided the legislative framework for child care in Ireland for the greater part of the twentieth century but, by 1991, the social and political situation with regard to children *at risk* had changed significantly as a result of a number of phenomena.

The 1991 Child Care Act is in total contrast to the 1908 Act which simply imposed negative duties to rescue children who had criminal offences committed against them, or who were being cruelly treated. Specifically the 1991 Act recognises that the welfare of the child is the first and paramount consideration (Part II, section 3:2, b). The rights and duties of parents are important, but due consideration must be given to the child's wishes.

Several influential reports have been published that have helped to shape the development of social care. These have been extensively reviewed and described by a range of writers (see, for example, Gilligan, 1991; Ferguson and Kenny, 1995; McElwee, 2001a). The most significant reports were the *Tuairim Report* (1966), the *Kennedy Report* (DoE, 1970) and the *Task Force Report on Child Care Services* (1980). All commented on aspects of social care provision and were influential in deciding on the type of education and training that social care practitioners should receive. In turn, this has led to changes in the skill-sets of practitioners, with less emphasis on some 'practical' skills (such as home-making and health care) and a greater emphasis on research, policy issues and academic knowledge. There has been — and still is — much debate about the virtues or otherwise of such a shift.

Social care has long been associated with residential child care. This emphasis has changed, especially with the decline of large institutions and the emergence of alternatives such as foster care and community childcare. In recent years, the field of social care has expanded greatly, in Ireland as elsewhere. It has been acknowledged that the types of skills and knowledge that social care practitioners exhibit can be constructively applied in other areas — such as in many aspects of the care of those with disabilities; in working with older people; and in responding to the needs of a very broad range of people from drug users to victims of domestic violence to refugees. Inevitably this brings social care practitioners into contact with other professions, including medical professionals, social workers and the

Garda Síochána. Participation by social care practitioners within multi-disciplinary professional teams is now quite common.

## WHAT PERSONAL QUALITIES DOES A SOCIAL CARE PRACTITIONER REQUIRE?

We can see from the definitions explored earlier that a social care practitioner has to have a broad range of personal and intellectual attributes. 'Academic' qualities include: a broad knowledge base in their field; the ability to work both independently and as part of a team; research skills; and a problem-solving approach. Much of social care education and training aims to assist students in developing these skills. The research outlined in Chapter 2 suggests that different attributes are seen as more important in different societies. In Ireland, for example, it is suggested that the ability to work as part of a team and to fit in to an organisation is seen as important, while in the Netherlands there is a lot more focus on the practitioner as an independent but accountable professional. It may be interesting to discuss why these differences in emphasis exist.

In addition, certain personal attributes tend to characterise practitioners — such as reliability and trustworthiness; altruism; empathy and compassion; and maturity. Social care practitioners must be open-minded and prepared to examine and perhaps even change their own attitudes towards others. It can be debated whether these qualities can be taught, or are somehow 'innate' in people who are attracted to social care practice as an occupation. Again, education and training may seek to emphasise and develop these qualities. But we can legitimately ask: Are good social care practitioners born not made?

As in all professions, there are several stages through which individual social care practitioners evolve. The developmental stage of the worker becomes defined in the context of interactions with others. As Garfat suggests:

> movement between stages represents a transformation in how the worker perceives, and acts within, interactions with the [client], in the context in which those interactions occur. The worker, in essence, experiences a transformation of perspective . . . Being, and doing, are modified as a result of this transformation of perspective. (Garfat, 2001: 4)

How a social care practitioner develops as a person and as a professional depends on a number of things:

- The quality of the practice environment
- The quality and consistency of professional supervision
- The philosophy of one's work peers towards the work, service users and their families
- The ability to be self-reflective in one's work

- The ability to take constructive criticism and turn this into 'best practice'
- A determination to keep up-to-date in reading and new approaches to work
- A willingness to be an advocate for the profession.

## WHAT QUALIFICATIONS DOES A SOCIAL CARE PRACTITIONER NEED?

In the Republic of Ireland, the professional qualification for social care practice is currently (2005) a three-year Ordinary Degree in Applied Social Studies. Many qualified practitioners go on to complete an Honours Degree in the field, and an increasing number progress to postgraduate qualifications. Professional-level courses in social care are offered at the Institutes of Technology in Athlone, Blanchardstown, Cork, Dublin, Dundalk, Limerick, Sligo, Tralee and Waterford, and at the Carlow College, as well as through the Open Training College (based in Goatstown, Co. Dublin, and specialising in the field of disability).

The government has indicated that in the near future all those wishing to work in the social care field will have to be professionally qualified — the BA Degree in Applied Social Studies will be the basic entry qualification. It is expected that those who are 'unqualified' will have to acquire the basic qualification. This is a major challenge to government and to bodies that employ social care workers.

A course of study in social care typically includes subjects such as sociology, psychology, social administration and policy, principles of professional practice, law, creative skills (art, drama, music, dance, recreation) and research methods. Many courses offer specialised modules in particular areas, such as community, youth or disability studies.

A key element of studying to be a professional social care practitioner is involvement in a number of supervised work practice placements of several months' duration. Some students already working in the field ('in-service students') may undertake their placements at work, closely supervised.

Social care students are challenged to develop academically through deepening their knowledge — professionally, by learning and practising social care skills; and personally, by developing a capacity to look at their own strengths and weaknesses in relation to the work.

## WHAT DO SOCIAL CARE PRACTITIONERS DO?

So, what do social care practitioners actually do? Anglin (1992) has observed that they work in two main areas:

*Direct Service to Clients*
- Individual intervention, counselling or therapy
- Group intervention, counselling or therapy
- In-home family intervention, counselling or therapy

- Office-based family intervention, counselling or therapy
- Assessment of child
- Assessment of family
- Child management
- Child abuse interventions
- Employment counselling or assistance
- Life-skills training
- Health management
- Education remediation
- Recreational leadership
- Arts and crafts leadership
- Counselling on death, dying
- Therapeutic play
- Parenting skill training
- Sexuality counselling
- Marriage counselling
- Stress management
- Lifestyle modification.

*Organisational Activities*
- Case management
- Client contracting
- Report writing and formal recording
- Court appearances/legal documentation
- Programme planning and development
- Use and interpretation of policy
- Individual consultation with other professionals
- Participation in professional teams
- Coordination of professional teams
- Contracting for services
- Supervision of staff, students or volunteers
- Staff training and development
- Public relations/community education
- Organisational analysis and development
- Policy analysis and development
- Financial analysis/budgeting.

A quick scan of the above lists will reveal the diversity of the role of a social care practitioner. If we were to prioritise, we might suggest that the main role of the practitioner is to *work alongside* service users to maximise their growth and development. The social care practitioner is also, crucially, an advocate for change.

## WHERE DO SOCIAL CARE PRACTITIONERS WORK?

In Ireland, social care practitioners may be employed in the state (statutory) sector (for example, for the Departments of Health and Children; Education and Science; or Justice, Equality and Law Reform); in what is termed the non-governmental sector (in organisations such as Barnardos, the Brothers of Charity, Enable Ireland and Focus Ireland, among others — many of which are, in practice, fully or partially funded by government); or in community-based organisations (such as community development projects or Garda youth diversion projects).

The Joint Committee on Social Care Professionals (JCSCP, n.d.) enumerated some 2,904 social care practitioners working across various sectors including community child care (71), staff in children's residential centres (1,214) and staff in intellectual disability services (1,619). Of these, just over 55 per cent hold what might be termed a professional qualification, with 14 per cent holding no quali-fications at all. This is similar to McElwee's (2000) findings in the residential childcare sector, which also enumerated 14 per cent of staff (or 105 practitioners) with no formal qualifications.

Social care practitioners make valuable contributions in emergent and devel-oping areas such as community development; Garda and community youth projects; women's refuges; County Childcare Committees; care of older persons; research and policy work. The breadth of chapters in this book reflects some of this diversity, though statistics for the numbers working in such areas are hard to come by.

In the new millennium, there has been a surge in the number of students applying for social care courses, paralleled by a dramatic expansion in the number of colleges that offer such an education. There is a danger of saturation at ordinary degree level and it is likely that this will ultimately lead to the development of more specialised courses in the future, with individual educational courses focusing on different aspects of care. Similarly students will probably elect to study for more specialised programmes at Higher Diploma and Masters levels.

At the same time, as indicated by the Joint Committee on Social Care Professionals, the pathways towards a social care education and training are increasingly diverse, and include school leavers entering courses through CAO and other routes; those with other qualifications seeking credit for prior learning; experienced workers already in the field but with no formal qualifications; and persons entering the profession as mature students with flexible training methods (JCSCP, n.d.: 21). Most social care courses actively recruit mature students (23+ years) and those who have completed relevant FETAC and BTEC/Edexcel courses within the further education sector.

## SALARY SCALES

Research suggests that in the human services, financial remuneration is not considered to be as important in determining career choice as job satisfaction, autonomy and working with people (McElwee, Jackson, McKenna-McElwee and

Cameron, 2003). Nonetheless, the salary scales for qualified social care practitioners were reviewed in 2001 and jumped by as much as 33 per cent. Previously, the salary scales ran from £16,761 (€21,300) to £22,900 (€29,000) for social care practitioners from base to house-parent status. This was a short salary scale, with little opportunity for personal or professional development, and did not entice people to enter or, importantly, to remain in the sector (McElwee, 2000).

Currently (as of 2005) salaries are in the region of €28,000 to €39,000 per annum plus allowances. Salary scales for more senior positions, such as childcare leaders, are in the region of €38,000 to €44,000 per annum plus allowances. It is of note that salary scales for broadly the same work can often differ quite considerably between the voluntary and statutory sectors.

## SOCIAL CARE: A CHALLENGING OCCUPATION

Social care work can be very challenging — emotionally and physically — and can mean working in some very difficult environments, but it can also be uniquely rewarding (see Chapter 16). Forewarned is forearmed, as they say. For example, the profile of children in residential care may often include multiple loss, rejection, deprivation, neglect and abuse. As a consequence, there can be a large gulf between desires, expectations and reality. An example of this might be working with young offenders in a custodial setting (such as a secure unit) where those in the service-user group (a) do not want to be there in the first instance; (b) have been removed from their place of origin and their families; (c) are locked up for a good part of the day; (d) are distrustful and resentful of perceived authority figures; and (e) are facing lengthy sentences. Here the work of the social care practitioner calls for a unique mix of skills and personal attributes.

*Risk* is now synonymous with child protection and welfare (Bessant, 2004). Attention is increasingly directed at what are variously termed 'high risk', 'high challenge' and 'at risk' children, with a child protection service concentrated on an even smaller number of cases at the heavy end of the (perceived) spectrum of risk. At the same time, professionals feel that they have been targeted by a media insistent on sensationalising stories of neglect. This can add to a general feeling of crisis and despair amongst professionals and the public (McElwee, 2000).

Neither is it uncommon for social care practitioners to fail to receive formal supervision on a regular basis; to receive verbal and sometimes physical abuse from service users; to work in under-resourced areas; not to report to their own peers; and to work unsocial hours. With increasing professionalisation and regulation of the field, there is a hope that many of these issues will be addressed in the future.

# WHAT IS THE DIFFERENCE BETWEEN A SOCIAL CARE PRACTITIONER AND A SOCIAL WORKER?

A common question asked by students relates to the difference between social care and social work. There are several differences. Social care practitioners train in the HETAC/DIT system, whereas social workers train in the university system. Social work training was always at degree level, whereas the social care degree came into being only in 1995. It was the norm to have professionally qualified social workers as part of teaching teams in the education of the next generation, but this became the norm in social care only towards the latter part of the 1990s.

Perhaps the major difference between social care and social work lies in the work orientation (Table 1.1). *Social care practitioners* will typically work in a direct person-to-person capacity with the users of services, sometimes called 'clients' and other times called 'service users'. They will seek to provide a caring, stable environment in which various social, educational and relationship interventions can take place in the day-to-day living space of the service user. An emphasis is on therapeutic work, but not in the context of more formal structured counselling.

The *social worker's* role is typically to manage the 'case' — for example, by arranging the residential placement setting in which a child is placed, coordinating case review meetings and negotiating the termination of a placement.

Table 1.1. Differences between Social Work and Social Care Work

| *Social work* focuses more on | *Social care work* focuses more on |
|---|---|
| • social and community networks<br>• social problems<br>• organisations and policies<br>• knowing about children and families<br>• a wide variety of societal groups and issues<br>• problem solving<br>• gaining power and societal influence | • individual and interpersonal dynamics<br>• human development<br>• people and relationships<br>• living and working with children and families<br>• specific needs of particular groups<br>• helping and growth process<br>• gaining self-awareness and personal growth |

*Source:* based on Anglin, 2001: 2.

It is possible for those with a degree in social care to qualify as a social workers via the postgraduate route. Universities may, and do, accept the BA (Hons) in Applied Social Studies as a basis for application to their postgraduate social work courses. There is no guarantee of entry and the universities continue to select their students according to their own criteria.

## CONCLUSION

Social care is a growth area in Ireland. It is demanding but rewarding because social care practitioners make a real difference in the lives of others. Formal social care had humble beginnings — located within a largely clerical or philanthropic context — but has expanded to include both the statutory and voluntary sectors. Social care practitioners are now trained and educated to degree level in thirteen colleges located across the country. Salaries and career structures have seen an immense improvement in recent times. The management and reporting structures in social care practice are moving towards an acceptance of the social care practitioner as an independent, autonomous professional. There is no better time to enter the social care profession in Ireland!

# 2
# Social Care: A European Perspective

Pelle Hallstedt & Mats Högström

## OVERVIEW

European curricula in social care have been designed in many different ways. Personal development has at times been given much space. Organisation and leadership are other fields that have been considered important. Some courses have tended to focus on the best way to be a proficient social care practitioner. In recent years, there has been a strong tendency to raise the academic or theoretical level of the curricula — the contents of study programmes have been changed. But what factors influence the content and design of social care curricula? Why do study programmes in social care vary in different countries? What is the impact of the content and design of the curricula on social care as it is carried out in the work field?

In this chapter, based on our current research (Hallstedt and Högström, 2004), we inquire into these questions. There are many possible answers. It is quite likely that the predominant model of social care practice in a country will influence the content of social care curricula, but this is not the only factor to influence what is included in the educational programmes. Other factors also contribute to decisions about what it is possible to insert into or erase from curricula — factors such as discourses of education and the academy; of professionalisation; and of marketisation. The following examination of the experience in a number of European countries aims to provide an insight into such interconnections. This may help you to place your own experience of social care education and practice in a broader context.

We first of all focus on the relationship between the social political system and the curriculum. Second, we refer to current discussions about social care practice as a disciplinarian and/or emancipative project. The reason for highlighting the first issue is that social care is part of national social policy. Social policies are dependent on how the responsibilities of welfare are distributed between the state, civil society and the market. Social policy, according to an influential categorisation by Esping-Andersen (1990), falls into three different regime-types: (i) the liberal welfare state; (ii) the conservative-corporatist welfare state; and (iii) the social democratic welfare state (also called the 'Scandinavian model').

We relate these different regime-types to curricula in social care in the Netherlands, Norway, and Ireland, and also make some references to the Swedish curriculum. Each programme for the study of social care is constructed in a particular social political system. Current discussions about professionalisation, or about options for social care workers in the market, or about academic demands, influence the design of social care courses. We discuss the interplay between the different factors, both theoretically and through an analysis of a range of European curricula in social care.

By way of conclusion, we argue that the content and design of a curriculum will have a substantial impact on the practice of social care practitioners. We locate these outcomes in relation to the two traditions that have dominated the debate about social care: discipline and emancipation. The discussion about discipline and emancipation raises problematic issues regarding *power*.

## THE DESIGN OF STUDY PROGRAMMES

What are the aims of social care work or — as it commonly termed in continental Europe — social pedagogy or social educational work? How should social pedagogy be planned and carried out? There are numerous views on this matter, held by different groups such as politicians, social administrators, social educational workers, and many others. Differences in views are as common within groups as between them. Different views on the content and aims are separated and developed into a number of homogenous ideas of social pedagogy. Ideas vary depending on the client or service user; the role of the client's social network; methods of work; the use of force or restraint, and other issues.

A central theme is the balance between the use of force or restraint and a therapeutic, care-giving kind of work. Each model of social educational work promotes its views in contrast to the others. This is how different discourses are built which become engaged in a power struggle over the definition of social educational work. The struggle for a central position occurs on different levels and employs different means: research findings; ethical discussions; and logical reasoning on the relationships between aspects like emancipation, autonomy and safety for the individual, and the use of force or restraint from an organisational perspective.

In this struggle, any one model strives to be considered the only reasonable one — beyond discussion. However, that position is only a temporary one, because the struggle for dominance in the discourse of social pedagogy will continue. The discussion about what is relevant, even what is allowed to enter into the discussion and who is allowed to take part in it, continues. There is a dialectic or two-way relationship between this ongoing discussion and debate and the practice in the field — the content and structure of the work that is carried out under the label 'social care work'.

The discourse of social pedagogy is one departure point for an analysis of the content and structure of study programmes. Another is the qualitative level of education. The traditional academic discourse, with its emphasis on a research basis for education, has become an important source of influence, reflecting the trend towards a higher average level of formal education in society. Other important discourses are: a professional discourse that stresses the uniqueness of the position as social care practitioner (see Chapter 4); the 'employability' discourse of vocational education; the emphasis on direct practical preparation for work; and the market discourse with its emphasis on a marketable and competitive product. The following sections examine social care/social education curricula in a variety of European countries, including Ireland, in relation to broader socio-political issues. The discussion will show that there is no single model of what social care or social pedagogy does or should embrace. This also impacts on how it is taught and learned.

## EXAMPLES OF CURRICULA IN SOCIAL CARE/SOCIAL PEDAGOGY

### Nijmegen, the Netherlands

In the Netherlands, there is a social profession known as *sociaal pedagogische hulpverlening* — literally, social educational work. Social pedagogy in the Netherlands is a mixture of youth work, residential work with a variety of target groups, and occupational therapy. Traditionally social educational work emphasises 'doing things' together with people in need.

As outlined above, each particular exercise of a profession, as well as the supporting curricula, has to be seen in context. The welfare discourse prevalent in Dutch society can be categorised as a mixture between the conservative-corporatist and the social democratic welfare state, though welfare researchers differ about where exactly to place the Netherlands. Esping-Andersen (1990) refers to it as a conservative-corporatist welfare state, but there are significant features of its welfare policies that bring it closer to the social democratic welfare state. Other researchers are more inclined to categorise the Netherlands as a social democratic welfare state; these include Goodin et al. (1999) who contrast the Netherlands with the United States (a liberal welfare state) and Germany (a conservative-corporatist welfare state).

A significant feature of the conservative-corporatist welfare state is its variety of different types and sources of social service. Thus the family, the church and voluntary organisations have traditionally been amongst the providers of social and economic assistance. Another significant feature of the Dutch society is its 'pillarisation': there are numerous subcultures such as religious (e.g. Catholic) and other social groupings that have had a substantial influence on Dutch society. Distinctive features of Dutch social provision are a huge number of voluntary social workers and organisations together with a society characterised by cultural diversity and a liberal view on social issues such as prostitution and drugs.

The Nijmegen study programme in social educational work is one of twenty in the Netherlands. The duration of the course is four years. The content and the form of the curriculum produce a certain kind of social educational worker. A student who is educated at the college in Nijmegen has achieved a 'professional identity'. This is gained through a focus on the individual student and the promotion of their self-awareness. Achievement of a professional identity means that Nijmegen graduates should be able to create a distinctive image of themselves in relation to other professional groups.

A discourse of professionalisation is here mixed with discourses of marketisation. A traditional academic discourse is not very visible in the curriculum — rather students' personal growth and self-awareness are emphasised. The consolidation of knowledge about oneself and self-awareness is accomplished through experiencing diverse situations. Artistic means (drama, music, sports and play, arts, audiovisual, and dance and movement) are used to help the potential social educational worker to encounter the client or service user in an appropriate way.

An important aspect of the professional identity of the care worker is the ability to decipher clients' needs, as well as how their requests for changes are to be met. The identity construction also enables the practitioner to dissociate themselves from the client; it is important not to be too close but yet to be 'on the same side as the client'. The fostering/disciplining elements are balanced in that the social educational worker takes the client's 'request for help' as a starting point for actions. How the client's request for help is dealt with by the social educational worker is the starting point in achieving an emancipating outcome.

## Lillehammer, Norway

In Norway, the term social pedagogy is used to describe two different professions: child welfare workers (*barnevernspedagoger*) and welfare nurses (*vernepleier*). The welfare nurses traditionally work with people with disabilities of various kinds, in particular those with learning difficulties. Recently the target groups were expanded to include older people with dementia, people with psychiatric problems, those with substance abuse problems and so on. This work takes place in many different institutional and, more commonly, community-based settings. The occupation of welfare nurse is licensed (see Chapter 4) which means that the curriculum is to a certain extent externally regulated. The child welfare worker works primarily with children and youth but also with other target groups, such as refugees, substance abusers and the mentally ill. This work also takes place in a variety of different settings, such as residential homes, youth clubs, after-school centres, and so on.

Child welfare workers, welfare nurses, and social workers are all educated to the same academic level, according to a common national curriculum, in 17 institutes of higher education across Norway. The study programmes are three years long. They are similar for the three groups and, to a certain extent, they are taught together in a common study programme (with a common first year).

The first national curricula for the two social professions were established in 1991 and replaced shorter, in-service training programmes linked to the big care institutions. Welfare nursing and child welfare are therefore quite well established as professional groups in Norway: training programmes for welfare nurses date from 1961 and from 1968 for child welfare workers.

The context of the Norwegian curricula is the Norwegian welfare society with its own distinct qualities. According to Esping-Andersen (1990), the Norwegian welfare state belongs to the social democratic regime-type. In short, this means that social rights are universal — they encompass all citizens without any prior means-testing. This approach can be contrasted to the liberal model where the state is responsible for assistance only to those proven to be in a needy situation. The social-democratic welfare type encompasses the middle class as well as the working class, whereas the liberal model is primarily directed towards the latter.

It is possible to detect some salient discourses in the curricula. One of them is what we may call a social political discourse. Its aim is that students should learn that all members of society have the same rights, independent of disability or any other impeding factors. Integration into society of those on the margins should proceed guided by the 'principle of normalisation' (Askheim, 1998; see also Chapter 19). On graduation, Norwegian students have achieved an identity as 'welfare navigator'; they are practitioners who can find a proper balance between clients' needs and society's demands. The welfare worker's mission is to guide the clients into societal norms as well as to be the initiator of changes in individual behaviour and of societal structures.

However, the principle of normalisation is not uncomplicated. There are tensions in the framework and legislation that make the principle of normalisation possible. One of the tensions is that there is a special legal framework for some groups of people, which states that the 'abnormal' should be given the same rights as the 'normal'. The aim of the legal framework is that when the aims are fulfilled, the framework should be erased. On the other hand, the aims are of a utopian quality, which means that special treatment of some groups of people will always be necessary. It has been a matter of debate whether the principle of normalisation has had any positive effects towards integration in the last decade of the twentieth century.

In order to counteract the totalitarian, paternalistic and homogenising tendencies within the principle of normalisation, the Lillehammer students are also taught about empowerment, an ideology that aims to tilt the division of power in favour of the client.

The second salient discourse in the Norwegian system is the academic. The studies at the Lillehammer College are characterised by the traditional division of subjects — into Sociology, Psychology and Law, for example. Many of the lecturers are researchers, and students write academic theses that give access to further education.

There are further discourses that compete with the social political and the academic. In one of the curricula — welfare nursing — a medical discourse intrudes, which makes it compulsory for the study programme to include certain elements that are not compatible with social political discourse. Divergent legislation and frameworks prevent the amalgamation of the two study programmes for welfare nursing and child welfare, though this has for a long time been on the agenda among staff and administrators at the college.

Another factor that influences the study programmes is the discourse of professionalisation. The workers' trade union brings pressure upon the college to educate one category of social workers, not three. From the point of view of the professional in the work field, this is a logical step, as the three groups of social workers (social workers, welfare nurses, and child welfare workers) are united in one union. But there are strong forces amongst the different categories of workers themselves which seek to preserve their separate professional identities.

## Sligo, Ireland

In Ireland, the most important area of work for social care practitioners is with children and youth — for example, in residential homes and special institutions, and work with people with learning disabilities. The work takes place in close relationship with clients; this, together with the typical client groups, places social care work in the tradition of social pedagogy.

The context for social care work, the social-political environment, has a number of original features. The Irish history of the twentieth century has had an impact on virtually all sections of society. Where the material interests of social classes have been the basis for political action in most European states, nationalism has overshadowed class interest in Ireland. Catholic and nationalist ideologies presented Ireland as a classless society with a culturally homogenous population (McLaughlin, 2001). Politics, including welfare politics, was naturally very much influenced by this.

Welfare policies in Ireland do not fit easily into the Esping-Andersen classification system. On the one hand, Ireland has certain features of the conservative-corporatist welfare state, where a comparatively large part of social work is fulfilled by the family, the church and private organisations. At the same time, on one of the central properties in the Esping-Andersen system, de-commodification, Ireland scored low. The conclusion was drawn that Ireland belongs to the category of the liberal welfare state, key features of which are means-tested aid, modest universal transfer, and modest social insurance.

Social care practitioners in Ireland are educated mainly in regional Institutes of Technology. In the Institute of Technology, Sligo, students follow a three-year ordinary degree programme with an optional additional honours degree year.

Sligo students are commonly inspired to see themselves as agents of organisations that foster people. In the terminology of the discourse of social pedagogy, the disciplinary side of the discipline-emancipation continuum is stressed. This is seen in the way adherence to the workings of organisations is emphasised. It is also present in the way theories of behavioural science are used. The relationship between practitioners and clients is presented in the curriculum as a tool of social educational work rather than, as is the case in some other traditions and approaches in social pedagogy, a central means or end in itself.

The curriculum has a tendency to form a special category for people referred to as 'clients'. Moreover, the student is on a different level from the client. The potential relation between the two is mostly asymmetrical.

Students are being 'coached' or inspired to take care of themselves. Self-awareness is an essential aim in the curriculum. This focus in assignments on students' self-monitoring — of their own progress, for example — is also present in Nijmegen. This is an example of how social control has moved to people themselves (Foucault, 1991). Another fundamental aim is to motivate students to adjust to the functioning of the workplace/placement. In many parts of the curriculum, the starting point for assignments or activities is the working of the organisation, not the client. In explaining what social care work is about, the curriculum repeatedly refers to 'transferring help to people in need'. Assignments tend to focus on the delivery of a service in an organisational framework.

Sligo can be placed in the orbit of discourses on different levels. One is the academic discourse that sets the limits for what is to be considered as an acceptable programme. Another is the professional discourse of social care that will be a basis for considerations of what the field (in terms of its unions, professional organisations and publications) will accept. The academic discourse could be seen as a means to advance the status of social care, not as an origin for fundamental changes in the profession.

## Malmö, Sweden

A fourth curriculum to serve as an example is the social work programme at Malmö University. In the first decade of the twentieth century, the Swedish Poor Relief Association launched a vocational training programme for the principals of poor relief institutions. In the beginning of the 1950s, the programme was divided into two separate training programmes: one for adults and one for children and youth. In 1959, the name of the certificate was changed from 'manager of orphanages' to 'social pedagogue'. In 1970, the curriculum in Social Pedagogy was launched.

The programme was three years long and was intended to cover the need for qualified staff in institutions and activity centres for children and youth with social, psychiatric, psychological, and physical disabilities. Students were also trained to become managers of such units. In 1983, the educational programme in social pedagogy was changed at the same time as new educational directions emerged. The educational programmes were at that time given full academic status. One of the new study programmes was directed towards people with learning disabilities, and another was directed towards the elderly. The core subject for all programmes was called Social Care; social pedagogy became a separate specialisation under this umbrella term.

Since 1983, the educational programmes have been changed several times (in Sweden — unlike Norway — there is no national curriculum. This results in great variety in the organisation and content of study programmes). In 2001, there was a major change. The core subject is now Social Work. The Department of Social Work in Malmö is divided into four specialisations: 1) social work specialising in multicultural aspects; 2) social work specialising in social education (social pedagogy); 3) social work specialising in social care (the elderly and functional impairments); 4) social work — administrative specialisation. All specialisations are three and a half years long. In four of the seven semesters, the content is the same for all four specialisations. It can be said that in Malmö the academic discourse has become more and more salient at the expense of vocational and professional discourses; this in turn affects the identity construction of the students.

We have earlier proposed that there are discernible identity constructions as a result of the curricula in Lillehammer and Nijmegen. We called them 'welfare navigator' and 'professional identity' respectively. In Sligo, no particular identity is promoted in the curriculum. Rather the curriculum is characterised by an effort to give students an adequate academic education and to make them 'employable'. This suggests that the potential employers set the standard for social care work.

What sort of identity do the Malmö students develop? We find this difficult to answer unambiguously. The students have been exposed to considerable changes; these have modified an identity that was not very clear from the beginning. The students have been moulded in different ways through vocational and professional ideas about the profession. Now, because of recent changes (since 2001), students and lecturers are to be acclimatised into an 'academic' social work discourse, but this has not yet been fully established in educational practice.

## SOCIAL PEDAGOGY, SOCIAL CARE AND SOCIAL WORK

There has been a long-running debate about the demarcation between social pedagogy/social care on the one hand and social work on the other. A recent contributor to the debate is Professor Sven Hessle. At a conference in Stockholm in 2002, he asked: 'What happens when social pedagogy becomes a part of the academic university discipline social work?' This question was particularly pertinent for the situation at the University of Stockholm, where the study of social pedagogy has been subsumed within the school of social studies. The situation is different in Malmö, as the department of social work was recently established alongside the long-established school of social studies at the nearby University of Lund.

In spite of different organisational conditions, similar issues arise. Curricula in social pedagogy and social care have traditionally had a strong vocational orientation. It is now obvious (in Sweden and elsewhere) that this vocational discourse is increasingly being replaced by an academic discourse related to social work. Another question arises: 'Are the centres for children, youth, the elderly, and the disabled in need of academically educated social educational workers?' This is a question that is often raised by both educational representatives and professional workers.

For us it is obvious that Hessle's question is relevant. He implies that the theoretical core that upholds social pedagogy, and that for a long time formed the demarcation line with social work, has vanished in the traditional academic settings. This theoretical core, according to Hessle (derived from Lorenz, 1994) could be found in 'self-directed learning processes' (Hessle, 2002: 2). This means that clients themselves are the ones who formulate needs and learn how to cope with and change life situations. The social pedagogical intervention is in the use of theoretical knowledge, combined with a communicative and reflective capability in the encounter with the client.

According to Lorenz (1994), this reflective and communicative competence, developed through the situation of living with people in need, is the foundation of social pedagogy. This is fundamental to social pedagogy as distinct from a social work discourse with its specific roots in many different disciplines with their own point of departures (Hessle, 2002).

This theme is elaborated by Eriksson and Markström (2003) who have strongly endeavoured to make the core of social pedagogy visible. They have carried out a sort of restoration of the forgotten roots of the social pedagogical approach. Other contributions, for example by the Norwegian Roger Mathiesen (2000) and the Danish Bent Madsen (1995), have contributed to revitalised discussions about the nature of social pedagogy.

From the descriptions in the literature, it is easy to get an impression of a highly emancipating attitude inherent in social pedagogy, compared to social work which is seen as more system-oriented. Nevertheless, in social pedagogy as well as in social work theory and practice, disciplining as well as emancipating actions are to be found. Careful micro-studies are required to find arguments to support the contention that social pedagogy is more emancipating than social work, or vice versa.

However, Hessle's point, which we can agree on, is that it is not possible to teach students to act in a 'social pedagogical way' solely through academic studies. Hessle has consequently a very pessimistic view on courses in social pedagogy — at least on those in Stockholm. There are reasons to take Hessle's worries on board and to give serious consideration to the question of how to make it possible to emphasise the core of social pedagogy in social work education without diminishing academic demands.

To conclude this section, we find that the Nijmegen curriculum aims at the construction of social pedagogues able to assert themselves in an open work field without a limiting framework. The thrust of the course in Lillehammer and of the curriculum in Sligo is rather to contribute to the creation of a corps of academically well-prepared welfare workers. Similar tendencies are seen in the Malmö curriculum, but also tendencies to adjust the education to changes of the welfare society such as privatisation, complexity, and an increasing number of alternative ways to organise welfare.

## DISCIPLINE AND EMANCIPATION

As we have seen, different study programmes can put the emphasis on various parts of the programme. Does this mean that the resultant social educational work carried out by graduates will vary accordingly? This does not have to be the case, since many factors will influence the development of the actions of the social educational worker, not least socialisation into the workplace. Still, the course will probably be a very important factor, especially when it comes to how the social educational worker will relate to clients or service users. This brings us to the question of how a study programme will prepare the students for meeting the client.

In the discourse of social pedagogy there are two main positions: discipline and emancipation. The former puts the emphasis on helping clients to create a viable situation in life, with the assumption that they need a certain amount of guidance. In contrast to this, emancipation has as its principal goal to help the client to come out of precarious situations and to remove the obstacles for an autonomous life.

*Discipline* and *emancipation* — the concepts seem like the extremes of a continuum. Let us look at the situation assuming that the most important aspect of social pedagogy is the relationship between the client and the social educational worker. What are the properties of this relationship? One vantage point is to investigate *power* in the relationship.

One way of investigating power is to see who has the power and who is subject to it. The pattern is obvious: the social educational worker has the tools of power; the client is in the lowest position. An example is the situation in a treatment institution where sanctions are multifarious, with dismissal as the ultimate threat. The predicament for the client is to adjust to the social educational worker, or else life will be unpleasant. Structural power is with the social educational worker.

Another way to examine power is to look at the use of power. This emphasis on the properties of power is a central theme in Foucault's (1991) writings on the subject, in which power is underlined as a movable instrument. People and organisations make the necessary adjustments in order to bring about changes in their environment. Foucault has shown how power has developed and changed its appearance over the centuries. It has changed from being clear and transparent to appearing in guises that are hard to detect. Open sanctions and threats of violence were replaced by surveillance and, ultimately, control moved to people themselves. This new form of control works through the influence on people of social standards for appearance, clothing, aspirations, expression and thinking. There is not just one standard, though. Discourses are constantly struggling for dominance. As noted above, the most effective form of dominance is that which does not appear as dominance. If we conceive of something as taken for granted and 'normal', we will not have the sense of being dominated at all.

In what way can this shed light on the relationship between the client and the social educational worker? First, both parties are subjected to influence from dominating discourses in society. These discourses and the power relation between them are in constant flux. The particular 'subject' (the client or the social educational worker) will act individually within the domain of the discourses, but may, even against their own will, be the conduit for dominating norms in society. Second, stressing the movable property of power, it might be the case that the client occasionally dominates the social educational worker, and not the reverse. One way of describing the relationship is to begin by investigating the resistance that the client could use in order to block the intentions of the social educational worker.

Let us return to the treatment institution. Usually the social educational worker holds the tools of power, but power always operates in a limited range. The client cannot be *forced* to recover! However, resistance from the client does not have to mean that they have a certain intention — they may simply reject what has been offered. This takes us to another aspect of power: that change can be accomplished through the use of power. It is common to conceive of power as something negative, but Foucault (1980) argues that it is possible to look at power without deciding whether it is in itself good or bad, rather just to consider what is accomplished through the use of power.

There are many channels of power. In the social care field, knowledge can be seen as a powerful tool. Most study programmes in the field contain the study of clients — of special target groups like people with learning difficulties, substance abusers, and elderly people. Indirectly clients can be reviewed in themes like communication, ethics and developmental psychology. To describe people through the use of classification systems, a regular procedure in social educational work, is a form of power in use. As Foucault suggests (1980), there is a close connection between power and knowledge.

Another important channel for power is the power over thoughts. They are organised in discourses, hard to detect for clients as well as for social care practitioners. For social care, 'the right way of thinking' and what is 'reasonable' must always be objects of scrutiny. For instance, is the liberal complementary form of social policy a suitable basis for care work intended for the emancipation of people? To leave people to themselves — is that the only way to support their emancipation? Could the extensive Scandinavian welfare system really be designed for the advancement of autonomy and independence? Or will emancipation turn out to be no more than attractive phrases contradicted by a practice more correctly described as discipline? How could the different study programmes be analysed in the light of the interplay between emancipation and discipline in the discourse of social pedagogy?

## THE WELFARE STATE AND CURRICULA IN SOCIAL PEDAGOGY

In this chapter, we have discussed four different curricula and their social political environment. The discussion can be summarised as follows:

- The Dutch curriculum has been developed in a social political environment characterised by great diversity and a modest governmental structure. The most representative property of the Nijmegen curriculum is the strong emphasis on the self-reliant and independent social educational worker. Artistic subjects, so central in the curriculum, serve two different aims — to expand the practitioner's self-awareness and to be used as a means in the communication with the client. Organisational matters form another important part of the curriculum. The student is prepared to function in a variety of work places. A general aim is to promote a strong profession;
- The Norwegian curriculum is located in a different social political environment. The course can be conceived of as part of the normalisation strategy of the Norwegian welfare state. It is more oriented to academic education than the Dutch course. Social Law constitutes an important framework for the curriculum. Empowerment is an important concept and students are trained to work together with the client in order to find an appropriate position in the welfare system;
- Sligo students are trained to use different means to analyse the client and the communication relationship between the client and themselves. Social, cultural and, in particular, psychological aspects are studied. Self-awareness is an important part of the study programme, but it is apparent that the aim is to make the student function in a position as social care practitioner in an asymmetrical relation to the client. This impression is accentuated by another observation in our study of the Sligo curriculum — that the organisation of social care work is the most common starting point. We find this to be compatible with the Irish social political environment with its mixture of government and privately organised welfare production.

The study of organisations is important in all the different curricula. The main difference between how the curricula consider the organisational environment is that in Lillehammer, government organisations are the most important, while in the other colleges, organisations in general are the objects of study.

The clients' interest is central in all the curricula. The difference between the curricula as to how this is treated is that in Lillehammer and Sligo, clients are approached top-down; in Nijmegen the approach is bottom-up.

Is it reasonable to impose education on a person? Is it reasonable to take part in the emancipation of a person? The answers are not obvious, certainly not if they must be produced without reference to criteria based on a set of values, values that will probably be parts of dominating discourses. To work for emancipation will, in this view, mean to promote discussions on related matters, such as: What are the properties of dominating discourses? What are the properties of the main channels of power? What are reasonable aims for social educational work? Is it justifiable to use force or restraint in order to reach those aims?

These matters have been discussed extensively (see Kelly, 1994). Questions have been raised about what is right and wrong in social care, about values and criteria. The manner in which these questions have been presented has often been criticised for not showing any criteria for decisions. This reluctance to point to something *outside* the discussion on the future of the client, their network, demands from the public, and other concrete problems takes us to the following conclusion on the central discourses in the field of social care: concepts like discipline and emancipation must always be objects of examination; they are open concepts and should always be examined in a concrete context.

3

# Child and Youth Care in North America

Grant Charles, Niall McElwee & Thom Garfat

## OVERVIEW

'Child and youth care work' [CYC] refers in North America to social care work that focuses primarily upon the wellbeing, as the name implies, of children and youth. It has existed for well over 150 years, although not always in a form that would be recognisable today. Indeed, the term itself is relatively recent. This chapter provides an overview of CYC in North America. It defines and describes child and youth care; traces the historical roots of the discipline; provides an overview of education and training programmes and opportunities; and discusses current trends and challenges that affect practitioners. The information and discussion in relation to the North American experience will provide an interesting and instructive counterpoint to your own understanding of social care — in particular, work with children and young people — in the Irish context.

## INTRODUCTION

It should be noted that the delivery systems for child and family services in which most child and youth care practitioners work are, quite often, philosophically and practically distinct from each other in Canada and the United States. This means that there has not been an equal development of the profession or discipline of CYC in both countries. But there is enough common ground to be able to provide an overview of child and youth care work across the continent. While there is a great deal of debate as to whether CYC in North America is a 'profession', a 'discipline' or a 'field' (Beker, 2001; Jull, 2001; Kreuger 2002; McElwee, 2003c) for the purposes of this chapter, the terms will be used interchangeably.

## HISTORICAL ROOTS

While it is difficult to locate with certainty the exact origins of CYC in North America, there are four paths along which the roots can be traced. The first is from the orphanages that were established in the 1700s in a number of communities across the continent. The original orphanages were run by religious orders such as the Ursuline nuns (Anglin, 2002). By the mid-1800s, as such orphanages grew in size, they began to hire lay staff, though often remaining under the auspices of religious orders. The lay staff tended to work directly with the children in the institutions.

Many of the children who entered these orphanages were not orphans in the true sense of the word, in that their parents were not dead. Rather, it was often the case that the parents were unable to provide adequately for their children because of poverty or illness. It was not unusual, for example, for men to be away from home for extended periods of time, working in the forests or fisheries or fighting in wars and, as such, they were unable to provide adequate support for their families. In these cases, children were placed in orphanages, usually on a short-term basis, until the financial situation of the family improved.

Child and youth care in North America can, in part, also trace its roots from the recreational and 'fresh air' movements that occurred across the continent at the time of the big waves of immigration that occurred in the mid-1800s. Millions of people immigrated to North America, primarily from European countries, but also from other parts of the world. Organisations such as the Young Men's Christian Association [YMCA], the Young Women's Christian Association [YWCA] and the Boys' and Girls' Clubs were founded, in part, to provide services to young people who came from backgrounds of poverty common in the greater immigrant population. While these organisations were not established to work exclusively with 'troubled' youth, they were among the first to do so in North America. They set up community-based recreational and social service programmes and residential youth homes as a means to help those young people, who would nowadays be termed 'at risk', to become productive members of society. As with the orphanages and residential schools, these services were generally set up within the context of a Christian orientation, though 'Y's' (YMCAs and YWCAs) and Boys' and Girls' Clubs tended to be run by lay people rather than members of religious orders.

A third historical foundation of child and youth care was within the 'correction' movement. Within this were found the industrial and training schools for juvenile delinquents, as well as the hospitals for the 'mentally or physically deficient' (Anglin, 2002). These facilities were usually, though not exclusively, run by state or provincial governments, as youth in both countries were not seen as a federal responsibility. Many of the programmes were set up as a part of or in conjunction with adult services. By the beginning of the 1900s, separate services for adults and children had been established. Though frequently serving children from urban centres, many of these facilities were built either in rural communities or on the outskirts of cities so as to hide these 'deficient' children from the eyes of society or to remove them from the corrupting influence of urban life. Even though North America was becoming increasingly urban, rural life was still idealised.

A parallel movement occurred with the establishment of residential schools for aboriginal youth in the latter part of the 1800s (Charles and Gabor, 1990;

Chrisjohn and Young, 1997; Fournier and Crey, 1997). These residential schools, while funded, for example, by the Canadian government in Canada, were run by Roman Catholic or Anglican religious orders. As with the orphanages, the facilities tended to be managed by members of religious orders such as the Oblates, while being staffed by lay people. The purpose of the schools was to assimilate aboriginal youth into mainstream society. While it could be argued that the purpose of each of the services was to assimilate children and youth into 'society' the residential schools were a deliberate attempt to destroy aboriginal culture. They separated young people from their families — in essence creating cultural orphans. The aim was to replace traditional socialisation processes with what have become known as Eurocentric values and beliefs.

It was within these programmes that child and youth care was born in North America. However, child and youth care is not the only professional group that came from these services. Recreational therapy, psychiatric nursing, rehabilitation services, correctional services and social work can also claim a portion of their origins within all or part of the above-mentioned types of programmes. It is also important to note that the roots of the profession were very ethnocentric, in that the organisations from which it grew tended to reflect the values and beliefs of the Anglo-Saxon elites of North America. Non-Anglo-Saxon people — whether they were, for example, aboriginal, Irish, Italian or Asian — were seen to be inferior and in need of assistance to become contributing members of society.

The organisations within which the 'original' child and youth care workers worked were reflections of their times, and those times tended to be moralistic and exclusionary; as such, they were often oppressive. This is not to say that some good work was not done. Indeed, many children owed their lives to the work of these original workers. But we cannot deny that assimilation, with all of the associated consequences, was a goal, and that the original workers were agents of these assimilation policies. It should also be mentioned that, with the exception of some of the programming by the 'Y's' and the Boys' and Girls' Clubs, the origins of child and youth care were in residential programmes of one sort or another.

It was not until the 1950s with the beginnings of the deinstitutionalisation movement that North America saw the beginnings of the professionalisation of child and youth care. As mentioned, prior to this time people in the institutions worked in positions that, while they reflected the later work of CYC practitioners, were not recognised as a distinct profession, discipline or field. As governments across North America began to close the large, supposedly impersonal institutions, they replaced them with specialised treatment facilities. This is not to say that there were not treatment centres prior to this time. Rather, there was a rapid expansion of such programmes. Many of the treatment facilities were administered by revamped organisations that had run the institutions, although there was a significant decrease in the number with formal religious affiliations. But many institutions disappeared overnight. Indeed, this was a thirty-year process with closures peaking in the late 1960s and early 1970s. Some of the correctional and hospital facilities are still in existence, though often on a much smaller scale than they were in their 'glory days'.

The new treatment facilities were smaller, more focused and more likely to be located in urban areas, as opposed to the rural location of the old institutions. They tended to be managed by professional rather than lay staff. It was within these programmes that CYC first began to be acknowledged as a discipline with specialised skills and knowledge. With this acknowledgment came a realisation that staff needed specific rather than generalised training and education.

## DEFINITION

Definitions of child and youth care have evolved as the field has changed over the years. Ferguson (1993) suggests that CYC, as a field, had its beginnings in residential care. Early definitions made little distinction between child and youth care and residential work. Since then, the field has expanded to include school- and community-based care; infant development; child life in hospital settings; juvenile justice; rehabilitation and recreation. Though we should record that the roots of CYC were not found only in residential care, it is also important to note that it has significantly moved into new areas in the past two decades — especially into community-based programming. In order to take this into account, a number of CYC organisations came together in the early 1990s to develop the following definition:

> Professional Child and Youth Care Practice focuses on the infant, child and adolescent, both normal and with special needs, within the context of the family, the community and the life span. The developmental-ecological perspective emphasizes the interaction between the persons and the physical and social environments, including cultural and political settings.
>
> Professional practitioners promote the optimal development of children, youth and their families in a variety of settings, such as early care and education, community-based child and youth development programmes, parent education and family support, school-programmes, community mental health, group homes, residential centres, day and residential treatment, early intervention, home-based care and treatment, psychiatric centres, rehabilitation programmes, paediatric health care and juvenile programmes.
>
> Child and Youth Care practice includes skills in assessing client and programme needs, designing and implementing programmes and planned environments, integrating developmental, preventive and therapeutic requirements into the life space, contribution to the development of knowledge and practice, and participating in systems interventions through direct care, supervision, administration, teaching, research, consultation, and advocacy. (Krueger, 2002: 14)

There has been much debate over the past twenty years as to whether CYC is a profession or a discipline. Those who would argue that it is a profession, or at least a developing profession, make their case based upon the uniqueness of the work performed with clients (see Chapter 4 for a further discussion on professionalism in an Irish context). Anglin (2001) believes that CYC is unique in that it focuses primarily upon the growth and development of children; is concerned with the totality of a child's functioning; has a social competency base; is based upon but not restricted to day-to-day work with children; and involves the development of therapeutic relationships with children.

On the other hand, Gaughan and Gharabaghi (1999) argue that while the ability of CYC staff to work in the daily life of children distinguishes CYC workers from other professions such as psychology or social work, this in itself is not enough to make CYC a profession. They suggest that CYC lacks a disciplinary epistemology whereby unique knowledge is produced by the field: rather it is borrowed from other disciplines. They also suggest that there is a lack of role distinction with other professional disciplines. These points suggest that CYC does not have control over a specialised or specific knowledge base and therefore is not really a profession. This debate has not been resolved and is likely to continue for some years to come.

## EDUCATION AND TRAINING

It is interesting that the thirty-year span in which many of the old institutions were closed or downsized saw a blossoming in the establishment and later expansion of formal higher educational programmes in child and youth care. In Canada, the Provinces of Ontario and Quebec were leaders in this area, with the establishment of two-year (in Ontario three-year) specialised educational programmes at the community college equivalent level (similar to Irish Higher Certificates and Ordinary Degrees). Similar diploma-level programmes were set up in a number of states and provinces, although, even thirty years later, there are still jurisdictions that do not have college-level training programmes. Despite a number of openings in recent years, university-level programmes in child and youth care are rarities in North America. Educational opportunities in CYC beyond the undergraduate level are almost non-existent. Among the exceptions are the School of Child and Youth Care in Victoria, British Columbia and Nova/Southwestern University in Florida which offer graduate and postgraduate education programmes. Canada is more developed than the US in terms of formal CYC educational programmes. Neither country has a formal accreditation process to ensure minimal quality for post-secondary programmes (Stuart, 2001).

While several institutions of higher learning offer formal educational training for CYC professionals, the majority of staff-members come to the workplace without professional training in the area. Anglin (2002) in his study of residential programmes in the Province of British Columbia, notes that a significant number of staff in a sample of residential facilities for young people do not have specialised tertiary-level training in child and youth care. Others may come from a number of post-secondary programmes that may or may not have any bearing on social care, while some have little or no education past high school. For example, in the Province of Ontario, only about half of the workers employed in the field have formal training (Gaughan and Gharabaghi, 1999). This is the case even though Ontario has a long history of providing post-secondary education opportunities in child and youth care. It also has the oldest and largest CYC association on the continent.

## CERTIFICATION AND REGISTRATION

To address the disparity in staff qualifications, some jurisdictions have begun to develop a certification process for CYC workers. The most successful in this area has been the Province of Alberta which has provided a certification process for government workers since 1979 and for all other CYC workers since 1985 (Berube, 1984; Phelan, 1988). The Province of British Columbia has developed a certification plan but it has yet to be implemented (Stuart, 2001). Certification programmes tend to be replacement programmes for formal education rather than supplementary programmes to formal education. For example, while it recognises formal education, the Alberta certification process has a grandfather clause for individuals who do not have formal education qualifications (CYCAA, 2000; Stuart, 2001). In other words, the certificate programmes are developed as a means to ensure a minimal training standard for front-line staff. They have not been developed as a means of professional registration as would be the case in some of the other disciplines in the caring fields. This ability to regulate educational expectations, entry qualifications and the use of the name of the profession is a central consideration in determining in North America whether a profession is truly a profession both legally and in the eyes of other professions.

## PROFESSIONAL ASSOCIATIONS

While the first CYC State or Provincial association was established in the Province of Ontario in 1959 (MacKenna, 1994), there has never been a time when all of the provinces and states have had active associations. At the peak in the 1980s, fewer than half of the US states had CYC associations (Krueger, 2002). But CYC workers in the two countries are represented by national organisations: in the US the Association for Child and Youth Care Practice [ACYCP] provides national leadership, while in Canada the same function is carried out by the Council of Canadian Child and Youth Care Associations [CCYCA]. While they are separate organisations, there is some cooperation between the two on matters of common interest. The two associations jointly sponsor an international CYC conference which is offered on alternating sites between the two countries. They also cooperate in the development of standards for certification.

Neither association has a high national profile, unlike their counterparts in professions such as social work, nursing, psychology or medicine. The CYC associations tend to have a much lower profile in terms of government lobbying. This is partly a result of a comparative lack of funds, but is also related to the low profile of the profession in the minds of the general public. Few people in either country are aware that child and youth care is a separate professional grouping under the general umbrella of the caring professions. This is, in part, the failure of the associations to formulate a strategy that will raise the profile of child and youth care.

A lack of public profile is not the only difficulty facing the Canadian and American associations. A disturbing trend over the past few years has been a significant decrease in the membership levels in many state and provincial organisations. This has corresponded with the disappearance or weakening of a number of the associations themselves. Unlike other professional or discipline-specific bodies, many of the CYC associations are dependent upon a small group of dedicated people for their survival or at least effective functioning. As these people move on, the associations often go into a period of stagnation or, in some cases, disappear altogether. A number of state associations have shut down in recent years (Krueger, 2002). The end result is a constant ebb and flow of the associations which makes such activities as effective long-term planning and lobbying difficult if not impossible.

Three other groups have been founded to contribute to the development of the profession in North America. The International Leadership Coalition for Professional Child and Youth Care Workers [ILCFPCYCW] was founded in 1992 to support the work of the associations (Krueger, 2002). CYC leaders came together to promote the field by assisting the ACYCP on such projects as the development of a national code of ethics and certification standards for workers. The code of ethics was developed so as to create a common guide for workers in their interactions with clients, by addressing such areas as responsibility for self, clients, employers and society (Krueger, 2002). The North American Certification Project [NACP] was initiated by ILCFPCYCW in conjunction with the two national associations to develop common certification standards for both countries. Two other CYC organisations worth mentioning are the Academy of Professional Child and Youth Care and the North American Consortium of Child and Youth Care Education Programmes (Ricks et al., 1991; Krueger, 2002). The first group consists of selected leaders in the profession, while the second represents educators from the various college and university child and youth care programmes. Both groups have been active in promoting issues relevant to the field.

## CONFERENCES

Though the roots of child and youth care go back many years, the first dedicated CYC conferences date only from the period of rapid expansion of the treatment centres. The Thisletown Conference in Toronto and the Valley Forge Conference in Pennsylvania were among the first forums at which CYC practitioners came together to discuss issues common to people in the field. From these early beginnings have grown a number of state, provincial, national and international conferences. The first national CYC conference in Canada was organised at the University of Victoria in Victoria, British Columbia, in 1981. The first international conference was held in Vancouver, British Columbia, in 1985. The international conferences are a co-operative endeavour between the Association for Child and Youth Care Practice and the Council of Canadian Child and Youth Care Associations. While there has been a decrease in the number of provincial and state conferences in recent years, the attendance at the Canadian national and the international conferences continues to be strong.

## JOURNALS AND ASSOCIATED WRITINGS

There are four major journals that promote child and youth care in North America. The first three journals are hard-copy publications. The *Journal of Relational Child and Youth Care* (formerly the *Journal of Child and Youth Care*) is a Canadian publication. The *Child and Youth Care Forum* and the *Journal of Child and Youth Care Work* are both published in the United States. *CYC-net* is a web-based journal, published monthly. Though published in South Africa, many of its contributors and readers are based in North America and it has a significant impact on Canadian and American workers. Many of the individual CYC associations also publish newsletters that contribute to their local memberships. Moreover, many publications in North America are directly concerned with child and youth care. While the specific works will not be listed here, it is worth mentioning some of the authors who have made a significant contribution to the growth of the field in recent years: Jim Anglin, Jerry Beker, Roy Ferguson, Gerry Fewster, Thom Garfat, Mark Krueger, Henry Maier, Penny Perry, Francis Ricks, Leanne Rose-Slade, Carol Stuart, and Karen Vander Ven are but a few of the individuals who have provided leadership to CYC in North America through their writings. Many also provide leadership in other areas. For example, Carol Stuart is a major contributor to the development of the certification/registration process in both countries.

## CHALLENGES

Many challenges face CYC practitioners in North America. They include the lack of a recognised professional identity, with a corresponding lack of respect from other allied professions. It is not as if the other professions are deliberately disrespectful towards child and youth care; rather, it is more that they are not aware of its specific role. The same tends to apply for governments across the spectrum of services: few acknowledge that CYC is anything but a job description, even in programmes that they run directly. In Canada, CYC is not recognised as a profession in the various provincial health discipline acts under which most of the caring professions are governed. More recently, the Provinces of Ontario and Alberta have made tentative steps to address this issue.

Lack of recognition is reflected in the low membership of child and youth care workers in their professional associations. The vast majority of CYC workers do not belong to a provincial or state association. This creates a circular problem as the low numbers of members mean that the associations have to survive on minimal budgets, which significantly handicaps their ability to lobby their respective governments for official recognition. This lack of recognition means that, unlike most other professions in the caring fields, child and youth care cannot demand mandatory registration, which in turn means that there is no money to assist in the lobbying efforts. Mandatory registration would go a long way to ultimately solving the whole issue of whether or not CYC is a profession.

One of the reasons why governments in Canada have not recognised child and youth care under the health services or related categories is that such recognition would result in an increase in pay for workers. While most governments have not even considered such recognition, those that have done so may have pulled back because of the increased costs related to such a decision. While this stance does not create a new problem for CYC practitioners, it does reinforce an existing one. The caring fields tend to be poorly paid in North America, and CYC is one of the poorest of the poor. This creates a high turnover in workers, as people are forced to look for other means of making a living.

In many ways, child and youth care is a young person's profession. Many people, regardless of where their hearts lie, leave CYC for other professions that have higher profiles and therefore more status and pay. It is not unusual for social workers, teachers and psychologists to have begun their careers in child and youth care but then to have moved on to their new profession. It is often these very people who have either contributed in some way to the leadership of the profession or who would have been likely to have taken a leadership role in the future — the very people the profession cannot afford to lose. CYC is seen as a stepping-stone profession where one can acquire excellent skills and knowledge that can then be used to be successful in other fields. This is beneficial to the individual worker but hurts the long-term development of the field.

Not only is there a high turnover in the field, but there is also a lack of males. Male staff-members are both hard to recruit and hard to retain, especially when the economy is healthy. This is a problem in many of the caring fields, but is particularly acute in child and youth care. The vast majority of students in the college and university programmes are female. This means that not only are men difficult to hire, but also the ones who are hired tend to be the least qualified in terms of education and training. This difficulty in hiring and retaining male staff is compounded by the fear that many males have of residents making false allegations of abuse. In North America, as in many jurisdictions, allegations of abuse have come from past residents of some of the institutions. Some of these are founded and some unfounded. There have been some situations where government investigations of abuse have been inappropriately conducted, with the result that quite innocent staff-members have been branded as abusers. This has created an atmosphere of fear that contributes to the turnover of male staff.

The high turnover of staff is not restricted to males. Both males and females leave child and youth care because of non-pay working conditions or the fear of allegations of abuse. An increasing problem, especially in the residential programmes, is the apparent changing nature of the behaviours of the young people. It would appear that there has been an increase in the amount of violent behaviour exhibited by young people in recent years. There is some debate about whether this is actually the case, but the perception remains. The result is the creation of working environments that are tense and sometimes dangerous. This also contributes to staff turnover, especially in the smaller programmes or in remote or rural areas where there may not be access to the same level of support that may be found in larger programmes.

There is no doubt that the working environments are potentially more dangerous, but this may not be related to an increase in violent youth. It may be a reflection of the numerous cutbacks in financing that have occurred in recent years in many states and provinces. This has caused the closure or downsizing of programmes, with the result that many young people are referred to services that are not equipped to meet their needs. This is compounded by cuts in staffing levels and training budgets. Such cuts contribute to people leaving the field as it becomes increasingly difficult to do one's job. As people leave, so does their collective wisdom. This causes a vicious circle that contributes to a downgrading of the quality of programmes. As experienced people leave, the knowledge of how to work with troubled youth also leaves, causing interventions to become more behavioural than relationship-focused. This, in turn, creates more situations that are about control rather than change, with greater consequent likelihood of violent rather than growth responses from young people. Unfortunately, there does not seem to be an end to the cuts in children's services. At a time when there has been an explosion in the number of young people coming into care across the continent, governments have been either freezing children services budgets or actively cutting them. This is having a significant impact on the field, as people are being asked to do ever more with less.

The cutbacks are also having an impact on hiring practices. Lack of funds is forcing many programmes to hire inexperienced or untrained staff in order to meet budget quotas. Even though CYC is not a high-paying field, experienced and higher educated staff tend to be paid more than uneducated or inexperienced people. The issue is compounded by a decrease in training and staff-development budgets — often the first to be cut in times of restraint. This is bad enough when staff-members are experienced and well trained, but potentially deadly when dealing with poorly trained or inexperienced people. Children have died in care in recent years in Canada during physical restraints because staff had apparently not been properly trained in the appropriate use of such interventions. For example, two cases currently under review in the Province of Ontario involve staff allegedly restraining children for inappropriate periods of time, using what have been long considered dangerous forms of holding. In both cases, the holds allegedly contributed to the death of children.

While the financial cutbacks are having the most significant impact upon child and youth care, there are also several other issues influencing the direction of services, and therefore people, in our profession. There is an increase in the demand by governments and funding agencies for proof that the money being spent on children's services is having an impact. This demand for programme and intervention accountability is primarily being dealt with through the development of service standards. Organisations such as the Child Welfare League of America and the Alberta Association of Services for Child and Families have long had standards of services that are used by many of the organisations that hire CYC staff. But what is new is that funders are expecting agencies and facilities to become accredited. There is not a uniform accreditation process in North America. Instead, there are accreditation bodies that are local, national or continental. The funders often dictate which accreditation body an individual organisation accesses. The aim of the accreditation is to improve service delivery. But at a time of staff cuts, the energy it takes for an organisation to become accredited often takes away from the work being done with clients. Few jurisdictions provide funding for agencies to go through what is often a lengthy and time-consuming process.

Related to the development of standards is the corresponding development of outcome measures. As with the development of standards and accreditation processes, the goal of outcome measures is service improvement. This long-needed initiative requires that interventions be performed on a planned and measured basis, rather than in the intuitive manner in which many interactions occur. Organisations such as the Canadian Outcome Research Institute and the Child Welfare League of Canada are active in the development of outcome measures and the corresponding measurement support systems for children's services programmes. As can be expected, there is some resistance by CYC workers to the development of outcome measures: although many support this initiative, not everyone wants to have their work examined or analysed. Similar resistance is evident among some people towards service standards and accreditation. But it is unlikely that governments and other funding bodies will back away from their demands in these areas. Accountability will be a strong force in children's services, and therefore in CYC, for at least the foreseeable future.

## CONCLUSION

The key challenge that faces child and youth care in North America is that of *change*. At the core of this process is the debate about the professional status of CYC. This is in some ways a false issue: what ultimately matters is whether the mandate of child and youth care is being met. CYC's mandate is to promote the healthy growth of children and youth; to help children and youth to become contributing members of society. This is not to say that the work to promote CYC as a profession is a wasted effort. Anything that contributes to the growth of CYC as a viable force within the caring fields will contribute to the wellbeing of children. Such initiatives help us to deal with changes demanded of us, and are clearly influenced by the massive change occurring in children's services and in North American societies as a whole. Perhaps this is fitting. A profession that has at its core the responsibility to promote change in young people is in itself inextricably involved in the process of change.

# 4

# The Professionalisation of Social Care in Ireland?

Perry Share & Niall McElwee

'professions . . . are all conspiracies against the laity.'

George Bernard Shaw,
Preface to *The Doctor's Dilemma* (1909)

## OVERVIEW

This chapter addresses the question of professionalisation and social care. It is quite likely that you have thought about yourself, now or potentially, as a 'social care professional'. Indeed, this term has been used a number of times in this text. Yet, what does it mean to be a professional? What are we saying about social care practice if we label it a profession? The term is not as simple as might first appear: it has a number of contested meanings and its use may reveal or hide important social processes and relationships.

In this chapter, we explore the concept of professionalism, pointing to how sociologists, in particular, have interrogated it. They have drawn attention to *power* as a key aspect of the creation and maintenance of professional groups. Professionalism is a concept that can be used in many ways by different social actors. We examine the place of professionalism within social care practice by posing some key questions: Is social care a profession and are those who provide it professionals? What are the implications of the answers to these questions? We discuss aspects of social care as a profession in the Irish context and suggest how it might develop in the future. Inevitably the graduates and practitioners of the early twenty-first century will help to shape this ongoing process.

## THE NATURE OF PROFESSIONALISM

Fundamental to an assessment of the professional status of social care is a critical analysis of the term 'profession' itself. Professionalisation is a process whereby an occupational group is able to claim special, or particular, status and power for itself. We recognise that certain occupational groups — in particular, doctors, lawyers and dentists — have traditionally enjoyed high *status* in society and also considerable *power*, both over their own lives and over the lives of others. This is generally reflected in significant levels of income and wealth. But how can we critically understand this process? How do certain activities, individuals or occupations become associated with the label of 'profession'? How does this change over time, and why is it that professionals tend to be highly favoured in our society?

There have been many attempts to provide a checklist of *traits* or qualities that constitute a professional — you could probably come up with a list yourself. Scottish residential-care expert Margaret Lindsay (2002: 76) bases her own definition of the term on a series of interviews that she undertook with 'a few people from the general public'. Her interviewees came up with a set of defining characteristics (Figure 4.1); the criteria produced by these 'ordinary people' are very similar to those identified by academic analysts of the topic. Lindsay's overview succinctly maps the territory of what professionalism might be. We will return to many of these themes later in this chapter, but also point to some other approaches that might help us to understand professionalism.

**Figure 4.1. Defining Features of a 'Professional'**

| Feature | What it Means | What does this mean in relation to social care? |
|---|---|---|
| **Learning** | Professionals have specific expert skills and knowledge; training is long and demanding and it requires hard work to build up the expertise required. | What specific knowledge, skills and know-how do social care practitioners have? |
| **Attitude** | Professionals have a calling or a vocation; there is a moral dimension and a sense of duty to others; this requires an active role in society. | Do social care practitioners exhibit a vocation? Do they act in society to further their profession? |
| **Responsibility and Autonomy** | Professionals have responsibility for what they do and are personally accountable for their work; they have a high degree of autonomy and have to exercise judgment. | Are social care practitioners autonomous? Are they accountable to society as a whole? |
| **Public Image** | Professionals are highly regarded and trusted by the public; they command trust, respect — even awe. | Are social care practitioners held in high regard by others in society? Do they enjoy status respect? |

*Source:* Lindsay, 2002: 76–7.

Sociologists have long been interested in the idea of professionalism. An early analyst of the phenomenon, pioneer sociologist Emile Durkheim (1858–1917), saw the development of professionalism as a way that the personal power and status of certain individuals and groups could be balanced against the needs of society. Professionalism was a trade-off: certain individuals could enjoy the status of being a professional, but they also agreed to be bound by certain *ethical principles* and a measure of accountability to society (Aldridge and Evetts, 2003: 548).

A later major sociologist, Max Weber (1864–1920), argued for a more critical approach to professionalisation. He saw it as a means whereby those with power and status could limit the ability of others to access these. Professionalism is thus a form of 'social closure'. Those who enjoy the membership of a professional group can make it very difficult for others to join them — for example, through establishing long and expensive courses of study; limiting the numbers admitted; discriminating against certain categories of person (such as women or members of particular religious groups); or through the creation of difficult and complex bodies of knowledge that people must master (such as having to learn Latin, or complex mathematics). This model of professionalism very much reflects the western experience of the traditional 'learned professions' of religious ministry, medicine and law.

Over the past forty years, the American writer Eliot Freidson has been the dominant sociological analyst of the professions. His primary work, *Profession of Medicine* (1970), has been followed by further discussions of the topic (1990, 1994, 2001) that have responded to criticisms of his initial analysis and have amended his theoretical and empirical approach.

As mentioned above, a very common approach to the analysis of the professions is to compile a list of key *attributes*. Such a list, based on numerous studies of the professions, could be the following (Williams and Lalor, 2000: 77):

- ownership of a recognised body of knowledge exclusive to that profession with development of new knowledge through research
- self-government through a body that sets and monitors its own standards of practice
- control of training and recruitment
- monopoly of practice in its own field of work with registration by the state
- conformity to moral and disciplinary codes of behaviour
- autonomy of practice and greater individual accountability
- a public ideology of service to a client group.

We explore these aspects further, in the context of social care in Ireland, later in this chapter.

In a brief paper prepared in 1990, Freidson suggests (1990: 3) that professionalism has two key meanings. First, it 'represents a more than ordinary commitment to performing a particular kind of activity' — this is the notion of 'vocation' voiced by Lindsay's interviewees. Second, it refers to 'the productive labor by which one makes a living, a full-time occupation that entails the use of some sort of specialized skill' — this echoes Lindsay's point about 'learning'. Only when these two attributes are *combined*, suggests Freidson, do we find a distinctive 'profession'. Thus a person might be very skilled at hairdressing, but we do not think of this occupation as a vocation. Similarly, a person might be a very dedicated carer, but we may not define them as 'professional' unless they have a particular type and level of training and education. This last example points to a very controversial issue in contemporary social care, particularly as the state attempts to 'regularise' the area through certification and registration — issues we examine in more detail below.

Freidson makes the further important point that a particular profession cannot, in the contemporary world, be thought of outside the specific and distinctive *institutions* of our society. Thus, one cannot be an intensive-care nurse without the institution of the modern hospital, nor a lawyer without the system of legislation, courts, tribunals, and so on. This applies even more so in the many countries of continental Europe where the professions are very closely linked to the state: for example, lawyers in countries such as France or Italy may be employed by the government rather than being private service-providers. Thus, it can be argued, it is impossible to be a social care professional unless you are connected to an institution of some sort that provides social care services.

The institutional dimension of professionalisation leads Freidson to stress the connection between professions and *work* — professions should be understood as particular types of occupations. But what is distinctive about these occupations is that the workers have a very high level of *control* over the terms, conditions and goals of the work they do:

> [T]he occupational group determines whom it recruits, how they shall be trained, and what tasks they shall perform. It has a monopoly in the labor market over a specific set of tasks, an exclusive jurisdiction. Furthermore, members of the occupation have the exclusive right to evaluate the way their tasks are performed and the adequacy of the goods or services their work produces. Neither lay executives in work organizations nor individual consumers have authority over the performance and evaluation of professional work. (Freidson, 1990: 14)

It is, argues Freidson, ultimately this level of control and autonomy over work that marks out professionals from those with other types of occupations.

Another important commentary that relates to issues of power comes from feminist writers. They have stressed the gender dimensions of professionalisation (some of these issues are alluded to in Chapter 8 of this text). The profession of medicine, for example, was at least partially founded on a process of replacing 'folk' knowledge about healing — largely maintained and used by women — with 'professional' knowledge that was exclusively the property of men. Thus the female occupation of midwife has come to be dominated by the male-centred practices of obstetrics and gynaecology (Ehrenreich and English, 1974).

Historically, 'caring' work has been undervalued by industrialised society, in comparison with 'productive work'. As Lynch and McLaughlin (1995: 254) argue: 'the conflation of the label "economic activity" with the label "work" means that the "non-economic" [including caring] work carried out by women is not defined as work at all'. This is a point that has been strongly argued in Ireland by the Carers' Association, which points to the massive benefit that the Irish state accrues from the unpaid and largely unrecognised work carried out by those who care for others. The devaluation of caring has in many ways been transferred to those who care as an occupation. It has historically been very poorly paid and is generally defined as 'women's work'. A recent study of the gender dimensions of the social care workforce in Ireland (McElwee, Jackson, McKenna-McElwee and Cameron, 2003) suggests that care practitioners' search for professional status has been hampered by such attitudes.

Overall Freidson (1990: 9) sees professionalism as a positive force in contemporary society, particularly inasmuch as it provides a 'third way' between government regulation, on the one hand, and the unfettered free market on the other. A crucial dimension that professionalism supports, according to Freidson, is a strong element of *trust*. Neither the free market nor a system of bureaucratic control, he suggests, can produce the unique relationship of trust that exists between a professional and their client.

## DISCOURSES OF PROFESSIONALISM

Recent discussions of professionalisation have focused on professionalism as a *discourse*. Aldridge and Evetts (2003) suggest that professionalism has become a way that both workers and their managers *talk about* work practices, a process that can have benefits — and drawbacks — for each.

They argue that 'professional' has entered the English language as a generic term that represents something good — a bit like the way the word 'healthy' is used in a promotional way to describe all sorts of food products. Thus, Aldridge and Evetts suggest:

> [T]he discourse of professionalism is now used as a marketing slogan in advertising to appeal to customers, in recruitment campaigns and company mission statements, in organizational aims and objectives to motivate employees, and has entered the managerial literature and been embodied in training manuals. (Aldridge and Evetts, 2003: 555)

As Freidson (1990: 2) had earlier pointed out, the term 'professional' is 'an ambiguous one, used more often symbolically and globally than precisely and concretely'. As a term, it is highly desirable — it makes workers feel better about what they do — but it may also be used by employers and managers to exercise control over employees' behaviour. Professional workers can be encouraged to work harder and longer, to 'self-exploit' themselves. They may be told that 'as professionals' they have obligations to the wider society that over-ride normal work demands — for example, they should stay at work until a job is finished, instead of knocking off at five o'clock, or they can be expected to bring home work at the weekends.

Following the work of French writer Michel Foucault (1926–84), Aldridge and Evetts argue that, today, professionalism has much to do with self-discipline and *self-management*. The successful employee today is one who self-consciously fits in to an occupational hierarchy, where:

> the community of fellow workers and the hierarchy of positions in organisations and other workplaces (such as peers, superiors and juniors) constantly reiterate and reinforce this sense of self and position as well as appropriate behaviours and work decisions and choices. (Aldridge and Evetts, 2003: 556)

In other words, much of 'being a professional' is to become accepted, by one's peers as well as the broader public, as working within a distinctive occupational community and having a professional self-identity.

These days the discourse of professionalisation is often used to bring about *change* in organisations and in occupations. This process is often linked to new forms of organisation, to legislation and regulation, to a greater emphasis on formal education and accreditation, and to new forms of technology, such as computerisation. This can be a difficult and conflictual process: 'an occupational identity crisis may follow, emerging as discontent particularly on the part of older and more experienced groups of workers' (Aldridge and Evetts, 2003: 556). This may become a major issue in the professionalisation of social care in Ireland and elsewhere.

Morrell (1999) has stressed the importance of seeing professionalisation as a dynamic and complex *process* and argues against the 'checklist' approach to professionalism. Rather, he suggests, professionalism is something that must be viewed as a result of *interaction* between groups in society. In other words, the extent to which a group can lay claim to professionalism is at least partly an outcome of its relationships with other groups: ultimately relationships of *power*. Whether or not nurses can call themselves professional, for example, is an outcome of their interaction, as an occupational group, with other groups such as medical doctors, legislators and health managers. Similarly, if social care practitioners are to attain professional status, it will be as much because of their interaction with social workers, Health Service managers and other groups, as it will be a result of the content of social care work itself.

## PROFESSIONALISATION AND SOCIAL CARE

In North America, authors such as Bettelheim (1950), Maier (1963) and Trieschman et al. (1969) long ago considered the question of social care work and the qualities of social care practitioners. Save for a small number of official reports (*Kennedy Report*, 1970; *Task Force Report on Child Care Services*, 1981), such an analysis has been missing in Ireland. The first book on childcare services was not published until 1991 (Gilligan, 1991) and a journal dedicated to the social care field (*Irish Journal of Applied Social Studies*) emerged only in 1998.

In 2004, the UK was in the middle of the process of professionalising social work, an occupational area that has much in common with what we call social care in the Irish context. Even as the Registration Councils for the profession in Britain were being set up, Harker (2004: 22) suggested it was 'ironic that social care has gained a national body to reinforce the boundaries of its profession, just as they are becoming more porous'. She argued that the 'social care approach' was moving beyond the traditional confines of social care work, and was increasingly being used in a broad range of settings — for example, in youth work, or drugs-action work. Thus, rather than being tied to particular institutions, social care was now better thought of as a set of approaches, ways of working or roles.

Thus, suggested Harker, 'now we expect professionals who work with young people to combine skills previously associated with youth and community work, social work, adolescent mental health and careers services'. This draws our attention to the fact that defining or establishing a profession is a complex and dynamic process that relates in contradictory ways to what professionals actually do and how they see their work.

So, can we talk about social care as a profession and, if so, in what ways? What are the implications of such a label? Much research of late has been directed into examining these questions (Krueger, 2002; Stuart, 2001; Williams and Lalor, 2000; McElwee, 2003c). A problem is that there is now only an emergent body of knowledge around individual and agency characteristics, agency treatment and intervention approaches and wider professional involvements. In other words, we do not yet have an extensive body of knowledge about what it is like to *work* in social care institutions (but see Chapters 16 and 22).

Caring includes an entire range of human emotions and experiences; social care practice may be distinguished from other caring professions by the condition of need; an attitude of concern; and intentional involvement in intervention (Ricks, 1992: 52). There are many different aspects of care, such as *caretaking* (providing for physical wellbeing), *caregiving* (physical care with special attention to the psychosocial aspects), *care interactions* (focusing on the use of self in communication to construct relationships) and *interventive* care (assessing situations, formulating goals, formulating applications and reflection) (VanderVen, 1992). Social care work can involve 24-hour care, 365 days of the year, acting as an advocate for children and youth; or working with emotionally and behaviourally challenging service users through the creation and maintenance of safe therapeutic environments.

Despite some agreement about what social care practitioners do, there is no clear, or agreed, international *definition* of social care. It was defined in 1998 by the Irish Association of Social Care Educators [IASCE] as 'the generic term used . . .

to describe services provided for children, adolescents, the elderly, for disabled persons and others in residential care, in day care and in the community' (Courtney, 1998: 2). More recently, social care has been defined in the Irish context by the Joint Committee on Social Care Professionals as:

> the professional provision of care, protection, support, welfare and advocacy for vulnerable or dependent clients, individually or in groups. This is achieved through the planning and evaluation of individualised and group programmes of care, which are based on needs, identified in consultation with the client and delivered through day-to-day shared life experiences. All interventions are based on established best practice and in-depth knowledge of life-span development. (JCSCP, n.d.: 13)

This is a rather prescriptive notion of social care: it outlines what social care workers do, or perhaps can or *should* do. It may or may not reflect what social care workers actually do.

In Ireland, the term social care practitioner applies to those with appropriate and recognised training who are recruited and employed in a professional capacity with individuals or groups in an agency, community or residential setting. In continental Europe, social care workers have a number of titles, many of which use the term 'social educator' or 'social pedagogue' (see Chapter 2). This term points to a rather different role: one that is more involved in educational and emancipatory practice: less about *care* for people and more about acting alongside them to *effect change*. This inevitably impacts on the notion of professionalism.

Such terms may help us to locate social care as an *occupation*, but what can we say about its status or otherwise as a *profession*? Stuart (2001) suggests that the work of social care practitioners can be distinguished from that of other 'related' professions such as psychology, psychiatry, social work and nursing by the following factors:

- It focuses on relationships with clients;
- It is practised in the milieux or socio-ecological contexts in which the client is located;
- It has a developmental perspective that accounts for development as a lifelong process;
- Its focus is on social competence rather than illness or pathology.

Knorth et al. (2002), drawing on both European and North American experience, explore various aspects of professionalisation in one particular branch of social care: residential care of young people. Many of these discussions and debates may apply more broadly to social care practice as a whole. They define professionalisation in the field of child and youth care as follows:

the extent to which practitioners and institutions are guided by sound knowledge and insight (into the nature, background and approach of the problems presented by clients) and express this by skilful and respectful treatment at the individual and organisational level. The foundation of this knowledge lies in systematised 'practice wisdom' and research-based data and theories. (Knorth et al., 2002: 3)

Such professionalisation is (in theory, though perhaps not very much in practice) reflected in public recognition and a set of working conditions and institutions. Professionalism, in this sense, can be contrasted with a *common-sense* knowledge ('everyone's qualifications') of how to care for others. It may also be distinguished from 'charity' or simple humanitarianism. Thus, as Knorth et al. (2002: 4) remark: 'in the western world . . . working with children whose developments are disturbed, and working with their parents, is generally seen as a profession that needs good professional education, appropriate support and "on-the-job" training'. Added to this are notions of accountability — professionals must be able to explain and account for their actions — and 'professional ethical standards and protocols'. The factors that for Knorth et al. (2002) constitute professionalism are illustrated in Figure 4.2.

**Figure 4.2. Sources of Professionalisation**

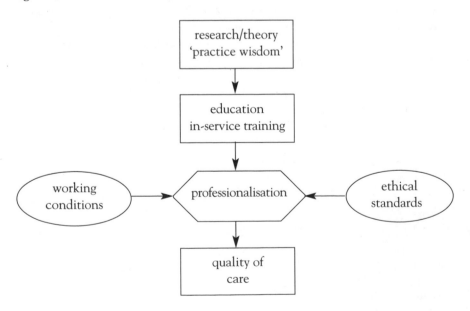

*Source:* Knorth et al., 2002: 4.

## CHALLENGES OF PROFESSIONALISATION

The process of professionalisation in social care can generate many challenges, such as the possible tension between professionalisation and *participation*. Looking at the example of youth work, Groen (cited in Knorth et al., 2002: 10) says: 'the wish for youth participation puts the whole traditional idea of professional under strong pressure. When a youth is (seen as) a co-expert, how does the professional with his [sic] knowledge and experience, position himself?' The same can apply in any area of care provision, where the client or service user has an input into the process of care. This draws our attention back to the issue of *power*. Is the power that social care practitioners claim for themselves of benefit to their service users, or to their detriment? Is it used to control others, or to facilitate their empowerment? These are important questions for social care practitioners (see Chapter 2 for some further discussion of these debates).

Drawing on both Israeli and European examples, Grupper (2002) points to the *economic* implications of professionalisation for residential care. An important aspect of any type of professional work is that it is expensive to produce and to purchase, as we have seen in Ireland in relation to the Tribunals of Inquiry, where lawyers' fees run to many millions of euro. Professional social care is also expensive: for example, in 2002, it cost the North Western Health Board €2.4 million to provide residential care for just eleven children in one year (NWHB, 2003). Grupper (2002: 67) argues that: 'the increase in costs [of care] has resulted in permanent pressure being placed on decision-makers and finance personnel to allow these services to be available only to a very small number of children, such as those with multiple problems and emotional disturbances, homeless youth and refugee populations'. As a result, care is *not* being provided to many who need it — especially as governments across Europe privatise and cut back on services.

The challenge, maintains Grupper (2002: 70), is to maintain high-quality professional services while containing costs. He suggests a number of ways to do this: for example, by ensuring better cooperation and coordination amongst existing professionals, but also by providing services through a mixture of trained, professional staff and non-trained or trainee staff. While not many would argue with the first of these suggestions, the latter raises many issues.

Lindsay sees professionalisation as an important issue for care workers — and for their service users. For her:

> [H]ow workers understand their role, how they define what they do at work, the values that are espoused as they work — all these will in turn dictate how they are perceived by other people — their colleagues, their managers, [clients] and society in general. And how these groups perceive these workers will affect how easily they are able to do their work. (Lindsay, 2002: 75)

This brings us again to the questions of status and power. Lindsay is saying that if care workers are recognised in a positive way by the broader society, this will follow through to the welfare of the people who are cared for. Colton (2002: 122) also sees professionalisation as driven by the 'need to improve the quality of care and the necessity of ensuring that residential workers are able to cope with the increasing challenge presented by very demanding [clients]'.

In the UK residential care sector, professionalisation remains an aspiration, not a reality: Colton (2002: 122) reports that 80 per cent of residential care staff are *not* formally qualified, including 40 per cent of managers of homes. Furthermore, the status of the care sector may be declining rather than improving, as the workforce is increasingly feminised (i.e. a higher proportion of women) and as the welfare sector as a whole is subject to increasing government monitoring and control (Colton, 2002: 124).

Within the North American social care landscape (see Chapter 3), social care — or child and youth care [CYC] — practitioners have also struggled for professional recognition. VanderVen (1992: 3) quotes the words of a caregiver: 'those persons who are the closest to clients and spend the most time with, and probably have the greatest effect on them are the child care workers . . . the least powerful, the least trained and the poorest paid'. Conversely the editor of the *Journal of Child and Youth Care Work* has commented: 'I do believe that we are closer than ever to consolidating our collective identity and securing widespread recognition for our work' (Mann-Feder, 2002: 3).

The North American Certification Project (NACP, 2002: 18) has attempted to define the professional role of CYC workers as practice that 'focuses on infants, children and adolescents, including those with special needs, within the context of the family, the community and the life span'. The role incorporates a developmental-ecological perspective that 'emphasises the interaction between persons and their physical and social environments, including cultural and political settings'. The Certification Project has involved an attempt to categorise and describe the core 'competencies' of CYC work, but a stumbling block has been the huge diversity of practice and resultant identities. Three key questions have been posed:

1. What does a professional child and youth care worker need to know?
2. What does a professional child and youth care worker need to be able to do?
3. What are the standards of practice in the field?

These are questions that still require a lot of research, discussion and debate.

## THE PROFESSION OF SOCIAL CARE IN IRELAND: A SHAKY FOUNDATION?

Whether or not social care as practised in Ireland can be described as a profession has been a point of ongoing debate (O'Connor, 1992; McElwee, 1998; Gallagher and O'Toole, 1999; Williams and Lalor, 2000; Byrne, 2003). Several key factors that both reflect and contribute to Irish social care's tenuous professional status have been identified:

- Social care employment is particularly subject to market forces. Employers, both statutory and non-governmental, operate highly variable standards in terms of qualifications for front-line staff. This can be seen in newspaper advertisements where agencies continue to indicate an acceptance of non-tertiary-qualified workers;
- Many of those working in social care have no tertiary qualifications at all;
- As an academic discipline, social care does not have its own distinct body of systematic knowledge (though this is changing, as evidenced by this textbook and the launch in 1998 of the *Irish Journal of Applied Social Studies*);
- Unlike many other professions, social care finds its educational home in the Institutes of Technology [ITs] and other similar colleges rather than in universities. The ITs are often seen in a negative light, and as inferior to the universities, by many in Irish society;
- The National Diploma/Ordinary Degree, rather than the Honours Degree, has long been considered appropriate as a base qualification, for example by the Health Service Executive, major employer of social care practitioners;
- There is no unified professional association that can claim to represent a majority — or even a substantial minority — of social care practitioners (though the Resident Managers' Association does represent over 60 per cent of managers of residential childcare units);
- There are several government departments involved in social care strategy, employment and policy development, and they rarely cooperate with each other in a coordinated way;
- There is no clear professional title or designation: over sixty different title designations are in current use (McElwee and Garfat, 2003b);
- There is a lack of occupational closure: anyone can legally call themselves a social care worker, though the government has indicated that it wishes to introduce registration of social care practitioners (DoHC, 2000).

Drawing on the set of attributes outlined earlier, we can assess the professional status of social care in Ireland. Although, as earlier suggested, the 'checklist' approach to analysing professionalism has been open to critique, this exercise may serve to raise some issues that future social care practitioners may wish to consider.

## Ownership of a Recognised Body of Knowledge Exclusive to that Profession

Is there a body of knowledge that could be said to represent 'social care' in Ireland? If so, is it exclusive to the field? This question could be answered in a number of ways. This textbook itself attempts to outline a body of knowledge: it was produced as a direct response to the question posed above. It aims to bring together in one place, for the first time, many of the key pieces of information and frameworks of analysis that pertain to the field of social care in Ireland. Previously social care students, educators and practitioners have had to draw upon a diverse but fragmented range of materials, such as government and agency reports, articles published in academic and industry journals and magazines; websites and a small number of research-based studies, published and unpublished. This body of knowledge has not been systematised, except inasmuch as it has been brought together in social care programmes of study. It would be difficult for an individual outside the field to access this information in a coherent or clearly signposted way.

As regards exclusivity, much of the knowledge within social care is shared with other professional areas such as social work, psychology and the health professions. Typically, social care courses draw on a broad range of disciplines, such as law, that have their own systematic and clearly recognised bodies of knowledge. It is difficult to identify a body of knowledge that is unique to social care in Ireland.

## Self-government through a Body that Sets and Monitors its Own Standards of Practice

The 'maintenance project' – that is, keeping the profession going as a profession — has been identified by Freidson (1994: 202) as an important aspect. In the field of social care, there has been very little success in this regard: the occupation remains fragmented, without a clear identity or organisational structure. A cause and symptom of this has been the relative failure to establish strong, representative professional organisations.

The main representative body for front-line social care practitioners has been the Irish Association of Care Workers [IACW], founded in 1972. The IACW has always struggled to secure the membership of more than a tenth of social care practitioners (McElwee, Jackson, McKenna-McElwee and Cameron, 2003: 79). It has had some input into policy-making; for example, it contributed to the 2002 Joint Committee's deliberations on the future of social care, but only as one amongst a number of stakeholders. In 2004, there was an attempt to reconstitute the IACW into a new organisation, the Irish Association of Social Care Workers [IASCW]. It remains to be seen whether this initiative is any more successful than its predecessor.

The Resident Managers' Association [RMA] was founded in 1932 and represents the managers of care centres for children and young people. Its mission is to 'provide a professional organisation for and of those responsible for the manage-ment of Child Care Centres; for establishing standards and ideals in the practice of child care; for the education and training of Child Care Workers; and for fostering public knowledge and appreciation of the service'. It publishes newsletters and other materials for its members; organises an annual conference and other occasional events; and represents members' views to governmental and other relevant bodies. It has seen considerable rejuvenation since the late 1990s.

The Irish Association of Social Care Educators [IASCE] is the newest repre-sentative body. It was founded in 1998 and represents the Institutes and colleges involved in the provision of higher education to the social care sector. It holds regular meetings of senior staff of the educational institutions; produces promotional and informational materials about social care; maintains a web portal, the Irish Social Care Gateway; and seeks to represent the interests of educators and social care students to government and others.

In recent years, these three associations have collaborated across a range of issues such as research and consultancy, publications, political lobbying and conference presentations. But they have no formal role in terms of setting standards of practice and monitoring. This is done externally — for example, in the provision of residential childcare by the Social Services Inspectorate; and in education largely by the National Qualifications Authority of Ireland [NQAI] and Higher Education Training and Awards Council [HETAC]. This situation can be contrasted with the region of Catalonia in Spain, where the social care profession is governed by an independent body made up of workers in the field and representatives of universities (Grupper, 2002: 66).

## Control of Training and Recruitment

The need for adequately trained staff in the social care sector has been consistently emphasised (Focus Ireland, 1996; Clarke, 1998: 82–93; McElwee, 1998). It is acknowledged that social care work is becoming more complex and demanding (Focus Ireland, 1996: 12). Training for childcare workers has been variously described as 'inadequate to the actual task' and 'very inadequate' (Focus Ireland, 1996: 17, 105). There remains a large proportion of people (about 45 per cent) working in the social care area who, though they may have extensive experience, are defined as 'unqualified' as they lack the basic educational training (Clarke, 2003: 3).

Until quite recently, most of those involved in the education of social care practitioners did not themselves have a background in this field; rather, they came from a diverse range of academic areas such as social work, psychology, nursing, sociology or business studies. As Lindsay (2002: 78) remarks: 'few other professional groups would expect most or all of those who educate new entrants to the profession to have no professional expertise themselves.' This situation is slowly beginning to change as degree-educated social care practitioners are able to compete for lecturing posts in academic institutions.

Differing selection and appointment procedures remain in operation throughout the country (McElwee, 1996). This has been a continual source of annoyance to many individual providers and, indeed, has been identified by the RMA as detrimental to the advancement of the profession. In reality, individual managers may contribute to the confused terrain by seeking specific alternative qualifications that relate to perceived needs in a unit or agency at a particular time.

## Monopoly of Practice in its Own Field of Work with Registration by the State

There is an important difference between certification and registration. Educational institutions *certify* the education and training of social care graduates. Certification can be seen as a process with a clearly defined set of standards that must be met through some form of external examination or assessment. Registration, on the other hand, is a legal concept whereby one registers with a body that has the backing of legislation. It is, in effect, a legal passport or licence to practise in a particular discipline.

According to Lindsay (2002: 76), registration of social care practitioners is not internationally widespread. In Ireland — as in many European countries, but not the UK — there has been a tertiary educational structure and process for the production of qualified social care practitioners since the 1980s. But the formal registration of social care practitioners is an issue that has been advanced only in the twenty-first century. In Ireland, after a long wait, the process of legislating for registration has commenced. The Health and Social Care Professionals Bill was published in October 2004. It remains to be seen how long it takes to finalise the legislation and to create the structures required for its implementation.

As the Irish government does (belatedly) move to register those involved in providing social care, this will inevitably impact on those already in the field — especially those seen to have inadequate educational certification. There is a major challenge for employers, government and educational bodies in responding to the needs of the 55 per cent of social care staff defined as 'unqualified' (Clarke, 2003: 3). It is also quite likely that there will be tensions between social care practitioners with different levels of educational certification.

## Conformity to Moral and Disciplinary Codes of Behaviour

In a number of countries, such as France and Belgium, specific *codes of ethics* govern the work of social care practitioners, whether formulated by the profession itself, or by outside regulators (Grupper, 2002: 66). In Ireland, the IACW developed (but did not finalise) a draft Code of Ethics, but it is unclear how many front-line staff have read this document or abide by it. In the meantime, individual Health Boards have published their own criteria, as have many agencies in the voluntary sector. Significant variation remains across the country with regard to this issue.

## Autonomy of Practice and Greater Individual Accountability

Today's social care practitioner requires skills in systems thinking and intervention, family development and dynamics and self-awareness in the area of family work. Many employed in front-line social care argue that their work is increasingly legalised and proceduralised because of the prevailing risk climate. Front-line workers also complain that much of their time is spent in writing up forms at the expense of working directly with service users. This situation will take some time to rectify as much of social care provision was unmonitored by the State for decades and there is no established history of self-regulation across the sector.

## A Public Ideology of Service to a Client Group

The notion of 'service' has long been at the centre of the concept of professionalism, even as it has been cynically exploited by some practitioners. Who might social care practitioners 'serve'? The vast majority of them are employed by statutory or voluntary bodies, so in many ways their immediate duty is to serve their employers. But to be a profession implies that there is a duty to serve the public also: here this might be interpreted to mean the clients or service users with whom the social care practitioners come into contact.

As an occupational grouping, Irish care practitioners have not expressed themselves very clearly in terms of their public service role. For example, they have a negligible presence in the media, which is more likely to contain 'shock horror' stories about child sexual and institutional abuse (McElwee, Jackson, McKenna-McElwee and Cameron, 2003: 73–4). In many ways, social care work is very much hidden — for example, there is no social care practitioner in Ireland with any sort of high public profile.

Within Irish social care there has been little of the debate that has been central to social work internationally (though fairly muted in Ireland) about whether the role of the care practitioner or social worker is to 'control' others, or to 'empower' them in relation to the oppressive structures of society (Skehill, 1999: 180–97). The term 'empowerment' is freely used in social care education in Ireland, but its implications are rarely recognised. To empower people is to facilitate them to challenge the process and structures that oppress them: in many cases, these may include the very same bodies (such as the health service or charitable organisations) that employ care practitioners. Empowerment then becomes a complex and highly political process.

## THE FUTURE

McElwee (1998) wrote of the search for 'the holy grail' of professionalism, but we might ask now if it is necessarily a good thing for social care. The list above indicates how social care in Ireland may — or may not — be moving towards some sort of professional status, but there are important issues to consider. For example, we have seen concern voiced about the financial impact of professionalisation. There are also worries about how it might impact on the caring relationship itself. Garfat (1998: 98) has noted: 'I don't want child and youth care to be a profession like other professions I know which tend to be more distant, dis-empowering and, yes, even non-caring'. There is a common fear amongst practitioners that if they become 'professional', they may have to swap some of the informal relationship-building qualities of care work for more 'efficient' and measurable practices.

Social care work requires a *reflective practitioner* — who can work well with service users, but also bases the work on a set of theories that are identifiable, recognisable and open to scrutiny. It is not enough just to 'do the work'. If social care practitioners want to be considered professionals, they must know why they have chosen a particular intervention or treatment as opposed to another. Practitioners should have a range of intervention tools and techniques to draw upon when faced with a situation. These should be based on best practice, not the limited knowledge base of one particular unit or community setting.

The issue of professionalisation has been around in Irish social care for a long time. It has begun to attract the attention of government which is, however slowly, beginning to pay some more strategic attention to the range of social care occupations and settings. The trade unions — including IMPACT and SIPTU — that represent many social care practitioners have begun to use the concept in order to improve the pay and conditions of their members. Employers have also started to use the term in recruitment advertisements.

However, it is crucial to the future of social care in Ireland that practitioners themselves engage seriously with the concept of professionalism and begin to discuss what it might mean. Are social care practitioners seeking to become another type of social worker, or nurse, or some other favoured 'professional' group, or are there other models that can provide a more liberating and — dare we say it — empowering form of professionalism? How might such an outcome be achieved? The social care practitioners of the future will be the ones to help determine the future of social care!

## CASE STUDY

Celia Gilmartin [not her real name] is a 31-year-old graduate of Waterford Institute of Technology [WIT] where she obtained a Diploma (1996) and a Degree in Social Care (1997). Celia undertook her placement experiences with children and youth 'at risk' in a special project in Limerick city in the first year of her Diploma. In her second year, she worked with CURA in Limerick city and, in her Diploma year, she worked with children with learning difficulties, in Waterford city. Thus, Celia worked in two different cities along the path to graduation, which she found useful in terms of differing cultures.

On obtaining a good result in her Diploma studies, Celia decided to undertake Degree-level studies, which moved her focus from front-line practice to management studies. On graduation in 1997 (with first class honours), she commenced work as a childcare worker in a private developmental facility in Waterford. She then moved to another childcare developmental centre which specifically targeted children from marginalised backgrounds. Celia was promoted to senior childcare worker and then deputy manager.    ➤

She then started to lecture on a part-time basis on the evening social care programme at WIT and secured a post as a community childcare worker with the South Eastern Health Board. She also started to present papers and workshops at various conferences and to publish in peer-reviewed journals.

In 2001, Celia relocated to the midlands where she again worked as a lecturer in personal development and social care on a part-time basis — this time with the Athlone Institute of Technology. She has recently been appointed Manager of a community development and day-care facility in Galway city. Thus, taking into account the fact that Celia has a primary degree, has worked in the field as a front-line worker and manager, has lectured at third level and has published, one could state that she has embarked on a road to securing professional status.

# Part 2

## Theoretical Approaches

5

# Attachment

Áine de Róiste

## OVERVIEW

Attachment theory has its origins in the latter half of the twentieth century in the
work of British child psychiatrist John Bowlby and American psychologist Mary
Ainsworth. It provides a framework, language and methodology for understanding
early relationships and their impact upon child development. In particular, it
attempts to explain the childhood origins of social and emotional behaviour. For
social care practice, attachment theory is a rich repository of concepts, formu-
lations and principles for understanding and working with children and adults who
have experienced adverse or disturbed relationships.

This chapter briefly defines attachment and indicates why an understanding of
the phenomenon is important for social care practitioners. It then outlines how
attachment theory developed, focusing in particular on the often controversial
work of Bowlby. It identifies some of the critiques of attachment theory, especially
from a feminist perspective, with particular attention to the maternal deprivation
hypothesis. It describes the process of attachment formation and outlines some of
the theoretical frameworks for understanding this process. It lists the various types
of attachment, then shows how an understanding of attachment may help in the
interpretation of adult relationships. The chapter concludes by re-inserting attachment into its social contexts, and with a discussion of its relevance to social care
practice — in particular, in the light of the concept of resilience. A case study
provides you with an opportunity to apply your understanding of attachment theory.

## THE MAIN ISSUES

Centrally attachment theory addresses:

- The significance of an early attachment to another for social and emotional
  development and relationships across the life span
- The negative impact of deprivation of an early attachment (maternal deprivation) or an insecure attachment
- Attachment as an inner organisation of attitudes, feelings and expectations
  about relationships — that is, a mental representation (the internal working
  model).

## ATTACHMENT: WHAT IS IT?

Attachment refers to the affectionate relationship or 'tie' a child has with its mother (or primary caregiver) while 'bonding' refers to the relationship formed by the mother with her child (Ainsworth et al., 1978). Fahlberg (1994: 14) defines attachment as 'an affectionate bond between two individuals that endures through space and time and serves to join them emotionally'. According to Bowlby (1951), it is a biologically based 'behavioural system', and the need for an attachment is as fundamental as that for food and water. What this system is has not been deter-mined, though research has identified neurobiological correlates of attachment (Kraemer, 1992; Schore, 2000). It should be cautioned that such correlational research (where the presence of one variable is linked with another) is not evi-dence of causation.

Central to attachment theory is the premise that a secure attachment inocu-lates a child against the harmful effects of adversity, while an insecure attachment places the child 'at risk' or may even of itself cause problems (Waters et al., 1993). Emotional regulation has its roots in attachment, in that the primary caregiver enables the infant to manage emotional tension and its release. If the primary attachment is insecure, emotional regulation may be damaged, leading to social and emotional problems (Kochanska, 2001).

Attachment behaviour is instigated by external threats and can be seen, for example, in 'the secure base effect', where the presence of an attachment figure enhances a child's confidence to explore and play. Attachment is not a phase of dependency to be 'got over', but rather a means of promoting security and independence. In Bowlby's words:

> [H]uman beings of all ages are found to be at their happiest and to be able to deploy their talents to best advantage when they are confident that, standing behind them, there are one or two more trusted persons who will come to their aid should difficulties arise. The person trusted provides a secure base from which his (or her) companion can operate and the more trustworthy the base the more it is taken for granted; and the more likely is its importance to be overlooked and forgotten. A healthy self-reliant person is . . . at one time providing a secure base from which his companion(s) can operate; at another he is glad to rely on one or another of his companions to provide him with just such a base in return. (Bowlby, 1973: 407)

A second way attachment behaviour can be seen is in 'proximity seeking behaviour'. For example, a child seeks to be near to their attachment figure, reflecting how attachment is adaptive in that it is a means to reduce stress, receive nurturance and promote safety and survival.

A third way is in 'separation protest' where a child protests at being separated from their attachment figure. This phenomenon arises at approximately six months and peaks at 15 months (Weiss, 1991). Related to this is 'separation anxiety', the fearful and fretful responses, such as 'clinginess', shown by the infant when the attachment figure attempts to leave.

## THE BACKGROUND TO ATTACHMENT THEORY

Bowlby drew on Freud's psychodynamic theory, on evolutionary theory and on ethology (the study of animal behaviour), particularly Lorenz's (1952) concept of 'imprinting': where young mammals and birds 'imprinted' or focused onto the first moving object they were exposed to during a 'critical period' post-birth. Studies of human infants showed the damaging effects of institutional care (Goldfarb, 1947), and research with monkeys (Harlow and Harlow, 1969) revealed the harm of being raised in isolation (including aggression, withdrawal and difficulties in mating and in caring for offspring). Bowlby (1953) applied these ideas to the human child, proposing that for social and emotional development, during the critical period of six months to three years, the infant becomes attached primarily to just one caregiver (this is called monotropism), usually the biological mother, who provides continuous loving care.

Feminist criticism has centred on the implicit assumption of the 'biological naturalness' of such an exclusive mother–infant attachment. Research with adopted children and with children from various cultures, has shown that in alternative forms of family structure and childcare (such as the kibbutzim in Israel), attachment is not restricted uniquely to the child's biological mother but may develop with others (Holmes, 1993). This may also occur outside the 'critical period' (since renamed a 'sensitive period') for attachment formation (Rutter, 1995).

The validity of monotropism has also been questioned. Currently, children are seen to have a hierarchy of attachment figures or an 'attachment network' of whom the mother is usually (but not necessarily) the most important (Holmes, 1993). After the mother may follow (in varying orders of importance) fathers, grandparents, siblings, care minders and possibly pets or transitional objects. In the absence of the most preferred, the child will turn to the next most preferred. They may also have different types of attachment with different persons (Kosonen, 1996). Typically, the mother–child relationship assists the child to understand feelings, to develop empathy and to develop coping skills (socio-emotional development). The father–child relationship, on the other hand, assists the child in their peer relationships and in the prevention of behavioural problems, illustrating how different attachment relationships contribute to emotional regulation (Steele, 2002).

## THE MATERNAL DEPRIVATION HYPOTHESIS

In Bowlby's words, 'the infant and young child should experience a warm, intimate and continuous relationship with his mother (or permanent mother substitute) in which both find satisfaction and enjoyment' (1951: 13). Any significant disruption in a meaningful relationship, according to Bowlby (1973), is experienced as a loss and — even as adults — whenever a love relationship breaks down, separation anxiety and grief ensue.

The 'maternal deprivation hypothesis' refers to Bowlby's contention that children deprived of their mothers (or mother substitutes) during the critical period, particularly those in institutional care, are likely to develop intellectual, emotional and social problems, especially antisocial and delinquent behaviour:

> [S]eparations, especially when prolonged or repeated, have a double effect. On the one hand anger is aroused; on the other, love is attenuated. Thus not only may angry discontented behaviour alienate the attachment figure but within the attached a shift can occur in the balance of feeling. Instead of strongly rooted affection laced occasionally with hot displeasure, such as develops in a child brought up by affectionate parents, there grows a deep running resentment held in check only partially by anxious, uncertain affection. The most violently angry and dysfunctional responses of all, it seems probable, are elicited in children and adolescents who not only experience repeated separations but are constantly subjected to the threat of being abandoned. (Bowlby, 1973: 288)

While research with children in daycare has not supported the maternal deprivation hypothesis, studies of institutionally raised children have identified negative consequences from not being raised by a mother or permanent mother substitute (Belsky and Rovine, 1988). In addition, some studies of infants cared for in poor-quality or full-time group daycare for the first year of life have shown negative effects. Poor-quality childcare was reported to increase the risk of insecure child–mother attachments. Low maternal sensitivity combined with sub-optimal childcare yielded a significantly lower number of securely attached infants. In contrast, being cared for by a relative yielded the greatest number of securely attached infants (Sagi et al., 2002). High levels of non-maternal care in the early years have also been linked with less harmonious parent–child relations and elevated levels of child aggression and noncompliance (Belsky, 2001). Research with both animal (Suomi and Harlow, 1972) and human infants (Clarke and Clarke, 1976), however, suggests that the negative effects of maternal deprivation can be overcome, which has led to attention being paid to the concept of *resilience*, discussed later in this chapter.

The link between early separation and disturbed behaviour has been cast in doubt. Rutter (1981) argued that Bowlby had confused maternal privation (children who had never received maternal care) and deprivation (children who had experienced a relationship with their mother but who had then lost it or been removed from her) and neglected attachment distortion (where the relationship is altered — for example, through separation or divorce). Whereas cases of maternal privation more predictably show problems, the consequences are more difficult to predict for cases of maternal deprivation and attachment distortion, as care from substitute others may ameliorate the effects (Howe, 1995).

Thus it may be that Bowlby overstated the case, that it is not any and every separation from the primary caregiver that is harmful but rather only certain types of separation. It has also been contended that Bowlby gave the notion of 'loss' greater emphasis than it warranted. For children of divorced parents, for example, the main risks stem not from loss per se, but rather from the discordant and disrupted relationships that tend to precede or follow the loss (Rutter, 1995). Feminist theorists have also raised concerns over the political motivation that may have lain behind the concept of maternal deprivation and the attention it received in post-Second World War Britain. They contended that Bowlby wanted to keep women at home and out of paid employment and that his theory contributed to a climate of guilt in mothers who were returning to work (Mead, 1962).

## ATTACHMENT FORMATION

Attachment formation develops from six months to three years. It is not dependent upon physical care but rather develops through interaction with the primary caregiver. In particular, it is related to interactions that involve relaxation after raised arousal — for example, comforting a crying infant (the arousal–relaxation cycle), and pleasurable interactions — for example, face-to-face games and cuddling (positive interaction cycle). The importance of parenting (caregiving) for attachment and the child's mental health cannot be overemphasised. As Bowlby stated:

> [C]hildren who have insensitive, unresponsive, neglectful or rejecting parents are likely to develop along a deviant pathway which is in some degree incompatible with mental health and renders them vulnerable to breakdown should they meet with seriously adverse events. (Bowlby 1978: 136)

Several features of both the primary caregiver and of the child are argued to be critical for attachment formation. Particular caregiver features critical for attachment formation include:

- *Warmth*
  Positive mood, emotional and physical closeness displayed in gentleness, positive tactile contact such as cuddling, emotional support and loving behaviour (De Wolff and Ijzendoorn, 1997).

- *Responsiveness*
  How quickly and appropriately the caregiver reacts to the child's cues — for example, signals indicating hunger, distress or excitement. For a caregiver to

be responsive, they need to be emotionally available to the child, not 'stuck away' in their own world.

- *Sensitivity*
An ability and willingness to recognise and interpret the infant's behaviour and emotional states from the infant's perspective and to respond appropriately, fostering harmonious, synchronous interactions (Ainsworth, 1973) — for example, ending a game when it is overwhelming for the child, or comforting a hurt child. To be sensitive, the caregiver needs to adjust their own behaviour to the needs of the child so that the behaviour 'meshes' or fits in with the child's behaviour.

  The maternal sensitivity hypothesis — that a caregiver's sensitive responsiveness is the major antecedent of infant attachment security — is central to attachment theory. Maternal sensitivity and communication have both been linked, albeit modestly, to secure attachment, while a lack of sensitivity, exemplified in maternal frightened or frightening behaviour (for example, when a caregiver has a psychiatric condition such as clinical depression) is linked to an insecure (disorganised-type) attachment (McMahan-True et al., 2001). But debate over how sensitivity should be assessed has contributed to a variety of different measures and thus it is difficult to compare research studies.

- *Consistency*
This refers to the extent to which the caregiver remains the same, behaving predictably and reliably. Research with children in daycare and kibbutzim has highlighted how teacher turnover with children aged 18–24 months has a negative impact on their security with their current teacher, illuminating the effect of disruption of early relationships upon future ones (Howes and Hamilton, 1992).

- *Self-confidence*
Research in Ireland has shown that maternal self-confidence and support from the spouse, when the child is 18 months, is a feature of mothers with securely but not insecurely attached children (Wieczorek-Deering et al., 1991).

Turning to the role of the infant in attachment formation, the infant is born prepared (socially pre-adapted) to be sociable and with reflexes — for example, crying and sucking — that facilitate proximity to and the responsiveness of a caregiver, usually the biological mother. An infant's temperament may also be influential in terms of the extent to which they synchronise or 'fit in' with the personality of the caregiver. As Santrock noted:

> [P]arents influence infants but infants also influence parents. Parents may withdraw from difficult children as they may become more critical and

punish them; these responses may make the difficult child even more difficult. A more easy going parent may have a calming effect on a difficult child or may continue to show affection even when the child withdraws or is hostile, eventually encouraging more competent behaviour. (Santrock, 1994: 235)

This illustrates a *transactional* perspective, recognising that attachment security is better predicted by examining a combination of caregiver and infant characteristics, rather than either alone. Sameroff and Fiese (1990) proposed that to understand attachment we must examine not just the characteristics of the child and the environment, but also the 'relationship context' and the transactions therein. It may be that attachment is dependent upon the 'right combination' or 'match' of infant and parental characteristics.

Securely attached infants tend to have a temperament with higher positive affect and lower fearfulness and have mothers higher on positive affect than insecurely attached infants. Children in this latter group were found to be more active and distressed with novelty and had more rigid, self-controlling mothers (Mangelsdorf et al., 2000) than their secure counterparts. But while the link between a secure attachment and positive parenting seems important, it is by no means inevitable (Rutter, 1995).

## ATTACHMENT AS A MENTAL REPRESENTATION: THE INTERNAL WORKING MODEL

According to attachment theory, an infant's experience of responses from significant others is the foundation of their 'model' of relationships — that is, how relationship behaviour is thought about (Lewis et al., 2000). For example, is someone's response construed as loving, controlling, ambiguous, dismissing or dangerous? Is a relationship development construed as positive, involving trust and love, or negative, involving the fear of rejection or abandonment? Bowlby called this inner organisation of attitudes, feelings and expectations, an 'internal working model' [IWM] that evolves in the light of attachment-related experiences across childhood and that guides relationship behaviour. It contains expectations about the self, the world and relationships which in a secure attachment buffer against future unsupportive and disappointing relationship experiences, while in an insecure attachment may contribute to future relationship difficulties (Waters, Weinfeld and Hamilton, 2000).

An insecure attachment may lead the child to view the social environment as hostile, unresponsive and untrustworthy and to see the self as inadequate and unworthy. The child is prone to be apprehensive, distrustful and fearful of relationships, with poor social skills, resulting in negative social experiences. In contrast with a secure attachment, the child is more likely to be optimistic, positive and trusting in relationships and to show good relationship skills (Lewis et al., 2000).

## TYPES OF ATTACHMENT

Mary Ainsworth and colleagues (1978) developed 'the Strange Situation' which classifies a child's type of attachment to its mother at the age of one year, by instigating overt behaviours that reflect an infant's IWM. The procedure involves the creation of a series of episodes in which the mother and child are together; the child is left alone by the mother; a stranger enters and approaches the child; the mother returns and is reunited with her child. The child's observed proximity and responses to the mother during the reunion episodes form the basis for classifying the child as one of the following:

## Secure (type b)

Typically 65–75 per cent of children can be described as secure, showing confidence in their mother's availability and responsiveness and a distinct preference for her over strangers (Waters, Hamilton and Weinfield, 2000). They seek out the comfort they need from their caregiver with the confident expectation that they will receive it. This is based on their experience that their caregiver is available whenever needed. Thus they develop the expectation that caregivers will be available when needed in the future. Secure children are less likely to have problematic behaviour and show more competent problem-solving, social interaction, confidence and independence than insecure children (Ainsworth et al., 1978; Matas et al., 1978; Elicker et al., 1992). They tend to develop open, flexible emotional expression and show a high level of positive emotions (Kochanska, 2001).

## Insecure-Resistant (type c)

These children tend to have a tetchy relationship with their mother, including elements of anger and resentment, characteristic of chaotic care. These children seek out their mothers yet simultaneously resist contact with them — that is, they display an approach–avoidance response after separation. When older, they are often clingy, possessive and overbearing, constantly seeking confirmation of the regard of others. They tend to perceive rejection and disfavour too quickly and develop heightened expressions of negative feelings indicative of poor emotional regulation (Kochanska, 2001).

## Insecure-Avoidant (type a)

Typically these children have experienced cold, rejecting parenting and tend to turn away from their caregiver under stressful conditions. They appear to be emotionally self-contained and not in need of care. Intimacy tends to be perceived as threatening and anxiety-laden, indicating a fear of feelings. This is also reflected in a pattern of minimising the expression of negative feelings — for example, fear and anger (Kochanska, 2001). These children show little understanding of the give and take of social interaction and appear as 'aggressively independent'. As adolescents and adults, they often place great value on non-attachment goals such as education and career.

## Insecure-Disorganised (type d; a classification added by Main and Solomon, 1986)

These children show marked and pervasive fear in the presence of their attachment figure and have usually experienced maltreatment and emotionally unavailable and unpredictable early care. They typically show contradictory behaviour in their relationship with their mother, including disoriented or disorganised behaviour — for example, a 'freezing' response, when distressed. They tend to perceive both the environment and their mother as threatening and unpredictable (Ainsworth et al., 1978; Main and Solomon, 1990; Dozier et al., 2001) and are prone to behaviour problems, including conduct disorder (Lyons-Ruth and Jacobvitz, 1999).

Caution must be exercised in the interpretation of these types, as every child is unique, and the relationship context in which each child grows up has many factors that influence the relationship. These attachment types should be considered as a light to illuminate behaviour as opposed to rigid fact. 'The strange situation' is also problematic as an attachment measure as it is culturally biased (Takahasi, 1990; McMahan True et al., 2001) and its validity is dubious. For example, it is doubtful whether the concept of insecurity and its classification is sufficient to cover all individual variation in attachment relationships (Rutter, 1995). Children with autism, who have severe relationship deficits, do not stand out from non-autistic children in 'the strange situation' (Rogers et al., 1991). In addition, debate persists over whether infant responses to the strange situation have more to do with temperament than attachment (Buss and Plomin, 1986).

## ATTACHMENT: CONTINUITY AND CHANGE

In the past, there was much interest in whether a child's attachment classification remained the same from infancy to adulthood. More recently, attention has shifted to viewing attachment as a dynamic process and to the exploration of factors such as parenting changes, care practices and life events which contribute to whether or not attachment classification changes (Hamilton, 2000; Lewis et al., 2000).

Change from a secure to an insecure attachment has been linked to family features such as parental discord or divorce, parental drug problems and maternal depression and abuse. Divorce represents a lack of parental availability and increased negative interactions between parent and child that may provide the child with a model that shows that close relationships cannot be counted on (Lewis et al., 2000). On the other hand, change from an insecure to secure attachment is associated with improved family functioning and presents the positive outlook that children can overcome adverse relationships to form a secure attachment with the same or other persons (Hamilton, 2000; Waters et al., 2000).

Family support services and other caregivers, such as extended family, may play a significant role in nurturing a secure attachment in the previously insecurely attached child. With respect to adoption, research has revealed that the majority of children adopted by four months display a secure attachment akin to their non-adopted counterparts. Children in care for at least eight months, and then adopted, show disproportionately more disorganised attachments and fewer secure attachments to their adoptive parents (Chisholm, 1998). This indicates the importance of timing of placement in care for a child's ability to form an attachment. Dozier and colleagues reported a greater incidence of insecure behaviours exhibited by babies placed in foster care after 20 months and concluded that:

> [C]hildren who have experienced relationship disruption are likely to develop disorganised attachment strategies unless they are in the care of nurturing surrogate caregivers . . . the experience of relationship disruption is so disorganising that only with the development of a relationship with a nurturing caregiver can the child begin to develop an organised attachment. (Dozier et al., 2001: 1475)

## ATTACHMENT TYPE: TRANSMISSION ACROSS THE GENERATIONS

The intergenerational transmission of attachment refers to the tendency of attachment patterns to be repeated across generations. For example, a mother insecurely attached to her own mother tends to have a child who is insecurely attached to her. Conversely, the mother who experienced a secure attachment to her own mother tends to have a child securely attached to her. How this happens is debatable. Research in behaviour genetics has reported that a particular genetic pattern seems to be associated with a certain type of attachment, notably the 'insecure-disorganised' type. This type is four times more frequent among children carrying at least one 7-repeat allele of the dopamine D4 receptor gene (Lakatos et al., 2002).

This research has yet to be replicated and validated. Many children may carry this genetic risk, but, having been parented sensitively, do not form an insecure attachment (Steele, 2002). Twin and sibling research has also failed to support a genetic basis for attachment as the similarity of siblings' attachment status is not significantly stronger the more genetically similar the twin or sibling is (Dozier et al., 2001).

More likely, attachment is transmitted via non-genetic means, such as the internal working model, which influences parental sensitivity and in turn the attachment formed. Related to this is the concept of attachment 'state of mind' — how adults process thoughts and feelings about their own attachment experiences. This has been reported to be the strongest predictor of an infant's attachment to biological or foster parents (van Ijzendoorn, 1995), more important even than age at placement (Dozier et al., 2001).

## ATTACHMENT AND ADULT RELATIONSHIPS

According to attachment theory, attachment security influences relationships across the life span. Indicators of attachment insecurity in adulthood include a lack of self-disclosure; indiscriminate, overly intimate, self-disclosure; undue jealousy; loneliness; and reluctance to make a commitment (Hazan and Shaver, 1994). The Adult Attachment Interview [AAI] was pioneered by Main and Goldwyn (1984) as a means of exploring the parental internal working models of parents, and rests on the premise that a mother's recollection of the quality of her childhood relationship with her own mother influences the quality of the relationship that she has with her child (van Ijzendoorn, 1995; Main and Goldwyn, 1998).

The AAI asks about past experiences and current thoughts and feelings regarding attachment. Healthy personality development is seen to require access to memories of painful experiences, in order to come to terms with them (Rutter, 1995). The questions assess the extent to which someone can examine their own speech, thoughts and feelings arising from the interview, in a reflective and balanced style, indicative of the ability to respond promptly and appropriately to a child's emotional signals. Four patterns of adult attachment have been identified:

### Autonomous Secure

An objective, open recall of early attachment experiences, positive and negative, with a clear valuing of relationships evident in the interview response.

### Dismissing Detached

Relationships are seen as of little importance, few childhood memories are reported and there is an absence of negative experiences, suggesting an idealised recall of childhood with little supporting evidence. Children of these parents tend to show an avoidant attachment.

### Preoccupied Entangled

Inconsistent, incoherent recall suggesting unresolved conflicts and an angry involvement with the attachment figure (whom they are still anxious to please) are evident in the interview. Children of these parents tend to show a resistant ambivalent attachment.

## Unresolved Disorganised

A very disjointed recall of childhood experiences with unresolved conflict or grief. Parents showing this pattern have often experienced neglect, abuse or a traumatic separation from their early attachment figure and have not worked through the mourning process. These parents are apt to exhibit frightened or frightening behaviour towards their own children, who are prone to a disorganised form of attachment (Main and Hesse, 1990). It is worth noting Steele's point that 'perhaps the most vital implication arising from research using the AAI is the essential need for victims of childhood loss and trauma . . . to be helped toward resolution of the complex feelings of guilt, anger, fear and confusion that so often haunt them' (2002: 521).

## Social Contextual Factors

> [J]ust as children are absolutely dependent on their parents for sustenance, so in all but the most primitive communities, are parents, especially their mothers, dependent on a greater society for economic provision. If a community values its children it must cherish their parents. (Bowlby, 1951: 84)

From this it is clear that Bowlby acknowledged the influence of social factors, such as economic and social support, on parenting. Children in care typically come from poor socioeconomic conditions and their families often have multiple social problems (EUROARRCC, 1998) which may impair attachment formation.

Child-rearing values and practices, which differ across as well as within cultures, also influence attachment. This was shown by research using 'the strange situation' (Clarke-Stewart, 1988; Takahasi, 1990) and by research that reported that support from grandparents enhances attachment security between adolescent mothers and their infants (Spieker and Bensley, 1994).

Acknowledgement of such cultural factors is even more significant now with the greater cultural and ethnic diversity of contemporary Irish society. Self-awareness also needs to be practised as a professional's own behaviour and beliefs influence what they perceive. As a consequence, it is important that cultural practices and attachment experience are explored across training in social care work.

# IMPLICATIONS OF ATTACHMENT THEORY FOR SOCIAL CARE PRACTICE

## The Maintenance and Development of Attachment Relationships

One of the most striking implications is that social care practice needs to support the maintenance and development of secure attachments in children. Children strive to form attachments even in the face of rejection, abuse or other adversity (Rutter and Rutter, 1993). Thus, as Atwool noted:

> it is important to base decisions about children in long-term care on a careful assessment of the child's perspective of their relationships with the significant adults in their lives . . . Children can only be protected within secure attachment relationships and a decision is required about whether this is possible via intervention targeted at the existing relationships or whether alternative placement is needed. (Atwool 1999: 49)

A key principle in child protection is that children should be separated from their parents or carers only after all alternative ways to protect them have been explored. It is agreed by practitioners that reunion with parents or other carers should always be considered. If it is decided to place a child in care, then, for the child's wellbeing, steps should be taken to support the child's sense of continuity in belonging to a family to which they feel attached and in which their sense of identity is maintained. Such steps might include contact with their family and important people from their past, and life-story work (Ryan and Walker, 1993). As Gogarty notes, access visits represent the point where 'the child bridges the need for security and attachment on the one hand and meaningful relationships from the past and perhaps the future on the other' (1995: 116).

In Ireland, 40 per cent (n=8) of a sample of children in residential care reported losing meaningful contact with their family since entering care, though the majority had at least fortnightly contact (Craig et al., 1998). Placements near the family home could be made a priority and greater flexibility and informality about parental visiting would be beneficial for the child's overall wellbeing (EUROARRCC, 1998). Such steps would help address the child's preoccupation with and concerns about their family of origin (Whitaker et al., 1984).

In emphasising that children need to feel cared about and to know that there are supportive people in their lives, attachment theory also confers great importance on the role of aftercare. In the *Madonna House Report* (DoH, 1996: 89), one young woman in care spoke of her loneliness when she went to live with a foster family after leaving residential care, as the staff never visited. Another person referred to 'one of the houseparents as being like a mother to him. He still brings her a present at Christmas. However she had not kept in contact with him'. A goal for childcare may thus be to enable children, including those preparing to leave care, to develop and sustain a support network made up, perhaps, of friends, relatives, aftercare workers and former foster carers (Gilligan, 1997).

It is also worth noting that, according to attachment theory, attachment may also be directed towards others outside the family, including groups and institutions. For example, a team, college or children's home can come to serve as a subordinate attachment figure. As Pearson (1996: 149) indicated, a children's home may become an attachment figure for a child, and forced separation from it can be distressing, inducing separation anxiety and anger. This highlights the importance of aftercare services in maintaining a continuing link between the child and home.

## The Need for Therapeutic Work

One of the strongest implications to be derived from attachment theory is the need for therapeutic work with children (and adults) who have experienced any disturbance to their primary attachment relationship. All care professionals should be aware that children cope with the loss or disturbance of their primary attachment relationship in a variety of ways. Bowlby (1973) identified three phases in the reaction to separation or loss — first, protest exemplified in restlessness, inconsolable crying and a regression to babyish behaviours, such as loss of bladder control; second, withdrawal into apathy and despair; and third, after days or weeks, detachment whereby the child shows some recovery and a return to play though relationships remain shallow and uncommitted. Upon reunion, the child displays clinging, crying, anger and even rejection of the parent. If the period of separation is not too long, these effects are not prolonged and the child returns to a normal pattern of behaviour (Howe, 1995).

The strength of the relationship broken and the abruptness of the separation are critical to understanding how the loss is experienced (Fahlberg, 1994). Some focus on achievement — for example, doing well at school — while others deny their hurt, which leaves them confused about their emotions. 'Yet others find that staying angry distracts them from their hurt and sadness. This may lead them to provoke anew the rejection that raised the upset in the first place resulting in repeated crises in their foster placements, schooling or residential care' (Clarke, 1998: 46). Many experience a grief response which needs to be worked through.

Children in group care have also been found to show an increased rate of resistance in their attachment to their mothers, which would need to be addressed in therapeutic work (Scher and Mayseless, 2000). Bowlby (1980) emphasised the need for children in care to have knowledge about their family of origin, to know the reasons why they had been taken into care, and the need for opportunities to work through separation grief and loss.

Methods to facilitate the 'repair' of the attachment process need to be considered (Fahlberg, 1994). These include counselling, grief work and direct work with children, involving life-story work, eco-maps, life-paths, creative techniques (use of stories, art, drama and play therapy) and programmes such as Batty and Bayley's (1985) 'In touch with children' (Fahlberg, 1994).

In order to break any 'intergenerational transmission' of an insecure attachment, as early attachment experience affects subsequent parenting, and because children in care may become parents themselves in the future, therapeutic work and training on parenting skills with young people in care is yet another implication from attachment theory.

## Quality Assurance and Professionalisation

Another implication of attachment theory is the need for 'good-quality' childcare and professionalisation of staff who work in any of the childcare sectors of employment. One of the most contentious issues explored in attachment research is the impact of daycare upon the child and mother–child relationship. While childcare in and of itself does not adversely affect, nor promote, the security of infants' attachment to their mothers, particular care features (including inadequate staff–child ratios and poor practice) may contribute to attachment and childhood difficulties (Steele, 2002). In advocating a greater value to be placed on childcare and on all who care for children, Bowlby's theory can be interpreted as accentuating the need for standards of care, quality assurance and training developments to advance professionalisation. The Irish Social Services Inspectorate [SSI] represents one means of quality assurance that is in place in Ireland today.

Bowlby's attachment theory can also be interpreted as encouraging a greater valuation of motherhood and the professionalisation of all who care for children (Holmes, 1993). Such professionals should be:

> skilled in understanding a deprived child's overwhelming needs; the craving for parental love; the need to idolise parents however flawed they are in reality; the importance of maintaining contact with absent parents, however fragmentary; the right to express pain, protest about separation, and to grieve loss. They must also be able to help parents in turn to recognise their children's and their own ambivalent feelings. (Holmes, 1993: 41)

Approved courses in Applied Social Studies represent one step in this professionalisation of the field (see Chapter 4). A professional organisation to represent staff is another. Further steps might include the development of a body of research knowledge and a statutory register of staff. According to McElwee (2000: 31): 'a national register would enhance the status of social care practitioners with regard to other disciplines and the political voice of the profession amongst the general public and counsels of the government'.

## Role of Family Support

Another implication of attachment theory is that family support work should be of paramount importance in promoting the care and welfare of children. Bowlby

(1978) recognised that interventions with children and/or their parents may have a positive effect upon the child's development and prevent the intergenerational transmission of attachment problems. For Gaffney et al. (2000), the presence of others (e.g. family support workers, grandparents) supporting the mother and child contributes to a mother, who was insecurely attached as a child, having a child who is securely attached to her. The mother's own previous childcare experience was also found to be influential to this change in attachment classification across the generations. Family support work involving interventions that enhance maternal sensitivity and responsiveness, in particular, may increase the proportion of secure attachments, thereby enhancing a child's development and reducing the risk of the child being taken into care (van den Boom, 1995).

## The Concept of Resilience

A final implication of attachment theory for care practice lies in the attention being paid to a child's level of 'resilience' and how this can be strengthened. Attention has been paid to this concept in trying to understand why some children cope better than others in dealing with adversity such as an insecure attachment. Resilience refers to 'qualities which cushion a vulnerable child from the worst effects of adversity in whatever form it takes and which may help a child or young person to cope, survive and even thrive in the face of great hurt and disadvantage' (Gilligan, 1997: 12). According to Gilligan, an excessive reliance on permanence has not been helpful as a principle in alternative care, as permanent placements have been more aspirational than actual. Instead, resilience needs to play a greater role in placement planning, especially for older children as it accommodates the complexity of childcare problems and needs.

Three factors are integral to resilience — first, characteristics of the child, for example, intelligence, self-reflection, temperament and self-esteem; second, a supportive family environment, including links with the extended family; and third, a supportive person or agency in the environment (Brown and Rhodes, 1991; Howe, 1995). Children in care who do well typically have an extensive and reliable range of social supports across the contexts of their lives (Gilligan, 2000a).

The term 'earned-secure' is used in assessing adult attachment to refer to persons who have overcome negative childhood experiences such as insecure attachments. While such persons parent effectively, they are, however, more at risk for depression, possibly because of the early adversity (Roisman et al., 2002).

## Relating to Children with Troubled Attachment Histories

Understanding and empathy are crucial for all helping relationships (Rogers, 1961). Becoming aware of your own attachment history and how you construe relationship behaviour is of major importance in working in social care. Working with children with troubled attachment histories may tap into unresolved separations or losses in a professional's own past. Fears of rejection and abandon-ment voiced by the child may be neglected because they are unresolved issues as well for a member of staff.

Staff-members also need to be aware that these children may have difficulties with the forging of trust and the development of intimacy and, as a consequence, will be slow about letting others get to know and become close to them. As a consequence, the importance of communication, personal development work and counselling in training cannot be overemphasised.

## CONCLUSION

In sum, attachment theory has made an immense contribution to our understanding of the significance of early relationships and how they shape the behaviour of the child and adult. The body of knowledge that is 'attachment theory' is still being added to, and ongoing research is expanding this ever more. You may like to use your knowledge of attachment theory to consider the case study outlined below, identifying, from an attachment perspective, what are the concerns in this case and how they might be addressed.

### CASE STUDY

Maeve is a 25-year-old mother who ran away from her family at 17. At present, she has a little contact with them but does not get on well with her mother, who she says 'does her head in'. Maeve placed her 3-year-old daughter, Eimear, in care after reporting to the social worker that she 'couldn't cope with Eimear's constant whining and crying, and anyway she doesn't even like me'. Eimear shows signs of neglect and it is clear that Maeve struggled to meet Eimear's needs even with the assistance of a family support worker who had helped her since Eimear's birth.

After Eimear was placed in foster care, her foster parents reported her to be a poor eater and sleeper, to stiffen when held and to be slow to comfort when distressed. After six months, however, she displayed improved eating and sleeping patterns and showed distress at separation and relief at reunion with her foster parents. Although she has not seen Eimear for six months, Maeve has now expressed a wish to see her again and this is to be discussed by the social work team.

# 6

# 'The Good Life': Ethics and Social Care

Damien Cussen

## OVERVIEW

'Happiness' and 'wellbeing' mean something to everyone, but are particularly meaningful in social care. These concepts originated in Greek philosophy and changed over time into the contemporary language of 'rights'. Two moral traditions grew from these roots: *deontological* and *consequentialist*. In this chapter, decisions made in social care settings are discussed, justified and criticised using theories and concepts stemming from these two traditions. The ideas of consequences, social utility and contract rights influence such decision-making. However, as shown in the case study in this chapter, for the social care practitioner, true justice results from respect for inalienable human rights based on the inherent moral value of the person and from the belief that humans can reap their potential only in a community of care.

## MAIN ISSUES

In social care practice, we see both consequentialist and deontological (rule-based) traditions at work. Some decisions are taken because the consequences of the decision are deemed to be 'good', either for the individual or for society. It is an assessment of the *effects* of an action or strategy that decides whether that action is a moral one or not. The idea of morality as a social contract that protects people's rights is also part of this tradition. On the other hand, the deontological rule or principle 'always show respect for persons' is observed not for any thought of consequences or contracts, but because it is in itself a core value or *moral principle*, seen as self-evident. Another way of expressing that core value would be to claim that people have a 'right' to be treated with respect.

## HAPPINESS! OH HAPPINESS!

The case described in the summary of an *Irish Times* report at the end of this chapter is of immediate interest to social care practitioners and students, as it highlights a 'system failure' that opens the social care system up to moral scrutiny from both inside and outside.

On 8 February 2003, *The Irish Times* reported on the death of 18-year-old Tracy Fay. Tracy's early home years were difficult and, at the age of 6, she left her mother's care and went to live with her maternal grandparents. At 14, Tracy began staying out all night. In 1997, she left home altogether and had her first contact with the Eastern Health Board's Out-of-Hours Service for homeless children. At 15, Tracy was pregnant, but her baby was taken into care at four months. At 17, she was pregnant again. Initially, both mother and child were placed in Orchard View, a group home, but this baby was also taken into care. On 20 January 2002, Tracy was reported missing by staff. Four days later, she was found dead outside the toilet area of a disused basement.

Questions can be raised as to whether justice was done, and as to whether any rights were infringed upon, in the series of decisions taken in this person's journey through placement. A brief look at the historical development of the concepts of 'wellbeing' and 'happiness' from early Greek conceptions to their current enshrinement in the United Nations Declaration of Human Rights will be undertaken before returning to the case study above.

## WHAT IS ETHICS?

The terms 'ethics' and 'morality' often occur interchangeably in common usage but there is a distinction between them (Popkin, 2000). A moral belief system is a set of beliefs that governs what we *ought* or ought not to do, whereas ethics can be seen as inquiring into the *justifications* or reasons offered for these beliefs. There have been many moral systems devised that offer advice on how to lead a good life. These systems are called 'normative' or 'prescriptive' systems of morality, as they contain norms or rules or prescriptions that tell us how we ought to live. A normative or prescriptive statement is one that contains the sense of the word 'ought', as in: 'you ought not to steal' or 'always tell the truth'. Why you ought or ought not to do these things will depend on the particular ethical justification offered by the moral system under consideration. A Christian and an atheist might both believe that telling lies is wrong, but their reasons for believing this are not necessarily the same.

If people in the street were asked to define ethics, they would probably give a variety of answers. If they were asked what they want out of life, their answers would probably come down to one thing: to be happy. The Greek philosophers, Socrates (470–399 BC), Aristotle (384–322 BC) and Epicurus (341–270 BC) also thought that the purpose of life was to be happy and to lead 'the good life'. They asked fundamental questions like: What are we on this earth for? What is our purpose or goal?

This way of looking at things is called 'teleological', as its focus is on purposes or 'ends' (in Greek, *telos* means end). A causal explanation, on the other hand, is the normal type of explanation given in science, and is our usual way of under-standing something. We feel that we have an adequate explanation for something once we know its cause. In biology, teleological explanations are still used. We do not ask what caused the liver but: What is the liver for? What is its function or end? As Korner (1977: 97) puts it: 'the possibility of a teleological biology is by no means regarded as absurd'.

The Greeks thought of nature and human existence in this way. Aristotle believed that once the end or purpose of human existence was known, it would also be clear how we ought to live (Guthrie, 1981). He held that we ought to live in such a way as to achieve our end or to fulfil our purpose. Once we know our purpose or end, actions are called 'good' if they bring us closer to achieving this end, and 'bad' if they do not.

Christian ethics also uses the notion of an *end* or purpose to human existence and has had a major influence in the context of social care and in education in general. Once the end is defined, the values or virtues that promote it are determined, as are the vices that can lead us astray. Another end or purpose that human beings might have — also influential in the context of social care — is that of psychological wellbeing (Maslow, 1954; Rogers, 1961). From this perspective, what we aim towards is becoming well-balanced and well-rounded individuals, autonomous and capable of independent living — in other words, happy people. Social care practitioners implicitly operate with the idea of ends; social care is essentially a purposive activity as it helps those who are not thriving or happy, by providing (or at least attempting to provide) opportunities to be happy and to lead a 'good' life.

## THE DUTY TO CARE

Deontological moral theories place the notion of *duty* at the centre of morality (Flew, 1984). An act is a moral one if it is done out of a sense of duty rather than out of consideration of the consequences of the act. Knowing what our duty is helps us to see clearly what the right thing to do is. Within a social care context (and beyond) there is general agreement (Beauchamp and Childress, 1994) that moral judgments should be governed by the moral principles of:

- Beneficence (the duty to act to the benefit of the client)
- Nonmaleficence (the duty to avoid causing harm)
- Justice (the duty to give to each according to their need)
- Autonomy (the duty to respect individuals' right to self rule).

The foundation for these principles is the idea that human beings have intrinsic moral value and hence are worthy of respect and care. While these principles are now enshrined in the United Nations Declaration of Human Rights, the notion of the intrinsic moral value of the human being was first expressed by the Greeks.

In what was termed the 'ethical turn' (Popkin and Stroll, 2000) in Greek philosophy, Socrates was among the first to focus on the concept of the good life or on how life ought ideally to be lived. He held that happiness, which he understood as *eudemonia* or human flourishing, was the aim of life and what we ought to strive for. Aristotle developed this concept further by defining eudemonia in terms of the development of human potential. In so doing, he saw the fulfilment of human potential as the pursuit of harmonious, holistic wellbeing (Blackburn, 2002). Eudemonia or happiness was an end that Aristotle saw as particular to human beings alone.

For Aristotle, what separated us from other creatures was our unique capacity for *reasoning*. We are rational animals and it is through the development of our distinctive capacities, as opposed to those we share with other animals, that we can achieve wellbeing. In this way, Aristotle emphasised the moral worth of the person, set out the criteria for membership of the moral community and provided the central tenet of the deontological tradition — in other words, the reason why we should bother to do our duty at all.

In the context of social care, the most likely interpretation of happiness is in terms of eudemonia or human flourishing. This idea embraces such notions as being happy in our actions, showing good judgment in the things we do, developing our potential and leading challenging and rewarding lives. It means being held in esteem by others as well as having regard for ourselves. It means being able to be happy with others. Aristotle saw that flourishing takes place within communities, within families and within relationships; that it takes place over time; and that the conditions must be right before human beings can flourish. Furthermore, he saw that there is a path to flourishing, since it does not happen instantly, and that guidance is necessary on this path (Blackburn, 2002). Aristotle's influence on social care philosophies should be obvious.

## PLUGGING ARISTOTLE INTO CHRISTIANITY

The moral life, according to Aristotle, was about the development of the virtuous character. In this regard, he recommended cultivating various virtuous habits like courage, justice or moderation. The thirteenth-century Catholic theologian, Thomas Aquinas, a follower of Aristotle, adapted this list of virtues to fit into a Christian framework. He added some more like the theological virtues of faith, hope and charity. In the seventeenth century, the German philosopher, Samuel Pufendorf (1632–94), in his *On the Law of Nature and of Nations* (1672), recommended that we reduce this list of virtues to three fundamental duties or obligations: duties to God; duties to oneself; and duties to others.

Under duties to oneself, Pufendorf included preserving one's life, pursuing happiness and developing one's talents, maintaining the Aristotelian focus on developing potential. Under duties to others, he included duties to family, social duties and political duties, pointing to the idea, as did Aristotle, that human flourishing takes place within communities. Social duties included not harming others, keeping promises and benevolence. Pufendorf based his version of duty theory or morality on 'laws of nature'. What he meant by it was 'as nature intended', which again uses the Aristotelian idea of end or *telos* as a form of explanation.

## THE CATEGORICAL IMPERATIVE

The most famous exponent of deontological moral theory or duty theory is Immanuel Kant (1724–1804). Whereas Pufendorf had seen three basic duties, Kant based the notion of duty on one foundational principle which he called the 'categorical imperative'. Even though it is but one principle, Kant gave different versions of it. One is: 'Act as if the maxim of your action were to become through your will a universal law of nature' (Kant, 1959: 44). Another: 'Act so that you treat humanity, whether in your own person or in that of any other, always as an end and never as a means only' (Kant, 1959: 47).

In any situation where we are unsure of what we ought to do or of what our duty is, according to Kant, we should apply the test of the categorical imperative. Duties like keeping promises and telling the truth can be seen as the right thing to do under the categorical imperative as can the injunction not to use people but always to treat them with respect. It is by reference to and observance of this single principle that we can know what our duty is and, hence, what the morally right thing to do is in any situation. Korner (1977: 134) quotes Kant as follows: 'everything in nature acts in accordance with laws. Only a rational being has the ability to act according to principles'.

Animals and other creatures do not act according to principles; only humans do. In this way, Kant reaffirms Aristotle's criterion for membership of the moral community: both philosophers see something special about human beings that places them above other creatures and thus makes them deserving of a respect and a value not granted to other living things.

Kant was writing at a time in human history called the Age of Enlightenment. Enlightenment here means the realisation that we are self-ruling beings, capable of discovering 'truth' for ourselves by use of our rational faculties. It was an assertion of independence from authorities (notably the Church) that claimed ownership of truth. The image of the human being as autonomous, rational, self-sustaining and equal emerges with Kant but comes initially from Aristotle. Human beings are now the kind of creatures that can bear rights and it is in Kant that the modern image of ourselves as rights-bearing, autonomous beings with inherent moral value is forged. This version of the human is now protected by legislation and is ideally embodied in social care practice.

## HEDONISM: EPICURUS AND THE PURSUIT OF PLEASURE

The concept of happiness provides the basis for the development of *consequentialism*: another route to the justification of moral decisions. Consequentialism leads to an interpretation of human rights as contractual, as arising out of a social contract, rather than as based on the inherent value of the human being. For the conse-quentialist, an action is deemed good or moral if it produces a *surfeit of happiness over unhappiness*. The root of this idea can be seen in Epicurus who defined happiness in terms of pleasure.

Epicurus is associated with the idea of hedonism — that is, of a life devoted to the attainment of pleasure. A hedonist is seen as someone who is self-interested, egotistical, as one who is a glutton for pleasure. Epicurus's name gives rise to the term 'Epicurean' and is used as a description of someone whose main aim in life is sensual enjoyment. The term 'epicure' in modern usage denotes someone who enjoys 'fine foods' and 'fine wines'. Although Epicurus is associated with advocating a life devoted to pleasure, this was not his true position. Rather, Epicureanism is a moral system based on an understanding of the 'natural state' of human beings (Popkin, 1998).

In this regard, Epicurus argued that the natural state of the human being was a state of pleasure, defined as the absence of pain. That is, pleasure is nothing more than the absence of pain. Epicurus regarded pain as the disruption of the natural state. It is freedom from pain that should be our goal; achieving this brings us into accord with nature. Actions that produce unhappy consequences are seen as immoral because they disrupt the natural order and bring us further away from where we should be.

## HOBBES'S SOCIAL CONTRACT THEORY: HEDONISTIC CONSEQUENTIALISM

Pain and pleasure surface again in the work of Thomas Hobbes (1588–1679) a descendant of the tradition of hedonism. Hobbes's view is often called *hedonistic consequentialism*, as it focuses on the consequences for each person of the behaviour of others (Flew, 1984). In Hobbes's view, people are inherently selfish; they look after their own interests first, even or especially at the expense of others. He claimed that because of our selfish and greedy natures, we are all at risk from each other. This fact, he argued, could provide an explanation for how society came about in the first place. It could be seen as a way of explaining what morality is.

In Hobbes's view, human beings are nasty, selfish and always act to maximise their own satisfaction. This kind of view is called *psychological egoism*. Hobbes argued that people always act in their own best interests: if there were no society or civil order or laws or morality (if we lived in, what he called, a 'state of nature'), our condition would be a war of all against all. The lives of men in this state of nature, wrote Hobbes in a famous phrase, would be 'solitary, poor, nasty, brutish, and short' (Hobbes, 1965: 169). He claimed that for selfish reasons alone, in the interests of self-preservation, it would make sense to agree to a social contract. The terms of this contract would be that power is handed over to an individual or group and, in return, this individual or group guarantees protection against aggressors.

The existence of law and police forces can be seen to emanate from this social contract, as can systems of morality. All come into being where the function of law and morality is to protect the individual from the encroaching aggression of others, be they neighbours or society at large. According to this view, if the contract between people and ruler is broken, the people acquire the 'right' to rebel. The social contract also gives rise to other rights, such as property rights or the right to life. The protection systems that are established, including the protection that morality offers, are there to enforce these rights. But these rights arise only within the social contract and do not exist outside or prior to the contract. There is no sense of an *inherent* value of human beings that makes them worthy of inalienable rights.

Morality, for Hobbes, arises out of the social contract and is based on the 'end' of protection. We can see what morality means here: asserting and defending rights; adjudicating between competing claims (justice); and paying compensation for transgressions of rights. The concept of rights as expressed here can be seen to impose a limit on the way we behave to one another. It imposes a 'moral floor' beneath which we cannot go in our treatment of each other. In a crude sort of way, Hobbes's focus on individual satisfaction works for the best of all, since considering the interests of all is the best (and safest) way of pursuing our own ends.

## THE GREATEST HAPPINESS PRINCIPLE: UTILITARIANISM

The focus on what is best for all is the central concern of another consequentialist strategy made popular in the eighteenth century, known as utilitarianism — now the most widely recognised expression of consequentialism. This approach emphasises that, when in conflict, the rights of the majority supersede the rights of the individual. This is also known as the 'greatest happiness principle'. According to John Stuart Mill (1991: 137), it 'holds that actions are right in proportion as they tend to promote happiness, wrong as they tend to promote the reverse of happiness'. Utilitarianism focuses on the consequences of actions and on whether these increase or decrease the amount of pleasure or happiness for everyone, including the actor. One reason for the popularity of consequentialist moral theories is that they appear to provide a scientific way to assess the morality of any action: the consequences of actions are publicly observable; we can see for ourselves what they are. Hence, utilitarianism is seen as an 'objective' way to calculate the morality of an act.

Within utilitarianism, a distinction can be made between *act* utilitarianism and *rule* utilitarianism (Flew, 1984). Act utilitarianism assesses the morality of an act on a case-by-case basis, tallying the amount of pleasure or pain produced by each act. Rule utilitarianism seeks compliance with a rule which, if followed, will yield a greater amount of happiness than pain for everyone. Modern utilitarians can use different terms to describe the outcomes of actions. 'What benefits people most', 'risks and benefits', or 'what is most favourable' or 'the greatest happiness' or even 'the satisfaction of preferences' are all terms that can be used to assess actions.

Utilitarianism's most famous exponent, Jeremy Bentham (1748–32), used the terms *pleasure* and *pain*. In his *Introduction to the Principles of Morals and Legislation* (1789), he wrote, 'Nature has placed Mankind under the governance of two sovereign masters, pain and pleasure.' To get over the problem of how to calculate the amount of pain or pleasure produced by actions, Bentham proposed what he called a 'hedonic calculus'. This was supposed to measure the amount of pleasure produced by an action in terms of its intensity, duration and frequency, among other things. According to this view, the amount of pleasure produced by, say, poetry could be the same as the amount of pleasure produced by getting drunk. This state of affairs led to a famous jibe by a contemporary of Bentham's that utilitarianism was a philosophy 'fit only for pigs' (Blackburn, 2002: 81).

## A PHILOSOPHY FIT FOR PIGS?

Utilitarianism does not have to be so negatively defined. In general, the operating principle of utilitarianism is: do those actions that produce the greatest good for the greatest number. But hospital wards have been shut down because of the principle of utility; it has condemned innocent men to remain in prison. According to this view, it is general utility or the public good that comes first.

The case of the Birmingham Six, played out in the English courts some years ago, could be interpreted in this light. All of the six were eventually proven to be completely innocent of the crime (causing explosions) of which they were accused. The presiding judge at the time, Lord Denning, could be seen as rejecting the appeal of the Six against their conviction on the grounds that allowing it would have meant admitting to huge levels of corruption in the nation's police force. This, in turn, would have undermined public confidence in the forces of law and order, a consequence bad for society. Denning said at the time:

> If the six men win, it will mean the police were guilty of perjury, that they were guilty of violence and threats, and that the convictions were erroneous. This is such an appalling vista that every person in the land would say: 'It cannot be right that these actions should go any further'. It is better to keep innocent men in prison, than let them go free and bring the system into disrepute. (cited in O'Neill, 2001)

The fact that this decision was later overturned could be interpreted along the same lines. Now the public good could be seen to be served by rooting out corruption in the police force.

Denials of individual justice and individual rights, as well as problems of weighing up good over harm, pose problems for the utilitarian, but this does not stop decisions being made at governmental level and at managerial level in public or state bodies that are guided and justified by the principle of utility. Resources are allocated based on perceptions of how the overall good will be served. This may result in the closing down of hospital wards or even of hospitals themselves in order to distribute resources in a way that benefits the overall majority. Nevertheless, justice for the individual and vindication of individuals' rights can come into conflict with the principle of utility.

## WHAT ARE MY RIGHTS?

*Rights* are a contemporary way of assessing morality or another way to talk about how people ought to be treated (Hinman, 1997). Rights can be seen as emanating from both consequentialist and deontological traditions, from Epicurean and Aristotelian roots. For the utilitarian and the social contract theorist, rights talk is acceptable if the granting of rights serves the purpose of increasing the general level of happiness in society. From this point of view, rights do not exist prior to the social contract nor do rights supersede the principle of utility.

It is within the Aristotelian tradition that the concept of rights as an inherent feature of human beings arises: we do our duty because we recognise the basic moral value of human beings. We recognise that human beings are part of a moral community and, as such, are deserving of respect. The notion of rights expresses this same point.

Human beings can be seen to have basic, natural human rights. John Locke (1734–1821) set out these basic rights in his *Two Treatises on Government*, a work that underpins the American Declaration of Independence and also influenced the ideals of the French Revolution. It is Locke's version of rights that informs the United Nations Universal Declaration of Human Rights. For Locke, we have three basic and inalienable rights: these are the rights to life, liberty and the pursuit of happiness. From these basic and inalienable rights others can then be deduced, such as the rights to property, free speech, freedom of movement and of religious expression (amongst others).

In this tradition, natural rights can be described as having four basic features; they are said to be:

- *Natural* — not invented or created by governments
- *Universal* — do not change from country to country
- *Equal* — everyone has them irrespective of gender, race, class or creed
- *Inalienable* — a person cannot transfer their basic rights (life, liberty, the pursuit of happiness) to anyone else.

The notions of duty and rights are interconnected. Within this tradition, there is no such thing as having a right without a corresponding duty or obligation; the right to basic health care or to education means nothing unless someone else (society) has the duty or obligation to ensure that these rights are enforced (Hinman, 1997).

# FREEDOM FROM AND FREEDOM TO

Rights impose correlative duties or obligations. One way of understanding these obligations is to describe rights as either positive or negative. *Positive rights* are rights to something, like the right to basic subsistence or to basic health care or the right to be educated. They impose a duty on the state to provide the means to fulfil these rights. *Negative rights* are freedom from something like interference in our right to free speech or freedom of movement or religious expression. Here, everyone and not just the state has a duty to refrain from interfering with other people in the exercise of their rights. Not everyone agrees with this distinction. A libertarian, for instance, is someone who thinks that there are negative rights only and that positive rights do not exist. According to this view, the state has no (or minimal) obligation to provide the means for upholding positive rights, and the only duties we have are ones of non-interference in other people's exercise of their rights. Freedom from interference in the exercise of free speech does not include the freedom to promote racism or to circulate pornographic images on the Internet or to shout 'Fire!' in a crowded theatre.

# HOW STRONG ARE MY RIGHTS?

One right overriding another implies that rights can be graded according to strength. The strongest rights could be called absolute rights in the sense that they cannot be overridden by any other type of consideration, such as utility or expediency. A person's right to life cannot be taken away, no matter what social utility arises from the use of their body parts. Some rights may be considered stronger then others. For instance, the right to self-defence can override someone else's right to life. An individual's right to ownership of property can be overridden by the state's right to eminent domain. It is a matter for debate (Hinman, 1997) whether there are absolute rights that cannot be superseded by other rights. If so, there can be only one, for if there were more than one and they clashed, there would be no way of deciding how to proceed. The debate on abortion can be seen in this light. It is because the mother's right to life and the foetus's right to life can both be seen as absolute, in this sense, that the issue is so contentious.

# JUSTICE AND CARE

Although rights are one way of patrolling our behaviour toward one another, critics of rights have asked how rights are to be understood within close relationships, families or communities (Gilligan, 1982). Rights focus on the individual and encourage a view of individuals as existing in isolation from one another. Rights can be seen as claims or entitlements an individual has against other individuals or groups. Rights can be seen as the moral minimum necessary in our interactions with one another. This moral minimum may be necessary for human flourishing to take place but it hardly *constitutes* human flourishing. In caring relationships, whether in a family or a residential setting, what is morally significant seems to be missed by an exclusive focus on the observance of rights. Genuine care for another's welfare implies more than the moral minimum. If the focus on rights is maintained, moral qualities like love, compassion and care are left unaccounted for. Among feminist writers like Gilligan, this debate has been cast in terms of a debate between justice and care. For Gilligan, justice is seen as a 'male' concept with its emphasis on rights, autonomy and liberty. The concept of care, then, is seen as a 'feminine' concept with its emphasis on relationships and compassion, following in the Aristotelian tradition of flourishing within a community of care.

Social care practitioners can see their work in terms of duties or obligations they have toward the client. They can see themselves acting on behalf of society in responding to the rights/claims of the client. At times, they may have to make decisions that favour the majority rather than the individual. Utilitarians think the principle of utility takes precedence over individual rights. Deontologists think justice for individuals is primary and that basic human rights can never be overruled on the grounds of utility. The area of applied ethics is the battle ground for these questions and conflicts. Abortion, euthanasia and assisted suicide are examples of issues where no agreement exists as to what the morally 'right' thing to do is. Similar questions and conflicts can be seen to arise in the case reported below.

## CASE STUDY

### A Life: Solitary, Poor, Nasty, Brutish and Short?

On 8 February 2003, *The Irish Times* reported on the death of 18-year-old Tracy Fay. The article stated that her early years at home were difficult and, at the age of 6, she left her mother's care and went to live with her maternal grandparents. At 14, with her grandmother dying of cancer, Tracy began staying out all night. In 1997, she left home altogether and had her first contact with the Eastern Health Board's Out-of-Hours Service for homeless children.

The article states that, according to social workers who dealt with her, Tracy had very 'special needs' and that 'she was like a child, fourteen going on four'. Though sexual abuse was never verified, one social worker described Tracy as 'dramatically sexualised by the time she came to us'. Towards the end of 1997, Tracy was placed in a hostel for young girls but left after five months. According to the article, Tracy had more than fourteen 'unsuitable placements', mainly B&Bs, between then and her death. A psychiatrist's report in 1998 found a 'very vulnerable girl in need of secure residential placement'. A second psychiatrist's report described the level of care for Tracy as 'disastrous', while a third described Tracy as feeling 'helpless and abandoned and incompetent to take charge of her life'. At no point, the article states, was an overall care plan devised for Tracy.

➤

At 15, Tracy was pregnant and reported by a friend to be 'delighted', but because of Tracy's poor parenting skills, her baby was taken into care at the age of four months. Tracy was reported to be 'in bits'. At 17, she was pregnant again and worried that her second child would be taken away from her. Initially, both mother and child were placed in Orchard View, a group home, but this baby was also taken into care. Tracy stayed on in Orchard View, even though, at 18, she was legally no longer the responsibility of the Health Board. On 20 January 2002, Tracy was reported missing by staff.

Four days later, according to the article, she was found dead 'amid discarded sleeping bags and dirty blankets, outside the toilet area of a disused basement.' She had been there at least 24 hours. The article ends with a comment from a social worker who said that a child had to be 'very tough to survive the childcare system. And Tracy wasn't very tough'.

### Applying the Concepts

In relation to this case study, a number of questions of a moral nature can be raised. For instance, could it be said that justice was done here? Was there an infringement or violation of rights? If there was, what kinds of rights were infringed? Were they contractual rights (consequentialism) or inherent, inalienable rights (Aristotle, Kant)? Was there a failure on anyone's part to fulfil their obligations? Was there a lack of morality in this situation, or was what happened immoral in any way? Was a duty of care not met?

Tracy Fay ended up in care at the age of 14. Could not something have been done beforehand to prevent this outcome? The Childcare Act 2002 sees care as a last resort, so the fact that she ended up in care at 14 could be interpreted to mean that the system had already failed her. Hence, it could be argued that a duty of care was not met and so this could be where justice was not done.

In dealing with contract rights, was Tracy denied her contract rights in any way? It would appear that individual key workers all 'did their job'. Fourteen placements were found for Tracy; she was supported while staying in B&Bs; she was monitored when she had her children. It could be argued that her contract rights were observed, even above and beyond the call of duty. Even though, at 18, Tracy was no longer the responsibility of the Health Board, it still took responsibility for her. It could be asked: Were the correct decisions and referrals made? Should she have been put into independent living (B&Bs)?

The article suggests that she was not ready for it. Tracy was described as someone with 'very special needs', as someone who was 'fourteen going on four'. It is possible that Tracy could have had, for example, a borderline intellectual disability, and hence she would not have been capable of independent living. Even if the right referrals were made, there was still, as admitted by the social workers, no overall care plan for Tracy into which these referrals fitted. Perhaps this was how justice was not done. Nevertheless, it could be argued that justice

➤

was done and that decisions taken in relation to Tracy were the best ones, given the circumstances. This was the best the Health Board could do given that it is understaffed and under-resourced. Hence, there was no moral deficit; on these grounds, there was no immorality. However, as admitted by social workers, Tracy was 'dramatically sexualised' by the age of 14. There was a suggestion of sexual abuse, though this was not verified. But was this suggestion investigated and dealt with within the system? Would the records show that this was done? Was the right decision made when it was decided to take both of her children into care? According to the article, this had a huge negative effect on Tracy. Perhaps here is where justice was not done.

In the judgment of the social workers, the fact that people needed to be 'tough to survive the system' points to a lack of care inherent in the system, but it also shows a moral questioning by social care professionals that indicates their concern for justice. In social care work, it is the idea of justice based on the inherent moral worth of the individual that matters. So even though Tracy's contract rights were observed, for the social workers quoted in this report, there was no justice because they saw Tracy's rights as a human being going beyond the contractual and any notion of social utility.

As evidenced by the their response to this situation, it is the Aristotelian model of social care worked out in terms of developing potentiality (a proper care plan) and respect that is of most relevance. For the social workers in this case, the justice that values the inherent worth of the person was not done; the potential that is everyone's right to develop was not reaped. It is the model of human flourishing within communities proposed by Aristotle that lets us see this outcome clearly.

7

# Gender, Sexuality and Social Care

Jacqueline O'Toole

## OVERVIEW

This chapter provides a broad overview of gender issues as they infuse the social care environment. It maps aspects of the debates on gender and social care that are becoming central both in the academic literature and in social care practice.

Use of the concept of social care requires a clear understanding of the contexts within which it is carried out and an understanding of the multiple meanings that exist amongst practitioners, educators, policy makers and employers (Gallagher and O'Toole, 1999: 70). It is clear that social care work involves a broad spectrum of specialised interventions in people's lives and further that it:

> is pivotal in the delivery of a range of residential, day and community social services particularly child care services for children at risk, services for children and adults with disabilities and other support services for marginalised groups. (Gallagher and O'Toole, 1999: 71)

In this chapter, we examine some gender-related issues that have implications for the meaning of and practices associated with social care in Ireland. Three important themes will be addressed:

- The *concept of gender*
- *Gender processes* in social care, including the meaning of care, the ratio of women to men working in social care, likely trends for the future and the implications of constructions of particular forms of femininity and masculinity within social care
- The notion of *sexuality* particularly as it may impact on social care work.

The chapter is written within a feminist sociological framework. This argues that gender inequality is an underlying feature of contemporary global societies and that such inequality needs to be analysed, explained and challenged.

# WHAT IS GENDER?

## Sex and Gender

Sociologists have conceptualised the relationships between women and men through a distinction between *sex* and *gender*. Sex is seen as a biological category that refers to the different physical and biological features that women and men possess, including genitals, chromosomal structures, reproductive systems and secondary sexual characteristics such as the distribution of body hair and breast development (Tovey and Share, 2003: 231). Sex is rooted in nature and gives rise to two categories: female and male.

Gender is viewed as a social category that refers to the socially constructed and variable notions of femininity and masculinity (Oakley, 1972). It is concerned with the socially ascribed characteristics associated with being female and male and with dominant ideas about what women and men should be like. At any time in any society, there may be much variation in understandings and expectations associated with the biological categories of female and male and the social categories of femininity and masculinity.

In recent years, the distinction between sex (nature) and gender (culture) has been challenged. Cross-cultural evidence suggests that simple binary oppositions of female/male and femininity/masculinity may not capture the complexities of gender in people's lives. Indeed, the divisions that are drawn may themselves be social constructions. The process of gender attribution, whereby we assign ideas about gender to females and males, is itself a social process that varies from one social setting to another: witness drag and transsexualism, for example. Each involves a transgression of historically given boundaries and notions of female/male and femininity/masculinity. It would seem that in the twenty-first century, the inevitability of sex and gender is no longer a certainty.

A final consideration concerns the acquisition of gendered identities. A range of sociological theories suggests that some form of socialisation is a key part of this process. From an early age — even just at birth — girls and boys are exposed to their society's understandings of gender: the process of learning about gender roles and identity begins almost at once. From parents, caregivers, the media, peers, the education system and culture come clear messages about gender differences.

However, the socialisation thesis, while interesting, is limited. A passive conception of the person is invoked. It is as if the child were a sponge waiting to be filled up by society and culture. There is a deterministic slant to socialisation that ignores the capacity of individuals to change, resist and alter dominant meanings in society. In addition, there is a sense in which gender identity becomes the central feature of a person's identity. Thus, although women may be differentiated according to social class, ethnicity and sexual preference, in socialisation theory, the fact that they are *women* appears to be the overwhelming constituent of their identity. Black, lesbian and post-modernist feminists have all questioned the validity of this assumption. Other identity indicators, such as social class, ethnicity and sexual preference, heavily influence the experience of being a woman or a man and mediate femininity and masculinity.

## How Do Perceived Gender Differences Lead to Gender Inequality?

From the late 1960s onwards, gender began to appear as an organising concept in sociology and elsewhere. Inspired by the Women's and Civil Rights Movements, academics and activists started to examine how almost all societies appeared to be organised in ways that benefited men more than women. It seemed to many social observers that women's and men's lives were radically different in various ways, including quality of life; experience of poverty; social status; access to income, education and employment; and participation in politics and economic life.

Women were perceived as second-class citizens whose main focus in life was the reproductive sphere, through maintaining and rearing a family, while men were viewed as somehow more important citizens, who concerned themselves with life in the public sphere of politics, culture and economics. Further, relations between women and men were immersed within these types of divisions. In Ireland, various movements and organisations, including the Irish Women's Rights Movement, began actively to challenge these assumptions and realities of everyday life and sought at both a policy and interpersonal level to overhaul what they saw as an unequal society that disproportionately benefited men (Connolly, 2002).

A key question that surfaced was why? Why did these unequal relations between women and men exist? It remains outside the remit of this chapter to tease out fully the complexities of the gender inequality debates. Rather, it summarises aspects of the main arguments and directs you to further material to flesh out the arguments in greater depth.

An *essentialist* view suggests that because of innate biological characteristics, women and men are differentiated biologically and socially. Men are seen as innately aggressive and goal-driven while women are seen as passive and emotional (Tovey and Share, 2003: 233). These differences have consequences for the lives that women and men lead, for the kinds of jobs they pursue and for their achievements in the private and public spheres. Essentialism points to 'natural' and unchangeable aspects of femininity and masculinity: women are perceived to be 'naturally' more caring than men; men are perceived to be 'naturally' more aggressive than women. Although this analysis has gained some support within the discipline of sociobiology, a significant difficulty remains: is it accurate to describe all women as passive and all men as aggressive when considerable variations exist — aggressive women and passive men, for example?

A second set of arguments sees gender inequality as socially constructed, as made in society and as linked to an understanding of power. In the 1970s, feminists focused attention on the *patriarchal* nature of western societies, to help explain continued unequal relations between women and men (Walby, 1990). Patriarchy is conceptualised as the systematic patterning of society in ways that men dominate, exploit and oppress women (Walby, 1990; O'Connor, 1998: 7).

In an Irish context, O'Connor (1998) enunciates an understanding of patriarchy as a system made up of six key structures of social relations that enable men to dominate women: paid work; the family and household; culture; sexuality; male violence; and state violence. Within the structure of paid work, women continue to experience vertical and horizontal occupational segregation that places them in lower-paid jobs than men, with less pay and status (see Bacik et al. (2003) for an account of women's experiences in the Irish legal profession). Vertical segregation refers to the notion that women are concentrated into the lower levels of the occupational hierarchy in terms of wages, status and authority, for example. Horizontal segregation suggests that women and men are allocated to qualitatively different types of careers and jobs.

Within the structure of male violence, social practices such as rape, violence within intimate relationships, and sexual harassment in the paid workplace serve to maintain male dominance and to control women's behaviour.

There are difficulties with the notion of patriarchy. It can be presented as a descriptive and universal category rather than one that is explanatory and historically specific. Such a descriptive nuance suggests that all societies have always been patriarchal in nature and organisation. This may tell us very little about the variation in gender relations that exists within and between societies or about the subjective experiences of women and men as they seek in their everyday lives to challenge the existence of structures that dominate them.

On the other hand, Tovey and Share (2003: 232) state that: 'it is certainly the case that all societies are differentiated by gender and have been dominated in various ways by men'. It may thus be a fallacy to ignore the important contribution that the concept of patriarchy offers as a descriptive and partial explanatory concept (Moane, 1999). Indeed, both Walby (1990) and O'Connor (1998) articulate accounts of British and Irish society respectively that clearly demonstrate the many ways in which each society is organised at an overall level to benefit men. Of course, every individual man may not benefit from this system, and not all women experience exploitation within such social arrangements.

To develop a more sophisticated understanding of gender differences and inequality, we can usefully turn to the work of Australian sociologist Connell (1987, 1995). Connell is concerned with the perpetuation of patriarchal social relations in the everyday lives of women and men. He argues that although gender is typically thought of as a property of individuals, it is necessary to move beyond this and conceptualise it as a property of institutions (Connell, 1987: 139–41). Gender, he argues, is a fundamental feature of capitalist societies that are run mainly by, and to the benefit of, men. Every society has a gender order comprising attendant hierarchies. This is made up of a historically specific division of labour; a structure of desire; and a structure of power, authority and control. Processes and practices of patriarchal control exist at each of these levels.

A variety of masculinities (some dominant and some not) and femininities are generated within the gender order. One such form of masculinity is *hegemonic* masculinity. According to Connell (1995: 76–86), only a minority of men practise this type of masculinity, and it involves active subordination of women and other men such as gay men. But he believes that most men gain an advantage from the subordination of women in terms of honour, prestige and the right to command: this is termed the 'patriarchal dividend'. The form of masculinity associated with this is *complicit* masculinity. Connell suggests that although the majority of men may not actively seek to dominate women, it is in their wider interests that traditional gendered ways of 'doing things' remain constant. Other forms of masculinity include *marginalised* (black men; working-class men), *subordinated* (gay men) and *resistant* (pro-feminist men) masculinities.

Some men view certain changes in society as an attack on their patriarchal privilege, but in Irish and other western societies, many others are challenging and changing notions of hegemonic and complicit masculinity. Overall, the concept of gender needs to be contextualised within a complex and sophisticated under-standing of patriarchal social relations as they exist in particular societies at particular times.

To summarise this section, a number of key points emerge:

- Gender is a significant and complex organising category in contemporary Irish and western societies, and is enmeshed in the social relations between women and men;
- Gender refers to the social construction of femininities and masculinities;
- Forms of femininity and masculinity vary both within and between societies at any one time and over time;
- At a societal level, gender is conceptualised as both a property of institutions and within a framework that emphasises the existence of a gender order where patriarchal relations exist to the benefit of men more than women and where men have greater access to powerful positions;
- At an individual level, because of variations in femininities and masculinities, both women and men may express and live gender in complex and diverse ways in their everyday lives.

## GENDER PROCESSES AND SOCIAL CARE

### The Language of Care

Gender is implicated in all social processes: it thus needs to be recognised that social care work is also a gendered sphere. The Irish social care literature has by and large ignored a theoretical and applied analysis of gender (see O'Connor (1992) and Gallagher and O'Toole (1999) for initial attempts at such an analysis). If gender is included, it tends to act as a synonym for either (usually) 'women' or 'men', instead of addressing the social relations between them. To explore some of the gender-related issues in social care, we first need to understand the 'language of care'. What exactly does care mean? As with gender, 'care' is difficult to define and has been strongly contested.

Unpacking the meaning of care suggests that there are inconsistencies in how the term is understood, with variables including who undertakes the care, who receives it, the relationship between the two and the social domain within which the caring takes place (Orme, 2001: 92). At a sociological and social policy level, care has come to refer to the provision of facilities and carrying out of tasks for those unable to do so for themselves. Carers are those paid to do this task (Orme, 2001: 93). But an understanding of care must also recognise those who receive care and the definitions they hold of the activities, tasks and relationships that unfold in the caring sphere. This type of analysis has made only a limited appearance in any of the care-work literature in Ireland.

One of the difficulties when teasing out the meaning of care is the distinction routinely drawn between paid and unpaid caring work (Gallagher and O'Toole, 1999: 78). By contrast, Walmsley (1993: 27) reports that in the Scandinavian countries the term 'care-giving work' encompasses all types of work where the caregiver provides consistent and reliable care for a person who, through age, infirmity or youth, is unable to care for her/himself. In the caring marketplace, different values are placed on similar skills according to who is using them, the criteria frequently being the gender and power of the worker.

Care work takes place along a continuum from informal to formal care. There is a significant interplay between informal and formal care *and* between gender and care in each sector (Lynch and McLaughlin, 1995; Feder Kittay, 1999). Figure 7.1 captures this interplay and illustrates some of the types of care that take place in each sector, as well as providing an example of care that could exist in the informal and formal sectors simultaneously.

**Figure 7.1. Types of Care**

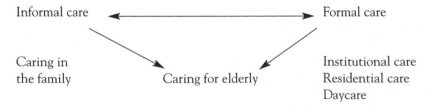

Gender relations impact on each of the sectors indicated in Figure 7.1 in terms of who provides the care, who receives the care, the relationship between them and the context of care. The relations between informal and formal care are also gendered in that assumptions about caring in the informal sector influence the provision and receipt of care in the formal sector.

It is mostly women who provide and receive care in the informal sector (Gerstel and Gallagher, 2001; Herd and Meyer, 2002). This is largely a result of constructions of femininity that see caring as an innate female quality. This has repercussions for the formal sector, as assumptions exist that it is only 'natural' that women will enter this field. Social care practice can, in some ways, be seen as a non-traditional occupation for men. It is seen as a 'caring' profession and, while some aspects of the work involve 'control' and surveillance, the emphasis on 'care' positions it as a feminised profession (Christie, 1998; 2001).

## Women and Men as Social Care Practitioners

Orme (2001: 14) believes that the connections between social care and gender are evident in that practitioners in this sphere work, in the first instance, within gender constructed social relationships. She suggests that it is the combination of social relations and power that makes the concept of gender useful when analysing social care. Further, understandings and constructions of femininity and masculinity explicitly and implicitly permeate the provision of care.

An emerging debate in social care concerns the small proportion of men amongst those entering the profession. It is interesting to note that an exploration of the meaning of both masculinity *and* femininity in caring contexts is at an early stage here. Key initial questions relate to the number of men working in the field; the role of men in social care; and the necessity of attracting more men into care. This requires ongoing research in an Irish context. Interesting work elsewhere suggests that a structural analysis of gender and attendant links with the notion of power provides a framework in which to analyse the roles women and man enact in the social care arena, both as carers and service-users (Cavanagh and Cree, 1996; Dominelli, 1997; Hanmer and Statham, 1999; Hearn, 1999).

An analysis of social care practice courses in Ireland shows that women dominate the membership of full-time programmes (McElwee, Jackson, McKenna-McElwee and Cameron, 2003). The consequences are manifold — an important one being that stakeholders are only now, in an Irish context, beginning to debate some of the issues, including 'making care work attractive to men'; men as carers; and the possible outcomes of care provision, service use and receipt.

As social care work involves the sharing of life-space, and encompasses management, therapeutic and personal care tasks (Graham, 1995), gender social relations are central. Anecdotal evidence from the profession indicates that women and men perform quite different roles when providing and using care and, further, that such roles are rooted in a particular construction of femininity and masculinity. In relation to men, Dominelli argues that:

> [F]eminists have been crucial in raising the problematic nature of masculinity for both men and women and revealed how men are limited in expressing the full range of their emotions and organisational skills because certain

characteristics have been defined as 'feminine' and out of bounds to them. (Dominelli, 1997: 111–12)

McElwee (2001b) and colleagues (McElwee, Jackson, McKenna-McElwee and Cameron, 2003) in their initial exploration of males in social care in Ireland, seem to agree, at least partly, when they suggest that, in the child and youth care arena, young people require women and men workers who are able to address the complexity of their roles and are willing to move beyond stereotypical constructions of femininity and masculinity. They state that men and women need to exhibit non-controlling, emotionally secure and facilitative characteristics.

McElwee and his co-researchers focus on men entering 'non-traditional' forms of work. Other research indicates that when men enter non-traditional occupations such as care work, masculinity may turn out to be a boon for them, as qualities associated with men become more highly regarded than those associated with women — even in predominantly female jobs (Cree, 2001: 153). Cree (2001) also observes that there are other advantages for men in non-traditional occupations: these include greater access to promotion; achieving more attention because of their small numbers; and being rewarded for an ability to express feelings and emotions which, it would seem, are taken for granted in women. More research is required in an Irish context which can interrogate masculinity and the potential impact of male privileging in the social care environment.

McElwee et al. do address important questions, not least of which is — what does it mean to be a male in social care? But a gendered analysis demands that this question be critically linked to a number of other questions including:

- What does it mean to be a woman in social care?
- How are gendered social relations enacted in the social care arena?
- What discourses of femininity and masculinity exist in the training of social care practitioners and in the social care work environment? What is the impact of these discourses on individual and collective social practices?
- How can men begin to address their positions in social care in a way that takes account of their privileged positioning *as men* in wider society? For instance, how is it that men, although considerably fewer in number than women in the education and training of social care practitioners, dominate the management positions in the educational institutions?
- An interrogation of *femininity* is also required.

There is little published material in Ireland that explores the gendered social relations that permeate interactions and interventions between social care practitioners and service users. A main goal of social care work is to empower those who use services to reach their full potential as human beings. As reflective practitioners, care workers must be aware of how their interactions might be underpinned by sexism and be connected to gender and power. To ensure non-oppressive practice, the generation of knowledge about gender and power, both in society *and in social care*, is necessary. Moreover, interactions and interventions between practitioners and users of a service must also be understood in the context of social class, sexuality, 'race' and ethnicity, and attendant power relations.

## SEXUALITY

## The Social Construction of Sexuality

Sexuality, like gender, is a social construction. There is not one 'true' sexuality or way of expressing desires; rather, there exists a variety of sexualities in all societies. 'Sexuality' is thus 'a diverse field of experience and behaviour that is brought together at certain times through a common body of language or discourse' (Tovey and Share, 2003: 259).

At different times in the history of societies, different meanings and practices emerge that guide our understanding and expression of sexuality. For instance, in many western societies, expressions of homosexual and lesbian sexuality have been negated and denied as they do not fit into dominant meanings of sexuality which emphasise heterosexuality as the norm.

Inglis (1998a, 1998b) suggests that there are powerful discourses moulding sexuality in Irish society. Discourses refer to dominant ideas and understandings about a topic — in this case, sexuality — that define how people experience and behave in their everyday lives. Such ideas become established as a knowledge or way of looking at the world. There may be a number of different and competing discourses at play at any one time: hegemonic and resistant masculinity, for instance. Discourses are linked to discipline. This means that individuals tend to be positioned in particular ways according to the discourses and may be forced to behave in particular ways through self-imposed or externally imposed discipline. Importantly, within any discourse, there is always the potential to resist the demands placed on individual experience and behaviour.

According to Inglis (1998b), some of the more powerful discourses that mould sexuality in Irish society are generated within the family, the education system, medicine, popular culture, religion, legal and political systems. He argues (1998a) that from the nineteenth century until the 1960s, the social construction of sexuality was immersed within discourses of sexuality promulgated by the Catholic Church, through the words and actions of bishops and priests. Sexuality was not so much hidden or repressed as talked about and enacted in a different sort of way from today. In particular, sexuality was viewed as a powerful force that needed to be regulated within the institution of marriage. The discourses linked sexuality to notions of sin, control, danger, guilt, suspicion, celibacy, purity, innocence, virginity, humility, piety and regulation that emphasised Catholic moral and social teaching (Inglis, 1998b).

The Catholic Church imposed a strict discipline of sexual morality where both men and women were encouraged to feel ashamed of their bodies. This imposition may have been experienced differently by women and men. Condron (1989) and Inglis (1998c: 178–200) state that women were expected to embody Catholic morality by being virtuous, chaste and virginal (Hilliard, 2002). If women contravened the conventions, strict sanctions were imposed. Observe the recent disclosures about the Magdalene Laundries where women were effectively incarcerated if they became pregnant outside marriage or were perceived to have been involved in 'morally unacceptable' behaviour (see, for example, Finnegan, 2004).

O'Connor (1998) suggests that historically women's sexuality was constructed around notions of reputation, marriage, childbirth/rearing and family. Since the foundation of the Irish state, women have grown up within a dominant understanding (discourse) of sexuality that specifies the woman as mother, as carer, as wife. O'Connor asserts that female sexuality continues to possess the following attributes: active heterosexuality; difficulties with contraception; an emphasis on the complex notion of 'love'; the experiences of sexual harassment; the stigmatising of abortion; powerful and contradictory messages around body image; sex being viewed as a consumer product and pressures against saying 'no'.

Dominant understandings of male sexuality were constructed around the notions of the uncontrollable and insatiable nature of sexual expression for men. Historically, in Ireland, male sexual expression was deemed powerful and a man's right to express himself sexually was, within reason, inalienable. Up until 1990, for instance, a man, upon marriage, had the right to demand sex from his wife, even if she resisted. In 1990, legislation was passed to criminalise rape within marriage and effectively remove the notion of wife/woman as male property. However, the experiences of many men in Irish society did not and do not conform to these dominant discourses.

Great change has taken place in the past thirty years with regard to sexual attitudes and practices. Sexuality has become public in Irish society: a new way of speaking by a variety of commentators has emerged to challenge and contest Catholic discourses of sexuality directly (Hug, 1999). Diversity, pleasures, preferences and choices have become the concepts that underpin the deployment of sexuality in contemporary Ireland. Freely available contraception; decriminalisation of male homosexuality; equalisation of age of consent between lesbians, gay men and heterosexuals; cohabitation; and the public celebration of sex in and outside marriage have all been part of the new discourses of sexuality.

Sexuality is 'out there' and 'in here': in the media, in the school playground, in the nightclub, in the minds and bodies of Irish people. Inglis (1998a) believes that what we now require is an analysis of Irish sexuality that describes and analyses how sexuality was and is seen, understood and embodied by participants in Irish social life. There are still substantial gaps in our knowledge about sexual attitudes and behaviour in Ireland. Much has changed in terms of sexual expression, including greater acceptance of the multifarious ways in which people live their sexual lives. But sexuality must be understood as linked to particular understandings of femininity and masculinity in society and to gender social relations and power.

## Sexuality and Social Care

We have seen that it is important to reach a better understanding of gender social relations in the social care environment. Similarly, the impact of sexuality must be addressed in social care. Social care work is constituted by the sharing of life-space. Expressions of sexuality thus permeate the everyday interactions of care workers and service users in a variety of ways that include touch, looking, physical stance, clothes and language. Within the social care setting, this can have major consequences for the level and type of interactions; concerns with and about behaviour; planning and controlling activities; developing care plans; specifying interventions; and general day-to-day living. As Irish academic studies of sexuality are limited, it is no surprise to find no published text or piece of research that deals with its impact in the social care environment in an Irish context.

This is not to say that sexuality has never been talked about in relation to social care. The topic has been addressed in the development of 'good' models of practice in the disability sector and within children's and youth centres. Some organisations have developed in-house programmes and policies with regard to people with learning difficulties and sexuality. These programmes and policies centre on self-advocacy in terms of sexual expression; protection of vulnerable people against sexual exploitation; age-appropriate sexual behaviour; development of relevant sex-education programmes; and responsibility in sexual behaviour. Such programmes have become particularly relevant in an Irish context with the many revelations of sexual abuse in institutional care. However, many such programmes and policies operate within a discourse of sexuality that has placed issues of regulation and control at the forefront. There is a need for ongoing research to tease out the implications of regulation and control for both the care practitioner and the service-user. The increasing emphasis in wider society on liberal attitudes to sexuality suggests that issues of self-advocacy and the role of appointed advocates are central to the debates on sexuality, especially as service users demand greater control over their sexual selves.

Managing sexuality and sex in human relationships is difficult. Humans have developed complex ways to manage and deal with their feelings in all kinds of relationships (Cavanagh and Cree, 2001). Since the mid-1990s in Ireland, *protection* has become a key element of the practice of social care work. The numerous accounts of sexual abuse have left social care practitioners and service users with a legacy so powerful it now guides the types of physical and intimate interactions that occur.

It is necessary to develop good practice models that protect all actors in these kinds of social relationships. It is also important to explore the links between gender, power and sexuality. McElwee et al. (2002) suggest, for instance, that women's and men's behaviour with regard to offering a supportive hug or a touch of hands is being seriously restricted lest it be misconstrued as a form of sexual harassment and/or abuse. This has serious implications for how care practitioners and service users interact. The issues are complex. On the one hand, the protection of service users and practitioners is paramount. On the other hand, a crying child, missing its parents, sometimes needs the security and intimacy of human touch. The fear attached to expressions of affection between practitioner and service user must be unpacked to uncover what this fear is about and where it comes from. Sex and sexuality are sometimes viewed as sensitive areas, too difficult to discuss with service users. Yet as many social care practitioners act *in loco parentis*, it will be necessary at some stage to deal with sexuality with clients.

As in all social relationships, it is imperative that social care practitioners develop an awareness of their own sexuality. Increasing awareness will help social care practitioners to acknowledge their own feelings and desires and how these affect their professional relationships with their clients. Social care practitioners must understand and acknowledge their own sexuality in order to work effectively and safely with others.

An important dimension of any discussion on sexuality is language. How people speak about sexuality and sex and the terms they use impact on social behaviour. Language usage is connected to power and the ability of certain people to speak for and about others. For instance, terms like 'slag' and 'slut' may have particular consequences for women's feelings and actions in their everyday lives (Lees, 1993; O'Toole, 1998). Terms like 'sissy', 'cunt', 'faggot' and 'queer' are currently employed as terms of abuse which, if used in the social care context (or indeed any social context), contribute to oppressive practices. Words for sexual behaviour and genitals carry considerable power. Social care practitioners must examine their own use of language and the use of language in the social care context to avoid perpetuating oppressive behaviours.

A final issue to consider with regard to sexuality and social care is the link between sexual preference, particularly homosexuality, and anti-oppressive practice. Tovey and Share (2003: 263) suggest that one of the more rapidly changing discussions around sexuality in Ireland relates to the experiences of lesbians and gay men. In 1993, sexual relations between men were decriminalised. Women had never been covered by the Victorian legislation that had criminalised sexual relations between men. Although equality legislation has been enacted to protect gay people amongst others, this has not necessarily meant that the everyday lives of gay people in Ireland are left untouched by anti-gay feeling and outright discrimination.

O'Carroll and Collins (1995) document aspects of the many and varied lives of gay people in Ireland, including their experiences of coming out, relationships, discrimination, national identity and sense of self. Despite significant changes in Irish society with regard to sexuality, there is still considerable work to be done to achieve an egalitarian existence for gay people. Further, the inequalities of gender that permeate wider society also infuse the lives of gay men and lesbians. Their experiences as gay are not symmetrical. Lesbians can experience discrimination on the basis of being women, just as gay men may benefit from being men within a patriarchal gender order.

Within care work, cognisance must be taken of the issues that affect gay men and lesbians. It is useful if social care practitioners develop an increased awareness of their own sexuality and attitudes to sexuality. Anti-oppressive practice — part of social care work training and practice in many countries, including Britain — demands that the lives of gay people be both protected and celebrated within the social care environment (Thompson, 1997). In the 1980s, social care education in Britain displayed an increased awareness of the impact of oppression and discrimination on service users and communities. There developed within education and training an emphasis on combating discrimination. This was part of a process that established these competencies as building blocks of qualifying and subsequent practice.

Social care training in Ireland does not, as of the time of writing, have models of anti-oppressive practice in its training and education programmes. While modules on equality are part of some social care programmes, they do not explicitly demand that students (or staff) sign up for anti-oppressive practices. Anti-oppressive practices refer not only to the need to challenge attitudes and practices towards gay people but also to challenge other ways in which people are discriminated against, including ethnicity, 'race', gender, social class, age, disability, education, marital status, family status and religion.

It is imperative that social care — in theory, policy and practice — revisit its founding principles to assess their relevance and contribution to anti-oppressive practice. It is only in recent years that learning about homosexuality has been removed from 'abnormal' psychology modules. Labelling anything 'abnormal' is questionable in the context of the need to explore the value of anti-oppressive practice.

An anti-oppressive module in the context of social care training could:

- Justify the development of anti-oppressive practice
- Identify the factors that underpin discrimination and oppression especially as they relate to social care work theory and practice
- Explain common concepts and issues across the various forms of discrimination including sexism, racism, ageism, homophobia and so forth
- Present the critical steps needed to construct a social care work practice based on principles of anti-discrimination and equal opportunities (Thompson, 1997: 2).

In summary, this section has explored some of the sexuality issues that pervade the social care environment. Sexuality is a complex feature of all human relationships and developing an awareness of how it impacts on social care is crucial. Further, increased awareness of sexuality will facilitate the discipline in developing anti-oppressive practices in relation to sexuality, racism, social class, ethnicity, age and disability.

## CASE STUDY

You are working in a residential home for people with intellectual and physical disabilities. This is a small group home/house attached to a large complex that includes a day centre, a recreation and leisure area and a number of other residential houses. There are four service users (two female and two male) and six staff (three female and three male) working in your residential home.

At a team meeting, a discussion takes place about one of the residents, Maria. Maria is 29 years old and has been living in this residential home for six years. She has been assessed as having the mental age of a 12-year-old, although you are not sure how this assessment was made.

It seems that last night, because of staff shortages and another house requiring some cover, there was no female on duty at bedtime. Last night, Maria had a bath and needed some assistance. As there was no female staff-member to attend, one of the male staff-members had to lift Maria from the bath and help her to dry herself and get to bed. You weren't sure how Maria felt about this but at the team meeting a female staff-member was complaining to Seán (the manager) about inappropriate behaviour, potential exposure to abuse, dignity and the importance of understanding Maria's needs properly.

Seán, the other male staff-member and one of the female staff-members were disagreeing, arguing that Maria didn't seem to mind at all and, in the situation that presented, someone had to assist Maria.

- Discuss the issues that arise in this scenario.
- Describe what you think good practice is in this situation.
- How can staff be encouraged to engage in good practice?

## CONCLUSION

This chapter has introduced an array of gender processes that are central to an understanding of social care work in Ireland. The focus has been on social care work from the perspective of the care practitioner. I have argued that gender is a complex concept, the meaning of which must be contextualised within an understanding of patriarchal social relations in wider society.

Forms of femininity and masculinity vary within and between societies. Their constructions within care work may provide an insight into how gender is understood within society generally. Despite the many and varied changes in Irish society over the past fifty years, discourses of femininity and masculinity persist in social care that conform to historically dominant meanings of both. Thus, it is more 'natural' for women to become care workers than men, as women are merely expressing their innate abilities to care.

If men do enter the profession, they are either lauded for their ability to go against the grain or expected to adhere to perceived traditional roles for men of surveillance and control. Of course, the complexities of social care work on the ground may suggest a much more complicated picture. Social care would benefit from more research to interrogate the relational categories of both femininity and masculinity as they are enacted by relevant social actors in the various social care arenas.

8

# Self in Social Care

Thom Garfat, Niall McElwee & Grant Charles

## OVERVIEW

Without the self there is no other. (Ricks, 2001)

This statement emphasises the tremendous importance of self in social care practice, for surely our practice is concerned with other. While the meaning of this statement will emerge as we move through this chapter, we want to state unequivocally at the opening that the social care practitioner in the field to help others has no choice but to know self, and to know self intimately.

The purpose of knowing self is not that one might develop as a finely tuned machine, sensitive to the nuances of need discovered in engagement with other. Nor is it to develop another tool in the arsenal of intervention — a trick of engagement we might carry into the arena of helping. Rather, the purpose of knowing self is that one might be, and be with, self in the encounter with other. It is in the experience of being with self that we find the opportunity to be genuinely with other, whether that other be child, youth or adult. When other experiences genuineness in an encounter with another human being, the door is opened for an alternative way of being in the world — a way of being in relationship that includes being with self. Ultimately we can find self only in interaction with other, in the context of relationship. The irony is that one needs to know self, and be with self, in order to be with other effectively, but one can truly know self only by being in interaction with other. Self and relationship are inseparable in effective social care practice. This is one of the apparent paradoxes of our field.

The purpose of this chapter is not to dwell on the philosophical aspects of self, other, relationship and helping. Although we would encourage anyone who wants to be a truly effective practitioner to do so, time and space limit such an exploration here. We encourage such enquiry as there is a relationship between the exploration of such issues and clinical practice; between the philosopher and the practitioner. We have never met an excellent practitioner who was not also concerned with the philosophical.

Here we explore what is meant by self in the field of social care; the perceived role and purpose of self; how self is seen as important and some of the ways that self and self-knowing might be developed. We conclude with some commentary on the 'use of self' in social care practice.

Discussion of self is by its very nature dangerously personal. This chapter will itself dwell near the edge of the personal, occasionally wandering into the territory of the personal self and experiences of the authors as we attempt to share a little of our own voyage. We will at times be clear, at times confused, at times serious and at times humorous. In short, we shall be, we hope, our selves.

## WHAT DO WE MEAN BY SELF?

> [I]n its fullest form this self is more than physical, more than emotional, and more than cognitive. (Fewster, 2001: 63)

We begin with the question, what is *self*? People use this word all the time. Think how it permeates our everyday discussions: 'I'll do it my-self'; 'he is lacking in self-esteem'; 'she is self-ish'; 'a worker should be self-aware'; 'to thine own self be true'. In the course of a day we may use the word self, standing alone or in conjunction with others, a dozen times, perhaps a hundred. But how often do we pause for a moment and ask ourselves (there it is again!): 'what is self?' Not often enough, we would argue. Yet attending to self is essential if we are to attend to other.

We could reach into the annals of philosophy and ponder the questions posed by great thinkers such as Socrates and Aristotle — but why bother? (See Chapter 6 for why we might!) For the self they discussed was the self as defined by their own space, time and context. Through the course of history the meaning, role and implications of self have changed, sometimes dramatically. Our interest lies in the helping and caring field, and more specifically in the field of social care, as it exists today.

Not long ago, any book about our field ignored the presence and role of self, except perhaps to make some comments about self-control or self-security. Yet today, any review of the literature, or of contemporary models of practice, reveals an overt concern with the self of the practitioner and youth or families. The central philosophical characteristics of the EirCan model of social and youth care practice (McElwee and Garfat, 2003a), for example, include:

- A focus on advocacy for clients
- A focus on the self of worker and clients
- A focus on connectedness, engagement and therapeutic relationship
- A focus on quality of service delivery.

Here we see a recognition of the importance of the self both of those who would help, and of the children, youth and families who are the focus of service delivery. The EirCan model, like many others, goes further to state that 'attention to self' is central to the effective helping process: in all parts of the system, from service design to delivery, a focus on the selves of the participants is essential. Self, then, has taken central stage in the social care process of both programme design and service delivery.

What do some of the contemporary writers in our field have to say about the self? Gerry Fewster is perhaps the most profound and prolific of these. He suggests that:

> [I]n its fullest form this self is more than physical, more than emotional, and more than cognitive. It is the sum total of all our aspects, and more. It exists at the core of our experience. (Fewster, 2001: 63)

Fewster argues that self exists at the core of our experiencing. Some might argue that self is the core of our existence, the centrality of what we are; in some respects like the hub of the wheel of human existence and experience. Yet it is not just the core — for that implies that self exists as a separate part of a person. It is rather the very *essence* of who we are (Ricks, 1989). Frances Ricks, another who writes frequently about the importance of self (and self-awareness), says that without self there is no other (Ricks, 2001). She argues that it is the self that forms the individual lens through which we perceive and interpret all of our experiences. In the absence of an awareness of the self, we cannot know if what we experience is 'real' or simply a projection of self onto other; a self-construction of other that may, or may not, have a basis in an objective analysis of who the other 'really' is. Self, then, is active, constant, and ever present.

When we talk like this about self, it is as if we were talking about something separate or distinct, like when we talk about my vision, my brain, or my kidney. Yet the writing in our field now suggests that self is not a separate thing from . . . well . . . self. Of course, this is where any discussion of self begins to get complicated. If we talk about self, for example, who or what is talking, or making the observations? How can I talk about me, as if somehow the speaker and the thing being spoken about are different? How can I reflect on self, if, in fact, I am self? Maybe, in the end, that is the best definition: *self is who we are*. In the quiet of the night, in the bustle of the day, in the intimacy of life, self is who we are. Self is the answer to the question, 'Who am I?'

'Who am I?' is a fundamental question for the social care professional. With time and experience in the field, we encounter situations that, if we are fortunate, demand we explore in depth the nature of our being. It is beyond the scope of this chapter to delve too deeply into this philosophical, some might even say existential, question. Suffice it to say that the question of the real or authentic self becomes increasingly important as one develops as a social care professional, or indeed, as one progresses, with reflection, through life. But of equal importance are the questions of 'Who do I appear to be?' and 'How can I discover more about my self?' It is to these that we now turn.

## ON THE PRESENTATION OF SELF

> [T]he professional recognizes that mood and attitude can affect performance, and so she or he comes to the work situation prepared to do the work. (Smiar, 1995: 38)

It has always been important in our field to address the 'presentation of self' in our work with young people and families. In earlier periods, concern about how we presented ourselves was focused on such issues as appearance, general conduct, general values or beliefs — as reflected in early attempts to define ethical guide-lines for the field. Social care workers were often screened to ensure that they held 'proper' values, were told what was 'appropriate dress', and monitored to ensure that their conduct reflected mainstream values and practices. In many areas, how we presented ourselves was very carefully determined and monitored by the agency or organisation for which we worked. If you were possessed of characteristics different from those dictated by the agency, you hid them carefully if you wanted to keep your job. Our concern with self was mostly limited to how we looked and acted, on the outside. Self was not really a well-developed concept in our field.

In the present time (we say it that way as we know it will change in the future), we mean something quite different by the term 'presentation of self'. We are now concerned with how the values, beliefs and characteristics of the individual worker show up in their interactions with youth and families. For, show up they do!

Imagine a social care practitioner who values family and believes it the most appropriate place for a young person to live and grow. This worker, in interactions with the youth and family, in case discussions, in team meetings, or any other aspect of her work, will manifest this belief through expression and action. In an individual interaction, for example, she will make reference to family, either implicitly or explicitly. In case discussions, she will constantly ask questions about family and try to move the plan towards keeping the youth at home. In team meetings, she will be a constant advocate for family inclusion. The values we hold position us to adopt a certain stance, to act in a certain manner.

Let us now imagine the same worker; let us assume that she also believes that the way to hold on to your job is always to be agreeable to your team-mates — especially your supervisor. Let us assume that she sees social care practitioners as insignificant in the grander scheme of things, as people who should not express themselves too loudly if they want to continue working.

Imagine her in a team meeting where the supervisor is discounting the importance of a young person's family and is making plans to move the youth into a permanent care situation. The practitioner believes that with some extra efforts the young person could be helped to return home. But she is now possessed of conflicting beliefs and the conflicting desires to act associated with each. On the one hand, she wants to advocate for more services and supports for the young person and family and, on the other hand, she wants to keep her good relationship with her supervisor. She also believes that the supervisor is more knowledgeable, more professional than herself. How might she present herself? Might she present as conflicted? Will she speak up? Might she leave the room? Might she act out? Might she just sit quietly thinking about how she can undermine the plan? Will she expose her conflict and ask for help? Imagine what she might do. Imagine, honestly, what you would do.

Whatever she does in this situation, this is the care practitioner's presentation of self — this is her self manifesting in the work environment. Who you are shows up in 'how you are'. Our values, our belief, our characteristics, are ever present. Thus it is imperative that we know our own values and beliefs, our characteristics, our attitudes, our way of making sense of things. If we fail to attend to these, they impact on our every decision in ways we might not notice. It is not that we think the practitioner should not have reactions, but that she should be aware of them as they occur.

## WHAT WE KNOW AND WHAT WE DON'T KNOW

[B]ecoming aware of how our beliefs, values, and ethics impact on us personally, we can also become aware of how they impact on our presentation to our clients. (Elsdon, 1998: 57)

We have emphasised that it is important to know ourselves: in order to be an effective and competent social care practitioner, we must be knowledgeable about who we are. But we do not always know everything about ourselves. Ironic as it may seem, it is probably impossible ever to know our selves fully. There are some things we know about ourselves, and some things we just don't know. There are some things others know about us, and some things they don't (and hopefully never will!) know about us.

In 1969, Joseph Luft introduced the Johari Window game, designed as an exercise to demonstrate the importance of discussion and feedback in developing open communications (Luft, 1969). Figure 8.1 illustrates a Johari Window relevant to self. In it we see that some things are known to self, and some things are not. Some things are known to other, and some are not. Let us look at the Johari Window for a moment in the context of working as a social care practitioner.

Figure 8.1. A Johari Window, Relevant to Self

|  | Known to self | Not known to self |
|---|---|---|
| **Known to other** | open | blind |
| **Not known to other** | hidden | unknown |

*Open* refers to what is known to self and known to other. This might include physical characteristics and, in working with youth and families, such things as the fact that the young person has broken the law; the parents are not living together; the mother is unemployed, and so on. It may also include things about the practitioner like where she works, how old she is, her previous experience — in other words, things that we all know about. Imagine an encounter between a social care practitioner and a young woman. What are the things we might expect them to know about one another?

*Hidden* refers to things that may be known to self but not known to other. From a parent's point of view, it may include such things as the fact that the father is having an affair (he knows it but no one else does); that the young woman is involved with prostitution; that she fears the father because of previous abuse. From the practitioner's perspective, it may include the fact that she is making her first home visit; that she is living with a man with a criminal record; that she is hoping to leave work early today. The hidden area covers territory that, at least for the moment, is not known to other. It also includes the myriad values and beliefs that a person holds and is not, for whatever reason, disclosing to the other. Imagine again the interaction between a practitioner and a young woman. What are the types of things that the practitioner may know about herself, that would be unknown to the young woman? What are the things the young woman might know about herself that would be unknown to the practitioner?

*Blind* refers to things that are known to other, but not to self. At first glance, this may seem strange. How could someone know something about me that I would not know? But a moment's reflection shows us that there are many things that other might know and of which we remain unaware. For example, a person might know that I get defensive when I am challenged, and I might not notice it. Or a person may be aware that I am hesitant in my speech, while I am unaware of this fact. In a family meeting, for example, a parent may notice that the practitioner is speaking quickly, but the practitioner may not be aware of her own speech or may even think she presents a calm and professional image. Equally, a practitioner may notice that the mother always glances at the father before answering a question. There are numerous things that, strange as it may seem, are known to other, but not known to ourselves. In the interaction between a practitioner and a young woman, what are some other things that one may know about the other that the other may not know?

*Unknown* refers to things that are known neither to self nor to other. For some it is hard to believe there could be aspects of ourselves that are not known to anyone, even ourselves. But suspend your disbelief for a minute and consider this example. Imagine that when you were very young you used to visit your grandmother, and when you were there, you felt relaxed and special because she paid a great deal of attention to you. Now, this was a long time ago and you hardly ever see her any more. But somewhere inside you, you have a special feeling about grandmothers. You don't notice it, you certainly don't think it abnormal, but there is a part of you that believes that grandmothers are good for young people. Now, you don't know this about yourself, and others certainly don't know it about you — unknown to self and unknown to other. But as a result of this experience, you may find yourself always exploring with families the possibility of a stronger connection between the young person and their grandmother.

Imagine an experience that you have repressed, like the fact that you were abused, or that you think, deep down, that you are not worthwhile. There exists the possibility that there are numerous things you don't know about yourself, and that others certainly don't know. When you work with young people and their families, there are things about themselves about which they are unaware, and about which you do not know. What are the other types of things that may not be known either to self or to other?

## NOTICING AND NOT NOTICING

This way of thinking also applies to how we pay attention to things. If you notice some things, and another does not, this increases the area in which some things are known to a person and some are not. The truth is that we all focus differently during the course of our experience, even if we share the experience together. Bandler and Grinder (1975) have demonstrated how some of us focus more on the visual, some on the auditory and some on the kinaesthetic (movement). Thus we might discuss a common experience and each have a different view of it. Three people go for a walk on the beach — when they come back, one talks about the sights (the colours, the shapes); another talks about the sounds (the crash of the waves on the beach, the howl of the wind); the third talks about the physical feelings she experienced (the sting of the wind on her face, the chill of the air). Three people shared the same experience; all come back with a different way of recording and talking about it.

One important aspect of the effective social care intervention is noticing (Garfat, 1998). An important part of training is noticing what we do notice and what we do not. In a programme one of us worked in, part of the interviewing process for potential workers was to have them go on a walk around the programme. The interviews then began with the questions: What did you notice? Why do you suppose you noticed that? The interviewer explored with the applicant things they did not notice and why that might be so. This type of exploration helps us to realise that we walk through the world with what have been called 'blind spots and blank spots':

> [B]lank spots are those areas in which we know that we need to know more. Blind spots, on the other hand, are areas in which our current theory, method, or perceptions prevent us from seeing something as clearly as we might if we didn't have that blind spot. In some respects they represent areas in which we need to know more but we don't know we need to know more. (Garfat, 1993: v)

The ability to recognise our blind and blank spots is an important part of the self-awareness demonstrated by effective social care practitioners. Without this awareness, we see only a portion of what exists, but think it is the whole.

We all see, as Ricks (1989) said, through our own personal lens. It is as if we arise in the morning and don our own particular pair of glasses, and through these unique lenses, we experience the world as we encounter it. Even though we have the experience together, some of it is known to you, some to me and, quite frankly, some to neither of us. But more about this later. For the moment, let us rest with the idea that, sophisticated as we might consider ourselves to be, there are things about ourselves that even we don't know.

## ON WHY IT IS IMPORTANT TO BE KNOWLEDGEABLE ABOUT SELF

> Work with youth is a process of self in action. (Krueger, 1998: 68)

It has been said, here and elsewhere (Garfat, 1994; McElwee, 2003a) that awareness of self is essential if the social care practitioner is to be able to distinguish self from other, so that she might know, as Fewster (2001) has said, 'where I end and the child begins'. Now this might seem a bit confusing. After all, as we stand facing one another, it seems clear to me that I am here and you are over there. We are after all, two separate entities, two separate beings. Or are we?

When you look at another person, what is it that you actually see? You see their physical presence; perhaps you see what they are doing. Let's go a little farther.

Imagine that you are approaching a young person to talk to her. You notice how she is standing, how her head moves, small gestures she makes. You notice the colour of her hair, the style of dress she sports, her jewellery and make-up. You watch and see how she responds as you approach her: perhaps she takes a half-step backwards, looks around her. From this you draw some conclusion, make some interpretations and assumptions. Perhaps you conclude from everything that you have seen so far, that she is a member of a particular sub-group of adolescent society. That she is anxious about your approach. That she is not sure about adults.

Stop here. The first half of the preceding paragraph was about the young person. The second half was all about you. As we take in information, there is a natural human need to make sense of it, to interpret it, to make meaning from what we experience. That is what was going on in the last paragraph.

As you approach the young woman, you take into consideration what you have seen. So, you slow down a little, perhaps making eye contact, trying to assure her that you are not a threat. When you are within an appropriate distance, you speak softly, telling her your name and why you were approaching her, again wanting to reassure her that you are no threat. Your judgment is that if she knows why you are approaching her, she may relax a little, taking the first step towards trust.

Once again, we would argue, your actions are all about you, and little about her. You are acting on your interpretations, your 'best guesses'. This is what happens when we interact with people. We interpret what we experience, and based on that interpretation, we act. But, not all of us interpret and act in the same way to the same situation. For it is true that one of us, approaching the same woman and seeing the same things, would respond differently. We might interpret, for example, that her behaviour is not a sign of feeling threatened but is rather an invitation to come closer, maybe even a subtle signal that she would like to go for a walk. What else might her actions be saying?

Why is it that we interpret things differently? Where are these interpretations coming from and how are they created? What influences us to perceive and interpret in a particular way? The answer is that we experience and act differently because of who we are. And each of us is different.

We each create for ourselves, through the course of time and history, our own particular way of perceiving and experiencing. How we perceive and experience is influenced by a number of factors, including, but not limited to:

- Our values and beliefs
- Our previous experiences in similar situations
- Our theoretical knowledge
- Our cultural experiences
- The characteristics of our upbringing
- The particular needs which are present at the moment.

From these we develop a way of perceiving, interpreting and then interacting with the world and those we encounter. A simple example should suffice to make our point here. Take the example of how the young woman looked around as we approached her. We see her do this and we have to make sense of it.

Now imagine that once in the past you approached a young woman and she did the same thing. As you talked to her, two men stepped out of the shadows and told you to leave. You felt threatened and frightened. In retrospect, you think you were lucky to escape without physical harm. As you approach this new young woman, and see the same action, your mind flips back to that previous experience and you wonder if the same thing is going on, if you need to be concerned for your own physical safety. But it is just a question as you compare your previous experience to this one.

You notice that you are doing this because you are self-aware — because in your work, you are able to notice when you are making associations between this experience and the previous one. You are noticing, as you are walking, how you are responding internally to what you are experiencing. You notice your own anxiety and realise that it comes from a previous experience. You separate this lingering anxiety from the current situation.

Now, imagine that you are not aware of how you are associating this experience with your previous one. As you approach the young woman, the same things are going on for you but you do not notice it. In those two cases, we ask, how might your final approach to the young woman, your first words, the tone and implication of them, be the same or different? For, different they would be!

All of us have had moments when we offered an interpretation to someone, only to have it rejected, to be corrected in our interpretation. Imagine you are talking with a family who has just had a son or daughter removed from home. Imagine you have had some experience with this. In your classes, you have 'learned' that it is always difficult for families when a young person is placed.

Perhaps you have recently been separated from someone in your own family and are finding it painful. Other parents with whom you have worked have cried over the separation. Based on these experiences, and your values and beliefs about family togetherness, you comment that it must be difficult for them. They laugh and say, 'Not at all. It is the best thing that has happened for us in years.' Different interpretations of the same event. If you had intervened, based on your assumptions about their experience, you would miss the mark with this family. The social practitioner needs to know self, and what is going on for self at any given moment, in order to be able to distinguish what is self and what is other.

## ON GETTING TO KNOW SELF

> [I]t's only through the investigation of our selves, our perceptions, beliefs, bias, philosophies, and ways of knowing that we will learn where our blind and blank spots lie. (Garfat, 1993: iv)

We hope that by now we have convinced you of the need for the competent social care practitioner to know self and to be aware of aspects of self that affect the interaction between practitioner and youth or family. You should have become aware of the implication that people are not ever fully aware of everything about themselves. Nothing about this is intended to imply a criticism of the individual. Rather it is a recognition that we all, living in the world we do, operate without a full awareness of self. After all, it is not typically a focus of our upbringing or our education. Indeed, if anything, our typical upbringing encourages us to keep the true self buried beneath the protective layers of our presentation. After all, the old adage runs, 'if you really knew who I was, you might not like me'. From the earliest age we are encouraged to keep many aspects of self hidden from other. Is it not understandable then, that we would also keep parts of ourselves hidden from ourselves? After all, to rephrase the previously quoted adage, 'if I really knew myself, I might not like who I am'. As we said earlier, this is not the place to delve into those deeper existential issues. But we could all benefit from a better knowledge of self if we want to work effectively with others.

## FIVE EXERCISES

Here we offer five exercises that might help the interested practitioner to develop a deeper knowing of self. These are neither all-inclusive nor absolute in their outcome. They are suggestions of things you might do in order to increase your awareness.

## 1. Go for a Walk

Go for a walk with a friend. Walk for about five minutes without talking. Pay attention to everything around you. After you have finished your walk, find a comfortable place to sit down and write. Still not talking, make a list of things you saw that you remember. Take about five minutes to do this. Once your lists are finished (you can talk now) share them with each other. Discuss:

- What you noticed that was the same
- What you noticed that was different from each other
- Any interpretations you made of what you saw.

Now ask yourself, and discuss, the following:

- Why, do you think, did you notice what you noticed?
- What memories of other events came to you while walking?
- How did you feel about this exercise?
- Why, do you think, did you not notice some things that your friend noticed?
- What are you learning while you are having this discussion?
- What is going on for you as you have this discussion?

## 2. Watch an Interaction

It is best to have at least four people for this exercise: two will interact, and two will observe. The two actors should engage in some form of interaction (real or role-play, it does not matter) for about three minutes. The observers should pay attention to body language, speech characteristics and so on. Once the interaction is completed, the observers discuss what they noticed, using the same types of questions as for the previous exercises. Once you have done this, also discuss the following:

- How was this exercise different from the previous one?
- How is it different to attend to more than one person at a time?
- Did you find yourself paying more attention to the verbal or the non-verbal?
- Why, do you suppose, did you focus where you did?
- What does this tell you about yourself?

Once the first pair has finished, switch positions and do the exercise again.

## 3. Use the Johari Window

Re-read the section on the Johari Window. This exercise can be as personal, or as safe, as you choose to make it. Remember, you are in control of what you choose to disclose, or even say, at all times. Pair up with another person. Take the Johari Window and:

- Think about the things about yourself that are known to both of you. Share some of these with each other. Once you have shared them, talk about what it was like to share these things. Be as honest as you care to be.

- Think about some of the things that are known to yourself, but are not known to the other. Write a few of these down and choose some to share with the other person. After you share a few of them with each other, talk about what it was like to share them with each other.
- Now discuss how the experiences of the two exercises with the Johari Window were different or the same. What makes the difference? Was there some part of this that was difficult for you? If so, why was it difficult?

Now move to the cell 'not known to self'. Think about what you know about the other person. Think about their manners, behaviours and characteristics of interaction. Write down some things that you think you know about the other person that they might not know. For example, you may have noticed that they were hesitant or shy, or spoke lower or faster, when telling you things they thought you did not know. Write some of these down. Now, share one or two of these with each other.

Now discuss how this was different or the same as the previous exercises with the Johari Window. Answer the following questions:

- How is it different to share with someone something you think they don't know about you, compared to sharing with them something you thought they did not know about themselves. How do you experience self-disclosure versus feedback?
- Which is easier for you?
- Which is harder?
- Why is that?

Now that you have gone this far, there are numerous opportunities open to you. You could, for example, look at how the cell 'known to self, known to other' has changed; or you could notice if and how your feelings towards the other are different; or you could notice if you learned anything new about yourself, like where your actions come from.

## 4. Answer Some Questions

Because you are interested in working with troubled young people and their families, complete the following sentences:

- Young people are _____
- Troubled young people are _____
- Troubled young people believe _____
- Families are _____
- The families of troubled youth are _____
- Caring is shown by _____
- Helping involves _____

Now answer the following questions for all of the above answers:

- Where, how, why did you develop that thinking?
- Who was the most influential in your developing this thinking?
- What is the implication of your thinking for your work?
- How will these beliefs show up in your work?

Imagine what it is like for others — young people, families — when we ask them to engage with us and disclose their life to us.

## 5. Notice Yourself in the Moment

This exercise is not for the faint of heart, or for those who believe that they know everything about themselves already. It is not that it is difficult; it is just that it demands a concentration and energy that some may not wish to give. We offer it here because we believe that all social care professionals need to practise attending to themselves in the moment in which they find themselves.

Pair up with another person. Sit down comfortably across from each other. What you are going to do is explain to the other person what you are experiencing, as you experience it. At an appointed moment, one of you will start to talk to the other. You begin, for example, with the sentence 'Well, here I am sitting in front of you and I am experiencing _____'.

As you notice anything you are experiencing — a thought, a feeling — share it with the other person. Pay particular attention to other experiences or people that come to you as you do this. Share everything that you feel comfortable sharing. At times, you may notice a thought, a feeling, or a memory that you do not want to share. In this case, simply say that you are noticing something that you don't want to share. But remember it for yourself for later.

Do this for about three minutes. When you are finished, take a moment to reflect on the experience and then discuss with the other:

- What it was like to do this
- What you learned from it
- Parts that were the easiest to share; parts that were the most difficult
- Anything else that you noticed.

Both of you should answer these questions. Then switch positions and repeat the exercise.

## OTHER THINGS YOU MIGHT DO

The above, of course, are simply five exercises that you might do to help in noticing, and getting to know, yourself. There are numerous other things you could do. For example:

- Keep a journal and note down whenever you find yourself having a reaction to something — in the journal, write about what you think is causing the reaction;
- With a friend, watch some children play, and then discuss what you both noticed;
- Ask someone who knows you how she experiences you;
- Offer some feedback to a friend;
- Look at the literature (music, art) you like and ask yourself why;
- Answer the following — honestly — Why am I attracted to this work — what do I hope to get out of it?
- Write an essay on 'Why Change Occurs';
- Identify interactions that scare you;
- Sit alone with no distractions for 30 minutes and see what comes up for you;
- Identify people with whom it would be easy for you to work, and those with whom it would be difficult. Explore the reasons why this is so.

There are numerous ways to increase your knowledge about yourself. It is, without doubt, one of the most important things you could do in helping yourself to develop into an effective practitioner.

We have attempted to offer just a few ideas about things you might do. In the end, you have to be able to identify the values and beliefs you hold; to identify what is occurring for you as it is occurring; to notice when you are feeling one way or another, and all nature of things. You also need to be able to notice when you are present and when you are not; to distinguish what part of your perceptions of other is about them and what is about you; to know when and how it is appropriate to disclose information about yourself and your experience and even to notice when you are being effective.

With time (and perhaps with age), knowing 'who you are' will become more and more important, just as it will become important to those with whom you work. There is no question in our minds but that one of the primary goals of working with people is to help them to explore their self and how they structure their experience of their lives. But in order for us to be able to go there with others, we need to be able to go there ourselves.

## ON THE UTILISATION OF SELF

> [I]f you are going to 'use' your self, then you need to understand your self. (Ward, 1998: 26)

The phrase the 'utilisation of self' has become pretty much a foundation statement in our field over the years. No one is really sure what it means, and perhaps the primary purpose is to make us aware that self, your own self, is the primary thing you have available in your work with others. But how it is typically phrased — 'the utilisation of self' — sounds like the self is some kind of tool you have in your array of techniques — one you can whip out when the time is right and with it weave your magic of helping. Nothing, in our opinion, could be farther from the truth. We want to step out on a limb here and say that we believe that the encounter of selves is the essence of the helping relationship. By being truly self with other, we are in the condition of helping.

In the earlier days of our field — well, not that long ago actually — the utilisation of self meant things like:

• Knowing when it was appropriate to self-disclose
• Drawing on your own experiences to allow you to understand the experience of those with whom you were working
• Noticing how you are feeling as a way of staying in touch with how others might be feeling.

Like many others in the field, we are now less concerned with such things, although we agree that they are very important. We are, however, more concerned about how we can 'be self' while in interaction with other. We focus on this because we believe that the more that the other person experiences us as genuinely being ourselves with them, the more likely they are to want to enter into a relationship with us that may be helpful to them. And the more likely they are to find their own 'self' while in that relationship.

By 'being ourselves', we do not mean doing whatever you want whenever you want to. Nor do we mean that we should encounter 'other' behind those defensive barriers of self-protection from where we normally present ourselves to the world. No. What we mean is that we are interested in being with other, complete with all our foolishness, fears, joys and curiosities, in a manner that genuinely reflects our inner, our whole, our genuine self, in response to being in relationship. Being 'I' in relationship with other. Being self in relationship for other.

Newer practitioners often wonder about self-disclosure. When is it appropriate, or not, to disclose information about yourself in relationship with a young person or family? Our first response is that if you are genuinely self in relationship for other, this is much less of a concern as you are guided by a connectedness of selves to know when it is or is not appropriate. But whenever you do disclose aspects of your self to another, you must do so always because it is seen as therapeutically useful, even essential to the process, in which one is engaged. We caution the newer practitioner against disclosing too much or too quickly as, in our experience, newer practitioners have a greater difficulty in distinguishing between their own needs (and wants) and those of the young person or family.

In reality, in the early stages of our professional development, many of our actions, while well-intentioned, are directed towards meeting *our own* needs — the need to be liked, to feel competent, to be equal, to be needed. These needs drive our early interventions often, unfortunately, without being present in our awareness. So, our answer to the question of when is it appropriate to disclose 'unknown to other' aspects of self would be sometime after you have developed a deep awareness of self in general, and in the moment. Because in the absence of a deep awareness of self, you cannot be sure if the disclosure is meeting your needs, or theirs. If you cannot identify clearly how your actions are for the other, then, in all probability, they are serving your own needs.

Drawing on your own experiences to help you appreciate those of other is also fraught with difficulty. While you may have had similar experiences to those of a young person or while you may think you know what the experience is like, until you are well able to know self, and to distinguish self from other, it will be difficult for you to appreciate how very much other is different from yourself. Until you are able to self-monitor, based on a deeper awareness, and to self-regulate, it is difficult to prevent your own previous experience from clouding your perceptions, and interfering with your actions.

In fact, we would argue, it is nearly impossible not to draw on your own experiences. In this field, we are so stimulated by our current experiences to revisit our old experiences that it is almost impossible to keep them from arising. It is not that you want to keep them from arising, but that you want to be able to notice them when they do come up and decide what to do at that time. That said, we encourage practitioners to seek similarities between their own experiences and those of the people they are working with as a way to allow personal experiences to arise, so that they might be explored and help the practitioner towards a deeper awareness of self.

## CONCLUSION

> [I]t hardly requires a postmodern leap to conclude, accordingly, that self is also other. (Bruner, 2002: 66)

In the end, we believe, there is only self. One cannot deny the presence of self, nor should one want to. If anything, we seek just the opposite — to have self fully present in our interactions with others. But it is not the superficial self that we are seeking — not the pseudo-self of everyday presentation, the cluster of defensive postures, positions and pretence that we so often hide behind in our daily lives.

We are interested in the self — if we might be so bold as to say it — that hides behind the daily posturing. We are interested in the genuine and profound self that is you as a human being — the one that arises and is touched in moments of interaction with others. The only way that self is going to be present when you work with others is if you work hard to know your self, to be aware of your experiencing as it is happening, and to take the risks necessary to expose your self to yourself. For it is only when you truly know self, that you might know other.

# Part 3

---

# Practice Issues

# 9

# *Legal Issues in Social Care*

Sinéad Conneely

## OVERVIEW

Law is a system and a body of rules designed to regulate human behaviour, to establish and maintain social order and to adjudicate on disputes. As such, it cannot be ignored by any professional group. For those who work in social care, it is impossible to ignore its reach. This chapter is an introduction to the Irish legal system, with particular emphasis on the operation of the courts. It outlines the system of rules known as family law, addressing the law of marriage and marriage breakdown, the private law of children and its public sister, child protection law. The body of rules that surrounds families is ever-changing and complex, but there are few occasions of human conflict that the law has not foreseen and for which it has not attempted to produce, if not the solution, at least the means by which one may be reached.

## INTRODUCTION

Social care students tend to approach the study of law with a little curiosity and much fear. Many come with preconceived notions that it is difficult to understand, boring, or completely different from every other course on their programme. They may feel it alienating, overly rational and objective, to the detriment of the caring approach to human problems encouraged in other aspects of their learning. In practice, they find few, if any, of these fears to be well founded; they tend to excel in the study of law precisely as it allows them to find real, practical and often imaginative solutions to everyday difficulties. The study of law gives a social care student confidence in their growing sense of professionalism and in their ability to comprehend and apply information. It encourages the emerging practitioner to be proactive in supporting clients who may have many encounters with the legal system. There is nothing for the social care student to fear in their law course, and everything to gain by embracing the challenges posed.

## THE ORIGINS AND OPERATION OF THE IRISH LEGAL SYSTEM

The Irish legal system is deeply rooted in the common law, a system of English origin that developed by means of itinerant judges travelling throughout the kingdom, applying the rules laid down by the king. The accumulation of legal rulings over time allowed the development of a coherent set of rules. This judge-based system contrasts with the legal system that prevails on the European continent, the Civil Law system, where codes of law were drawn up and applied to the letter by the judges.

In England, it was also possible for litigants to appeal to the Lord Chancellor to deal with a case according to the 'justice and equity of the matter', where the common law was too rigid to cope with the case. This developed into a separate court of law, the Court of Chancery, and eventually the rules of equity became well established. The two branches of law — common law and equity — were fused into a unified court system, where either set of rules could be applied by the courts.

The doctrine of precedent or *stare decisis* emerged in order to create an element of continuity, uniformity and predictability in the law. It ensures that judges abide by the decisions of higher courts. The judge examines the *ratio decidendi* (the reason for the decision) of the earlier case and is bound to follow the judgment of a higher court, where the facts of the case before the court are sufficiently similar. Judges are not obliged to follow all prior decisions of another court. A distinction may be drawn between binding authority, which a judge is obliged to follow, and persuasive authority, which a judge may or may not choose to follow.

A binding authority is a decision of a higher court on point, while decisions of courts of equal jurisdiction, foreign courts and inferior courts are merely persuasive. The difficulty for lawyers lies in the fact that most courts will not state the *ratio* of the case expressly, but leave it to be discerned from a reading of the case. It has been said that determining the *ratio* of a case is more art than science, but there are several general principles that always apply. The ratio is based on the facts of the case and the rule applied is limited by those facts. This allows lower courts to avoid the system of precedent by arguing that the facts of the case before them are sufficiently different to preclude the application of precedent.

A judgment may contain other statements of law known as *obiter dicta*, statements that are not of direct relevance to the decision. These statements do not bind lower courts under the system of precedent, though they may be persuasive, particularly if delivered in superior courts and closely reflect the facts of the case before the lower court. A finding by a later court that a statement is merely *obiter dicta* frees the court from *stare decisis* and allows it to make an alternative ruling. This flexibility may seem to give judges too much power to avoid the operation of precedent, but remember that any judicial pronouncement, even the long-established common law rules, may be altered or destroyed by legislation.

The rules developed by judges continue to be an important source of law in this jurisdiction, but have been eclipsed to a large extent by other sources. Since independence, the primary source of law is legislation passed by the Oireachtas (Dáil Éireann and Seanad Éireann) and signed into law by the President. The sole and exclusive law-making powers for the state are vested in the Oireachtas. Judges do continue to play a role in interpreting and applying legislation and common law rules.

Our legal system diverged in a fundamental way from the British model when the people of Ireland adopted a Constitution in 1937. *Bunreacht na hÉireann* 1937 is the foundational law of the land that gives legal validity to all the institutions of the State, regulates the exercise of power and confers fundamental rights on citizens. It takes precedence over all other law, common law and legislation, and any rule that conflicts with a provision of the Constitution may be declared invalid by the High Court under Article 34. Legislation and common law rules that predate the Constitution become part of Irish law only to the extent that they are consistent with its terms. The Constitution can be amended only by constitutional referendum of the people of Ireland.

Of ever-increasing significance to the Irish legal system is the law-making function of the European Union [EU]. This law enjoys supremacy over all conflicting national law, including constitutional law, and the Irish Constitution has been amended to ensure that no European law may be found to be in conflict with it. Article 29 states that no provision of the Constitution invalidates laws enacted, acts done or measures adopted by the State that are necessitated by the obligations of membership of the EU.

## THE STRUCTURE AND JURISDICTION OF THE IRISH COURTS

Article 34 of the Constitution provides that 'justice shall be administered in courts established by law by judges appointed in the manner provided by this Constitution and, save in such special and limited cases as may be prescribed by law, shall be administered in public'. Thus, the Constitution holds the principle of public justice dear, though whole areas of civil law have been excepted from this principle, particularly in family law, and proceedings are instead held *in camera*.

The Constitution envisages the setting up of courts of first instance and of appeal, a High Court and a Supreme Court. The courts of first instance had to include a court of local and limited jurisdiction, and the District Court meets this criterion. It is the lowest court in the hierarchy and its judges hear cases locally and sit without a jury in criminal cases. The District Court deals with issues of juvenile crime, under the Children Act 2001 and, when hearing charges against children (under 18 years), is known as the Children's Court. This court sits at different times and days from the ordinary sittings of the court. It has the power to order the convening of a family conference or to refer a case to the Health Board (now the Health Service Executive). The civil jurisdiction of the District Court is limited to cases where damages claimed are less than €6,348. The District Court is important in family law matters and deals with issues relating to guardianship, custody and access, spousal and child maintenance, the family home, domestic violence and proceedings to take children into the care of the Health Service Executive.

Ireland is divided into eight circuits, each with a Circuit Court. This court deals with indictable criminal offences by judge and jury. The vast majority of serious crimes are dealt with in this forum since the Circuit Court hears all indictable offences not triable in the Central Criminal Court. The Circuit Court hears civil cases where the damages claimed are between €6,348 and €38,000 and it hears appeals from the District Court in both civil and criminal cases. The Circuit Court is very significant in the area of family law, since it not only deals with issues that may be raised before the District Court, but may also hear cases concerning judicial separation, divorce, nullity, succession, wardship, declarations as to marital status and as to parentage, and disputes between engaged couples.

The High Court, described by Article 34 of the Constitution, has full original jurisdiction in civil and criminal matters, and power to determine all questions of law and fact. Significantly, legislation may be challenged in the High Court on grounds that it is contrary to the provisions of the Constitution. This power, known as constitutional judicial review, is of enormous significance in the defence of constitutional rights and guarantees, and has impacted greatly on the development of Irish law since 1937.

When the High Court is exercising its criminal jurisdiction, it is known as the Central Criminal Court. Criminal cases tried in this court are confined to murder, attempted murder and conspiracy to murder, treason, piracy, rape and aggravated sexual assault. The High Court hears civil claims for damages of over €38,000, and appeals from the Circuit Court in civil cases and appeals by way of case stated from the District Court. It is also significant in the area of family law: it exercises a concurrent jurisdiction with the Circuit Court in family matters and has exclusive jurisdiction in the areas of adoption and child abduction.

Any decision of the High Court, including a decision on the constitutional validity of legislation, may be appealed to the Supreme Court, the highest court in the land. The President can refer a Bill to the Supreme Court to test its constitutionality under Article 26 of the Constitution. In addition, the High Court and the Circuit Court may consult the Supreme Court, by way of case stated. It is a collegiate court — with always more than one judge presiding. As a result, several judgments may be handed down in any particular case and the decision emerges from the majority view. Family matters come before the Supreme Court only by way of appeal from the High Court and appeals by way of case stated from the Circuit Court.

The Constitution provides for the establishment of special criminal courts wherever the Government is satisfied that the ordinary courts are inadequate to secure the effective administration of justice and the preservation of public peace and order. The Special Criminal Court is such a court and the rationale for its existence is the belief that the independent functioning of juries might be undermined by subversive organisations, though its remit also extends to 'ordinary' crime. As a result, it tries cases in the absence of a jury and in the presence of three judges drawn from the High Court, the Circuit Court and the District Court.

Criminal appeals from the Circuit Court, the Central Criminal Court and the Special Criminal Court are heard by the Court of Criminal Appeal, which consists of three judges drawn from the High Court and the Supreme Court. Cases may be appealed from this court to the Supreme Court.

## THE FAMILY IN CONSTITUTIONAL LAW

Article 41 of the Constitution views the family as the natural and fundamental unit group of society, in possession of inalienable and imprescriptible rights. These are antecedent and superior to all positive law: they cannot be given away or abandoned by lack of use or by the passage of time. Family rights are antecedent to positive law; they exist before the creation of law and exist as an aspect of innate humanity.

It is beyond argument that the family protected by the Constitution consists only of the family based on marriage, and all other forms of family composition are excluded from the confines of Article 41. In *The State (Nicolaou)* v. *An Bord Uchtala* [1966] IR 567, a case that concerned the right of a natural father to oppose the adoption of his child, the Supreme Court thought it quite clear from the provisions of the Article that the family referred to was one founded on the institution of marriage and the Article's guarantees are confined to this group.

The non-marital family continues to fall outside the ambit of Article 41, though its members may have other family rights under Article 40.3 of the Constitution, which deals with the personal rights of citizens. All children, whether marital or non-marital, have the same Constitutional rights, though the court may find that the rights of the marital child are located in Article 41, while the rights of the non-marital child are to be found in Article 40.3.

Generally, family members have a right to each other's company, though it may be possible, following the referendum in June 2004, to deport the non-national parents of an Irish-born child, where this is in the interests of the common good, even if this means that the child will be deprived of either their parents or their right to reside in Ireland. There is a right of privacy within marriage, specifically in the area of family planning, and married couples have a right to procreate. The courts have used Article 41 to strengthen the cause of equality between the partners of a marriage. Generally speaking, all members of the marital family have rights, so that the rights of parents are not absolute and may be controlled in their exercise by the courts acting in the interests of children. The autonomy of the family has been supported by the courts, and parents may give or withhold consent to medical treatment of their child, unless their actions are detrimental to the welfare of their child. See *North Western Health Board* v. *W(H)* [2001] 3 IR 635.

Article 41 is also significant for its inclusion of the grounds for divorce in the text, and for the protection of the role of women within the home. The latter has always been contentious on policy grounds and it seems that it does not give women any direct claim on family property or assets.

Article 42 deals with the question of education, but also concerns the family in a very real way, since the State acknowledges that the primary and natural educator of a child is the family. It guarantees to respect the inalienable right and duty of parents to provide, according to their means, for the religious and moral, intellectual, physical and social education of their children. Parents are free to provide this education in their homes or in private schools or in schools recognised or established by the State, but the child must receive a certain minimum level of education or the State may intervene to protect the child. The factors to be taken into account when determining whether a minimum education is being provided in the home were laid down in the *Director of Public Prosecutions* v. *Best* [2000] 2 IR 17, and they include the personality of the child, the quality of home education, the response of the child compared with the child's response to any other education that they may have received, and any adverse effects on the child of continuing in home education. Children have a right to free primary education, guaranteed by Article 41, until they have reached 18 years of age.

The provision goes on to say that, in exceptional cases, where the parents for physical or moral reasons fail in their duty towards their children, the State will endeavour to supply the place of the parents, with due regard for the natural and imprescriptible rights of the child. This is very significant as it establishes the constitutional basis for the right of the State to take children into care, where this is deemed necessary in the interests of the child. It may be difficult for a child to compel the State to act, at least where they fail to show that their constitutional rights have been violated (*TD* v. *Minister for Education and Others* [2001] 4 IR 259).

## THE LAW OF MARRIAGE

It is evident from the discussion of the constitutional position of the married family that the law of marriage is of central importance in Irish family law. Indeed, legislation has been very slow to recognise cohabitation in the absence of marriage, despite the growing numbers of people who choose to cohabit. This may be because of an abundance of caution with regard to the Constitutional position of the married family and a fear that legislative efforts to support cohabitation would be seen to promote it at the expense of the institution of marriage.

Costello P, in the High Court case of *B* v. *R* [1995] 1 ILRM 491, restated the traditional common law definition of marriage as 'the voluntary and permanent union of one man and one woman for life to the exclusion of all others'. Thus, marriage must be between members of the opposite sex, intended for life, and voluntarily contracted by parties with capacity to contract. Irish law does not countenance the notion of polygamous marriage. In addition, persons wishing to marry must be over 18, must be free to marry and must also be outside the prohibited degrees of relationship, of consanguinity (blood) or affinity (marriage).

The formalities that must be observed in every case in order to have a valid marriage are those of the jurisdiction in which the marriage takes place and the marriage will not be recognised by any country if it does not comply with local formalities. Since the Family Law Act 1995, it is necessary for all persons intending to marry within the Irish State to give at least three months' written notice of the intended marriage to the appropriate Registrar. There is a possibility of court exemption prior to the ceremony, but a failure to comply will result in the marriage being null and void.

## Marital Problems and Ending Marriages

The most important purpose of law is to provide a set of rules and a forum for conflict resolution. There are few areas in life where more conflict arises than in the family setting. Such conflict can take the form of physical or psychological violence, and the law has sought to grapple with this issue, though not always successfully. Domestic violence legislation is interesting as it differs from the general norm of family legislation in that it protects unmarried cohabitees, parents of adult children and others who reside together in non-contractual relationships. Even in this context, the fear of undermining marriage is evident and it may be suggested that the legislation fails to give adequate protection to very vulnerable sectors as a result.

When marriages break down completely, couples have numerous ways to respond, legally speaking. They may seek to have their marriage annulled by the courts, where grounds exist under the law of nullity; they may come to an arrangement between themselves, which deals with the terms of the separation; they may go to court to seek a judicial separation or, after four years' separation, they may choose to get a divorce. The route out of a marriage is a complex issue that comes down to the individual needs and preferences of each couple.

## Domestic Violence

Civil remedies for domestic violence are located in the Domestic Violence Act 1996 which, in theory at least, offers broad protection from abuse to spouses, dependent children, cohabitees and others in domestic relationships, including the parents of adult children. It aims to ensure the safety and welfare of persons at risk, with welfare defined to include the psychological welfare of the person in question.

The most radical remedy available to the court is the barring order. This directs the respondent to leave the place where the applicant or a dependent child resides and prohibits them from re-entering until such time as the court specifies. The order may also prohibit the respondent from using or threatening to use violence; molesting or putting the applicant or a dependent person in fear; or attending at or in the vicinity of or watching or besetting a place where the applicant resides (stalking).

An application for a barring order may be made by:

a) A spouse, or former spouse;
b) A cohabitee who has lived with the respondent as husband or wife for at least six months during the nine months immediately prior to the application. A

cohabitee may apply for a barring order only where s/he has an interest in the property equal to or greater than the respondent's interest;

c)  The parent of an adult respondent.

An application may be taken on behalf of a dependent child, to include a child of the applicant or respondent or both, an adopted child, a child to whom either party is *in loco parentis* (in place of parents) and disabled persons who are unable to live independently of the applicant. The order may be sought in the District Court or the Circuit Court and can last up to three years.

It is possible to obtain an interim or pre-trial barring order under the Domestic Violence (Amendment) Act 2002 on an *ex parte* basis (without the other side present) where the court considers it necessary or expedient to do so in the interests of justice. The order and the evidence on which it is founded must be served on the respondent as soon as practicable and the order has effect only for a period of not more than eight working days.

A safety order may be obtained under section 2 of the Domestic Violence Act 1996. This order does not compel the respondent to leave the residence, but it orders the respondent to refrain from using or threatening to use violence, molesting or putting the applicant or any dependent person in fear and prevents the watching or besetting of the place where the applicant or any dependent person resides, if they do not reside with the respondent. This order can last for up to five years. The application may be made by:

a)  A spouse
b)  A cohabitee who has lived with the respondent for six out of the twelve months immediately prior to the application
c)  The parent of an adult respondent
d)  A person of full age residing in a non-contractual relationship. This would include same-sex couples, for instance, but would exclude landlords and their lodgers.

Safety or barring orders may be made by the court when it considers that there are reasonable grounds for believing that the safety or welfare of the applicant or any dependent person so requires it. There are no statutory guidelines in the Act that address when the court should consider that this standard of proof has been met and so it has a considerable degree of discretion in the area.

A protection order is available under section 5 of the Domestic Violence Act 1996. The order does not compel the respondent to leave the home, but does prevent the respondent from using violence or threatening to use violence, from molesting or putting the applicant or any dependent person in fear. The respondent will be ordered not to watch or beset the place where the applicant resides. This order can be granted only while the parties wait for the outcome of barring order or safety order proceedings.

In all cases where dependent children are involved, section 7 of the 1996 Act empowers the court to consider making an order under the Child Care Act 1991, if this is more appropriate. The court may adjourn the case and order a Health Board investigation into the child's circumstances. Unfortunately, this provision may serve to discourage abuse victims from seeking help. The court may also look at issues of maintenance, custody and access, without a separate application.

Section 6 of the Domestic Violence Act 1996 empowers the Health Service Executive [HSE] to seek a remedy on behalf of an aggrieved person who is too traumatised to proceed. They can seek an order only where the person would have been entitled to apply for the remedy under the legislation. The HSE must have reasonable cause to believe that the victim has been subjected to molestation, violence or threatened violence or otherwise put in fear for his or her safety or welfare. They should ascertain the wishes of the aggrieved person or the dependent child and those wishes will be taken into account by the court. This provision is very useful and has been used by the HSE where a child is a victim of sexual abuse by one parent and it is better to remove the abusive parent from the home than to take the child into care. The court will examine if an adult carer is willing and able to provide reasonable care before making an order on behalf of a dependent child.

All orders under the 1996 Act are enforced by the Garda Síochána. The gardaí may make an arrest without warrant if an order is breached. The local Garda station will receive a copy of any order made under the 1996 Act. The Court also has power to deal with an infringement.

Clearly, the 1996 Act is an extremely important and useful piece of legislation in combating violence in the home, but it is not without its limitations. Specifically, numerous categories of victim are unprotected by the Act, including persons who have obtained a decree of nullity, cohabitants who do not satisfy the residence requirements for a safety or barring order or the property requirements for a barring order, adult siblings who want a barring order, persons who have a child but do not cohabit, persons who want to bar an adult child where the property is owned by the child or who wish to bar a person who is not their child, such as a son-in-law. The HSE's power to make an application on behalf of another is very useful, but is constrained by the need to show that the person would be entitled to make the application on their own behalf. So, for example, the HSE cannot take an action on behalf of a cohabitee who does not have a share in the residence.

## Nullity

The law of nullity has been unusually important in this jurisdiction because of the absence of divorce, since a nullity decree from the Irish courts allows a couple to remarry. It is significantly different from a divorce decree in many respects. A decree of nullity means that a marriage is null and void from its inception, as it lacks some vital component. A divorce is the dissolution of a valid marriage, usually some time after its inception. Since the couple were never actually married if a nullity decree is granted, the ancillary relief available on separation and divorce is unavailable to them. The fathers of children of annulled marriages remain their guardians, under the Children Act 1997.

The grounds of a nullity decree must exist at the time that the marriage was entered into by the couple, rather than at some later date, when the relationship began to break down. In all cases, the courts will presume that a marriage is valid and it is for the petitioner to prove clearly that the marriage is a nullity on the balance of probabilities.

A marriage may be declared void or voidable. A void marriage never existed at all — it is void *ab initio* (from the beginning). In theory at least, the parties may remarry even in the absence of a nullity decree, since they were never really married in the first place, but it is usual to get a decree for the sake of clarity. Where the ground for nullity renders a marriage void, any interested party may take an action, not just the 'spouses' themselves. A voidable marriage is valid until the decree of nullity is granted by the courts, and then the marriage is retrospectively invalidated. Only the parties to the marriage may seek a nullity decree on ground that the marriage was voidable, and proceedings cannot be instituted after the death of one of the parties.

There are three broad grounds upon which a marriage may be declared void:

1. Non-observance of formalities, such as the failure to give three months' notice of intention to marry to the Registrar of Marriages.
2. Lack of capacity. This relates to the common law definition of marriage and includes situations where a party is under 18, is already married, or where the parties are within the prohibited degrees of relationship or are of the same sex.
3. Lack of consent. This is by far the most important ground for a claim that the marriage is void. Consent to marriage must be the fully free exercise of the independent will of the parties to the marriage. The courts have identified numerous situations where this consent has been vitiated, including:
   a) Mental incapacity;
   b) Intoxication;
   c) Fraud, mistake and misrepresentation — for instance, where a man conceals his homosexual orientation from his wife until the marriage;
   d) Duress and undue influence, where the parties did not give full, free and informed consent to the marriage. An example would be where a young couple is pressured into marriage because of a pregnancy, or where one party forced the other to marry by threatening suicide;
   e) Limited-purpose marriages, such as a marriage to gain citizenship.

A nullity decree that declares the marriage voidable may be obtained on two important grounds.

a) Impotence, either physical or psychological
b) Inability to enter and sustain a normal marital relationship, such as when one party suffers from a mental illness, a drug addiction or is homosexual.

The law of nullity has not stagnated, but has been developed by the courts to take account of modern knowledge, sometimes controversially. It remains to be seen if the rapid development of nullity will continue in the face of the availability of divorce in Ireland.

## Separation Agreements

The parties to a marriage that has broken down may choose to draw up a separation agreement that governs their new arrangements, in order to avoid having recourse to the courts. The agreement is then incorporated into a deed of separation. They may negotiate the terms of the agreement with the help of a family mediator or their solicitors. Generally, an agreement will contain a provision that the couple will live apart from a certain date, which is useful if either party wishes to obtain a divorce at a later date. Other common clauses include a non-molestation clause, which provides that neither spouse will molest, disturb, interfere with or annoy the other; a clause that deals with spousal and child maintenance, guardianship and custody of children; property and succession. In relation to the latter issue, spouses will usually renounce their rights under the Succession Act 1965. Agreements will also deal with the issue of income tax and indemnify each spouse from future debts and liabilities incurred by the other.

Where an agreement has been breached, the plaintiff spouse can bring an action for damages. The Supreme Court, in the central case of *P O'D* v. *A O'D* [1998] 1 ILRM 543, recognised that a separation agreement amounts in law to a binding contract and, as such, bars subsequent proceedings for a judicial separation. Thus, the extensive range of financial and property reliefs available from the court on application for judicial separation are lost to the couple who have a separation agreement. A spouse may still seek a divorce from the courts and will have the legal remedies opened up to them at that time.

## Judicial Separation

A judicial separation is a decree awarded by the courts, which releases the couple from the obligation to cohabit. Significantly, the Judicial Separation and Family Law Reform Act 1989 and the Family Law Act 1995 which govern this area of law also provide for extensive powers in the area of ancillary relief and financial provision. A judicial separation does not entitle the spouses to remarry. An application for a judicial separation is usually made to the Circuit Court, though it may be made to the High Court if very substantial property is involved. There are six grounds for a decree of judicial separation outlined in section 2 of the 1989 Act, namely:

a)   The respondent has committed adultery;

b)   The respondent has behaved in such a way that the applicant cannot reasonably be expected to live with the respondent;

c)   There has been desertion by the respondent of the applicant for a continuous period of at least one year immediately preceding the date of the application. Note that this includes constructive desertion, where conduct on the part of the respondent causes the applicant to leave the home and live apart from the respondent with just cause;

d)   The spouses have lived apart from one another for a continuous period of at least one year preceding the date of the application and the respondent consents to the decree being granted;

e)   The spouses have lived apart from one another for a continuous period of at least three years immediately preceding the date of the application;

f)   The marriage has broken down to the extent that the court is satisfied in all the circumstances that a normal marital relationship has not existed between the spouses for a period of at least one year immediately preceding the date of the application.

The importance of the decree of judicial separation lies less in the decree itself and more in the availability of ancillary relief from the courts at the time of application for the decree. These reliefs will be examined in the context of divorce.

## Divorce

Section 5(1) of the Family Law (Divorce) Act 1996 provides that a divorce may be granted only where the spouses have lived apart for a period of or periods amounting to four years during the previous five years, there is no reasonable prospect of reconciliation between the spouses and proper provision has been made for spouses and dependent members of the family. A person can be 'living apart' from their spouse while still residing under the same roof. In M McA v. X McA, Unreported High Court 21 January 2000, McCracken J in the High Court confirmed that the facts of a particular case may show that the parties were living apart in the same house, mainly based on the mental attitude of the parties. Ireland operates a system of no-fault divorce.

Once a divorce decree is granted, the parties are no longer spouses and may remarry. They continue to be joint guardians of their children, unless the court grants a declaration that one parent is unfit to have custody. They lose inheritance rights under the Succession Act 1965, though they may still take proceedings under the Domestic Violence Act 1996.

The Court may also make orders under the Guardianship of Infants Act 1964 regarding custody of and access to dependent children where either a judicial separation or a divorce is granted.

Once proceedings for divorce or judicial separation have been instituted, either spouse may seek preliminary court orders for the protection of their person or their interests, including protection under domestic violence legislation, orders relating to custody and access to children, or for the protection of the family home under the Family Home Protection Act 1976. The court may also provide that a party pays maintenance pending suit — that is, until the trial date. The court can also prevent dishonest dispositions of property designed to reduce the assets available to a spouse.

The Court will try to achieve an equitable distribution of assets and ensure financial provision for dependent members of the family at the time of the decree. There are numerous tools at the disposal of the court in this regard including:

1. Periodical payment and lump-sum orders for the benefit of a spouse or the dependent members of the family;
2. Property adjustment orders that provide for the transfer of property from one spouse to the other for their benefit or the benefit of dependent family members;
3. Financial compensation orders that provide financial security for a spouse or dependent member of the family where they have lost a potential benefit on divorce. This allows the court to direct a spouse to provide life insurance for the other spouse;
4. Pension adjustment orders that enable the splitting of pensions between the parties;
5. Miscellaneous ancillary orders that allow the court to provide that one spouse will occupy the family home to the exclusion of the other for a specified period, and the court may direct the sale of the home and division of the proceeds of any such sale between the spouses.

The court may also extinguish succession rights where a judicial separation is granted, though a spouse may still ask the court to make provision from the estate of the other when a divorce decree is sought.

The court will look at numerous factors when it decides the issue of financial provision. These include the resources of the parties and their obligations; the standard of living enjoyed by the family; their ages and the length of time they have lived together; their past contribution to the family, including their work in looking after the home and caring for the family; the effect that their marital responsibilities have had on their earning capacity. It will also examine their conduct; accommodation needs; the value of any benefit forfeit by the spouse when the decree is granted; and any rights the spouse has under statute law. The discretion of the court is extremely wide in matters of family law. The philosophy of the Irish legislation is against the concept of a clean break in the context of marital breakdown. Finality is hard to achieve and the court retains the power to vary or discharge orders made at the time of judicial separation or divorce.

# CHILDREN AND THE LAW

Since family law concentrates on the law of marriage and the ending of marriage, child law is often neglected as an area of interest within the discipline. It is not that the law does not cater for children; it is simply that students of family law tend to focus on the aspects that relate to adults and their concerns, rather than the legal needs and rights of children. Social care students can afford no such luxury and it is vital to become acquainted with child law from a very early stage of contact with the course. There are numerous aspects of law that impact directly or indirectly on children's lives. Few encroach more than the topics approached in this section: the rights of parents to access and custody; the rights of the child to protection, usually from parents; and the law of adoption. Child law may be divided between public law and private law. Private legal issues usually arise where a couple separate and disagree over the future arrangements for children. It is primarily concerned with the relationship between parents. Public child law is more concerned with the relationship between parents and the State, where a child is not properly cared for within the family.

## Parental Disputes

The married parents of a child have automatic joint guardianship — that is, they are vested with all the rights and responsibilities that are involved in bringing up a child. Guardians have the right to be consulted on all matters relating to the welfare of the child, such as education, health, change of name and religion. One of the rights involved is a right to custody — that is, the right to physical care and control of the child on a day-to-day basis. Access is usually granted to the parent who does not receive custody of the child, and is viewed as a right of the child.

When a dispute arises between parents in relation to the upbringing of a child, usually when parents separate, the court must decide the issue on the basis of the welfare of the child, under the Guardianship of Infants Act 1964. The District Court and the Circuit Court may determine disputes between parents on matters that affect the child's welfare under the 1964 Act, and the court also has the power to determine child custody and access issues in judicial separation and divorce proceedings. In all cases, the welfare of the child is first and paramount; this includes the 'religious, moral, intellectual, physical and social welfare' of the child. The 1964 Act does not include reference to the emotional welfare of the child, though the court will take this into account.

The situation is different where the parents of a child are unmarried. It is important to remember that Irish law does *not* recognise the relationship of cohabiting couples as a 'common law marriage', and their financial and property disputes are resolved as if they were strangers. Unmarried parents do have support obligations towards their children and the courts will resolve disputes in relation to the upbringing of children.

The unmarried mother of a child is automatically the legal guardian of the child and is both the legal and constitutional custodian of the child. The unmarred father has no automatic rights, though he may become a guardian by a number of routes. If the mother of the child consents, there is a special informal method of appointing the father as a guardian, which involves only signing papers in a solicitor's office. If she does not consent, he can still apply to the court to be made joint guardian with the mother, and the court will make a decision on the basis of the welfare of the child. Where the natural father becomes a guardian in either case, he has all the rights and responsibilities that attach to this position. The natural father always has the right to apply for custody or access under the Guardianship of Infants Act 1964, in the absence of guardianship.

## Child Protection

The legislation that deals with child protection is the Child Care Act 1991, which requires the HSE to promote the welfare of children in its area who are not receiving adequate care and protection. The courts are obliged to give precedence to the welfare of the child as the 'first and paramount consideration' but must also have regard to the wishes of the family, the wishes of the child and the principle that it is generally in the child's best interests to be brought up in his or her own family. The first duty of the HSE, therefore, is to try to ensure adequate care by supporting the family, rather than removing the child. Where parents consent, a child may be maintained by the Health Board as long as his or her welfare demands it. The arrangement may be terminated by the parent at any time. No court proceedings are necessary in this context.

It may be necessary to protect children in emergency situations. The gardaí have the power to remove a child to safety where there are reasonable grounds for believing that there is an immediate and serious risk to the health or welfare of the child, and it would be insufficient for the protection of the child to await the application for an emergency care order by the HSE. The gardaí may enter the premises without a warrant and take the child to the local regional office of the Health Service Executive who must make a court application for an emergency care order at the next sitting of the District Court. An emergency care order lasts for a maximum period of eight days and the order may be made without notice to the parents. The court must be satisfied of an immediate and serious risk to the health or welfare of the child.

The more commonplace care proceedings are contained in Part IV of the 1991 Act. The HSE may apply for a care order that commits the child to its protection for the term of the order. The court must be satisfied that the child has been or is being assaulted, ill-treated, neglected or sexually abused, or the child's health, development or welfare has been or is being or is likely to be avoidably impaired or neglected and the child requires care and protection that they are unlikely to receive unless the order is made. When a care order is made, the HSE may control the child as if it were a parent. It may give consent to medical examination or treatment or the issue of a passport, for instance.

An interim care order may be made pending the hearing of the care order before the court. The HSE should make arrangements for access by parents and other relatives, though the court is empowered to preclude access where necessary to safeguard the child's welfare. Where a child has been unlawfully removed from care, the HSE may seek Garda assistance in searching for the child and returning the child to lawful custody.

The HSE may, alternatively, seek a supervision order that authorises it to visit the child at home to satisfy itself as to the child's welfare. The court may make this order where the child has been or is being assaulted, ill-treated, neglected or sexually abused, or the child's health, development or welfare has been or is or is likely to be avoidably impaired or neglected and it is desirable that the child be visited periodically by or on behalf of the HSE. On making the order, the court may give directions as it sees fit, concerning the care of the child, such as requiring the parent to bring the child for medical examination. The order may last for a maximum period of 12 months, but may be renewed on application by the HSE.

The Children Act 2001 introduces a new special care order that is designed to provide care for troubled or unruly children. It inserts a new Part IV(A) into the Child Care Act 1991 and obliges the HSE to seek a special care order in all cases where it appears that a child needs special care that they are unlikely to receive unless an order is made. Before applying for this order, the Board is required to convene a family conference. A special care order will be granted by the court where the child's behaviour poses a real and substantial risk to his or her health, safety, development or welfare, and the child requires special care or protection that they are unlikely to receive unless the court makes such an order. The HSE must take such steps as are reasonably necessary to prevent the child in special care from causing injury to themselves or others or from escaping from the special care facility. The maximum period of the order is 12 months but it may be renewed where the conditions that gave rise to the original order still exist. The Act also provides for emergency special care orders and permits the Garda Síochána to deliver a child into the care of the HSE.

## Child Abduction

The law has also endeavoured to protect children where they have been removed from their place of habitual residence across international frontiers, usually by a parent, without the consent of the other parent or in defiance of a custody order. It may also involve the lawful removal but wrongful retention of a child in another jurisdiction. Ireland is a party to two International Conventions in the area of child abduction; the Hague Convention has worldwide application and can be activated in the absence of a court order establishing rights of custody, while the Luxembourg Convention applies to members of the Council of Europe and requires a court order to be activated.

Both conventions are primarily concerned with securing the speedy return of the child to the place of habitual residence, on the basis that the best interests of the child are served by the prompt return of the child to the jurisdiction of origin. They establish a Central Authority in each signatory state to facilitate the operation of the Conventions and both emphasise that a decision under the Convention is not a determination of the merits of a custody or access issue. These international instruments have force of law in Ireland as a result of the Child Abduction and Enforcement of Court Orders Act 1991.

Legal applications in this area are heard by the High Court, which can declare the removal or retention wrongful or unlawful and order the return of the child. The merits of a custody or access issue are not examined and there are few and limited arguments that may be made to prevent the return of the child. The court may decline to return a child under the Hague Convention where there is evidence that the abduction is not wrongful, in that the abducting parent had the consent of the other parent, or where the parent claiming that there has been abduction significantly delays in instituting proceedings for the return of the child. In addition, it is a defence to proceedings for the return of a child that the person having the care of the child was not actually exercising custody rights at the time of the removal or retention, and the courts may refuse the return where there is a grave risk that the child would be exposed to physical or psychological harm or would otherwise be placed in an intolerable position. The child's own wishes may be taken into account where the child has attained sufficient age and maturity.

If a parent in Ireland suspects that their child may be abducted, they should seek a court order under section 11 of the Guardianship of Infants Act 1964, prohibiting the other parent from removing the child from the jurisdiction without the prior approval of the court. The parent may then object to the issue of an Irish passport for the child, or the court may require the surrender of a passport where one has been issued. If a child has been abducted out of Ireland, the parent should try to establish the whereabouts of the child and contact the Irish Central Authority — located in the Department of Justice, Equality and Law Reform — for assistance.

## Adoption

Adoption breaks the legal relationship between a child and his or her natural parents and creates a permanent legal connection with the adoptive parents. Orders are made by the Adoption Board, An Bord Uchtála, which also has the power to recognise foreign adoption orders and to assess the suitability of persons who wish to adopt in other jurisdictions. The Adoption Acts 1991 and 1998 deal with the recognition of foreign adoptions.

An adoption order may be made in respect of a child who is an orphan, a non-marital child, or an abandoned child where High Court proceedings have established that the parents have, for physical or moral reasons, failed in their duty towards their child. A mother will usually place a child for adoption with an adoption society and she will be requested to sign a formal agreement to place, and her agreement should be free and in the full knowledge of the consequences of placing the child for adoption. A final consent to adoption is not valid unless the child has attained six weeks of age. The consent of the natural father of a non-marital child is not required, but under the Adoption Act 1988, the adoption society is obliged to make reasonable effort to involve the father during the pre-placement stage. If he objects to the placement, it is deferred for at least 21 days in order to allow him to make a guardianship application to the courts. If his application is successful, his consent to the adoption is required.

The High Court can make an order empowering the Adoption Board to dispense with the consent of the parent where a valid agreement to place is in existence and where this is in the best interests of the child, under section 3 of the Adoption Act 1974. In addition, it is possible for the High Court to permit the non-consensual adoption of a child, including a marital child, where the parents have failed in their duty towards their child for a period of not less than 12 months immediately preceding the making of the application. This failure must be total; it must be likely to continue without interruption until the child has reached the age of 18; and it must amount to an abandonment of all parental rights in respect of the child. It must be established before the court that because of this failure it is appropriate that the State as guardian of the common good, should supply the place of the parents. This requirement stems, of course, from Article 42 of the Constitution. The action is taken by the Health Board under the Adoption Act 1988.

## CONCLUSION

The discussion of child law, from parental disputes to adoption, brings us neatly back again to the centrality of marriage. It is possible to free a marital child for adoption only under the very strict terms of the Adoption Act 1988, while the consent of a parent to the adoption of a non-marital child may be waived by the court where a valid agreement to place exists. So often in family law, we arrive back at Article 41 of the Constitution, the protection of marriage and the married family as an underpinning foundation of Irish family law. Students need to be aware that this is only a short tour of some aspects of the area of family law, but I hope that it is enough to whet the appetite of the budding social care professional and to convince even the sceptical that law, in theory or in practice, is not be feared.

10

# The Social Care Practice Placement: A College Perspective

Kevin Lalor & Judy Doyle

## OVERVIEW

The aim of this chapter is to examine the supervision, management and operation of social care students' practice placements, and to make explicit the roles of the student, the placement supervisor and the college tutor. Social care students may be placed in a wide variety of statutory and non-statutory agencies — for example, group homes for children and adolescents, special schools, high-support care, community development centres and daycare and residential services for people with learning disabilities. Placements are an integral component of all courses in social care. The student, the college tutor and the placement supervisor are central to the student's placement experience and form a triad in practical and academic communication.

**Figure 10.1. The Tripartite Relationship between Student, Supervisor and Tutor**

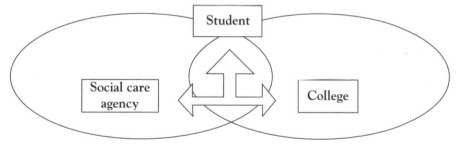

The triad of placement supervisor, college tutor and student (Figure 10.1) is central to the 'learning by doing' model adopted by social care courses. The practice placement is the interface between theoretical knowledge and practical experience of hands-on work. Individual thresholds of stress, strengths and weaknesses are explored and tested at the coalface of social care practice. Coping mechanisms are enhanced and developed. The student placement should offer a secure environment for learning and imparting of knowledge.

## THE KEY PLAYERS

The placement supervisor is generally an experienced, qualified social care practitioner who has undertaken to supervise the student's work practice in the particular agency. The college tutor is generally a member of the lecturing staff who monitors the student's progress with regard to course requirements. Finally, and most importantly, the student is registered on a programme of study and is committed to becoming an effective social care practitioner.

In this chapter we shall examine:

- The purpose of the practice placement
- Key events before the practice placement
- Key events during the practice placement
- Key events after the practice placement.

The chapter is illustrated with case studies and a particular focus is given to coping with challenging behaviour.

## WHAT IS THE PURPOSE OF SOCIAL CARE STUDENTS' PRACTICE PLACEMENTS?

The purpose of the practice placement is to expose the student to the practical world of social care work in a controlled manner, in order to facilitate the acquisition of practice skills. The goal is to link theory to practice and to aid learning through the acquisition of practice skills. Consequently, placements are designed to encourage the development of a professional social care practitioner who is:

- Able to work therapeutically with clients
- Reliable, responsible and observant
- Capable of problem solving
- Competent in effective and efficient decision making
- Able to implement and evaluate the effectiveness of treatment programmes
- Sensitive in their communication with vulnerable people
- Aware of their own value system and able to respect the value system of clients
- Able to use initiative
- Aware of the needs and rights of various client groups
- Able to respond appropriately and effectively to collective and individual needs
- Skilled in forming relationships and communicating with others
- Able to work constructively with colleagues
- Able to maintain confidentiality
- Able to keep records and use case files.

Initially, placement may prove a daunting prospect. It may be the student's first experience of the world of work; it may be their first exposure to a client group of which they have various misconceptions, apprehensions and stereotypes; they will almost certainly find the work physically tiring and, finally, it may trigger a host of unexpected emotional responses. We shall examine these issues in further detail in case studies later in the chapter.

Accordingly, the practice placement is an aspect of social care education that must be carefully managed. Though fortunately rare, negative placement experiences can lead to profound student discouragement, even to the extent of leaving the social care area altogether. This chapter examines issues that must be considered before, during and after the practice placement so that we might maximise the number of students who find their placement a positive, rewarding experience.

## KEY EVENTS BEFORE THE PRACTICE PLACEMENT

The supervision of students by their college tutor begins on their first day in college. It should involve individual and class tutorials, the development of relationships with lecturers and the monitoring of pastoral and academic wellbeing. In this section, we examine a number of important considerations for the tutor to consider before a student is allocated a social care placement.

## 'Quality of Fit'

An early consideration for the college tutor is the compatibility of the student's abilities with the requirements of the agency. Whilst a majority of students will adjust reasonably well to most working environments, there are exceptions. Very occasionally, a placement will be terminated because of gross unsuitability. Whether it is as a result of the particular demands of an agency or because of the personality of a given student, student-placement 'fit' needs to be given serious thought. Tutor familiarity with the demands and expectations of various agencies is useful here. A college tutor will strive to build up a knowledge of social care agencies that can provide high-quality supervision of students. In certain circumstances, a student might present certain traits that are particularly demanding of supervisors. For example, a student may have failed practice placements in the past or shown resistance to instruction. Some supervisors pride themselves on being able to provide a positive learning experience for students who have had unhappy experiences previously.

The preferences of the student must also be considered. Ideally, a student should experience as wide a range of social care agencies and client groups as possible. This provides them with a wide overview of the range of social care work situations. Students should have the opportunity to express preferences for particular client groups. Occasionally, a student will have overwhelming apprehensions about a particular client group, often as a result of circumstances in their own backgrounds. Such fears must be respected, and students should not be placed in a position where they are positively fearful on work placement. Of course, confronting mild apprehensions is an important aspect of practice placement and is usually resolved satisfactorily. Indeed, there is a strong sense of empowerment to be had in overcoming initial apprehensions and learning to be comfortable with, and work effectively with, a particular client group.

## Garda Clearance

You should be made aware of the legal frameworks, national standards and guidelines on child protection and welfare that are relevant to the area of social care practice.

Garda clearance against any criminal record on the prospective student may be required. Increasing numbers of agencies require students to have obtained a Garda Clearance before the placement commences. Your tutor will advise you about this.

## The Pre-placement Visit

The placement supervisor will be concerned that the student is mature, committed, amenable to instruction and reasonably comfortable with the client group. In order to determine this, a pre-placement visit should be arranged. In addition to allowing the supervisor to screen students, it also plays a very important role in allowing the student to determine whether a placement is workable. Students should arrange this pre-placement visit themselves so that they can begin to take control of, and responsibility for, the placement. It should be impressed upon students that it is *their* placement and their responsibility to ensure that it is as rich and as rewarding an experience as possible.

It is useful for students to bring a CV to this meeting so that the supervisor can keep on file a record of the relevant previous experience of the student. They may also wish to contact character references for the student.

## The Pre-placement Seminar

When students have been matched with suitable agencies, it is useful to hold a seminar to discuss the roles and expectations of supervisors, students and tutors alike. Such a seminar is an opportunity to consider a range of important issues.

* *Professionalism*
  The minimum standards of behaviour expected of students on placement must be made clear, such as expectations about punctuality, reliability and confidentiality. As we have already mentioned, the practice placement may be

the student's first experience of the world of work and they may need clear guidelines. The pre-placement seminar is a useful forum to make clear expectations vis-à-vis:

- *Punctuality and attendance*: The student's working week should be that of the social care staff in that agency.
- *Dress*: The majority of agencies take a relaxed, informal stance on the issue of dress. However, supervisors do not always approve of typical student garb.
- *Smoking*: It is not acceptable in the presence of children and will not be permitted in most enclosed workspaces.

It goes without saying that students should adopt a kind, sympathetic approach to clients and that house rules should be consistently applied. Students must appreciate the importance of treating clients with respect. In the case of residential care, the student is working in what is a home environment.

- *Recognising Your Limits*
  A desire to 'make a difference' is a natural and commendable aspiration of many social care students. However, such an aspiration is sometimes the product of an insufficient grasp of the complexities of the cases they are likely to encounter. A more realistic understanding of the nature of care work will decrease the likelihood of disillusionment and disappointment in not achieving the elusive 'breakthrough' after a matter of weeks.
  The emotional aspect of care work should be recognised. Students will come from a variety of backgrounds and will be varied in their maturity and ability to deal with upsetting cases. It helps to acknowledge that, almost by definition, social care staff work with vulnerable people. This is also an appropriate time to discuss strategies for dealing with upsetting incidents at work. The importance of outside interests, informal support through discussion with others in the field, and the more formal support of tutors and supervisors should be stressed.

- *Befriending of Clients*
  Another natural tendency for students is to strive to be popular and well-liked. Of course, the primary goal of social care practitioners is to be effective in their interaction with their client rather than to be liked. A common pitfall is that a student may become so friendly with clients that they lose the separateness necessary to function professionally. A not infrequent example is where a student becomes drawn into 'slagging' and overt criticism of staff, thus undermining their own position as a student on placement.

- *Evaluation*
  Ultimately, a judgment will be made as to the student's performance. The particular college's procedures for such an evaluation must be made clear to

students. Sometimes students fail a placement or the placement breaks down. The alternative arrangements that may or may not be made in these circumstances should be made clear.

- *Altruism*
  Does it really exist? The pre-placement seminar is a useful opportunity to question our motives for becoming involved in social care work. Jungian psychologists suggest that there is a strong link between our impulses to help people and our own need for power. As Hawkins and Shohet explain:

> The role of helper carries with it certain expectations. Sometimes clinging to our role makes it difficult to see the strengths in our clients, the vulnerability in ourselves as helpers, and our interdependence . . . [we must] face the good and bad, pure and impure motives in ourselves before we can help others. (Hawkins and Shohet, 1989: 8)

## Pre-placement Check-list for Students

- Be professional in your dealings with agencies. Remember, you are an ambassador for your college and your course.
- Be aware of the legal framework, national standards and guidelines on child protection and welfare that govern the area of social care practice.
- Recognise your limitations.
- Mind your own feelings and emotions.
- Do not 'befriend' clients.
- Be aware of your duty of care towards your client group.
- Be aware that Garda clearance may be sought.
- Be open to advice and constructive criticism. Ultimately, your performance will be formally assessed.

## KEY EVENTS DURING THE PRACTICE PLACEMENT

Once the placement begins, the day-to-day management of the placement shifts to the student and supervisor, although the college tutor retains an important role. Let us consider the roles of each part of this triumvirate.

## The Role of the Supervisor

Supervisors who agree to monitor students' practical learning have undertaken to provide an appropriate induction programme for students. At a minimum, this should involve introducing the student to staff and clients, familiarising the student with the aims and objectives, work practices and roles of different personnel, guiding the student through the physical layout of the agency and clarifying the agency's rules and ethos. The supervisor should:

- Establish mutually agreed goals and learning objectives towards which the student will work during the placement. Preferably these should be formalised in a written document that can be reviewed periodically;
- Develop a relationship of trust and confidence with the student;
- Encourage the student to identify their learning needs and target their related goals;
- Set aside time for an agreed regular meeting with the student to give feedback on their progress and discuss issues arising out of placement;
- Make an end-of-placement report. Students should be involved in this process and should be aware of the contents of the report before it is sent to the college.

Student–supervisor meetings should be predictable — at a set time each week. Some agencies claim to be habitually 'tearing busy' or 'in a crisis' and find difficulty in providing students with adequate supervision. The suitability of such an agency for a student placement should be carefully considered.

Writing of social care staff supervision, Skinner highlights the important link between supervision, good practice and integration of learning in residential care:

> Residential staff should always receive supervision from their line manager, covering both their day to day work and their professional development. Such supervision is not a luxury; it is a prerequisite for good practice and sound management. Regular individual supervision is always difficult to achieve with the constraints of a staff rota, and is extremely vulnerable to any kind of crisis large or small. But it is the means by which staff can integrate learning and experience. (Skinner, 1998: 76)

Weekly student–supervisor meetings should be held, (a) to facilitate feedback to the student, and (b) to provide an opportunity for students to discuss their performance. The student and the supervisor should keep a written record of the salient points discussed at such meetings, and future learning needs should be identified.

The Irish Association of Social Care Educators [IASCE] handbook, *Working Models: A Manual for Placement Supervision*, states that 'student supervision is about carefully and systematically planning, monitoring, facilitating and supporting the student's own development towards professional practice' (IASCE, 2000: 7). Student–supervisor interaction should be an exercise in constructive criticism. It is not a forum for 'showing off' or 'nagging.' Nor should students perceive comments as a 'put-down' or an affront to their ability. Rather, it is an opportunity for the student to benefit from the guidance of an experienced professional. This requires openness, honesty and a degree of humility on the part of both student and supervisor (see Chapter 11 of this text for further discussion of supervision in social care).

## The Role of the Student

The student has two primary roles whilst on practice placement. The first is to strive to make the placement as rich a learning experience as possible — to seek and heed guidance and instruction, where necessary, and to bring a positive attitude to dealings with colleagues, clients, and their families.

A second role is to monitor the quality of the placement. For various reasons, the student–supervisor relationship may become unsatisfactory. The student may feel that they are not being given adequate opportunities; they may find that a supervisor leaves because of holidays, illness or maternity leave. In such instances, it is primarily the student's responsibility to communicate such developments to the college tutor so that a solution can be arranged.

A further role of the student is as ambassador for their college. Whilst each student should be taken on their own merits, the reality is that agencies will build an impression of a particular college and its courses based on its previous experiences with the college's students.

## The Role of the Tutor

During the placement, the college tutor will continue to monitor the student's placement experience. This may be by way of small group discussions around relevant issues or by way of one-to-one tutorials. The tutor must be alert to issues that might require their intervention and be available to students to deal promptly with any such issues that might arise.

A further function of the tutor is to arrange the placement visit, where the student, supervisor and tutor will meet formally to discuss the student's placement experience to date and decide on future targets and placement objectives. Whilst the visit shall be arranged between the supervisor and tutor, the supervisor should ensure that the student is informed and adequately prepared for the visit. It should be stressed to students at all times that they should be open, honest and straightforward in their dealings with supervisor and tutors. It is only in this way that emerging difficulties can be identified and managed. In the words of the IASCE handbook (2000), students must 'work through' rather than 'get through' the placement.

## Case Studies

Having examined the role of each of the actors, let us examine the experiences of Eve and Adam, which typify the experience of first-year social care students embarking on their first placement. Both Eve and Adam's student placement experiences are very similar despite the very different introductions they had to social care work (one planned, the other more chaotic). The issues being raised are similar and are quite common for a first-year student in social care practice — such as self-doubt in relation to one's competency, skills, concerns regarding behaviour management, health and safety needs, role definition, identity and belonging. Typical questions pertaining to self-doubts include:

- Can I accomplish this task?
- Am I able for this type of work?
- How can I cope with such bizarre behaviours?
- Will I be taken seriously if I try to be assertive?
- Where do I fit in on the team?
- How safe am I in this environment?
- Are the families involved aggressive?
- Will I be informed as to what the organisation expects of me?
- Can I speak honestly with my supervisor?
- How do you know when care practice is holistic?
- Will I get good feedback from the team on my assessment form?

## CASE STUDY 1: EVE'S STUDENT PLACEMENT

Eve began her first-year student placement on her eighteenth birthday. It was a residential care unit known as Brookwood. This unit catered for six boys and girls manifesting emotional and antisocial behaviours, and ranging in age from 9 to 15 years. Eve was unsure what to expect in this placement other than what she had learned during her first three weeks in college. However, her introductory meeting with the service manager had gone well the previous week, and Eve liked the house so she was confident that her planned induction meeting would go well on her first morning in Brookwood.

Upon Eve's arrival at Brookwood, a 15-year-old boy, Jason, was being admitted to care in an emergency situation following the death of his grandmother with whom he had always lived. Jason was very distressed at the loss of his grandmother and also at not being allowed to live at home on his own or with his father in London. As Jason needed a lot of support and reassurance on his arrival at Brookwood, Eve's induction meeting was curtailed and deferred to another day, and was not as informative as she had hoped. Consequently, Eve found herself at the coalface of residential care work sooner than she had anticipated.

Two children needed a lot of help with homework; another child was upset that his mother had not attended his access visit the previous evening; and two teenage boys were demanding to be driven to football training. From Eve's perspective, her first shift on placement was moving at a hectic pace, with little time for guidance or to ask questions. One particular child was demanding a lot

→

of Eve's time and attention, so that she felt she was not sufficiently engaging with the other children.

At the end of a busy shift, Eve sat down with her newly appointed supervisor and discussed the events of the day. Eve's supervisor, who had been unobtrusively monitoring Eve's progress, was conscious of Eve's need for information and guidance. Eve had a lot of questions for her supervisor such as:

- Why could Jason not go to London to live with his father?
- Why was Jason verbally abusive when people were trying to help him?
- Why were the children behaving in such a demanding way?
- Why did the children's mother not attend their access visit?
- Why were the two younger siblings living in residential care?
- Jason is such a nice child — why did foster care break down for him?
- Do the children always need such time and attention at bedtime?
- Why was the 15-year-old not allowed to go to the disco with her friends?
- Why did the Asian child get extra assistance with her skin and hair care?

Eve's supervisor (who had supervised many students in the past) started by giving her Brookwood's Service Provider's Policy Document to read. This allayed many of Eve's anxieties. It answered many of her questions, such as

- What is the Purpose and Function Statement of the agency?
- Are students allowed to read the service users' case files?
- Is there a dress code to which I should adhere?
- What is the service provider's policy on Garda clearance for students?
- May I read the organisation's Health, Safety, and Welfare Statement?
- Are the service users allowed to take all phone calls from family and friends?
- Am I in danger of contacting Hepatitis B?
- Is it safe for me to take the young people out on my own?
- May I attend team meetings?
- Is there a job description and job specification that I can read?
- How often can we meet for supervision?

Parallel to this process, the supervisor was providing emotional support by explaining the context of the service users' lives and the allied dangers and difficulties encountered by them. She also explained to Eve the need for practitioners to separate personal and professional lives, so that when in work we are 'work-focused' and learn the ability to keep our professional lives within the context of work. It is not helpful to carry home with us undue worries or difficulties encountered through the course of duty, hence the need for debriefing and effective supervision that should help us to separate our work life from our personal lives, as much as practically possible. We must guard against becoming enmeshed and ineffective in our professional lives.

# CASE STUDY 2: ADAM'S STUDENT PLACEMENT

Adam's case study will serve to contrast with Eve's experience of introduction and induction to student placement.

Adam arrived on his first morning in placement half an hour early. He had time to absorb the environment and, although apprehensive, he was looking forward to working in a daycare centre with people with learning and physical disabilities. The manager and Adam's new practice supervisor formally introduced Adam to the organisation by way of an 'information meeting.' The Service Provider's Policy Document and a 'questions and answers' session were provided, followed by a guided tour of the workshop area where the more active service users were engaged in activities. Some people were learning basic cooking skills; others were putting candles in boxes; while others were sealing envelopes. Adam agreed to spend the remainder of the afternoon working alongside his supervisor. Some of the most striking first impressions for Adam were:

- The importance of remembering when the service users were to have their medication and by whom it had to be administered;
- Differentiating between the medical care team and the role of the social care team — who is responsible for what, when and where?
- Being aware of dietary needs and who could digest what. Again, the differentiation of roles and responsibilities of the nursing staff, the cooking staff and the social care practitioner needed clarification for Adam;
- Stairs and electrical appliances pose a serious risk to certain clients — Adam was conscious of his need to be alert and vigilant at all times;
- The repetitive language and behaviours of many of the clients;
- His difficulty in understanding the speech of some of the service users;
- The large amount of reading material to be addressed and retained on care files.

Adam noted that some people attending the workshop were non-verbal in their communication; consequently he observed how social care practitioners used sign language and picture association in order to communicate effectively with their clients. He felt somewhat overwhelmed at the prospect of learning such a lot of new skills, not just in the area of communication, but also in all aspects of care for people with disabilities. The physical, emotional, medical, educational and recreational aspects of the clients' lives, parallel to the administrative role of social care practice — such as recording, planning, monitoring and tracking — were all aspects of practical hands-on practice that Adam was observing and mentally noting on his 'to do list'.

There seemed a lot of questions to ask and to remember for Adam's meeting with his supervisor. Consequently, he decided to note in his placement journal what he regarded as essential information for his meeting with his supervisor. Certain questions had already surfaced in his mind, such as:

→

- What are the short- and long-term goals and objectives of the clients' placements in this workshop?
- What planned progression can be established for these clients' future care?

Adam was not too unduly worried about his first day on student placement, though he was more acutely aware of his lack of knowledge in the specific area of work with people with disabilities. A dual process of knowledge acquisition was now becoming apparent to Adam, one being his need to read material related to theory and practical information in this area and the other being his need for information and guidance from his supervisor on routines and application of theory in a working environment.

When Adam met with his supervisor at the end of his first day, there was evidence of some anxiety as Adam explained his confusion about his role definition in certain situations and circumstances. Adam was also concerned about losing face or appearing ignorant about this particular field. All such apprehensions were noted for discussion with his supervisor along with some questions for his college tutor to assist him through this crucial engaging week of student placement.

The supervisor, however, was impressed that Adam was already on the road to identifying a substantial number of his deficits in knowledge within the disabilities sector. Such deficits were translated into self-paced learning objectives for Adam's first year on practice placement. It was decided that Adam would use his placement journal to monitor his progress or difficulties in specific areas, and that weekly supervision would serve to track and address these milestones in learning. By the end of the placement, an evaluation of stated goals and task achievement would serve to acknowledge Adam's overall completion and acquisition of knowledge in the assessment report format.

## Coping Strategies for Challenging Behaviour

Finally, let us examine the issue of challenging behaviour. Behaviours that cause most difficulty for social care students and experienced practitioners can be the areas of violence, self-inflicted injuries and child sexual abuse. Violence can pose a personal threat, while sexual abuse and working with the manifestation of very challenging behaviours in the aftermath of sexual abuse can be daunting. Often as a result of biological-family and foster-care breakdown, multiple challenging behaviours may be manifested. Experienced social care practitioners are highly skilled in addressing such behaviours in a very firm but kind manner. They are equally skilled at imparting such knowledge to students in a role-modelling manner. Consequently the student learns to:

- Observe the offensive behaviours;
- Stand back from the manifesting behaviour and put the action into context;
- Avoid reacting to, or escalating the behaviours;
- Become aware of the verbal and non-verbal body language that pre-empts such behaviours;
- Become aware of the triggers that have provoked such behaviours;
- Respond in a calm manner that de-escalates the impending crisis;
- Remove peers who may be inciting the behaviours;
- Take responsibility and action that helps restore calm to the environment;
- Talk to the child/young person following the incident to help resolve conflict;
- Aid the person in looking at alternative methods of dealing with strong feelings and actions.

Student and practitioners alike must remember that the young person may re-enact their past life experiences, whether they are living in residential care or are on a supervision order at home. Consequently, it is usually learned patterns of behaviour that we are observing. Often, such patterns have been a way for the child to survive past life experiences, or are a reaction to the trauma, rejection, abuse, hurt and pain that they are experiencing. By projecting their anger, emotional turmoil, sadness, anxiety and confusion upon their caregivers, the child's expectation is that we can handle these horrible feelings for them. That is, the challenging behaviour is often a cry for help. Although difficult to deal with or to comprehend at times, it is far healthier in terms of outcomes if the child is supported in expressing such feelings as opposed to suppressing them. It is also an opportunity to form attachment with a child/adolescent at the de-escalation point in the arousal–relaxation cycle, where the child is often emotionally drained from the outburst, relieved of their tension and open to forming attachment and bonding to the person who has stayed with them through this frightening cycle.

Consider the example of a child in residential care who has been promised a visit by her mother on her birthday. On the day, the mother rings to cancel the visit. The girl becomes very upset. She smashes a window, scratches her arms, breaks dishes, bites her key-worker and kicks a hole in a door. Eventually, with gentle and persistent persuasion, she falls asleep in her key-worker's arms and, upon awakening, sighs and groans loudly and says so sadly, 'Oh, I wish you were my mammy. . . .'

A young person who has experienced sexual abuse can at any time experience flashbacks where incidents are recalled in explicit detail; such painful memories prove very difficult for the person to cope with. A range of behaviours may manifest for such individuals — for example, inappropriate touch, sexualised play, offensive language and overt aggressive behaviour. The experienced social care supervisor will engage the social care student in understanding the background to these behaviours in a safe environment. Consequently, when the student encounters the reality of these behaviours, there will be an enlightened understanding of the reasons why the person is acting in this manner.

Challenging behaviour may also be manifested by clients who have psychiatric illnesses, addictions or learning disabilities. Social care workers may be shouted at, lashed out at, or even hit. There are no easy responses, theoretical words, or magic wands that can eradicate other people's pain, or teach us how to cope and work with such case scenarios. College can prepare the nurse for her first experience of a patient dying; the doctor for her first experience of having to inform family that a loved one has died; the social worker for his first experience of having to remove a child from its family. Similarly, challenging behaviour will be covered in college for social care practitioners. But it is not until the student has actual hands-on experience of such behaviours that they will truly understand the meanings of what they have learned, or can have an understanding of how they are expected to respond so that they can establish coping mechanisms for the future. This is where knowledge and practice truly intertwine and become embedded in the mindset of the social care graduates of the future.

## KEY EVENTS AFTER THE PRACTICE PLACEMENT

The evaluation of a student's performance as 'satisfactory' normally concludes the practice placement. A student assessment form will be completed by the supervisor, in the presence of the student, and should be countersigned by the student. Generally speaking placements are assessed on a pass/fail, rather than graded, basis. Each student should be assessed at their own level — that is, a mark of 'Satisfactory' does not indicate that performance is that of a 'satisfactory' care practitioner, but that it is of a 'satisfactory' student of care work, at a particular stage of development.

The student evaluation is primarily the role of the supervisor, but it is the college tutor who will present this result to the college examination board. Thus, the tutor must be satisfied that it is a fair assessment of the student's performance.

Two further tasks remain for the college tutor. The first is to elicit feedback from students on the quality of supervision that they received on placement and the overall quality of learning experience. This helps to ensure that the agencies where students are placed are in a position to offer high-quality supervision and learning experiences to students. The second task is to coordinate a supervisors' meeting. Generally, this will involve inviting supervisors to attend a seminar where feedback on the management of student placement can be discussed. It is a useful opportunity to invite a guest speaker to speak on a topic related to supervision in social care.

## THE END RESULT

The staff team in an effective practice placement agency will collectively support and be inclusive of the student on placement, while the supervisor will support the student in this sharp learning curve. This is a dual process that should result in the student blossoming in the following areas:

- Self-knowledge and open accountability
- Proficiency in being an advocate on behalf of the client
- Confidence and competency skills
- Critical incident analysis
- Interpersonal relationship skills
- Clarity of role, role expectation, and task acquisition
- Reduced anxiety with an awareness of personal potential stressors
- Effective and efficient aspiration towards standards of excellence in their duty of care towards service users and their families
- Awareness of their role as a team player
- A moral and ethical awareness of their use of power and control while working with vulnerable people
- Ability to handle fear and worry
- Awareness of professional obligations in role-modelling respectful behaviour to both service users and colleagues in practice
- Awareness of the unpredictable nature of the work and the need to look towards positive solutions that are based on consultation and participation with the key players
- Being child-centred with an awareness of the relevant legal framework, and the United Nations Convention on Human Rights and the Rights of the Child
- Being a proactive advocate on behalf of the service users in relation to protection and welfare
- Being proactive in opposing oppression, discrimination, racism, and acknowledging ethnicity.

A checklist of core competency skills is detailed below (Table 10.1).

Table 10.1. Core Competency Skills of the Social Care Worker

| Communication | Assessment | Planning | Intervention | Self-awareness |
|---|---|---|---|---|
| • observation | • needs of service users | • situation analysis | • immediate needs | • stress management |
| • active listening | • prioritising essential needs | • objective setting | • long-term needs | • objectivity |
| • questioning | | • prioritising goals | • attachment issues | • empathy |
| • clarifying | | | • self-harm/abuse | • calm in crisis |
| • validating | • risk analysis | • keywork management | • education | • reflective judgment |
| • summarising | • monitoring work climate | • time-management | • confidence building | • appropriate use of power |
| • evaluating | | • policy knowledge | • self-esteem issues | • control of emotions |
| • report writing | | • procedures and laws | • positive identity | • externalising abuse/stressors |
| • sensitivity to literacy | | • care plans | • social skills | • identification of coping strategies |
| • team work | | • role of family action plans | • life skills | • avoidance of collusion |
| • links to other professionals | | | • aftercare | |
| | | | • independent living skills | • ongoing need to upskill |
| | | | • impulse control | • consistency |
| | | | • anger management | |

## CONCLUSION

In conclusion, one of the most important attributes that any student of social care can have is a good sense of humour, for while social care work can find practitioners working with some of the most vulnerable families in our society, where sadness and poverty abound, there will also be good times with positive outcomes. Such good humour can prove invaluable and has often been used appropriately to ease tense situations.

When working with crisis, it can be easy to be wise in hindsight. Sometimes there is a sense that all the experience or learning in the world will not prepare us adequately for certain work-related circumstances. However, one can often look back and feel a sense of achievement when, finally, that child happily returns home, or is doing well in foster care; or an adolescent is successful in her exams; or Mum succeeds in giving up alcohol. Truly, such rewards are the essence of social care work.

11

# Using Professional Supervision in Social Care

Eileen O Neill

## OVERVIEW

Professional supervision is an integral part of effective practice for many social care practitioners, while for others it can remain an irregular and confused experience. To ensure that supervision is used as a positive resource, it is necessary to understand fully its purpose and functions. It is necessary to accept that both supervisor and supervisee share responsibility with the organisation for its effectiveness.

As far back as 1951, Bettelheim identified the need for supervisory support for staff who worked in residential childcare settings. Exactly fifty years later, the National Standards for Children's Residential Centres (2001) in Ireland echoed this by identifying the standard that:

- All staff-members receive regular and formal supervision, the details of which must be recorded; (2.13)
- There is an effective link between supervision and the implementation of individual placement plans. (2.14)

The inclusion of these criteria as a standard has led to supervision becoming a reality for those working in residential childcare services, although how participants experience supervision can differ considerably. Those working in community-based services or those employed in the disability sector do not have such a mandated requirement for their supervision, although, in recognition of best practice, some such organisations ensure that supervision is available.

This chapter focuses on how to use supervision to ensure that it is a positive resource that benefits staff at all stages of their career while contributing to the ongoing development of the organisation. This facilitates practice that is accountable and relevant to the needs of those who use the services at times of need in their lives.

Attention is paid in this chapter to the following:

- Professional supervision — Why have it? What is it?
- Three functions of supervision and a *dual-focus approach*

- Using professional supervision as a student
- Using professional supervision as a staff-member
- Using supervision as a supervisor.

## WHY DO WE NEED PROFESSIONAL SUPERVISION?

Society in general has become more demanding of service provision, with an increased expectation for quality and standards. Legislation has placed a higher requirement for accountability in all areas of working and public life. Key statutes in the area include the Safety, Health and Welfare at Work Act 1989; the Freedom of Information Act 1997; and the Protection for Persons Reporting Child Abuse Act 1998. Coupled with these, a number of scandals that have emerged in the past decade, in political life, in the business world and in professional services, have highlighted the need for a recognised framework for accountable practice and for the ongoing development of practitioners in a supportive environment. Professional supervision, when provided and used effectively, contributes to this.

In summary, the following factors indicate why professional supervision is deemed necessary:

- Professional task — the professional dimension to a discipline requires recognition, structure and monitoring. Supervision is part of accepted practice in a number of disciplines: psychology, occupational therapy and social work, as well as social care;
- Inquiry reports — inquiries into service deficits and abuse in the past identify the absence of regular, formal supervision for a range of staff in the health sector (Leavy and Kahan, 1991; McGuinness, 1993; Laming, 2003). The recommendations of these reports strongly advocate the responsible availability and use of regular, structured supervision, particularly for those working in the areas of child care and protection. Evidence of learning from the gaps and mistakes of the past must be integrated into responsible practice;
- Accountability — practitioners must be accountable and held accountable for what they do and for how they do it. Employers need to have established structures that facilitate this process;
- Workers are recognised as a vital resource — investment in the human resources of services can aid staff retention and is recognised as beneficial for effective and improved delivery of services. Research (Sinclair and Gibbs, 1998) suggests that supervision is important for staff morale. This is particularly important at times of high staff turnover. People are more likely to stay in a job where they feel valued and good about what they do;
- Continued Professional Development [CPD] is perceived now more than ever as a necessary component for practitioners at all stages of their career. Qualification is an entry requirement and it is necessary to develop skills and self-awareness further in order to become a truly competent worker;

- Duty of care and recognition of demanding work — supports and structures to enable staff to work in demanding and potentially stressful working environments are recognised and accepted as necessary.

## What is Professional Supervision?

Professional supervision is a partnership process of ongoing reflection and feedback between a named supervisor and supervisee/s to ensure and enhance effective practice. Provided in a supportive manner, it offers a structured opportunity to discuss work, to reflect on practice and progress and to plan for future development.

In describing supervision as a *partnership*, it is implied that both participants have responsibilities. When entering any partnership, it is necessary for both people to be aware of what is expected of them and of what they can reasonably expect from the other. The partnership of supervision requires that there are clearly identified expectations on both sides. Coupled with expectations come responsibilities.

Examples of responsibilities shared by both supervisor and supervisee include:

- Preparation for supervision
- Contributing to the agenda
- Starting on time
- Using the allocated time fully
- Honest two-way feedback and communication
- No interruptions
- Ensuring that postponement is rare.

Describing supervision as a *process* indicates that the functions of supervision need to permeate beyond the supervision meeting and become integrated into practice. This process of supervision is evident when the supervisee leaves supervision with something to think about as well as identified objectives for their practice. Experiencing supervision as a process is more likely to contribute to the ongoing development of the participants and, potentially, of the service.

*Reflection* and *feedback* are recognised as key components in all supervision. Reflective practice is regarded as a means to develop self-aware professionals who possess the maturity and insight to learn from their experiences — the positive experiences as well as those that require improvement. Participating in supervision provides the opportunity for reflection on the detail of day-to-day practice as well as on any significant events that may have occurred. Reflecting on practice with another can lead to greater objectivity through exploration and feedback. Feedback in supervision is a two-way process — both supervisor and supervisee share responsibility for its effective use.

The core process of supervision takes place in regular, planned, structured time, between a named supervisor and supervisee/s. This time provides an opportunity to ensure the standard of service and care to those who use the services, and facilitates the practitioner's development in a supportive manner. Some circumstances may require additional supervision — for example, in response to a particular change or difficulty. At such times, it is important that responsive supervision is available.

While supervision in social care generally takes place on a one-to-one basis, it is useful if attention is also paid to the supervision of the team as a whole. Service delivery is dependent on the manner in which the team functions, and teams can benefit greatly from the opportunity to reflect in a structured way on their practice, with a view to identifying the strengths of the team and the areas that need further development.

Confusion has existed for some people regarding supervision. One reason for this has been the many and varied ways in which supervision has been experienced by practitioners. On the one hand, it has often been experienced solely as a response to a concern or crisis, thereby becoming associated with problems only. This is a limited view of supervision and has contributed to negative interpretations and uses of what can be a positive and proactive resource. On the other hand, many practitioners have found supervision to be nothing more than 'checklisting' to make sure that they have carried out certain tasks. This can lead supervisees to feel that they are back at school, having their homework corrected — not very empowering for adults with responsible workloads!

Supervision will be used effectively only if its functions are identified and understood from the beginning of one's career and if supervisor, supervisee and organisations share common and realistic expectations regarding its implementation. To this end, it is necessary to know what supervision is *not* as well as what it *is*.

Supervision is *not*:

- A casual activity which takes place over a cup of coffee
- A chat
- An optional extra
- Counselling
- Appraisal
- A grievance session
- A telling-off
- Something that happens only when there is a problem
- Something that happens only when there is nothing else to do.

Supervision *is* a regular opportunity to:

- Reflect on the daily work — the process as well as the content;
- Discuss any particular responsibilities of the supervisee;
- Monitor and ensure the quality of practice;
- Identify and further develop understanding and skills;
- Seek and receive support and feedback;

- Consider the impact of the work;
- Keep up-to-date with agency changes and requirements;
- Be constructively challenged;
- Identify areas for further professional development and implement a professional development plan.

## Three Functions of Professional Supervision

Accountability, support and learning are the three main functions of professional supervision:

- *Accountability* for effective practice and service delivery. It is important that practitioners are accountable and are held accountable for their work;
- *Support* for the individual staff-member to carry out their work in a demanding work environment;
- *Learning* and ongoing development and self-awareness of the participants.

Each of these three functions needs to be present in a balanced way over time if supervision is to meet its objectives. The skilled supervisor is aware of this and has the ability to zone in on a particular need the supervisee may present, while remaining focused on the overall functions. The overlap between the three functions is apparent in the majority of situations brought into supervision.

**Figure 11.1. Balance of the Functions in Supervision**

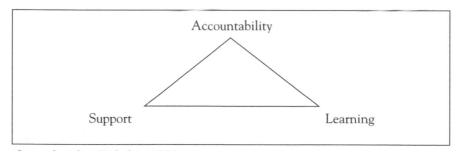

*Source*: based on Kadushin, 1976.

Regular overemphasis on any one or two components will not lead to the best use of supervision.

- If the main focus is on *accountability* to the exclusion of the other two functions, there is a risk of 'check-list' supervision becoming the norm. This will monitor to a certain extent the content of the practice of the individual but fails to pay due attention to the wider picture. Some managers may overemphasise this function, as ensuring accountable practice of others is the remit of the manager. But the supervisor must be aware of the fit between accountability and the other functions if supervision is to be truly effective;

- If *support* is the primary objective of supervision, there is a likelihood that such support may become a crutch for the individual while they move from one difficulty to another. Recently appointed supervisors or those who supervise colleagues can overemphasise the support function at times, at the expense of the other two. Professional supervision must facilitate the supervisee in a supportive manner but must also be about more than support if it is to ensure the ongoing development of accountable practice;

- When *learning* is regularly the main objective in supervision, there is a risk of it being viewed as a teacher/pupil input. In such situations, the supervisor is expected to be the source of all knowledge and the supervisee the receiver of the information. This can eventually lead to the supervisee, although well informed, having limited opportunity to develop through self-reflection and responsibility. Ongoing and lifelong learning are recognised as necessary in today's workplace. Supervision provides a regular and structured opportunity to integrate the learning from everyday work experiences.

## DUAL-FOCUS APPROACH

Supervision has, in the past, for many practitioners, frequently had a single focus. It focused either, on the one hand, on their responsibilities with particular attention paid to checking up on the work or, on the other hand, it provided a forum to focus solely on themselves with little if any attention paid to the details of the work. Neither of these approaches on their own leads to effective supervision. Rather, a combination of both promotes the best use of the supervision.

Maintaining a *dual-focus approach* ensures an operational and a developmental focus. The operational aspect considers the task of the work: the detail of practice with attention to the particular responsibilities of the individual in the context of their job description. The developmental aspect considers the person who carries out the job: the person themselves as a practitioner.

**Fig 11.2. Dual-Focus Approach**

| Operational Focus<br>is on<br>The **Task** of the job and the<br>tasks of the work | Development Focus<br>is on<br>The **Person** who carries<br>out the job |
|---|---|
| *Examples include*<br>• The purpose and function<br>of the service | *Examples include*<br>• The impact of the work on<br>the person |
| • Job description and<br>responsibilities | • The skills and strengths<br>of the supervisee<br>• Areas for further development |
| • Policies and procedures | • Reflection on practice, ideas |
| • The client group – assessing<br>needs, direct care | • Working as part of a team |
| • Care plans, key-work,<br>recording and report writing,<br>time-management | • Formulating, implementing<br>and evaluating a professional<br>development plan. |

*Source:* O Neill 2001.

Professional supervision is an effective resource at all stages of one's working life — from student days to experienced professionals in senior positions. The next part of this chapter introduces Maria at three different stages of her career and considers her use of supervision at each stage.

## MARIA — USING SUPERVISION AS A STUDENT

Maria is a student on an Applied Social Studies course. So far, she has enjoyed her studies, particularly the varied nature of the programme with its mix of theoretical and practical subjects. She knew that practice placements were part of the course and was looking forward to this new experience with a mixture of anticipation and apprehension.

Preparation for placement had taken place throughout the year in lectures which had considered the purpose and function of placements and the roles of the college, the student and the workplace (see Chapter 10). Maria had visited the workplace, as required, in preparation for the placement. She had met the manager of the service and the staff-member who was to be her direct supervisor for the next twelve weeks.

She was aware that regular, structured supervision was a requirement of all placements and, despite all she had been told in class about what this would entail, she was not sure what she thought about it. This was not helped by the mixed messages she was getting from fellow students and friends:

- One person had experienced supervision as a friendly chat with her supervisor with whom she worked daily. The supervisor was herself less than a year out of college. After the first few weeks, this chat began to be more and more casual and less and less focused on the work. The student found this enjoyable at a personal and social level but not helpful in using the placement as the learning opportunity it was meant to be;
- Others had very limited contact with their supervisor whom they met only for periodic, brief supervision meetings, because of frequently cancelled appointments. The students felt that the meetings were rushed and only went through the motions of what supervision should be — there was little investment by either in making them work. In fact, the students felt they did not need to make any effort at all as the supervisor did most of the talking anyway;
- Supervision was experienced differently again by others who worked with an experienced member of staff as their supervisor. Although working together most days provided the opportunity to discuss aspects of the work as they arose, they also met, uninterrupted, once a week to reflect on themselves and on the work and to plan for the coming week. These students felt they had been challenged to do better and, therefore, supervision was a worthwhile experience — although not always easy.

With all of this in mind, Maria was curious as to how she would experience supervision in her placement. Although she had been told that the agency to which she was going had a clear supervision policy for staff as well as students, she was also aware that policy and practice did not always match.

Remembering from her placement class that both supervisor and supervisee are together responsible for how supervision is experienced, Maria realised that she had a part to play in making sure that she got from it what she wanted and needed.

On the first morning of her placement, Jane, who was to be her supervisor for the next twelve weeks, met Maria. Jane, who had been working in the centre for almost three years, explained that she had set aside an hour later in the morning for them both to sit down together and consider the details of how the placement would be structured. Maria was given a copy of the centre policy on student placements and on professional supervision, for consideration later. In the meantime, Maria was shown around and introduced to members of staff and to three adolescent boys who were residing in the centre at the time. So began her placement.

From the beginning, there was an expectation that all those working in the service, regardless of their experience or position, would participate in regular structured supervision at least every four weeks. The policy and practice matched perfectly in this regard, as supervision was incorporated into the working day for all.

Maria was told in the first meeting with her supervisor that they would meet weekly unless one or other were sick or there was an immediate crisis; in the latter case, supervision would be rescheduled for later in the day. The purpose of these meetings, as outlined in the policy and identified by the supervisor, was to enhance the placement experience through regular reflection and feedback, in order to ensure that Maria began to look behind what she was seeing and experiencing and develop her understanding and self-awareness in the process.

In the early weeks and based on the experiences of her friends, Maria was somewhat sceptical about what she was told concerning the frequency and expectations regarding supervision. She also experienced more than a little apprehension, as she feared that supervision might turn into nothing more than a litany of her mistakes and transgressions.

Maria and her supervisor did, in fact, meet weekly throughout the twelve-week placement, and also had two extra meetings to ensure that the support and direction she needed were available to her when a particular crisis occurred.

Because supervision happened regularly and frequently, as planned, Maria quickly became comfortable with meeting her supervisor and discussing all aspects of her placement experience. Her supervisor helped Maria to consider the range of things that were included on the agenda. Examples of these were:

- The policies of the particular service and how they impacted on direct practice;
- The needs of adolescents in general and how such needs can be met in a group care setting, while also taking into account the specific needs of each young person and the reasons for their admission to care, as well as care plans, keywork, working with families;
- The value of undertaking ordinary everyday tasks for and with young people;
- Identifying her own strengths and skills and the areas she needed to develop further for professional practice. Maria received regular, balanced feedback throughout her placement. Her supervisor spoke honestly to her; highlighting areas of concern or difficulty and how she could improve while also affirming, with specific examples, Maria's strengths and skills, as appropriate.

There was a clear focus on integrating reflection on practice at all stages of her placement experience. This introduced Maria to the practice and process of reflective practice which was to stand to her in her future career.

## MARIA — USING SUPERVISION AS A STAFF-MEMBER

Having qualified eighteen months ago, Maria now works as a social care practitioner in a residential childcare service, with young people aged 12 to 16 years. She is one of a team of eight staff who work closely with teachers, psychologists and social workers to ensure wide-ranging services to the young people and their families.

Maria finds her work satisfying and challenging in equal measures. Working with young people who present with such acute needs and individual behaviours ensures that every day is different, with no likelihood of boredom. Although in her second year out of college, Maria finds that she is still constantly developing new skills and gaining new insights.

When Maria arrived in the service, her induction highlighted that she, like all staff, would participate in structured supervision every four weeks. Again this information brought up a mixed response in her. It reminded her of her previous experiences of supervision as a student and she wondered what would be expected of her by her new supervisor. She was somewhat apprehensive as she could not imagine what she would use supervision for once she became familiar with the work. In chatting to other staff, she began to pick up that some staff used supervision to discuss the keywork they were involved in, or to look at a report they had to prepare — this sounded straightforward enough; others used it, they said, as a 'sounding board' — this sounded rather vague to Maria who could not fully imagine what that meant.

Molly, who worked as one of two childcare leaders on the team, was Maria's supervisor from the outset. The first supervision meeting explored their previous experiences and ideas of supervision and examined its purpose and function within the service. They discussed the possible uses of supervision and examined the service policy regarding how the details would work between them. The meeting concluded with both of them signing a brief contract of commitment to the supervision process.

Before they finished, Maria was asked to consider what she had taken from the meeting and realised that she was more relaxed and clearer about supervision:

- They would meet once every four weeks for one hour — this was outlined in the policy and in keeping with residential services generally;
- The meeting would be recorded on the agency recording form at the end of each meeting. They would both be involved in the recording, which they would sign. The form would be kept by Molly, and Maria could access it through her or through the line manager at any time;
- The agenda, to which they would both contribute, would be decided at the start of each meeting;
- Information shared between them would not be discussed with the rest of the team members. Both had a responsibility to highlight with their line manager any difficulties that might arise if they were unable to resolve them together;
- Although supervision received a high priority within the service, it was acknowledged that there might be some circumstances that might require postponement of an occasional meeting. In such an event, they shared responsibility for rescheduling the meeting as soon as possible;

- Supervision would be reviewed between them at least twice a year. This would give them both an opportunity to give and receive feedback on how each of them was experiencing supervision, what was working and what needed to improve.

On reflection, Maria also felt that she had begun to get to know a little about her supervisor from some of the discussions they had shared. By now, she was surprised to find herself looking forward to the supervision to come, her apprehension somewhat lessened but not gone.

In the early days of supervision, Maria used the time to ask questions concerning the policies of the organisation and to find out more about what to do in certain situations with the young people and when working with their families. Her supervisor responded at times with very specific information and direction. At other times, Maria was asked her opinion on a situation, and then her response was further discussed relating to a specific area of the work.

Maria always arrived to supervision with a list of items for the agenda. At times, this was drawn up in a panic just prior to supervision, with little thought given to preparation in between the meetings. But Maria was happy that she could think of things to talk about. Molly was careful to facilitate her in reflecting on her actual practice and the rationale behind this last-minute approach. Through supervision, Maria became more self-aware. She realised that she had a responsibility to plan for the meeting in order to get the most from it. This would benefit her in a realistic manner within her practice.

Her supervisor helped Maria to identify the skills that she was using and to develop further her ability to cope with all the new experiences she was meeting in day-to-day practice. Through reflecting on events within her area of work, Maria was guided to recognise alternative strategies for managing both young people and her reactions and interactions.

Using speculation, with her supervisor asking 'what if' questions, helped her to explore new approaches to practice in the safety of supervision. She no longer felt afraid to voice suggestions and opinions and grew in her ability to participate in team meetings as a result. Her skill in advocating for young people was also developed through supervision. As she grew more self-aware, her supervisor was better able to challenge her around scenarios and thus encourage her to move out of her 'comfort zone', to consider new ways of working.

At one of their regular review sessions, her supervisor used feedback to identify changes in Maria and her practice. Through a mutual exchange of reflections on her practice, they were able to create a picture of Maria's development to date. She was both surprised and delighted by some of these changes. This helped her to recognise that her confidence had improved significantly, although she also acknowledged her need to continue to develop. Using this information, they focused on identifying areas for Maria's ongoing development in the coming year. Her supervisor assisted Maria in formulating a Personal Development Plan [PDP].

Maria's main objective was to become more competent in understanding the 'bigger picture', so that she could avoid her tendency to get bogged down in one aspect of a situation. They broke this overall objective into specific tasks that related to her daily practice and current workload. These included:

- Considering the children in her care within the context of their families
- Examining the wider regional and national policies and legislation that inform practice
- Looking at her skills and how transferable they were to other client groups and areas of work
- Reflecting on her own attitudes and how they impacted on decision making.

These were incorporated into the process of supervision over the coming months. This gave Maria a particular focus for her work and contributed to her increased motivation. She also began to use supervision in a more responsible way.

## MARIA — USING SUPERVISION AS A SUPERVISOR

It is now three years since Maria first qualified. She has recently successfully competed for and been appointed to the post of Childcare Leader within the unit. She is aware of the wider organisational issues associated with working in the service and is familiar through her practice with the policies and procedures and their implication for effective service delivery.

Her experience in supervision has helped her to progress to this stage. In recent months, she has reflected on the skills necessary to achieve promotion to this senior post. She was encouraged by her supervisor to examine her motivation for seeking more responsibility and to identify areas she would have to do further work on to be effective in the role. This ensured that Maria continued to work within a context of awareness around her ongoing development achievements and needs. As part of her new role, she has supervisory responsibilities for Childcare Workers. Although looking forward to the post in general, this is one aspect about which she has some apprehension.

She has learned to use her supervision consistently to deal with the realities of her experiences. In this way, she is able to voice her concerns and anxieties about her new role within supervision. Together with her supervisor, she identifies skills necessary for her to become an effective supervisor for other staff. These include:

- Listening
- Reflecting
- Supporting
- Prompting
- Questioning
- Guiding

- Problem solving
- Time management
- Feedback.

Through discussion and prompting, Maria becomes aware that she already uses these skills in her everyday work. To be an effective supervisor, she now needs to focus on her use of these skills, and to develop a methodology for transferring these into her role as a supervisor. Attending the forthcoming training for new supervisors within the organisation will help this. In addition, Maria's ongoing supervision with her own supervisor will play a crucial part in her ability to become a good supervisor.

Working with her supervisor, Maria realises that one of her main anxieties, as a new supervisor, is that she will be expected to supervise staff-members with whom she previously worked on a peer level. Her supervisor helps her to recognise that maintaining the balance between the three key aspects of supervision — namely support, learning and accountability — is the priority at this stage. She knows that it would be all too easy to slip into the supportive, empathetic role and fail to question, challenge or direct practice.

It is here that remembering the principles of the *dual-focus approach* will inform her own practice as the supervisor. The important point to keep in focus is that the two facets of practice — namely the task and the person *in* the task — must both be examined and reflected upon.

In discussing her concerns with her supervisor, Maria is challenged to consider her own first impressions of supervision, subsequent actual experiences and their impact on her attitudes to being a supervisor. Through her reflection, the importance of developing a clear framework within which she can commence and continue the process of supervision with her new supervisees is highlighted.

As she prepares for her first supervision meeting, she establishes a plan for this framework, identifying certain areas for inclusion. This she discusses with her supervisor as follows:

- The need for both supervisor and supervisee to tune in to each other's expectations and experiences of the supervision process
- The need to identify what is meant by professional supervision to ensure a shared understanding from the outset
- The need to explain and establish clearly the ground rules and practicalities and policies relating to meeting for supervision
- The drafting and signing of an agreed contract for supervision
- The process and practice of recording together a summary of the supervision
- The need to provide the proper environment for effective supervision. This includes an interruption-free zone with no external pressures to distract either party — no phones or mobiles, no bleepers, no callers.

In keeping with the principles of supervision, Maria feels secure to discuss with her supervisor, on an ongoing basis, any concerns she may have regarding her own role as a supervisor. Through continuous reflection and challenge, Maria develops her knowledge, awareness and confidence as a supervisor in her new role. This is not always easy and, at times, she becomes aware of just how skilled her supervisors have been throughout her career to date:

- She was facilitated to develop at her own pace;
- She was encouraged to question and also to consider her own opinions;
- She was supported and did not feel judged at times of doubt and confusion;
- She was challenged to improve in specific areas;
- She received regular feedback as a matter of course. This feedback was always presented clearly and was relevant to her practice — at times it was affirming and at other times it was corrective;
- She received direction and guidance.

Maria realises that good supervision did not happen by chance. It required sustained, focused effort on behalf of the supervisor; realistic commitment by the organisation; and active, responsible engagement by the supervisee. Both supervisor and supervisee have a responsibility to make sure that the supervision they engage in is good supervision. To achieve this, they have to commit responsibly to honest, respectful communication, feedback and reflection.

Working with people at times of vulnerability or need in their lives demands self-aware practitioners of the highest calibre who are in touch with their own strengths and limitations. Active and responsible participation in regular, structured supervision can contribute to this at all stages of professional life.

# 12

# Working with Victims of Violence and Abuse

Grant Charles, Niall McElwee & Susan McKenna-McElwee

## OVERVIEW

Many of the children and families we work with in the field of social care have experienced violence at some point in their lives, either as victims or as perpetrators. Many of the behaviours we see exhibited by the young people in our care, or by members of their families, are manifestations of the consequences of violence. Indeed, the effects are so prevalent that it is easy not to realise that the problems presented to us on a daily basis are often the result of violence and abuse. Sometimes, as the saying goes, 'we cannot see the forest for the trees'. We spend so much time in social care practice dealing with the behaviours associated with the various forms of violence that we fail to see the common thread and understand the similar needs of diverse client populations. Violence is woven through many aspects of social care. This chapter provides an overview of violence and abuse. Included will be definitions and a description of the consequences of violence and abuse, as well an outline discussion of potential staff responses.

## DEFINITION

One of the factors that contribute to the confusion about violence in the minds of many people in the field of social care is the tendency of researchers, practitioners and policy makers to attempt to place the many forms of violence into *distinct* classifications. For example, many on college courses learn about physical and sexual abuse, or physical assault and sexual assault, as if these were distinct classifications independent from one other. As another example, we are taught to use the term violence to identify attacks against others, without much focus, if any, on the various forms of violence against the self. The end result of so classifying violence is that we develop interventions and programmes based upon dichotomies rather than similarities. This leads to a duplication of services that is costly both in financial and human terms.

Some years ago, one of us ran a residential programme for adolescent sexual offenders. The emphasis was almost exclusively upon the 'offending' behaviours of the young men in the programme. The lack of success in working with these offenders made it clear that something was missing in the treatment process. It was only after the programme started to address the fact that many of the young men had themselves been sexually victimised that long-term positive change was noted. The close relationship between victimisation and perpetration was missed in the beginning as the focus was on a classification of violence rather than understanding the relationship across the spectrum of abuse (Charles et al., 1995; Charles and McDonald, 1996; Sanders, 1996). To work successfully with the young men we had to deal with both the violence that had happened to them and the harm they had caused others.

There are many examples of the tendency of interventions and systems to be focused on only one form of violence — each comes with corresponding evidence of failure. Another example is the ineffectiveness of many of the interventions that deal with male 'batterers' in family violence situations. Despite years of effort and investment, there is evidence that many of the interventions, such as individual psychotherapy or anger-management groups, do not have much success in preventing spousal violence (Bancroft and Silverman, 2002; Jacobson and Gottman, 1998). This is, in part, because many of the programmes try to deal with the violence of the perpetrators without addressing the root cause of the problem, which in many cases is the victimisation of the individual as a child (Whitfield et al., 2003).

## TOWARDS A DEFINITION OF VIOLENCE

It is critical to have a definition of violence that covers a range of behaviours. We can then sub-categorise the various forms of violence within the overarching definition. Violence can thus be conceptualised as part of an interrelated set of behaviours. In the broadest sense, violence can be defined as any actions or words intended to hurt someone or oneself. This definition is broad enough to encompass all aspects of violence. It includes both violence against others and violence against self. It also includes violence through word and not just deed. It is only recently that verbal abuse and emotional neglect have been acknowledged as being as potentially damaging to the individual as physical abuse (Brunner et al., 2000; Crosston-Tower, 2002). Even the witnessing of violence against another can have long-term consequences for the observer, as we have begun to recognise with children raised in families where there is spousal battering (Bancroft and Silverman, 2002; Gleason, 1995). Moreover, violence is about not just the action but also the *threat* of action.

Violence can be placed in two categories: violence against others and violence against self. There are two primary, yet overlapping, forms of violence against others. The first, physical assault, is defined as an intentional physical action that causes or can be expected to cause physical or psychological harm. The second, sexual assault, is an intrusive sexual act or threat that causes or can be expected to cause the victim physical or psychological harm. In each case, the threat of harm in itself is an act of violence.

We see no real distinction between assault and abuse. There are some legal and social distinctions, but in terms of the acts or threats of action and the potential consequences, there are no real differences. There can be an overlap between the two sets of behaviour. For example, there is often violence or a threat of violence in sexual assault cases.

## VIOLENCE AGAINST SELF

Violence against self can be defined as self-effected bodily harm. It can take many forms including substance abuse, eating disorders, self-mutilation and suicide (Charles and Matheson, 2003). Each form of violence against self can cause physical and psychological damage to the individual every bit as severe as that caused by others. Despite this, these behaviours are often not seen as forms of violence. This is unfortunate as it is difficult to formulate effective interventions if one does not understand the dynamics of the observed behaviour. By failing to conceptualise self-harm as a form of violence, it is possible to miss a link between violence against self and violence by others. As with those who are violent against others, people who are violent towards themselves are often the victims of earlier harm. Perpetrators of violence are often self-harmers themselves. For example, we have observed a relationship between suicidal behaviour and young men who are violent towards others. This is but another example of the interconnection between violence across traditional classifications of violence and abuse.

While we do not intend to explore the theories as to why people commit violent acts, it is important to note that there are many explanations that range from the genetic (Leyton, 1986) to feminist perspectives (Driver, 1989). There is no universally accepted theory of violence: It may be that the fragmentation of the concept of violence may prevent the development of a theory that would explain its root causes. Having said that, one must be aware that several of the consequences of violence appear to contribute to the development of violent behaviour — something we know manifests itself in social care practice on a daily basis.

Some violence is purely predatory, but much is reactive (Bloomquist and Schnell, 2002). The problem is that we often fail to see it that way. What we see is an explosion of emotion without an understanding of what internally triggers the violence. What looks to us like an overreaction is often cognitively justified by the individual who is feeling attacked. What looks to us like offensive action may be considered defensive by the perpetrator. Indeed much of the violence we see and experience in, for example, residential settings, is reactive in that the individual who perpetrates it is trying to defend themselves. Let us provide an example from practice.

Ian, a social care practitioner in a residential setting, went into Gráinne's bedroom to say goodnight. As he approached her bed in the semi-darkness, she started to shake. Ian didn't observe this behaviour because of the lack of light in the room and, as he got closer, Gráinne threw a book at him, which had been on her nightstand, and started screaming. To Ian, this looked like unprovoked violence. To Gráinne, in her mind, this was a prelude to the sexual victimisation she had experienced from her father for many years as a child. She was simply defending herself. Ian, of course, had no intention of abusing her but failed to realise that she associated a man coming into her room at night with her past victimisation. He ended up giving her a consequence for the 'assault' against him even though from her perspective it was a purely defensive act. By responding only to the surface violence and without attempting to understand the underlying causes, he lost an opportunity to help her to deal with her past victimisation.

It is important to see that the violence that we observe is often an historically appropriate response, but in an inappropriate setting. We would all support a young person who defends herself against abuse. Indeed, we would encourage it. The problem is that what would be considered appropriate violence in one setting, such as an abusive home, gets generalised to other settings such as residential programmes, where the threat of abuse is not present. The threat is not present but the historical fear is, with the result that we see a great deal of misinterpretation of intent on the part of young people. A simple touch on the hand of a young person by a staff-member, in a show of support, is misinterpreted as an intrusive act and generates an explosive defensive response (Charles et al., 1993).

It is also important to note that the reaction to violence, other than any physical damage caused, is entirely subjective. People react and respond to violence in different ways depending upon their interpretation of the situation and of the actors involved. Factors such as who the perpetrator is, past experiences of violence, levels of support available and the degree to which the act changed the 'worldview' of the person all influence the response (Bloomquist and Schnell, 2002; Garnefski and Arends, 1998; Hyman et al., 2003; Tremblay et al., 1999; Wekerle and Wolfe, 2003).

Why this is important to note is that many social care practitioners tend to conceptualise the supposed impact of violence according to an unproven hierarchy within which certain forms of violence are deemed to be worse than others (Charles, 1996). For example, sexual assault is seen to be worse than bullying, even though we know that both can have similar long-term consequences for the victim. Sexism also seems to play a role in our reactions: violence between adolescent males is minimised as 'boys will be boys' even though it is the most common form of victimisation (Mathews, 1996). Both the 'hierarchical' and 'gender' views skew our response to victims of violence in that we risk invalidating someone's reaction to abuse by placing our interpretation onto their own reaction.

# CONSEQUENCES OF VIOLENCE

There are several potential consequences of violence, including behavioural, psychological, interpersonal, self-perceptive, academic, sexual and spiritual reactions (Hawke et al., 2003; Litrownik et al., 2003). Often, victims of violence exhibit a range of interconnected responses (Wekerle and Wolfe, 2003). The particular response depends upon the subjective interpretation by the victim. This is influenced by factors such as the age of the victim, the relationship of the victim to the perpetrator and the gender of the perpetrator. It is also influenced by how resilient the young person is and their past experiences of violence (McElwee, 2001c). A major influence on how a person is impacted upon by violence is whether they are exposed to a single traumatic event or to a more prolonged and repeated trauma (Hawke et al., 2003). Keeping in mind the subjective nature of the response, those who are the victims of ongoing violence often suffer the most damage and exhibit the widest range of responses.

Young people who are most likely to have an adverse reaction to violence include those who experience greater stress, unpredictability, uncontrollability, real or perceived responsibility and betrayal (Draucker, 1995; Wyatt and Newcomb, 1990). Also included are those with prior vulnerability factors such as genetics, early onset and long-lasting childhood trauma, lack of functional support and concurrent stressful life events. In addition, those who report greater perceived threat or danger, suffering, terror, and horror or fear and those with a social environment that produces shame, guilt, stigmatisation or self-hatred are also at high risk for having long-term adverse reactions to violence. This helps to explain why victims of sadistic perpetrators are often severely traumatised by their experiences. The combination of terror and shame is a powerful prelude to long-term consequences (Charles, 1996).

While it is possible that one could have little or no reaction to an act of violence, in most cases there is at least some short-term reaction. Terr (1990) reports that this may include recurring thoughts or nightmares about the event; changes in sleep patterns; anxiety or fear and/or being on edge; being easily startled or being overly alert. Some victims report feeling depressed, sad or run down while another short-term consequence may include having memory problems especially related to the event, feeling scattered or unable to focus and having difficulty making decisions. Other consequences include feeling irritable, easily agitated, angry or resentful, often in combination with periods of feeling emotionally numb, withdrawn, disconnected or different from others. Some victims report spontaneous crying, a sense of despair and hopelessness or not being able to face certain aspects of the trauma. Short-term reactions can turn into long-term consequences if the person does not have sufficient external and internal resources to assist them to cope with the traumatic event. The internal resilience of the individual is important as is the support of friend, family or professional helpers (McElwee, 2001c).

There are several long-term consequences of violence (Litrownik et al., 2003; Wekerle and Wolfe, 2003). Transition from a simple reaction to a long-term consequence can be said to have occurred when the particular behaviour becomes a regular rather than a reactive form of interaction with oneself, others and the social environment. Initial reactions to the violence are integrated into the individual and become part of their personality and associated behaviours. It then becomes more difficult to work with victims (Flannery et al., 2003) — the associated feelings and behaviours are much deeper than the original reactions, the person is more guarded and defensive and often unaware that the reason they act the way they do is a result of the initial violence.

In terms of longer-term psychological reactions the individual can have extreme and repetitive nightmares, anxiety, phobias and psychosomatic complaints such as stomach aches, headaches, enuresis and encopresis. Any victim of violence can experience long-term self-hatred and shame but these are most likely to be present in victims of sexual assault. Victims can also exhibit general fearfulness and a specific fear of others of the same gender as the abuser (Wekerle and Wolfe, 2003). They can experience depressive symptoms and long bouts of sadness and social withdrawal, as well as associated feelings of isolation and stigmatisation (Flannery et al., 2003).

In chronic ongoing experiences of violence, such as those associated with severe child abuse, young people report high rates of dissociation, intrusive thoughts, suicidal ideation and acute phobias (Brunner et al., 2000). They often have serious levels of anxiety, fear, depression, loneliness, anger, hostility and guilt (Malchiodi, 1997). It is not unusual to experience distorted cognition with chronic perceptions of danger and confusion, illogical thinking and inaccurate images of the world (Campbell and Lewandowski, 1997). Victims can have shattered assumptions about the world and find it hard to determine what is real or unreal. This is related to an increased likelihood of difficulty in thinking through or resolving problems, especially those of an interpersonal nature (Charles and Matheson, 2003). This makes it much harder to build relationships, even though victims may be desperate to make connections with others. Another consequence of violence is a significant increase in rates of psychiatric disorders (Flannery et al., 2003; Owens and Chard, 2003).

There are several long-term behavioural responses to violence that can become integrated in victims over time. Children may experience developmental delays and exhibit clinging behaviour, extreme shyness and fear of strangers (Wekerle and Wolfe, 2003). These may continue through adolescence into adulthood. Young people may have trouble socialising with peers and may constantly fight with or bully younger or weaker children (Baldry, 2003). Related to this is poor school adjustment and disruptive classroom behaviour, with accompanying truancy and running away behaviour (Herrera and McCloskey, 2003).

Victims of violence are more likely to engage in self-destructive behaviour such as self-mutilation, delinquency or prostitution and early use of drugs/alcohol, substance abuse/dependence and risky sexual behaviour (Dennis and Stevens, 2003; Elliot et al., 2002; Hawke et al., 2003; Kaukinen, 2002). Female victims are more likely to experience school-age pregnancy and eating disorders (Charles, 1996; Waller, 1991). Those victimised are also at higher risk of attempting suicide (Garnefski and Arends, 1998).

Victims of violence often turn to violence as a response to what has happened to them (Brezina, 1998; Flannery et al., 2003). Young people who have been victimised are more likely than others to turn to criminal behaviour (Brezina, 1998). Those who have been sexually abused are at a greater risk of themselves becoming sexual abuse perpetrators (Bentovin, 2002), while those who have been physically abused are at higher risk of physically assaulting others (Herrera and McCloskey, 2003). Thus, violence can create a cycle of violence that is passed from generation to generation and person to person.

There are various other behavioural responses including passivity, over-compliance, rigidity, fear, distrust, and paranoia (Wekerle and Wolfe, 2003). These can contribute to the misinterpretation of others' motives: the innocent reaching out of another person to them may be seen as a prelude to further violence or exploitation. Some victims of violence exhibit chronic 'leakage', where they constantly have to tell others their 'story' without ever resolving their negative experience.

Victimised young people are also at higher risk of academic problems such as lower overall school performance test scores and lower language, reading and maths scores (Kinard, 2001; Eckenrode et al., 1993). They frequently work and learn at below-average levels with greater risk of disciplinary problems and suspensions from school. Such young people also tend to be less future-oriented and have fewer and lower educational goals and vocational expectations (McKenna-McElwee, 1996).

Sexually victimised young people often have great difficulty in relation to sexuality and sexual development (Dolan, 1991). Younger children may engage in simulated sexual acts with siblings or peers as well as inappropriate sexual behaviour (Friedrich, 1993). In this, one can see the roots of later sexual offending behaviour (McClellan et al., 1996). Sexual victimisation exposes children to premature sexual knowledge and behaviour. Some young people engage in open or excessive masturbation, excessive sexual curiosity and frequent exposure of the genitals. In adolescence and later in adulthood, it is not unusual for people who have been sexually victimised to continue to display sexually maladaptive behaviour such as sexual disorders, promiscuity and general dissatisfaction with sex (Briere and Runtz, 1990). It should be noted that many of these behaviours can be observed in people who have been otherwise maltreated.

Victims of violence also experience more interpersonal problems than their peers, often having insecure attachments to parents and caregivers and few close friends (Karr-Morse and Wiley, 1997). This is largely because of the difficulty of trusting others — a result of the pain that has been caused to them. The more chaotic and unpredictable the environment, as is often the case in unsafe homes or communities, the more difficult it is to trust others. Victims often report overly sexualised or overly conflicted relationships because of a fear of intimacy associated with a lack of trust and an inability to reach out to others.

Those who have been victimised, especially over long periods of time, may have self-perception distortions such as extremely low levels of self-esteem and inaccurate body images. This can lead to eating disorders (Charles, 1996; Waller, 1991). Many report an overwhelming sense of guilt or self-blame for the abuse, with an accompanying sense of chronic self-disgust and self-hatred (Charles, 1996). Many fail to develop a cohesive sense of identity, creating an endless search for a connection within which they can find themselves. This leaves them vulnerable to exploitation and further abuse. Victims also report feelings of being out of control. This may be countered by constant attempts to be in control, often achieved by abusing others or themselves. Young people who self-mutilate are often attempting to gain control over their bodies and their lives by choosing when and how to hurt (Charles and Matheson, 2003).

Victims may also experience a loss of faith not just in themselves but also in others and the world at large (Shipman et al., 2003). This can be compounded if the young person has been victimised by a member of the clergy (Sipe, 1990). Violence impacts upon the worldviews of the individual and can cause a loss of love of life that leads to what can be called a spiritual crisis. This can take many forms, from losing faith in a divine being to struggling to find any meaning in life. This creates a restlessness that contributes to the rootlessness often seen in people who have been exposed to violence. This spiritual crisis is often overlooked in social care settings as we move to the establishment of secular organisations, yet it is perhaps the most significant consequence of abuse. Without a sense of spiritual connection to a divine being or even to a sense of a greater good, young people can lose or fail to develop a purpose in life. The pain that this causes can lead to self-destructive behaviours and the striking out at others both verbally and physically.

For some young people, the impact of the violence has been so severe that they develop serious long-term psychiatric illnesses that significantly impact upon their ability to function (Hyman et al., 2003; Owens and Chard, 2003). One of the most common conditions connected with victimisation is post-traumatic stress disorder [PTSD]. While often associated with people in war zones, it is a common reaction of people who have experienced violence of any sort (Wolfe et al., 1994). Though it can be triggered by a single traumatic event, it is often seen among people who have been victimised over a long period of time. In these situations, the person has usually been both terrorised and dehumanised enough that they have no sense of mastery over their lives. As a coping mechanism, they develop long-term dysfunctional reactions. People with PTSD exhibit some combination of the following (Brown, 1994):

- Recurrent and distressing recollections
- Recurrent distressing dreams
- Acting or feeling as if the event was recurring
- Intense psychological distress at exposure to symbolic cues
- Physiological reactivity to symbolic cues
- Efforts to avoid thoughts, feelings or conversations associated with the trauma
- Efforts to avoid activities, places or people that arouse recollections of the trauma
- Inability to recall important aspects of the trauma
- Markedly diminished interest or participation in significant activities
- Feeling of detachment from others
- Restricted range of affect
- Sense of foreshortened future
- Difficulty falling or staying asleep
- Irritability or outbursts of anger
- Difficulty concentrating
- Hyper-vigilance
- Exaggerated startle response.

While the diagnosis of PTSD is more complex than just an observation of the abovementioned symptoms, it is important to note that many young people in residential care exhibit or report similar difficulties in their lives. It may be that many of them are experiencing a long-term, ongoing form of PTSD that has gone unnoticed. By the time they are admitted into a residential programme, the reactions are so ingrained that even they do not realise that it is anything other than how they have always been. What is important from the perspective of social care is that an inexplicable overreaction that a young person may have to our words or actions may be a PTSD response to what would otherwise be an event of minimal significance.

Another common long-term reaction to violence is dissociation (Wekerle and Wolfe, 2003). This is a psychological escape from an overbearing situation within which one can neither fight nor flee. The person retreats into their mind until such a time as it is safe to come out. To the observer dissociation often looks like a blank stare. Social care practitioners can observe young people going into dissociative states during times of high stress, when recounting abusive experiences or when external environmental cues trigger a memory of the event. To someone who does not realise what they are seeing, the young person may look as if they are not paying attention or caring about what the other person has to say, when in fact they have gone to a psychological place of safety.

## WORKING WITH VICTIMS OF VIOLENCE

While it is not the purpose of this chapter to discuss specific interventions with young people who have been victimised, we will give a general framework for intervention that establishes some boundaries. Charles (1996) has outlined a framework for working with victims of severe abuse. Many of the points in this model can be used throughout our work with any young person who has been victimised. Within this framework are dynamics common among victims of violence, along with a positive outcome for each. In our interactions with young people, we need to help them move from the dynamic or reaction to the positive outcome. There are various ways to reach the positive outcomes specific to the individual victim. The point of the framework is to ensure that all our interactions are purposeful and goal-oriented. It is the interaction that builds the relationship that in turn helps the young person to move from a place of trauma to a place of being a productive and contributing member of the community. Some form of the dynamics (listed below) appears to be present in victims of violence, although their extent and how they manifest can vary from person to person. They are most easily observed in young people who have been victims of ongoing violence and abuse. All the previously mentioned consequences of violence cluster in one or more of the dynamics of shame, betrayal, powerlessness and terror.

The first dynamic — shame — refers to the sense of humiliation and degradation experienced by those who have been victimised. Many victims feel shame whether from the type of abuse perpetrated or from the sense of defeat or weakness that results from a physical assault. A positive outcome, in regards to this dynamic, would be for victims to reach a state of respect where they value and respect themselves, as well as being valued and respected by other people. Respect means developing attitudes and behaviours that are not self-harming and that do not leave them open to exploitation by other people.

The second dynamic — betrayal — refers to the victim's sense of loss of trust, in others and the social systems. Redevelopment of trust is the desired positive outcome in relation to the dynamic of betrayal. This means developing a belief in oneself as well as in other people. Trust in oneself means being able to learn to accept one's existing strengths and one's ability to develop new skills. Trust in other people means being able to accept formal and informal support from other people when needed. Trust means being able to access and develop appropriate resources.

The third dynamic — powerlessness — refers to the encompassing minimisation of the victim's needs by the perpetrator. The needs and desires of the perpetrators of the abuse came before those of the young person to the extent that it appears that many of the victims believe that they do not deserve to have their needs met. This is not to say that the victims are completely powerless. They often have limited control, but this is often manifested through 'symptoms' such as eating disorders, self-mutilative behaviours or striking out against others. The control tends to be in terms of themselves rather than in terms of their relationships or social environment. The positive outcome for this dynamic is for the person to develop an appropriate level of control or mastery over their life. This means developing a belief that it is acceptable to have one's needs met without having to be submissive to the desires of others. It means being able to develop mutuality in relationships, whereby both parties are able to achieve need fulfilment in a non-exploitive manner.

The fourth dynamic — terror — refers to the sense of acute fear that is experienced by victims, especially if they were children at the time of the violence. Many victims do not feel safe with others. The positive outcome of this dynamic, therefore, is the development of a sense of safety. This appears to mean that the individual needs not to feel helpless any more. The young people need to develop a belief that they can, through their actions and choices, make their social environment safe and non-threatening. It also seems to mean learning to recognise the components of a safe environment.

Our actions with victims of violence have to be purposeful and related to their expressed and unexpressed needs. This requires a rigorous examination of our interactions and the environments we create, not from the viewpoint of a particular theoretical framework or programme perspective, but through the eyes of those who have been victims of violence. For example, how would isolating a young person from others because of acting-out behaviour be interpreted by the individual? Would it be seen as a way to calm them down or as a means of control similar to that used by the person who victimised them? The distinction is critical if our goal is to help the young person move past the abuse.

## DEALING WITH VIOLENT SITUATIONS

It is our experience that when working with victims of violence, it is important to reduce, as much as possible, the power differential between the staff and the young people. Many of those we work with have grown up in social environments where 'might is right' and any attempt to overpower the individual through word or action recreates the power dynamics of their past and reinforces their current patterns of behaviour. This is not to say that young people should not be held accountable for their actions. Rather, it is about the interactions we have with the young people. Is our interaction about control or is it about teaching more appropriate ways of dealing with life? Keeping this in mind, we should give the young people as much control as possible over their lives by providing as much choice as possible. Throughout any intervention, but especially one where emotions are running high, it becomes important to engage in dialogue with the individual, to explain clearly what it is you want and the reason behind it and to listen carefully to any concerns the person may have. By doing this, we recognise that the young people are experts about themselves.

It is important to keep these principles in mind at all times, but critical when dealing with a violent situation. At times when violence has occurred, or is at risk of occurring, *calmness* becomes the key word. Anything other than a calm response risks escalating the situation further. It does not matter whether one actually feels calm inside, but rather that one appears calm to the young person. One's calmness sets the tone for the interaction and models an alternative way to deal with feelings. The rules for interaction in an explosive situation are: stay calm; do not try to control the situation; lower your voice and response; and, unless others are in danger of harm, consider leaving as a way of de-escalating the moment. It is also important, whenever possible, to ask for assistance from another staff-member. If more intrusive measures are needed, such as if another young person is at risk of harm, it is critical that a plan be established and followed prior to the intervention to ensure the safety of the young people and the staff-members. A reactive response places all of the parties at risk of injury. When intervening in a violent situation, staff-members need to be protective of themselves and the young people. They need to expect the unexpected, recognise client triggers and recognise their own triggers.

## REACTIONS TO WORKING WITH VICTIMS OF VIOLENCE: SOME PRACTICAL ADVICE

Students or staff can have a number of reactions when working with victims of violence. Some relate to the fear of personal harm or of an actual physical assault. While fear is a common emotion felt when working with potentially violent young people, assaults happen much less frequently. Though they are relatively rare, there should be a written plan on how to deal with such occurrences. If a student or staff-member is traumatised by an assault, they may require professional assistance to deal with their reaction. In most cases, students and staff can receive all the support they need from the professionals on their team or in their workplace. This peer support, when exercised well, can be a powerful counteraction to the assault.

For peer support to be exercised successfully, we suggest a few guidelines to be followed. First, it is important to remove the student(s) and/or staff from the scene of the assault and thereby limit the person's exposure to sights, sounds and odours coming from the incident. Next, the student or staff-member should be given water or juice to drink — for physiological reasons, but also as a gesture of nurturance. Someone needs to stay with the person to help keep them grounded and as a statement of support. The person who is staying with the student or staff-member needs to encourage the individual to talk about what happened. To do so, they need to be accepting of the story by listening, paraphrasing the story and reflecting the feelings the individual expresses. The support person needs to ask open-ended questions, seek clarification of the experience when necessary and summarise their own understanding of the story.

In terms of the peer-support process, let the story be told without interruption. Reassure the individual that their feelings and thoughts are normal. Many people who have been assaulted feel they have stepped out of the realm of human experience and that there is something wrong with them because of how they are feeling. It is important to commend them for telling about their experience. Have them identify a strength they showed in response to the incident. This helps the person to see that they have a number of strengths that can be activated to deal with the situation. Finally, inquire about the support network they have outside work, and ensure that they get home safely. These same interventions can be used when dealing with young people who have been recently assaulted.

In many ways, dealing with the aftermath of an assault against a student or staff-member is easier than addressing the fear that student or staff can also feel when working with young people who have been victimised. Fear is but one of the many negative emotions that we can experience in our work but it is a core one in that it can build up slowly and without notice until we have a serious aversive reaction. When this is combined with the impact of listening to the very trying and emotional stories that young people in our programmes tell us about their experiences, it is not unusual for students or staff to begin to feel overwhelmed.

It is as if each moment of fear or each telling of a story is a single drop in a glass of water. Before someone realises it, and without any advance notice, the glass overflows, and the person has become consumed by the experience. This form of secondary traumatisation can have severe repercussions for the person if they do not get the support they need. Its effects can parallel those of an actual assault. People who experience such a reaction need support both at work and at home. The support needed will be different for each person, from peer assistance to professional help, but if the person is not helped, the long-term ramifications can be serious.

## CONCLUSION

One of the central themes among the young people we work with in social care settings is that of violence and abuse. Many children and youth have been victimised, some over long periods of time, with severe consequences to them in terms of their social development and worldview. Many, in turn, have become perpetrators of violence. It is part of our job to try to help them to move past the violence and to become contributing members of society. Unfortunately, our task is limited by how researchers, practitioners and policy makers have, variously, tried to classify violence and abuse into distinct categories. It is our premise that violence is *always* a subjective experience for the victim and that the reactions to violence are an experience common to all victims. We believe that before student social care practitioners can work successfully with victims, they need to understand these common dynamics and be able to respond to them in a planned, systematic manner. It is only through such an approach that we can assist the young people in our care to move to a point of safety and from there to a place of contribution.

# 13

# Enabling Young People through Consultation

Cormac Forkan

## OVERVIEW

As a social care practitioner, working with young people across varying settings is often a possibility. Considering this, the overall aim of this chapter is to examine a process whereby young people from a socially disadvantaged background were enabled, through a process of *meaningful* consultation, to bring about change in their area. Specifically the chapter addresses:

- The social context in which many children experience contemporary society
- The various international and national methods that have been used in an attempt to help young people to overcome issues they face
- A hands-on-experience of the process of enabling young people.

The chapter opens by referring to some of the major social transformations that have occurred in Irish society since the 1930s — ones that are now clearly visible in contemporary Ireland. It suggests that, despite the obvious advantages associated with the social change of the past 80 years, segments of Irish society are feeling more and more 'at risk' from issues such as poverty, school drop-out, divorce and suicide. A perception of 'risk' has emerged as a result of a plethora of ideas, including that parents are often forced, through economic concerns, to trade off their time with children for monetary rewards.

A key component of risk is not being enabled or having the social skills to deal effectively and in a positive manner with one's own issues and those of society. Several EU and Irish government attempts to respond to such needs are outlined. For a future social care practitioner working with young people, a key role must be that of enablement. The chapter outlines how, drawing on an example from Blanchardstown Youth Service, young people were enabled, in a practical way, to bring about real change in their own local area.

## EVIDENCE OF SOCIAL STRAINS

> The notion that far-reaching change is taking place in the structure of . . .
> society is now rather commonplace . . . the growth of urbanization of the
> population, the rising technicality and bureaucratisation of work, the general
> upgrading in standards of living, the spread and increasingly higher attainment
> levels of education, and the heightened self-awareness and rise of minority
> groups, have created serious social strains. (Sheldon and Moore, 1968: 3)

One might think this a description of key issues that face Irish society at the
beginning of the twenty-first century. This presumption would be incorrect, as the
extract is, in fact, from an article — 'Monitoring Social Change in American
Society' — written over 30 years ago. However, many of these social strains have
become even more evident and pronounced in today's world, particularly in Ireland.

The changing nature of Irish society has resulted in Ireland having fewer legal
marriages, a rising cohabitation rate, higher-than-ever rates of separation and
divorce, more single-parent families and more homosexual unions (Tovey and
Share, 2003: 148). One of the biggest changes experienced in the past 30 years has
been the massive increase in the number of women engaging in paid work outside
the home. From 1971 to 1991, the number of women in the workforce grew by
100,000. However, between 1991 and 1997, the number of women at work grew
by another 120,000 (CSO, 2000). These somewhat crude data-snippets describe a
very different Ireland from the one being constructed by de Valera's protectionist
policies and enshrined in his vision of frugal comforts, in the 1930s (see Arensberg
and Kimball, 2001).

## UNDERSTANDING SOCIAL CHANGE

Trying to understand social change has been core to the enterprise of sociology. As
the trajectory of social change has advanced with growing speed over the past fifty
years, this search for understanding has become more intense and focused.
Sociologists soon came to the realisation of something very important — that the
much-sought modern society spurred on by economics and globalisation was
accompanied by *unintended* consequences that had the potential to be destructive
to the 'fabric of society'. Numerous social impact studies have been completed to
establish the extent of this potential harm, with Putnam's (2000) study of change
in American 'social capital' over a 30-year period being one of the most notable.

Several generic themes have emerged, of which the notion of 'risk' has been
amongst the most prominent. In modern-day Ireland, for example, many people
feel 'at risk' from sources they see as totally outside their own control, such as
toxic-waste dumping, potential nuclear war or global warming. On a more micro-
level, people feel 'at risk' from more immediate sources, such as school drop-out,
poverty, street violence, family break-up, suicide and a host of other family-related

issues. We cannot open up a national newspaper without constant references to risk.

For example, recent figures (Battell, 2003) relating to education from Waterford City and County pose serious questions. The figures illustrate that in 2002 the number of early school leavers [ESL] in Waterford has remained as consistently high as in the previous two years and higher than the national average. The latter stands at 4 per cent while the figure for Waterford is 7 per cent. Of ESLs in Waterford, 73 per cent were boys; 27 per cent girls; 61 per cent of male ESLs had a Junior Certificate as compared to only 37 per cent of their female counterparts. There are increasing numbers of older male ESLs (aged 17–18). While these figures relate to Waterford, they are a microcosm of the national trend for those young people deemed to be most at risk.

When sociologists began to analyse the array of figures relating to 'risk', in conjunction with those for education, it came as no surprise that children and adolescents were identified as most 'at risk'. For many, especially those who unreservedly welcomed the advent of postmodern society, these results created quite a shock, as to talk about risk in the context of social development seemed paradoxical. But, commenting on the general home-life and lifestyle of children in Ireland, Abbott and Ryan (2001: 52) point out that many children 'now spend far less time with those adults who love them and more time with professionals whose job it is to educate them'. In the United States it has been reported (*Washington Post*, 27 September 1999: A8) that since the late 1970s, the time spent at work by American fathers has risen by 3.1 hours per week, with an increase of 5.2 hours for mothers. The resulting emergence of the phenomenon of 'latchkey kids' reflects a situation where parents/guardians are forced, through economic concerns, to make a trade-off between time with their children and increased financial income.

The obvious question is, if these trends continue, what will be the consequences? It is both common and professional knowledge that younger children and teenagers need 'quality time' with adults they can trust and talk to about pertinent issues they face on a daily basis. But teenagers in contemporary society spend much of their lives dealing with people who really do not know them as individuals. Because of the proliferation of post-second-level education, the period over which the teenager remains dependent on their parents or guardians has lengthened considerably. Conversely many children are expected to be independent and 'stick up' for themselves, sometimes without the support of their parents or guardians. The transition from childhood to adulthood is now more confusing and daunting than ever before for many 'at-risk' young people.

In 1998, Hirsch published a study, conducted over a five-year period, of a group of suburban adolescents in America. Her results, poignant as they were at the time, are testament to the paradox in terms of social and economic development and its effect on some young people. She said:

The most stunning change for adolescents today is their aloneness. The adolescents of the Nineties are more isolated and more unsupervised than any other generations . . . not because they come from parents who don't care, schools that don't care, or a community that doesn't value them, but rather because there hasn't been time for adults to lead them through the process of growing up. (Hirsch, 1998: 19–20)

This sense of aloneness has resulted in an increasing number of young people acting out their emotions in a way harmful both to themselves and to the society in which they live. Current concerns relate to drug and alcohol abuse, teenage pregnancies, depression and suicide. Many of these problems are related, resulting in a more complex set of issues for contemporary society.

## WELLNESS

Over the past two decades, the 'wellness' of young people across Europe has been tracked using a number of indicators, such as the extent to which young people indulge in illegal drug use, tobacco and alcohol consumption, and crime. If alcohol is taken as an example, authorities in Europe are becoming increasingly concerned by the extent of alcohol abuse among its young people. More than 55,000 people aged 15–29 die in Europe each year as a result of alcohol-related incidents. While the trends in each country differ, research has shown that within Europe, there is a general trend towards 'wider tolerance, and even approval, among young people for intoxication' (Global Youth Network, 2002: 1).

Many commentators believe that the increase in excessive and binge drinking is caused both by the young person's search for a 'buzz' and by the drinks industry's introduction into the market of designer or fashion drinks. According to an international survey on drinking patterns of young people in 2000, Irish children as young as nine are beginning to drink (*Irish Times*, 24 July 2000). The general finding was that between the ages of 15 and 17, 61 per cent of boys and 52 per cent of girls had used alcohol. The abuse of alcohol among young people in Ireland is so widespread that it is commonplace for pupils to miss school completely or turn up to school with a hangover. Commenting on the abuse of alcohol among young people, the Association of Secondary Teachers of Ireland [ASTI] has stated that alcohol abuse is now far more widespread than any other form of drug abuse (*Irish Times*, 26 June 2000).

## RESPONDING TO 'RISK'

Acutely aware of the need to help young people across Europe to deal with these specific social issues, the EU Commissioner with responsibility for Research, Innovation, Training and Youth, hosted a two-day conference in Brussels in November 1997. The conference aim was to hear the concerns of 120 young people, aged between 13 and 18, from across the various member states. As Cresson, the Commissioner in question, stated, 'We wanted to listen to European young people and let them take part in preparing the next generation of community programmes.' A key policy initiative that emerged from this was the 'Youth for Europe' programme. This programme specifically targeted people from disadvantaged backgrounds. Its overall aim was to create an 'equal society without economic and informational imbalances, a society without obstacles to mobility for young people' (*Irish Times*, 18 November 1997).

Four years later, in 2001, the European Commission launched the White Paper *A New Impetus for European Youth* — one of the first EU attempts to recognise and deal with specific youth issues. As Devlin (2002: 4) notes, the underlying aim of the paper was 'to put in place the right conditions to enable young people in Europe to see themselves and behave more as supportive, responsible, active and tolerant citizens in plural societies'. Central to the White Paper is the concept of 'enablement'. Taken at its simplest, to enable means to provide someone with adequate power, means, opportunity or authority to do something. Most children, when deemed able, are taught how to go to the toilet on their own, how to brush their teeth and how to wash their hands. In essence, they are enabled. But, as outlined above, many contemporary children have not had the opportunity to learn the necessary life skills to deal with issues in their family, education, relationships or even more basic areas such as self-belief, self-esteem and confidence. In a sense, they have never experienced the process of enablement.

In a broader sense, sociologists and educationalists realise that if young people are missing out on basic life skills, there is little hope that they will be able to participate in issues relating to the society in which they live. In its 1994 policy document, *Towards the Development of a Comprehensive Youth Service*, the National Youth Council of Ireland [NYCI] states that through participation in youth work, many young people can successfully experience enablement through the various programmes and activities on offer. The document notes that:

> The principle of participation is crucial if the aim of enabling young people to become critically aware and active citizens is to be achieved. [Participation] . . . goes beyond youth work, having equal validity in the broader life of communities and society at large. It requires real commitment and openness to change on the part of the adults who work with young people since it means, in effect, a sharing of power. (NYCI, 1994: 13)

Over the past decade, it has become clear that Ireland faces a key challenge in ensuring that all young people are enabled to participate fully in their lives and in their society. In an attempt to respond to this, the government has introduced such measurers as the Youth Work Bill (2000), the National Children's Strategy (2000) and the National Youth Work Development Plan (2003). Each illustrates the growing importance the government places on the resolution of these issues.

# ENABLING THE REAL PARTICIPATION OF YOUNG PEOPLE

How, in practice, can young people be enabled to such an extent that they can have a real and meaningful impact both in their own lives and in the society in which they reside? Why might such a question be important for a future social care practitioner? According to Gilligan:

> Caregivers, teachers and social workers should remember that the detail of what they do counts. The rituals, the smiles, the interest in little things, the daily routines, the talents they nurture, the interests they stimulate, the hobbies they encourage, the friendships they support, the sibling ties they preserve make a difference. All of these little things may foster in a child the vital sense of belonging, of mattering, of counting. All of these little things we do, these details, may prove decisive turning points in a young person's developmental pathway. (Gilligan, 2000b: 18)

The next section of this chapter will describe a situation where young people were enabled to bring about change in their own lives and in that of their community.

Since the 1980s, Foróige, the National Youth Development Organisation, has provided many youth-based programmes and activities for young people in the Greater Blanchardstown Area [GBA] including the Blanchardstown Youth Service [BYS] and other associated youth projects. Since the 1970s, the population of the GBA has grown from approximately 3,000 to 49,780 in 2002. In conjunction with this very rapid population growth, several key changes and trends have been identified within this area (BAP, 2001; BAP, 2002; RAPID, 2002):

- In 1996, the unemployment rate in the GBA was 18 per cent, having fallen to 8 per cent in 2002. Despite this, Tyrellestown, Mulhuddart, Coolmine and Corduff still have exceptionally high rates of unemployment. In general, dependency ratios are twice the national average;
- While there is a huge demand for childcare and family support services in the area, most people on low to modest incomes cannot afford the existing services. In particular, this has stopped many women from pursuing further education or obtaining work outside the home;
- Nearly one-third of the population (32 per cent) is under 15 years of age, this being 10 per cent higher than the Dublin average and twice the national average. Therefore, the need for youth-based programmes and facilities is a primary concern in the area;
- The ESL rate is 50 per cent above the national average, with 33 per cent of those who have a formal education leaving school on or before the age of 16. Furthermore, only 16 per cent of the population has completed third-level education;
- Though the area has experienced growth in housing development, the local authority is unable adequately to meet the need for housing;

- Lone parents account for 15 per cent of the total households in the area;
- In April 2000, there were 330 asylum seekers in the locality;
- There are approximately 196 Traveller families in the area, constituting 1.65 per cent of the population of the GBA. The lack of Traveller accommodation is an area of considerable concern.

To help mark the twentieth anniversary of Foróige in the GBA, it was agreed to 'provide a mechanism for young people to have a voice in Blanchardstown in 2003' (Forkan, 2003: 7). This was guided by the fundamental purpose of Foróige: to enable young people to involve themselves, consciously and actively, in their own development and in the development of society. To help make this happen, BYS in conjunction with the Blanchardstown Youth Forum, a representative body of voluntary groups, and the Junior Youth Forum, which helps young people involved in voluntary groups to exchange ideas, set out to talk to 600 young people aged 12–18. The specific aims of the process (Figure 13.1) were recorded in the subsequent report *Youth Perspectives* (Forkan, 2003). These are examined in more detail below:

**Figure 13.1. *Youth Perspectives*: The Research Process**

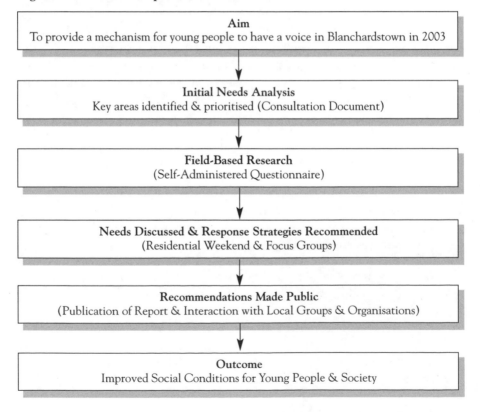

**Aim**
To provide a mechanism for young people to have a voice in Blanchardstown in 2003

**Initial Needs Analysis**
Key areas identified & prioritised (Consultation Document)

**Field-Based Research**
(Self-Administered Questionnaire)

**Needs Discussed & Response Strategies Recommended**
(Residential Weekend & Focus Groups)

**Recommendations Made Public**
(Publication of Report & Interaction with Local Groups & Organisations)

**Outcome**
Improved Social Conditions for Young People & Society

*Source:* Forkan, 2003: 9.

1. *Identify the key issues for young people in their lives in the GBA.*
   The first step in enabling young people to have a voice in their area involved consultation. During the summer of 2002, BYS consulted with young people involved in their summer programmes and courses. As part of the consultation, it was explained to the young people that Foróige, which operate BYS, was now 20 years in Blanchardstown. To mark this occasion, it was decided to produce a report that would investigate the key issues that face GBA young people in modern-day society and then help them to air their views to the locality in an attempt to resolve these issues. One hundred and fifty young people were given a sheet of paper outlining six potential areas of importance for young people, and were encouraged to prioritise the issues from most important to least important. In addition, they were asked to identify a list of any other issues that they found to be important for young people.

2. *Prioritise these issues.*
   Following this, the Junior Youth Forum met with this author and BYS staff to analyse the consultation document. The top three issues identified by the young people were 'drugs, alcohol and tobacco'; 'crime and safety'; and 'racism and discrimination'. These issues were then used as a basis for designing a questionnaire. The draft questionnaire was piloted with members of the Junior Youth Forum.

3. *Research the issues.*
   Following this, a sample of 470 young people was chosen from across the GBA, to whom the questionnaires were distributed. A response rate of 90 per cent was achieved. There is not space here to report full results of the research, but key results relating to the topic 'alcohol and tobacco' are now presented as a paradigm. From these, the reader may appreciate the extent and level of the issues raised by the young people in the area.

*Research Results*
Eighty-three per cent of females in the 16–18 age group indicated that they drank alcohol, with 79 per cent of males in the same age range doing so (Table 13.1). The figures reveal that approximately 40 percentage points fewer of 12- to 15-year-olds drank alcohol compared to the 16–18 age cohort.

Table 13.1. Use of Alcohol, in GBA, by Age and Sex

| Age Categories | Do you drink alcohol? | Male % | Female % | All % |
|---|---|---|---|---|
| 12- to 15-year-olds | yes | 46 | 39 | 43 |
| | no | 54 | 61 | 58 |
| 16- to 18-year-olds | yes | 79 | 83 | 81 |
| | no | 21 | 17 | 19 |
| All | yes | 60 | 57 | 58 |
| | no | 40 | 43 | 42 |

*Source:* Forkan, 2003.

With regard to the frequency of drinking, the majority of the males (34 per cent) and females (34 per cent) who indicated that they drank alcohol, did so on a weekly basis (Table 13.2). When the two age categories were compared, it was found that the majority of those in the 16–18 cohort who drank alcohol did so on a weekly basis (38 per cent) with drinking several times a year being the most common option for the 12–15 age group (29 per cent).

Table 13.2. Frequency of Alcohol Drinking, by Age and Sex

| Age Categories | Frequency of drinking alcohol? | Male % | Female % | All % |
|---|---|---|---|---|
| 12- to 15-year-olds | Daily | 2 | 0 | 1 |
| | Several times a week | 8 | 8 | 8 |
| | Once a week | 28 | 28 | 28 |
| | 1–3 times per month | 23 | 26 | 24 |
| | Several times a year | 30 | 28 | 29 |
| | Other | 9 | 10 | 10 |
| 16- to 18-year-olds | Daily | 2 | 1 | 1 |
| | Several times a week | 21 | 11 | 15 |
| | Once a week | 40 | 37 | 38 |
| | 1–3 times per month | 24 | 32 | 28 |
| | Several times a year | 5 | 12 | 9 |
| | Other | 10 | 7 | 8 |
| All | Daily | 2 | 1 | 1 |
| | Several times a week | 15 | 10 | 12 |
| | Once a week | 34 | 34 | 34 |
| | 1–3 times per month | 24 | 29 | 27 |
| | Several times a year | 16 | 18 | 17 |
| | Other | 9 | 8 | 9 |

In terms of smoking, 16–18-year-old girls smoked more than any other group (40 per cent) (Table 13.3). In comparison, males in the 12–15 age cohort smoked more (25 per cent) than the older group of males.

Table 13.3. Smokers, by Age and Sex

| Age Categories | Do you smoke? | Male % | Female % | All% |
|---|---|---|---|---|
| 12- to 15-year-olds | yes | 25 | 27 | 26 |
| | no | 75 | 73 | 74 |
| 16- to 18-year-olds | yes | 24 | 40 | 32 |
| | no | 76 | 60 | 68 |
| All | yes | 26 | 33 | 29 |
| | no | 75 | 68 | 71 |

When the figures relating to the rates of drinking and smoking are compared, the figures show that just under one-third of the entire group surveyed stated that they smoked (29 per cent). Double this amount (58 per cent) said that they drank alcohol. While there were more drinkers (n=248) than smokers (n=128) among the respondents (Table 13.4), the majority of those who smoked did so on a daily basis (85 per cent) whereas the majority of those who drank did so on a once-a-week basis (34 per cent).

**Table 13.4. Frequency of Smoking and Alcohol Drinking**

| Frequency of Action | % Smoking Tobacco | % Drinking Alcohol |
|---|---|---|
| Daily | 85 | 1 |
| Several times a week | 6 | 12 |
| Once a week | 1 | 34 |
| 1-3 times per month | 2 | 27 |
| Several times a year | 3 | 17 |
| Other | 3 | 9 |
| | 100 | 100 |

4.  *Reflect and discuss the findings of the research, and develop strategies on how to respond to these issues.*

    Once the questionnaires were returned, a preliminary analysis was undertaken. This information was then used at a residential weekend in October 2002, with 60 young people from across the GBA. The aim of the weekend was for the young people to discuss the preliminary findings of the survey and then draw up a list of recommendations on how best to resolve the issues identified in the survey. The 60 young people attending the weekend were divided into six groups with each research area being discussed by two groups. In addition to this, two separate focus groups on the same topics were held, with a group of Traveller boys and girls and a group of 'new settlers' in the area. The residential weekend and the focus groups allowed for qualitative comments to be added to the quantitative results that came from the survey.

In relation to alcohol and tobacco, the following recommendations were made by the young people:

*   **Alcohol-Free Nightclub.** It was recommended that the GBA needed a nightclub for young people, styled on a real one. This would be a place where young people could go and alcohol would not be available. There could also be separate hours for 15- to 18-year-olds and under 15s, as this might encourage the older teens to attend.

- **One Big Youth and Leisure Centre**. This should be a smoke- and alcohol-free zone. It should also contain a coffee shop where young people could hang out. A leisure centre would help the young people to stay healthy.
- **Change the Attitudes of the Garda**. Give the Garda more training for dealing with young people, particularly the methods they use for dealing with drinking habits. There also needs to be some monitoring of gardaí to make sure that they are dealing with situations in the correct fashion.

5. *Make recommendations to various agencies/bodies in the GBA on how to respond to these issues and communicate these through a variety of media.*

   Subsequent to the collation of the recommendations made by the young people, the *Youth Perspectives* report was written. The primary purpose was as a tool to be used with the various agencies in the GBA, to place the ball of social change in motion. On 22 January 2003, Minister for Children Brian Lenihan was invited by the young people to launch the report. As pointed out by the Minister, 'Giving a voice to young people and children is the first goal of the National Children's Strategy, to which the Government is fully committed'. The project gave young people in Blanchardstown the opportunity to voice their opinions about the community in which they live and, more importantly, to become proactive in improving their community.

   Having presented the report to the Minister on behalf of all young people in the area, and in order to raise awareness further, the young people performed a short sketch they had written, which addressed many of the key issues that had emerged through the process. Since the launch and publication of the report, young people representing the process were invited to become part of many of the key community, voluntary and statutory agencies in the area. Involvement of this kind always runs the risk of being tokenistic, but the fact that young people have been enabled through the process to represent themselves locally, must surely be regarded as an enormous success.

## CONCLUSION

A total of 23 key recommendations emerged from the research process. These recommendations give credence to the underlying philosophy of Foróige and BYS, that if young people are enabled, as they have been in this case, they can 'consciously and actively' look at how best to better their own lives and that of society in general.

Over the past decade, there has been a considerable increase in the use of the term 'youth participation' in research reports similar to this one, strategic policy documents and in youth-based programmes and proposals. Kearney (2002: 10) proposes a number of reasons why this term is now central to Irish youth work. These include the use by local government of a 'consensual approach to decision making'; acknowledgement in society of the rights of young people, as set out in the UN Convention on the Rights of the Child; and continual evolution in the application of the Child Care Act (1991), culminating in the National Children's Strategy.

The question remains as to how recommendations from a process of this kind will be used to bring about the desired social change. More to the point, will they become 'dormant entities', left on a shelf to gather dust? The key to the overall success of this process lies in a simple definition — how the agencies in the GBA define the notion of 'process and product' will largely determine the eventual success of this consultation. Up until recently, the end result or product was often the primary concern for many employers, educationalists and policy planners. But organisations such as BYS have realised that in addition to striving to reach an end product, equal acknowledgement of process is vital to the conscious and active development of young people and society. By acknowledging this process, it is possible to see that the results and recommendations from this study impinge on three areas of the young person's life — namely, the family, the peer group and the community (Figure 13.2).

**Figure 13.2. The 'Appropriate Product-Process Model'**

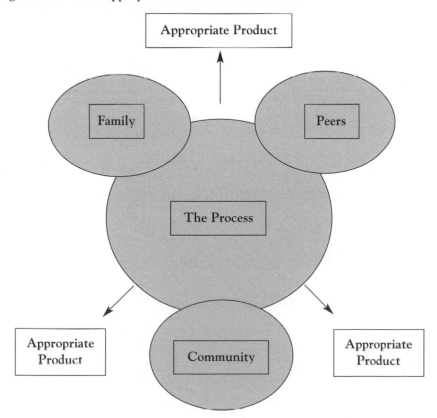

If the relevant statutory and community/voluntary organisations work together with the young people to achieve these recommendations, in a *process*-based way, the needs of young people will be met in a planned and consensual way, rather than in the historical reactive fashion, evident across communities in Ireland. In essence, this would be an example of real youth enablement and participation that would have the potential to create positive change across the family, the peer group and the community.

For Duffy:

> Put bluntly, life is simply life, good and bad. Full of ups and downs. Moral highs and lows. Perhaps there is no such thing as the good ol' days. Like those long summers we think we had, but which never show up on old weather charts, all they are, are our own edited highlights of the past, with the bad bits left out. (Duffy 2002: 14)

It is the responsibility of all of us to ensure that, in the future, young people can look back on their life experiences and be sure that the long summers did actually exist and that, in reality, their recommendations were allowed to make a real difference to themselves and to their community. The process of enablement that underlies the success of such a goal must surely be the core focus for any social care practitioner who is privileged to work with young people.

## 14

# Leadership and Teamwork in Social Care

Patrick McGarty

## OVERVIEW

This chapter addresses some of the issues related to teamwork in the management of social care work. It suggests that the team has become a key way of organising work, not least in social care environments. A shift away from more individualistic approaches to work inevitably leads to challenges as well as benefits: teamwork may involve new tensions. In particular, a team means bringing together people with different talents, attitudes and styles of working; a number of such styles are outlined. The remainder of the chapter examines the concept of leadership, contrasting it with the notion of management. In conclusion, it is noted that team-based approaches are likely to become more prominent in social care practice.

## INTRODUCTION

In recent times, the pace of change in social care services in Ireland has been rapid and has affected everyone from management, to front-line staff, to end-users. Ongoing restructuring in relation to planning, organisation, funding and delivery of services has presented new challenges for social care practitioners, and the expectations placed on managers are now many and varied. Government policies now emphasise accountability, quality and the integration of health and social care services in a dynamic work environment.

Health and social care services are not a conventional service industry, yet managers face the normal dilemmas of any industry in relation to staffing, resourcing and budgeting. The fact that social care managers operate within a legal and increasingly structured framework means that they need to be not only supervisors of professional good practice, but also monitors of compliance of agreed care procedures. In this unique and often challenging environment, managers must work closely with their staff. In this context the importance of human relationships in the workplace should never be taken for granted (Henderson and Atkinson, 2003). In particular, the notion of teams and teamwork is most important. Strategic planning in health and social care recognises the contribution of teams in the sector: multidisciplinary teams rather than individuals will become the building blocks of organisations pursuing health gains (Doherty, 1998).

One of the consequences of the growth of such teams is the emergence of tensions based on conflicting allegiances and professional backgrounds. While education and training in social care and social work now emphasise teamwork, many professionals still act as sole practitioners, and may have only a limited understanding of the implications of teamworking.

## WHAT IS A TEAM?

Kazenbuch and Smith (1993) describe a team as a small number of people with complementary skills who are committed to a common purpose, a set of performance goals, and an approach for which they hold themselves mutually accountable. Teamwork represents a set of values that encourages listening and responding constructively to views expressed by others; providing support and feedback; and recognising the interests and achievements of others. Teams may be assembled to carry out a variety of roles on a short, medium or long-term basis. In a social care environment, effective teamwork will ultimately shape the quality of service delivered to client groups.

In its broadest sense 'team' is a concept familiar to everybody, but the term is often confused with other groupings. Confusion surrounding the term has led some commentators to suggest that it is often used in a manipulative way by employers to achieve increased productivity from their workforce (Morley et al., 1998). Every workplace has groups that range from senior management teams, to project teams to functional teams, but a title in itself does not necessarily constitute the team. The entire workforce of any large and complex organisation is rarely a genuine team, but is often described as such.

It is a common mistake to confuse teams with other forms of workgroups. Generally, the latter's performance is a function of what its members do as individuals. Where a team differs fundamentally from a workgroup is the requirement for both individual and mutual accountability. Teams rely on more than group discussion, debate and decision; on more than sharing information and best-practice performance standards. It is the extra dimension of teamwork that makes possible performance levels greater than the sum of the individual bests of team members. Simply stated, a team is more than the sum of its parts (Kazenbuch and Smith, 1993) (Table 14.1). In social care environments, some of the strongest teams develop vision, direction, momentum and common purpose, working with the most difficult of client groups.

Table 14.1. Not All Groups are Teams: How to Tell the Difference

| Workgroup | Team |
|---|---|
| • Has strong, clearly focused leader | • Has shared leadership roles |
| • Has individual accountability | • Has individual and mutual accountability |
| • The group's purpose is the same as the broader organisational mission | • Has a specific team purpose that the team itself delivers |
| • Has individual work-products | • Has collective work-products |
| • Runs efficient meetings | • Encourages open-ended discussion and active problem-solving meetings |
| • Measures its effectiveness indirectly by its influence on others | • Measures performance directly by accessing collective work-products |
| • Discusses, decides and delegates | • Discusses, decides, and does real work together |

*Source:* Kazenbuch and Smith, 1993.

While a team can be defined as a group of individuals who share goals and work together to deliver services for which they are mutually accountable, team members are often interdependent, despite their differentiated roles. The composition and skill set of a team should ensure that there is appropriate diversity to undertake the necessary team roles. Skills balance in all teams can be categorised into three main areas — functional expertise, problem solving/decision-making skills, and interpersonal skills.

In common with most work environments, team members in a social care environment may have similar functional expertise, but often lack decision-making or interpersonal expertise. An appropriate skills mix will often complement the skill-set deficits of a colleague and fellow team member. While the skills mix is an important factor in team effectiveness, the team role — the part that someone plays within the team — is most important. Belbin (1993) defines a team role as a tendency to behave, contribute and interrelate with others in a particular way. The behavioural-based model of team role developed by Belbin suggests that effective teams need to have a range of participants who play very different roles within the team structure. Nine team roles ranging from the Plant (creative, imaginative and unorthodox) to the Monitor/Evaluator (sober, strategic and discerning) all contribute to team effectiveness.

No one person can have all the attributes, but the combination of different individual roles will contribute to a high-performance team. Belbin's different role types allow for individual weaknesses. These weaknesses can be compensated for by other team members.

## Table 14.2. Team-Role Descriptions

| Team Role | Contribution | Allowance Weakness |
|---|---|---|
| Plant | Creative, imaginative, unorthodox. Solves difficult problems. | Ignores incidents. Too pre-occupied to communicate effectively. |
| Resource Investigator | Extrovert, enthusiastic, communicative. Explores opportunities. Develops contacts. | Over-optimistic. Loses interest once initial enthusiasm has passed. |
| Co-ordinator | Mature, confident, a good chairperson. Clarifies goals, promotes decision making, delegates well. | Can be seen as manipulative. Offloads personal work. |
| Shaper | Challenging, dynamic, thrives on pressure. The drive and courage to overcome obstacles. | Prone to provocation. Offends people's feelings |
| Monitor Evaluator | Sober, strategic and discerning. Sees all options. Judges accurately. | Lacks drive and ability to inspire others. |
| Teamworker | Co-operative, mild, perceptive and diplomatic. Listens, builds, averts friction. | Indecisive in crunch situations. |
| Implementer | Disciplined, reliable, conservative and efficient. Turns ideas into practical actions. | Somewhat inflexible. Slow to respond to new possibilities. |
| Completer Finisher | Painstaking, conscientious, anxious. Searches out errors and omissions. Delivers on time. | Inclined to worry unduly. Reluctant to delegate. |
| Specialist | Single-minded, self-starting, dedicated. Provides knowledge and skills in rare supply. | Contributes on only a narrow front. Dwells on technicalities. |

*Source*: Belbin, 1993.

While the benefits of working together are well known, building teams and achieving effective teamwork is often difficult. Teamwork will not work in every instance. Among the barriers often highlighted are intra- and inter-professional rivalries that can occur in social care environments. Interpersonal differences, lack of teamwork training and competing priorities of the organisation will also contribute to ineffective teamwork. A common barrier outlined in all literature is the lack of an effective leader to lead the team. In their study of teams in medical practice, Furnell et al. (1987) concluded that the notion of overall leadership is implicit or required when professionals work as a team. Thus the team can be seen as a group of people with a designated leader who may or may not consult with others, and who may override their recommendations. In contrast, a team may comprise a group of people from different professions with equal clinical authority in their own particular areas of competence, and decisions about clients' care and treatment are arrived at by consensus; no single member is able to override others. In practice, many teams operate somewhere between these two positions (Furnell et al., 1987: 167).

## LEADERSHIP

Leadership is the process of influencing others to work willingly towards the objectives and goals of a group, team or organisation. Leaders are the powerful drivers, the visionaries and the influencers in a group, who often bind together competing interests in the pursuit of a particular goal. Academic debate has centred on arguments in relation to the difference, if any, between leadership and management. Some would see these terms as synonymous, as leadership is part of the management role. Mintzberg (1979) contends that the distinction between leadership and management is blurred as the roles overlap. He asserts that leadership is but one dimension of a multifaceted management role. Many other commentators would argue that leaders and managers play different roles, and make different contributions to organisation development and direction. They contend that leaders have followers while managers have subordinates.

Those who make a clear distinction portray the leader as someone who develops visions and drives new initiatives, and the manager as someone who monitors progress towards objectives to achieve order and reliability (Huczynski and Buchanan, 2001). The leader is prophet, catalyst and mover-shaker, focused on strategy, while the manager is operator, technician and problem solver, concerned with the routine here-and-now of goal attainment (Bryman, 1986). The leader establishes vision and direction, motivates and inspires, while the manager establishes plans, designs and staffs the organisation structure, controls performance and produces order. Consistency and predictability are the hallmarks of a manager, while often the very opposite qualities describe a leader. Kotter (1990) contends that there are clear distinguishing factors between both functions (Table 14.3).

Table 14.3. Leadership versus Management

|  | Leadership Functions | Management Functions |
|---|---|---|
| Creating an Agenda | Establishes direction: Vision of the future, develops strategies for change to achieve goals | Plans and budgets: Decides actions and timetables, allocates resources |
| Developing People | Aligning people: Communicates vision and strategy, influences creation of teams which accept validity of goals | Organising and staffing: Decides structure and allocates staff, develops policies, procedures and monitoring |
| Execution | Motivating and inspiring: Energises people to overcome obstacles, satisfies human needs | Controlling, problem solving: Monitors results against plan and takes corrective action |
| Outcomes | Produces positive and sometimes dramatic change | Produces order, consistency and predictability |

*Source*: Kotter, 1990.

Kouzes and Posner (1987) argue that there is a clear distinction between the process of managing and the process of leading. It is the difference between getting others to do and getting others to *want to do*. Leaders do this by being credible; they establish this credibility by their actions — by challenging, inspiring, enabling, modelling and encouraging.

What then makes a good leader? Leadership theory has usually revolved around three areas — trait theory, style theory and contingency theory. Early theories assumed that certain psychological and physical *traits* made for good leaders. Qualities such as initiative, self-assurance, appearance, imagination, sociability and decisiveness have all been proposed as leadership traits. While trait theory has had many proponents, many of the attributes outlined describe patterns of human behaviour rather than personality traits. Difficulties with this area revolve around the inability of writers to establish a consistent set of traits or attributes. Leadership, which ultimately is concerned with influence and power, is difficult to analyse in terms of personality traits (Huczynski and Buchanan, 2001). Despite trait theory being discredited in many academic quarters, many managerial selection schemes and testing procedures still operate on a trait basis in identifying potential managers.

Style leadership theorists argue that employees will work harder for managers who employ certain *styles* of leadership. Organisation psychologists in Michigan and Ohio State Universities in the 1950s identified two pillars of leadership behaviour: employee-centred behaviour that focuses on relationships and employee needs; and job-centred behaviour that focuses on the end result of getting the job done. The Michigan and Ohio studies developed the notion of democratic and autocratic leadership styles, and identified two types of leadership behaviour — consideration and initiating. Consideration is leadership behaviour that involves participation in decision making and involves trust and support for the workforce. In contrast, the initiating structure is a pattern of leadership behaviour that emphasises performance and goal attainment, and expects workers to follow instructions. Likert (1961) applauded the benefits of considerate performance leadership and outlined four different styles of leadership, ranging from dictatorial, autocratic to democratic and laissez-faire (see Table 14.4).

**Table 14.4. Leadership Styles**

| |
|---|
| System 1: *Exploitative autocratic*, in which the leader<br>• Has no confidence and trust in subordinates<br>• Imposes decisions, never delegates<br>• Motivates by threat<br>• Has little communication and teamwork. |
| System 2: *Benevolent authoritative*, in which the leader<br>• Has superficial, condescending trust in subordinates<br>• Imposes decisions, never delegates<br>• Motivates by reward<br>• Sometimes involves subordinates in solving problems. |
| System 3: *Participative*, in which the leader<br>• Has some incomplete confidence and trust in subordinates<br>• Listens to subordinates but controls decision making<br>• Motivates by reward and some involvement<br>• Uses ideas and opinions of subordinates constructively. |
| System 4: *Democratic*, in which the leader<br>• Has complete confidence and trust in subordinates<br>• Allows subordinates to make decisions for themselves<br>• Motivates by reward for achieving goals set by participation<br>• Shares ideas and opinions. |

*Source*: Likert, 1961.

These four divisions of management-style effectiveness will ultimately depend on the leaders themselves, the particular work environment and the subordinates. In care environments, where decision making may often in practice be centralised and bureaucratic, a democratic style that emphasises participative group action would be seen as the more appropriate leadership style.

While it is recognised that an employee-centred participative and democratic style of leadership is favoured by most employees, proponents of contingency theory argue that one leadership style may not be effective in all circumstances, but is contingent on the particular situation in which a manager finds themselves. According to Fielder (1967), a leader's effectiveness is dependent on a number of factors, including the leader's personality, whether the leader is motivated by relationships or task completion, whether the leader has control and influence in the workplace, and by wider environmental factors. O'Grady (2001: 348) poses the question, 'Does it not follow, however that the person most suited to be a leader will be the one who can detect the leadership style required in any given situation and then effectively apply that style?'

Contingency theorists argue that effective leadership styles wholly depend on the particular situation. Organisation structure, characteristics of employees, the nature and complexity of the group's task, reward structure, nature of work contracts, and external environment all contribute to unique situations that ultimately influence leadership style. Because of this uniqueness, no one leadership style is superior. Despite the fact that there is no 'one size fits all' leadership solution, research has consistently proven that a considerate, participative leadership style is the most effective.

Reflecting on leadership qualities, Dixon concluded:

> One comes to the simple truth that leadership is no more than exercising such an influence upon others that they tend to act in concert towards achieving a goal which they might not have achieved so readily had they been left to their own devices. The ingredients which bring about this state of affairs are many and varied. At the most superficial level they are believed to include such factors as voice, stature and appearance, an impression of omniscience, trustworthiness, sincerity and bravery. At a deeper and rather more important level, leadership depends on a proper understanding of the needs and opinions of those one hopes to lead, and the context in which the leadership occurs. It also depends on good timing. Hitler, who was neither omniscient, trustworthy nor sincere, whose stature was repellent, understood these rules and exploited them to full advantage. The same may be said of many good comedians. (Dixon, 1994: 214–5)

In the increasingly complex work environment of social care, participative management approaches have been emphasised, reflecting broader social and political trends. Social care work environments are changing, and now leadership functions are often no longer concentrated in a formally appointed manager. Leadership functions in social care often revolve around decentralised structures and semi-autonomous self-managing teams where a coach or facilitator role has now replaced the role of leader (Huczynski and Buchanan, 2001). The traditional notion of leadership, which assumed that leaders were men, has now been reversed. Women's perceived qualities of intuition and a willingness to engage with feelings are the capstones of twenty-first-century leadership styles. The emphasis on the 'soft skills' of enthusing, inspiring, coaching and facilitating has ensured that women are often more suited to leadership roles.

## CONCLUSION

In the overall context of social care, the service is focused on a wide range of client groups. The quality of service a client group experiences depends crucially on the skills, knowledge, experience and teamwork of the staff who deliver the service. Managers must realise that teamwork does not necessarily suit all situations, but the emphasis on the team is a growing phenomenon in the work environment. This does not mean that teams will dominate and subsume individual opportunity or formal hierarchy and bureaucracy, rather that they will often enhance existing structures without replacing them (Kazenbuch and Smith, 1993). Leadership behaviour will not be confined to those with formal leadership roles and titles, but will be dispersed across the organisation to front-line staff-members who may be required to adapt their style to fit the particular situation.

With participatory management in the human services on the increase, a new model of leadership is in the ascendancy, one that emphasises collectivism over individualism, inclusion over exclusion. Pine et al. conclude that:

> [N]o other variable is more critical to the success of efforts to involve staff in organisational decision-making than leadership at the top. In short, leadership attributes of vision, optimism, shared values and commitment, valuing a team approach (but knowing when to use it) and trust, are critical factors for success in involving others in decision-making and participatory management. (Pine et al., 2003: 120–21)

With an increased emphasis on the team approach, there must be clear guidelines in relation to training, structures, working relationships and career structure for those who undertake responsibilities well beyond their traditional roles. In this workplace of the future, effective teamwork and leadership will ensure that social care services will be better prepared to meet the challenges of this new environment, and ultimately improve care services to all client groups.

15

# Aftercare

Rose Doolan

*Who Cares?*
Constant years of tight held hand
And dominant guidance
Following bewildered on the
Red tape lead of boroughs' policies.
Systematically filed, regularly tested,
Separated safely to a distant spot.
Suckling on the eager breast of care,
Systematically cuddled, caressed, enclosed.
To what end this mothering protection?
To produce
a weak
unprepared
inexperienced
child,
To face
a hostile world.

Peter Mangan (*Who Cares News*, 4 December 1978)

## OVERVIEW

This chapter explores leaving care programmes for young people after they depart
from children's residential centres. It highlights aftercare programmes that are
effective, as well as the challenges that face young people in relation to aftercare
services. The young person's experience of aftercare programmes is presented
throughout the chapter, based on research carried out by the author. The dichotomy between 'effective aftercare' and 'challenges to effective aftercare' is described.

## INTRODUCTION

For the purpose of this chapter, 'aftercare' is defined as the support received by
young people after they leave residential care. This support, provided through
aftercare programmes, may begin while the young person is still in residential care
or may be provided by an outside agency.

The Child Care Act (1991) places responsibility on the state to promote the welfare of, and to protect, children. It empowers the relevant Health Board to provide support for children until they leave residential care, but there is no statutory obligation to provide aftercare. The Act outlines how a Health Board may assist a young person leaving care. This may include visiting; providing support while in education; assistance in finding a trade; and 'by cooperating with housing authorities in planning accommodation for children leaving care on reaching the age of 18 years' (Child Care Act 1991: 24). But the legislation outlines what a Health Board *may* provide rather than what it *shall* provide in relation to aftercare support. In legal terms, the word *shall* creates an obligation, while the word *may* suggests that support can be provided at the discretion of the Health Boards. According to the *Youth Homelessness Strategy* (DoHC, 2001b), the provision of aftercare for the young person leaving residential care is currently viewed as an optional extra.

The 1991 Child Care Act states that the age of leaving care is normally 18 years. Section 45 of the Act further states that if a young person at the age of 18 remains in full-time education, the Health Board may continue to provide assistance, though the Irish Social Services Inspectorate [SSI] (2000) reports that education is not prioritised in residential settings. My own experience as a social care practitioner is that few young people remain in residential settings past the age of 18.

A comprehensive, structured approach to aftercare is essential. In Ireland, the concept is new and only at a developmental stage. Only half the residential centres inspected by the Social Services Inspectorate in 2002 (SSI, 2003) had in operation planned programmes for leaving care. There is no database of services, nor any up-to-date statistics in relation to the number of young people leaving residential care.

If appropriate support services are not provided to assist young people in their transition to adulthood, they may re-enter the care system via services for the homeless or through the judicial system. Kelleher et al. (2000) have carried out the only Irish national study on the subject of leaving residential care. They report that: 'one third of young people leaving the care of the Health Boards and over a half of those leaving special schools for young offenders experience episodes of homelessness or spend time in detention centres at some stage during their first six months [after leaving care]' (Kelleher et al., 2000: xvi).

This chapter is based on research (Doolan, 2002) carried out with five participants in a non-residential care centre. The research concludes that aftercare programmes are paramount in meeting the individual needs of young people who move on to independent living from residential care. The support required includes educational, social and emotional aspects, as well as the development of tangible independent living skills. The earlier in the young person's life these programmes commence, the more effective the result.

The aftercare service provided by the centre studied is a highly structured and skill-enhancing programme. Staff-members provide unconditional support for as long as the person attending the service requests it. This is of immense importance to the participants as the service is tailored to meet their individual needs. It offers young people a variety of educational activities that include a wide range of sports, literacy, crafts and computer skills. The activities are run in tandem with individual counselling and family support.

A primary goal is to reintroduce young people to education and training. The centre aims to provide programmes that will empower young people to take responsibility for their future outside the residential setting. It has no age limit and is therefore accessible to adults in their early to mid-twenties. Groups of young people attend the service on specific days and times, depending on their age.

The research specifically focused on the older group, of 16 years and over. While a case study of one of the participants is provided, the experience of all five young people is referred to throughout the chapter. In order to ensure confidentiality, the name of the young person in the case study has been changed and the aftercare service is not identified.

## CASE STUDY: AFTERCARE FROM MARK'S PERSPECTIVE

Mark is 22 years old. He has been in and out of residental care throughout his life. At the time of the research, he was living with his mother and sister, but previously lived independently. He has two childrern who live with their mother. Mark regularly spends time with his children. He has been attending the aftercare service for ten years and acknowledges the support that it has given him over the years:

> By the time I was eighteen I had two children . . . so that was quite a young age to have two children you know. I got major support from this place [the aftercare service] like helping me out with the kids and all that and they taught me about, well basically about being a father you know, taught me some skills about how to become a father cause I wasn't prepared to become a father.

Mark elaborates on how the programme provides emotional support for him as he struggles with heroin addiction:

> I am a heroin addict and Tom [staff in the aftercare centre] was the first person I told . . . so with that and another staff-member who is gone now they gave me great support and this other staff got me into NA meetings and actually he came to the meetings with me . . . which was brilliant just to know there is someone there with you.

Mark also describes how recreational and educational activities promote a better understanding of life:

→

We do a lot of research on a lot of things which is good to get people to have more of an understanding of life that's important.

According to Mark, access to counselling was of enormous benefit:

It gave me counselling when I needed to talk about my own problems, it was a support system for me and for me going back to home and making sure that I sort of live the life that I need and get the basic stuff that I need.

Mark has completed his Leaving Certificate. He outlines how the aftercare service supported him while he was at school:

Yep I done my Leaving Cert, both my Junior Cert and my Leaving Cert, and that was through this place as well, the help I got with the likes of computer skills and being able to do my homework in here and having teachers coming in here and all that. I found this place very good, you know, because I had so much on my mind with my own personal problems and I was going to school and I wasn't concentrating and I was acting out an awful lot, sort of running away from my own feelings of what was going on at home and when I was falling back at school this place just sort of picked me back up again, you know. It made me catch up on my skills that I had lost out on. So I reckon, you know, if it wasn't for this place I probably wouldn't have even stayed in school.

Mark talks about how the programme helped him to live independently and how he gained confidence while attending the service:

I learned how to money manage, you know, stuff like that, how to look after my kids, be a responsible person to myself . . . I've learned one thing from this place: if you don't look after you, you won't be able to look after your kids or your family either . . . I find that this place gave me an awful lot of confidence, you know, I'm not saying I was very quiet but confidence to me is very important and this place gave me a lot of confidence to be social about life, about learning about life.

Mark was very clear about the impact of the aftercare service on his life:

I need this place. I don't think I could survive without this place . . . this is my safe house, this is where I come if I need to talk or if I need to do something for myself . . . This is my safe home.

Five young people attending the aftercare service were interviewed. The analysis of data revealed two distinct categories: (i) effective aftercare, and (ii) challenges to effective aftercare. Many sub-categories evolved from these, as illustrated in Figure 15.1.

**Figure 15.1. Effective Aftercare and Challenges to Effective Aftercare**

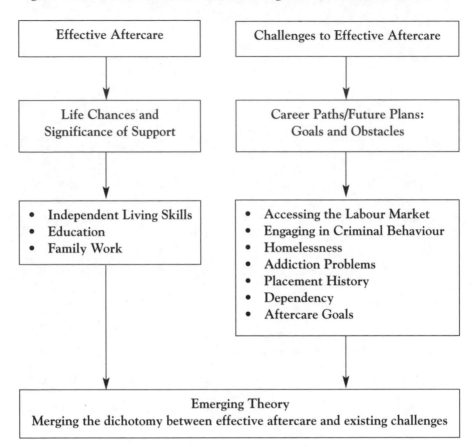

## EFFECTIVE AFTERCARE

Notwithstanding a lack of provision of aftercare services, it is clear that such programmes, when made available, are of paramount importance in allowing young people to live independently after leaving the care system. The *National Standards for Children's Residential Centres* (DoHC, 2001c) promotes the development of aftercare provision. Section 5.35 of the *National Standards* states:

> [T]wo years prior to a young person reaching the legal age of leaving care the care plan will outline the preparation and support in place for the young person. Included will be the named person who will maintain contact with the young person after they leave the centre, the financial support available to the young person, the living arrangements and support available in times of illness, crisis or seasonal celebrations. (DoHC, 2001c: 19)

## LIFE CHANCES AND THE SIGNIFICANCE OF SUPPORT

Life chances reflect the impact aftercare programmes have on the young person's transition from residential care to independent living. Ordinarily, most young people who leave their family home at the age of 18 do so to attend college, start a new job or to go travelling. Most receive continued financial and emotional support from their family. Most young people leaving care do not receive this level of support. Fahlberg (1994: 222) poses the question: 'Who will be this individual's family of resource?' According to participants in this study, the aftercare programme provides such support. Mark describes how the programme offers him space and time to talk about his problems, support in times of need, and encouragement in times of success.

Many young people living in residential care are very apprehensive about reaching their eighteenth birthday. This is not a time for celebration, rather a time when they are forced to face the realities of adulthood. Many do not feel at all prepared to do so:

> The eighteenth birthday is huge for us. While others are looking forward to their eighteenth birthday I dreaded it. There are big emotions around it; you don't know what the next step will be. When I turned eighteen I knew that was it. Most social workers don't keep people on. I often thought that I would have been better off putting up with the beating at home. (young person quoted in Kelleher et al., 2000: 12)

This point is reiterated by Garnett (1992) who suggests that young people brought up in the care system are expected to achieve a much higher level of maturity and independence than would normally be expected of their peers living at home.

Participants in the study commented that the staff-members working in the aftercare service are friendly. An informal relationship with staff assists young people in socialising with others. The young person feels at ease talking about difficulties and enjoys the programme. The fact that the service has no cut-off age is of enormous importance to Mark and other participants. This unconditional support is reflected in Mark's description of this as his 'safe home'. The 'open-door policy' adopted by the service is of enormous benefit in meeting the individual needs of the young person.

It is important that those who avail of aftercare services do not become solely dependent on the programme for support. In view of this, the programme networks with outside agencies where participants may also seek support and find resources. It develops links and networks on behalf of the young person in the provision of holistic care, thus impacting in a positive way on their life chances. Coyle (1998) outlines the importance of such networks, where aftercare services rely heavily on resources and partnership with other agencies. From Mark's perspective, links were forged with agencies that provided specialised support for his addiction problems (counselling and NA).

Mark has attended this aftercare service for ten years. Other participants have also attended the service for a significant number of years, implying that it is flexible and individually tailored to meet young people's needs: they choose to attend the service. The individualised approach concurs with Stein and Carey's (1986) recommendations. They suggest that such programmes should address the different aspects of the individual, including their personal, political, psychological and material needs and rights. But they further suggest (1986: 131) that aftercare services should help to tease out the contradictions between the position of those leaving care and what is expected of them. They report that an: 'expectation that most of the young people would achieve an independent and adult life was largely contradicted by their necessary dependence on other agencies for help, support or control'.

The aftercare service in the study attempts to address such contradictions. In Mark's case, assistance with parenting skills helped him to understand what is expected of him as a parent — this was a specific programme tailored to meet his needs. The programme in itself provides a setting where the young person can meet others and form friendships. Recreational activities act as an informal medium for the teaching of social skills. Mark suggests that such activities promote a better understanding of life.

Stein and Carey (1986) recommend that recreational and social activities for the young person leaving care need to be financially accessible, as most care leavers have little money to spend on socialising. The aftercare service provides financial support for Mark and all of the participants. This allows them to engage in recreational activities, enhancing their life chances in the process. Coyle (1998) concurs that aftercare programmes should be informed and planned in such a way as to ensure that people are fully involved in informal opportunities in their daily lives. She outlines that this promotes and enhances the young person's skills and abilities.

## INDEPENDENT LIVING SKILLS

To help young people negotiate some of the practical issues associated with care leaving, such as budgeting, shopping and home management, Coyle (1998: 46) advocates that aftercare programmes need to incorporate a task-centred, information-giving approach: 'for young people to be successful on their own, there are various intangible skills and attributes that they must have — social skills, decision making, self esteem.'

A wide range of skills to promote independent living is taught — formally and informally — on the described programme. This has greatly benefited the young people who attend. Tangible skills such as cookery, laundry, personal hygiene and budgeting are included in the programme, while intangible skills such as communication, coping and social skills are described as beneficial by the participants. Mark and the other participants see such tangible skills as essential to living independently. They say that intangible skills also play a central role in programme provision.

Stein suggests that the concept of empowerment needs is pivotal in aftercare programmes. He emphasises that for such programmes to be effective, they must be based upon engagement, negotiation and participation, and must be guided by the question, 'How will this empower the young person?' (Stein, 1992: 7). The philosophy of empowerment appears to play a central role in the programme in the study. Mark describes how the programme teaches communication skills, so encouraging him to fulfil his goals and enhance his confidence.

## EDUCATION

Kelleher et al. (2000) found that 60 per cent of young people in care left school at 15 years or younger. Education is thus a key factor in the provision of an effective aftercare service. Stability in care combined with the support and encouragement of carers results in longer years of school attendance for children in residential services. In addition, retention within the educational system allows aftercare supports to be provided. Key elements for the educational success of young people attending an aftercare service include consistency and a strong interest in the education of each child. This often means taking on an advocacy role and addressing practical measures that encourage learning and study. Participants acknowledged the supports provided by the aftercare service in relation to the education system. Mark attributes his success at school to the support provided by the service, including tuition, attending school meetings and homework supervision.

The success of young people in formal examinations is an important aspect. But success in educational terms takes on a wider context that includes helping young people to feel confident in their abilities, both academically and socially. Benefits of education are more diverse than just academic attainment. Young people who leave school early are disadvantaged not only because of the lack of formal qualifications, but also in terms of the social success of progressing through school with their peers.

## FAMILY WORK

There was a varied response by participants in relation to the level of involvement of families with the aftercare service. Those involved in the service recommend that it commence work with families earlier, in order to open the doors of communication in relation to their progress. At the time this study was completed, three of the participants had moved back to living with their families. The programme maintains links with a counselling service for the benefit of participants and their families. Mark was in receipt of long-term support and assistance with regard to family issues.

Kelleher et al. (2000) found that a third of young people who had left Health Board care had returned home to their families, but this can lead to high levels of personal distress. Past experiences whilst living at home may resurface. Furthermore, young adults experience difficulty in adjusting to community and social networks. Stein (1992) argues that there is a tendency for young people to return home having spent a considerable length of time away from their family. He notes that maintaining links throughout care and identifying strengths and sources of support within families should be a key factor in any care or aftercare plan.

Gilligan argues that working with families involves a complex mix of skills, likely to encompass re-engagement, negotiation and mediation. Family support involves addressing issues raised by 'gender, cultural diversity and by complex social problems' (Gilligan, cited in Canavan et al., 2002: 28). Gilligan promotes an 'inclusive vision' when supporting families, one that incorporates and interlinks elements from a wide variety of fields including community development, education (adult and child), social work, criminal justice, social employment, early childhood services and local area regeneration. Parents and siblings need to be involved in the aftercare plan.

It is important to acknowledge that the young person needs to guide social care practitioners as to the level of engagement and involvement they want with their families. Stein argues that:

> [Y]oung people in care have experienced a troubled background involving family difficulties and abuse. Despite the best intentions of those providing care, young people in the care system often experience further disruption perhaps resulting in the loss of links with their family and their native community. (Stein, 1997: 3)

Problems experienced by young people after leaving care, such as loneliness, place demands on social care professionals to be 'additionally' accessible, to provide all types of helpful advice at the appropriate time. For any aftercare programme, the involvement of families may prove challenging and time-consuming. But if the young adult is to live outside residential care, either at home or independently, the support of family, together with participation in an effective aftercare programme, is essential.

## CHALLENGES TO EFFECTIVE AFTERCARE

There is a dichotomy of service provision in relation to aftercare services from the young person's perspective. My research highlights the advantages of aftercare programmes, but also identifies the challenges that an aftercare service is faced with.

## CAREER PATHS/FUTURE PLANS: GOALS AND OBSTACLES

When asked about career paths and future plans, participants described the many challenges that make the transition to independent living difficult. These include accessing the labour market, engaging in criminal activity, homelessness and drug addiction, placement history, dependency on the programme and lack of aftercare goals.

## Accessing the Labour Market

According to Stein, there are key areas of difference between the care leaver and other young people:

> [Y]oung people leaving care have to be independent at a much earlier age; have lower levels of educational attainment and post-sixteen further educational participation rates, higher unemployment rates, unstable career paths and higher levels of dependency on welfare benefits and early parenthood. (Stein, 1997: 59)

The aftercare service actively encourages the young person to seek employment. Participants who had left residential care outlined their difficulties in accessing the job market and in steering their career paths. Mark is the only participant in this study to have secured long-term employment. The challenge for the service is to support participants to access the job market and to remain in employment. Kelleher et al. (2000) recommend that aftercare programmes should encourage young people to increase their educational and vocational skills in order to avail of job opportunities. Kelleher et al. (2000) and Stein and Carey (1986) found low levels of employment and poor educational attainment among care leavers.

The aftercare service helps those applying for jobs. Participants use the resources provided, such as the teaching of computer skills, to access the job market. Most participants express a desire to work; their interests and talents are encouraged. Participation in the programme increases young people's confidence with the ultimate objective of enhancing their employment opportunities.

## Engaging in Criminal Behaviour

One participant interviewed revealed that in order to get money, he is involved in crime. He suggests that prison may become part of his future. Kelleher et al. (2000: 129) revealed that two years after leaving Health Board care a quarter of young people had been sentenced to prison. These young people attempt to attain societal goals by deviant means, conforming to Merton's (1968) theory of social deviance. Merton proposes that a person internalises social values such as goals to succeed, to climb the social ladder and to make a career. As a result of being removed from their home, a young person's social structure has been disrupted. Their economic and educational position acts as a constraint to achieving in society, in turn leading to criminal behaviour. For Merton (1968: 185), much criminal behaviour is 'the expression of a situation in which man has accepted social goals but lacks legitimate means of reaching them'.

## Homelessness

Kelleher et al. (2000) found that two years after leaving Health Board care, two-thirds of young people had experienced episodes of homelessness. For many young people, leaving care can mean anxiety, fear and loneliness. One explained: 'I was nervous about leaving care and could not sleep at night. I was terrified of moving into the private rented sector. I did not think I could cope . . . I did not feel ready to live on my own. Yet I did not want to share with strangers' (quoted in Kelleher et al., 2000: 117). One young person involved in crime seeks help in relation to accessing the housing market. Being homeless hinders him from accessing jobs or training and forces him to engage in criminal activity to survive.

It is vital that facilities are established to provide accommodation and support for young people who have left care as they struggle in the initial months of independent living. The *Youth Homelessness Strategy* (DoHC, 2001b) advocates the provision of accommodation such as 'scatter flats' — supported accommodation in existing housing complexes run by the local authority. The *Strategy* highlights the key role of local authorities in tackling the accommodation needs of young people leaving care.

Participants living at home with their families reported that options in relation to rented accommodation were not available to them, because of high financial costs. They aspire to live independently in the future. For Mark, living independently has become a reality and he is moving into a flat with friends, with the support of the aftercare service.

Stein (1997) found that schemes working with young people who had difficulties in securing accommodation were able to help the vast majority to find 'good' places to live within two years of leaving care. This was achieved by assessing both the nature of accommodation and the young person's views as to its suitability based on their current needs. Smith (1994) and the *Youth Homelessness Strategy* (DoHC, 2001b) argue that local authorities should adopt a 'specialist' and 'comprehensive' housing approach in meeting the needs of all young people, including those leaving care.

The availability of suitable and affordable accommodation will have an impact on the young person's involvement in criminal activity. Young people in this study feel that having accommodation is the start that leads to employment and independence. The aftercare service supports the young person seeking accommodation by making available a database of suitable accommodation, by promoting the young person's right to suitable accommodation, and by recognising the effect housing has on other aspects of their lives.

## Addiction Problems

One young person described how the programme supports him in drug rehabilitation and emphasises the importance of this support in order to help him to stay off heroin. Kelleher et al. (2000: 125) found that a third of young people leaving Health Board care experienced addiction problems. My research revealed the enormous value participants placed on drug education provided by the aftercare service. The challenge for the service is to keep abreast of developments in relation to drug awareness. In educating young people of the dangers of drugs, through videos and games, the programme allows participants to judge for themselves the risks involved.

## Placement History

Participants revealed that there was a tendency towards 'multiple placements' prior to leaving care. These findings concurred with a study by Garnett (1992) who suggested that young people were likely to have considerable movement and disruption prior to leaving the care system. The challenge for the aftercare service is to support the young person by working through difficulties that may stem from multiple placements. Stein (1992) argues that multiple placements have an emotional impact upon young people. Changing carers, friends, neighbourhoods, schools on several occasions with little consistency in the young person's life creates difficulties.

Participants who spoke about their experience of care expressed dissatisfaction and dislike for previous placements. One young person was angry about inconsistency in relation to staff turnover. It is important to acknowledge that multi-placement issues need to be addressed in the residential care system through comprehensive care planning and the resourcing of appropriate placements. Clarke (1998) reveals that care staff-members face uncertainty about the appropriate level of contact they should have with young people in residential care. This uncertainty poses difficulties for the young person in the development of secure relationships. The young people interviewed revealed that they felt ill-prepared to leave care at the age of 18 and expressed disillusionment when talking about the support and contact received from previous placements.

The challenge for aftercare programmes is to address the issues raised in relation to multi-placements in order to promote a healthy transition from childhood to adulthood. Aftercare programmes must promote a positive sense of identity. A sense of security for young people leaving care can be achieved by ensuring that there is no ambiguity as to the support that will be available to them after they leave care. The *National Standards for Residential Care* (1995) outlines that a key member of staff needs to be named as the person who will continue to link with the young person upon leaving care. The availability of support needs to be tailored to meet each young person. Ordinarily there is no time limit placed on the support provided by parents to their children in the transition from adolescence to adulthood.

## Dependency

Parker (1980) argues that the quality of care a child receives can reflect the quality of life they have upon leaving care. This is supported by the findings from my study. Participants tend to depend on the programme in relation to financial support, emotional support and money management; institutional care remains part of their life. An expectation of continued support appears to be a normal reaction when leaving care. One participant stated that he expected the Health Board to provide financial support in relation to housing, and almost all young people interviewed were welfare dependent.

One young person stated that he expected to re-enter the institutional care system by going to prison in the future. Mark described his reliance on the after-care service for support in order to stay off heroin. The aftercare service attempts to address the challenge of dependency by ensuring that support is provided to service users through planning and negotiation.

It was apparent that money management was a problem for some of the participants in the aftercare programme. Stein and Carey (1986) also found that money and its management came high on the list of difficulties. It is likely that the dependency revealed in the study in relation to budgeting skills stems from the lack of responsibility placed on the young person in residential care to manage their own money. Chakrabarti and Hill (2000) echo this argument and suggest that young people living in residential care are not given the opportunity to budget.

According to Chakrabarti and Hill (2000), total responsibility for money matters continues to be part of the social care practitioners' remit. In this study, one participant relied on the service manager to help him manage his money. Aftercare services are presented with a challenge when devising a programme to help the young person deal with money matters. Appropriate training must be devised in this respect prior to leaving residential care. Young people would then perhaps have a better knowledge of the standard of life they could afford.

## Aftercare Goals

Participants showed a lack of ability to communicate their expectations from an aftercare service. They were unsure of how to make a start to live independently or of their future goals. One identified housing as a priority in the transition from care to independent living, but could not offer any suggestions as to how the service could facilitate him in the attainment of affordable accommodation. Pinkerton and McCrae (1999) point out that accommodation was a huge concern for the young person leaving care.

Another area of concern identified by the young people was that they did not feel ready to leave care at the age of 18. One participant suggested that the Health Board should reconsider this cut-off point as he felt he was forced to leave care at this age. Stein (1997) found that very few young people remain in care placements beyond the age of 18, and indeed a majority leave at 16 or 17 years of age. The challenge for aftercare is to support the young person at this difficult time, by instilling confidence and encouraging maturity.

## CONCLUSION

The term 'aftercare' implies that the young person has finished care and is no longer in need of it. The terms 'continuing care' and 'transitional care' are useful ways to express that leaving care is part of a lengthy transition from childhood to adulthood. Irish policies need to reflect the need for aftercare services, so that those leaving residential care are faced with fewer challenges and greater opportunities. It is important to note that a comprehensive policy on leaving care is available within the HSE Eastern Region (ERHA, 2004). It is hoped that it will guide residential centres in relation to best practice.

Aftercare programmes should begin early in residential settings. It is important to maintain contact with family and neighbourhood of origin, helping the young person to cope with issues in their lives. From the moment of entry, clarity is required as to the reasons why a young person is living in residential care, as this impacts upon their choices or future plans when moving on to independent living.

A focus on skills such as cooking and cleaning is of secondary importance to young people leaving care. Speaking as a former social care practitioner, I feel that in residential care too high a value is placed on tangible skills and not enough on the development of the young person's self-esteem, confidence and resilience in the face of feelings of loneliness and isolation. Tackling such issues must be a priority for aftercare services. Working in a collaborative way with families and other agencies is vital.

Specific provision by government of a housing programme conducive to the needs of young people leaving residential care is also essential. A young person who has appropriate accommodation has a greater chance of a successful transition to independent living. There needs to be an acknowledgement that providing aftercare support is far more economical than providing long-term institutional care via the judicial system or homeless services.

Aftercare programmes can act as a preventative strategy to preclude future social problems. The provision of effective aftercare programmes can benefit both participants and society. Challenges to effective aftercare may be overcome by identifying and addressing the needs of individuals from the time they enter residential care. Preparation for independent living should not begin at 16 but should be continuous throughout the young person's life in care.

Throughout the research, the young person's transition from care and their ability to manage independent life was examined and evaluated. Implicit in the research is an examination of the effects of residential care itself and how the young person living in care is prepared for leaving. It has identified deficiencies in the Irish system for young people leaving residential care. It emphasises the importance of programmes that attempt to address those issues.

To overcome successfully the challenges of living independently, young people need the support of an effective aftercare programme. The Irish system is evidently in the embryonic stage in this respect. Despite a general acknowledgement of the need for aftercare services, priority and resources have yet to be given for their development. There is a need for interdepartmental cooperation in the provision of such services. The responsibility for their provision does not completely rest with the Health Service Executive, but is a state-owned task that encompasses housing, welfare and education departments. Mark and other participants in my research outline the importance and the significance of the aftercare service in their lives. Unlike many other young people leaving residential care, they have had the opportunity to attend an aftercare programme. Other young care leavers may not be so fortunate. It is time that we ceased to view aftercare as an optional extra; instead it must be valued as an essential component in the successful transition from residential care into independent living.

16

# Working in Social Care

Danny Meenan

## OVERVIEW

This chapter explores some aspects of working in social care, with a particular emphasis on residential childcare. The author has had 16 years' experience of working in this field, as front-line worker, manager and educator. The chapter outlines some of the key features of residential care as a sector, emphasising the vulnerable nature of those young people who enter the system, and the challenges posed for those who practise in this area. The types of skills required of practitioners are outlined, as are some of the key personal attributes that contribute to effective care practice. The complex and challenging — yet ultimately rewarding — nature of the day-to-day work is explored. The importance of self-care is emphasised. The chapter concludes with an examination of training and development of social care practitioners. It emphasises that the development of a culture of continual improvement is crucial, to the development of a more effective and fulfilled social care workforce; to better organisations in the field; and, most importantly, to a better care experience for those who enter the system.

## INTRODUCTION

There are many aspects to working in the field of social care. Throughout society some individuals and groups will always require a form of help, support and care. The role of the social care practitioner can be as diverse and varied as the group of people to whom they provide valuable services.

Community and primary care services are non-acute aspects of the health service. They encompass health and social services. The primary care strategy sets out to reconfigure and strengthen this provision of healthcare. Social care practitioners play a key role here. Many such practitioners are at the heart of the community, providing a necessary service to people in need in a variety of settings, such as daycare, community work, supporting people in their homes, supporting young people and adults with disabilities and their families, and residential care both for young people and for vulnerable adults. This work can be both rewarding and challenging; it offers a variety and range of duties every day.

Providing care and support for people in need is not an office-based role with a 39-hour week — it could be a 24/7 service. Vulnerable people do not stop needing care and support after five in the evening. Many require ongoing intervention and guidance to help them cope with the trauma and stress of their particular situation or circumstances. Others just need to feel that they are not alone.

The aspect of social care that I will explore further, from a practitioner's perspective, is residential childcare. I have worked for over 16 years in this field in both the voluntary and statutory sector in Northern Ireland and in the statutory sector in the Republic of Ireland, for the North Western Health Board. Throughout this time, I have experienced residential childcare from a variety of perspectives — as a childcare worker, centre manager and a service manager. These various roles have offered me great learning opportunities, have helped me to develop my expertise and ability and have allowed me to demonstrate my practitioner and management skills and ability to make sound judgment calls.

## YOUNG PEOPLE IN RESIDENTIAL CARE

Children and young people enter into residential care for a number of reasons, such as abuse, neglect or foster care breakdown. They may live in unsafe environments where their protection cannot be guaranteed.

Many young people in residential care can experience deep-seated feelings of loss, separation and abandonment. They may carry the baggage and scars of multiple placements and transfers of bases where they have not had opportunities to build trusting relationships or invest in emotional security. Fahlberg (1994: 160) discusses how unresolved separations can interfere with the development of future attachments. She suggests that the new attachments that young people make are not meant to replace the old attachments — they can coexist.

This is also true for young people in residential care. For a number, prior negative experiences with adults and other caregivers have led them to develop their own coping mechanisms. These may prevent the development of further attachments, either out of loyalty to birth parents or as a means of self-preservation.

The role that residential workers play in the lives of young people in care is of vital importance. The smallest aspects of everyday caring can make a difference and have a great impact. In this process, the residential worker adopts many guises, such as teacher, mentor, role model, friend and advocate, to name just a few. It is incumbent on every social care practitioner to remain professional, to be efficient, and to carry work through to all the various agencies with which they make contact.

The role the residential worker plays may be a far cry from the role of the other adults that these young people have known throughout their short lives. Some may have had to learn to be self-reliant as a result of extended periods of neglect or being left alone, and may tend not to trust adults readily. For many, the apparent containment of a mainstream residential centre with its rules and responsibilities may prove difficult to adhere to and can lead to potential areas of conflict. For some young people, residential care may be the best option, as living within a foster care placement may constantly remind them of the dysfunction of their own families, adding to their pain and frustration. Residential care can also be seen by the young person as a temporary base, away from their home, where they can explore specific issues that caused their family to break down.

While there are many common factors that lead to young people coming into care, everyone in residential care has their own unique set of circumstances. Each young person is an individual and should be treated accordingly. Residential workers often find it difficult to come to terms with the fact that some young people will present particular behaviour as a way to avoid an exploration of the reasons for their admission into care. The presenting behaviour is what is dealt with and the underlying reason is not disclosed. This can lead the worker to feel frustrated and sometimes lead to feelings of self-doubt.

It is essential that where the social care practitioner is unable to identify or explore the core reason for behavioural problems, they recommend referral to an appropriate discipline such as psychology or child and adolescent mental health. All residential workers must understand that some young people in residential care may *never* fully discuss their true feelings or how the emotional impact of their past experiences has affected them. The simplest triggers — a song on the radio, a phrase someone uses, the smell of a particular perfume or cologne — may bring memories flooding back. These can be the precursor to a violent outburst or a retreat into their inner space. The important thing is to let these young people know that there is someone who will be there for them when they feel that they are ready to talk. This is a personal journey which, for some young people, may take many years to travel.

## RESIDENTIAL CHILDCARE SKILLS

So what are the skills that are needed to equip residential workers in their role? For Clough (2000: 23), one of the challenges of working in residential childcare is to define what is specific and distinctive about it. He suggests that in residential houses there is a mix of physical care, holding and the development of self. I agree with Clough that residential care should provide a good place to live, where residential workers can respond in everyday activities in ways that are therapeutic and life-enhancing.

In order to explore key skills, I discussed with other residential workers the qualities they perceived to be important and that would assist them in their work with young people. The following skills and qualities were identified:

- Non-judgmental
- Team member
- Good communicator — oral and written
- Good listener
- Problem solver
- Patient — remaining calm in crisis

- Aware of self
- Caring nature
- Assertive
- Open to learning new things
- Understanding
- Creative and imaginative
- Sense of humour.

Key words such as 'rewarding', 'demanding' and 'challenging' were used to describe their work with young people in residential care. Some people see their work in residential care as more of a vocation than employment. They emphasise staying focused, and being consistent and dedicated, even in the most difficult times, to help make a difference in young people's lives, rather than just coming to work as a means to an end.

For many residential workers, residential care can be a mind-opening experience. Many initially find it difficult to comprehend what some children and young people have already experienced in their short lives: more than many other adults, including staff themselves, will experience in a lifetime. In my discussion with residential workers, they talked about how, in the beginning, it was difficult to rationalise how adults could treat children and young people with such contempt and cause so much pain. Residential care 'opened their eyes' to personal trauma and behaviour that they never knew existed.

So how do we prepare ourselves to work in this environment? I am sure that many residential workers would support the development of the theory related to this work. A professional entering residential childcare experiences a very sharp learning curve that requires quick thinking and ingenuity on a daily — sometimes hourly — basis. For many, the theory studied at college does not always match the reality of working in a residential centre. But it does give you an understanding of why some young people behave in the way they do.

We, as adults and staff, need to afford young people, including those in residential care, the opportunities to explore issues and learn from life experiences and, indeed, to make mistakes. Sadly, we also have to realise that some young people, in residential care, as a consequence of their experiences prior to admission, may never change their behaviour or break the spiral of negative or offending behaviour, no matter how many safety nets we provide.

Social care ethics directs us to support and be proactive in young people's development, safety and journey to adulthood. It is an integral part of a job to network with other agencies, while being fully cognisant of children's confidentiality. It is imperative that we document and record accurately any information that will help and enable the choices and opportunities for the young person.

## RESIDENTIAL STAFF

The issues of self-awareness and professional boundaries are always a contentious issue for those who work in residential care. There is always a need to remain safe, but provision of a high quality of care can sometimes leave individual staff in vulnerable situations. Communication among the team is a very important aspect in residential work. Sharing of ideas, consulting with others, consistency and continuity of approach, with all staff following agreed protocols and policies, cannot be emphasised enough.

Residential workers must be aware of what we bring as individuals to residential work. All people have their own prejudices, beliefs and ethics, and residential workers feel that we have something to offer the young people we work with — why else would we be there? But our experiences and life events must not colour our vision nor lead us to make judgments, just because we feel we know better or feel we have experienced a similar emotional trauma. We must always remain open in our outlook and see each young person as an individual who will react differently in a variety of similar situations. We must work at their pace and level of understanding to help them to deal with issues.

Many residential care workers are faced with situations that challenge their thinking and force them to think more laterally and constructively. Residential teams are usually made up of a variety of individuals who have stories to tell and experiences to share. There should always be opportunities to grow and develop — both personally and professionally. There is a requirement for strong elements of trust and open communication between team members, as each individual social care practitioner needs to feel a sense of support and security from others at times of heightened anxiety or aggression within a centre. Knowing that someone is there to assist you through particularly difficult situations can be the factor that gives residential staff the impetus to continue with a particular course of action. Structures, routines, consistency and clarity of actions are all important aspects of team cohesion.

As already emphasised, team cohesion and consistency are important factors, given the nature of the residential task. The shift system, if not organised properly, can allow different staff-members to work in significantly different ways. If the same rules are not applied by all staff, in a consistent manner, this can potentially lead to confusion and frustration for the young people, as well as difficulties in staff relations. Failure to maintain equilibrium of approach can be reminiscent of the previous experiences of some young people. They may quite naturally play off one set of staff-members against the other. Communication is vital, and properly structured handover meetings between shifts reduce the opportunities for manipulation and potential conflict. Some centres that have a high turnover of staff may reflect the previous turmoil in some young people's lives and reinforce the inconsistency and lack of constancy in their lives.

Throughout my social care career I have worked with many residential care workers who were at different points in their careers — students on placement, new young unqualified staff, people with many years of life experience, recent graduates, and others with years of work experience. They all agreed that you actually have to work in residential care to experience the emotional roller coaster that it can be. But they also stress how rewarding, worthwhile and enjoyable it is to make a positive contribution to the lives of children and young people.

## SELF-CARE

One of the most important issues about working in residential care is the issue of self-care. This of course is an issue not solely for residential workers, but given the pressure and stress that this type of work creates, it is an area that some people may neglect.

Self-care means that every individual must take responsibility for their own safety and wellbeing. We cannot provide adequate and appropriate care for others, particularly troubled children and young people, if we do not make time to look after ourselves. It could be said that as we are the only person who is constantly with us, we must always be the one to care for ourselves.

Self-care in this environment is closely linked to self-awareness. Individuals must remain acutely aware of their own limitations and levels of tolerance and anxiety. The ability to recognise incidents of high anxiety in ourselves may take some time actually to master, but if we are not careful and continue to work, oblivious to our mood and ignoring the indicators, this may lead, in time, to feelings of complete exhaustion and occupational burnout.

Many people do not recognise that they are suffering from stress. They think that these feelings of rushing adrenalin and high anxiety are part of the job, and in some circumstances, the stimulus that keeps them going. Failure to recognise that you are under pressure can often lead to additional issues in the workplace. For some people, this could mean making rash decisions or reacting in an unaccustomed manner that may lead to the further deterioration of a situation that can spiral out of control. The young person can end up feeling, and reacting, defensively, and neither side is willing to back down with the fear of losing face.

Over the years I have worked in residential child care, I have seen enthusiastic, eager and bright-spirited people coming to work in the service. Everyone wants to do their best for these young people and can become quite attached, even to the young people who constantly challenge them and stretch their patience to the limit. People generally get support and guidance from other team members, and the longer-serving members of the team often find themselves in the position of mentor and emotional supporter during times of upset and frustration.

Good support through supervision is vital for all residential staff (see Chapter 11). Supervision should not be a place that simply evaluates your plan of work for your key child and organises your next time off. It is an opportunity to explore the impact of particular situations and events and how they have affected you on all levels, and a place to plan how you will deal with similar situations better. I have found that at times people will avoid exploring specific issues in supervision, as they often fear letting their guard down. They wonder how their manager will view them if they really say what they are feeling or thinking.

I feel that it is healthy to explore all the emotions that negative situations may generate; individuals may often remain emotionally stunted if they do not fully express the issues that contribute to their frustrations and distress. In meeting the needs of residential staff in my service, I have introduced the services of an external clinical supervisor who provides that particular place where the safety valve can be opened and personal issues can be released and explored. Many staff-members have found this method of self-exploration in a non-work environment very therapeutic and have stated that it gives them the opportunity to explore specific issues and frustrations in a freer manner, without the fear of feeling professionally vulnerable. We all need to have this opportunity to explore the specific issues that residential care can throw at us as; without it, our vision may be clouded, our opinions misjudged and our work with young people tinged with misunderstanding.

These feelings are often stronger after an aggressive outburst, where a lot of anger is displayed and even physical assaults take place. No one comes to work to be assaulted or verbally abused, but the fact remains that in residential care it is an occupational hazard that cannot always be prevented, but must never be condoned.

When children and young people have been traumatised, they can act out in aggressive and unpredictable ways. For many young people, it is an open expression of the inner turmoil that one manager described as being akin to 'a volcano before it erupts'. It is unhealthy for anyone, particularly troubled young people, to repress anger and hurt, as they will often erupt at times when you least expect it.

Children and young people are naturally active, and boredom can often lead to frustration and an inappropriate response to the simplest of requests. Residential workers need to be proactive in promoting ways that facilitate young people in letting off steam. We, as residential care staff, have the responsibility to ensure that this happens in a safe environment and that we provide a steady stream of activities to facilitate it.

As in all professions, people have a certain working style or forte that leads them to work in particular environments. Some people prefer to work with younger children, others with adolescents. Some enjoy the revolving door of a short-stay or assessment centre as opposed to the longer commitment of medium- to long-term care. No matter which environment you choose to work in, be that mainstream, high support or secure care, remember that you are not working in a vacuum — other professionals are there to support and help you both inside and outside the service. Do not feel undervalued or intimidated by the seniority of other professionals. Residential childcare practitioners have the best knowledge of the young people in their care; after all, they are with them almost every day, experiencing the variety of emotions that are displayed. It is important that you share your knowledge clearly and confidently, as you are also a very important contributor in the decision-making process and can influence the development of plans for the young people under your care.

## TRAINING AND DEVELOPMENT

As part of my research in Health Services Management (Meenan, 2002), I explored issues of career and personal development with a cross-section of currently employed residential staff. We discussed a number of issues that related to their work in residential childcare, and each person was given an opportunity to discuss their particular journey in the service, highlighting significant highs and lows during this time. Each person's story contained both positive and negative personal perspectives. While all workers have different personal experiences, there were many similarities in their professional experiences.

Training was a key theme that emerged — in particular, the appropriateness of the training that was delivered. Discussion with employees regarding what training they would find most useful had been highlighted prior to the training taking place. Prior to the training, all residential staff had been involved in a training needs analysis. Through this process, they had decided on the areas of learning and development that they felt would meet their needs. From the discussion, it was clear that the training provided had, as a consequence, been very beneficial and relevant to their work setting.

The residential staff also stated that the issues raised and discussed at length during the training could be immediately put into practice, and they adjusted their approach to work situations accordingly. This gave a good indication that the training was understood and its practical application was appropriate to the setting. The residential staff also felt a part of the service and it helped them to gain a better understanding of their work environment and the young people for whom they provided a service.

Interestingly it was not just issues of childcare that were identified as positives from the training, but also the team-building training sessions. These have been of great benefit in helping staff to gain a more constructive understanding of the team process and the dynamics involved in working in groups.

This process of training and development initiatives encompasses an improvement in service provision, supported in the government's *Action Plan for People Management* (DoHC, 2002a) in the health service. A recurring theme identified in relation to training was the feeling that many of the participants felt more confident in carrying out their duties and also felt that they could better contribute to decision-making processes that involved other professionals. They had identified issues in the past of feeling inadequate and not feeling that their contribution was required or considered, but now the consensus seemed to be one of more confidence in these settings. However, the major issue of not having the recognised social care national qualification still impacted on some occasions, compounded by frustration at not being able to advance in their career.

Induction into the service was another bone of contention. For individuals who commenced work in the service in recent years, there appeared to be a better structure and approach to induction compared to earlier experiences of not being given direction, support or guidance. This had added to feelings of stress, inadequacy and working within a vacuum. Different forms of support and guidance introduced in recent times have helped to create a better structure, but there are still some areas where some staff felt that this would need to be further developed.

*Variety* in roles and responsibilities was identified as an important factor. There was a sense that individuals wanted to try different areas of employment in the sector but felt hindered by the qualification bar. This could also be an indication of stress levels within the service, given the number of people looking out for alternatives to the highly stressful conditions related to working in residential childcare. This desire for variety could also be seen as a positive, with individuals expressing an interest in gaining more skills in different areas, which they could in turn introduce into their own work setting, with a view to improving current work practices.

It is good to hear that people are open to the idea of change and the development of new skills and approaches, but it is important to balance this with the need for some measure of stability and consistency, given the intensity of the client group with which they work. People did seem to equate the acquisition of new skills as change and progress, but felt they needed to take more time to consolidate the skills they had acquired to date, before venturing on a constant stream of alternative approaches to the residential childcare task.

It was interesting that individuals had aspirations and career goals that were generally achievable. Some appeared to be identifying a number of different options that they wished to explore before making a definite decision about their next career move. The majority of the issues presented did involve much further training, particularly professional training, but were firmly placed in the career future of the participants and seen by many as the precursor to career progression. All of the participants linked this to improved practices at work, leading to the provision of a better quality of residential childcare for the young people.

There was a collective agreement that this was the beginning of a continuing process from which people felt they would benefit, if plans could be agreed for each individual that were specific to their own needs. This concurs with Armstrong and Murlis's (1998) discussion that lifelong learning is part of the learning and development vocabulary and should be agreed to meet individual and organisational needs.

Overall, I found the process very interesting and was pleased to witness an obvious interest in career development and skills development that could lead to an improvement in service delivery. The challenge is to discover how to develop a system that encourages the development of staff-members who will acquire expertise and remain in the service. This may mean a radical change in the way we plan and develop services but it may also be a further indication that better consultation with the key stakeholders in the service is required, together with agreement on an optimum framework for future development.

Training and development of residential staff is vital if we are to diminish the mistakes of the past and provide a caring and supportive environment that will help children and young people to develop and flourish, both emotionally and physically. The support of suitably qualified staff to undertake this process is an important factor that will inform the effective provision of residential care.

The fact that formal qualification was high on the agenda is no surprise, as for all staff it is the primary focus of future career advancement and a means to gain equity with other professionals in the sector. What was also positive to see was that the group saw their own self-development as linked to the development of the service and an increase in the quality of interventions that could be facilitated. Personal issues also featured in discussions around career development, especially issues that related to family commitments and the feeling that the nature of residential work and any future developments and training initiatives should take cognisance of this.

The *Action Plan for People Management* (DoHC, 2002a) also discussed the concept of forging stronger links with the education sector in Ireland, and this was an important factor for this group in particular. The Social Services Inspectorate (SSI, 2002) stated that there should be ongoing training and development for residential staff and that staff should be supported in completing qualifying training.

## CONCLUSION

The identification of individual care practitioners' learning and development needs is an important factor to consider. It is important that the identification of these needs is in line with the objectives of the service and the needs of the young people. An appropriate management structure needs to be established that will provide opportunities for career enrichment and enhancement as a means of retaining expertise and specialisation within the social care service.

Training should be provided on an ongoing basis, with opportunities for reflection, so that skills are updated regularly to ensure consistency and continuity of approach. A system of mentoring, coaching and shadowing is vital and should be an integral aspect of the induction process for new staff and also a way to develop new skills and gain experience in specific areas of interest, such as therapeutic interventions or approaches to team development and cohesion.

The best way to achieve organisational objectives and strategies is through the ongoing development of the front-line care workers who provide the service. In turn, the calibre of the people employed in any service, and the quality of the working life that they enjoy, will directly influence the quality of the service that will be experienced by the service recipients.

All health and social care agencies must now ensure that they provide opportunities that will facilitate the current and future development of appropriately skilled and trained staff. Health and social care agencies are becoming increasingly aware of how important it is to retain staff in certain sectors. Issues like career management as a tool to develop staff can be an effective way to address this issue. The development of staff and the investment in people and their future are integral in the overall shape of a good human resource management structure. As we live in a fast-moving and ever-evolving world, it is important that organisations, including health and social care organisations, continuously develop their staff so that they remain up-to-date with regard to new approaches and techniques.

The Office for Health Management (DoHC, 2002a) states that if we are to achieve the best return from investments, it is important to invest in the right areas. To this end, a strong emphasis is placed on issues of training and development. These are seen as areas of investment that organisations make in themselves and their employees that will at least ensure their own survival and, more usually, ensure that the maximum potential is attained for both the whole organisation and individual staff.

The future of any residential service should be developed in such a way that it offers choice, quality care and therapeutic intervention for the children and young people. The provision of support systems for social care staff, such as external clinical supervision and stress management, should be provided on an ongoing basis. This process should be transparent and supported by management throughout the sector.

The process of career development should be seen as a continuous process that is revisited and assessed at regular intervals. It should be part of a culture that promotes and empowers individuals to recognise the importance of change and development, not just for the sake of it or as part of a once-off strategic intervention. It must recognise the efforts that people undertake in striving towards the sustained growth of a quality service that provides the best possible care and therapeutic interventions for one of the country's most vulnerable client groups.

17

# Integrating Social Care and Social Work: Towards a Model of Best Practice

Colm O'Doherty

## OVERVIEW

This chapter begins by examining the current alignment of social care and social work and tracing their development. A model of best practice is then proposed that takes account of:

- The discrete formation characteristics of social work and social care
- Current issues and trends in the caring field.

It is argued that the potential now exists to establish a unified approach to standards across social care and social work. Changing professional roles and identities compel practitioners to develop new languages and forms of organisation that offer greater levels of accountability to users. These mould-breaking formations promote 'cultures of collaboration' and give high priority to equality and democratisation. This may result in an expanded practice repertoire as these developments offer scope for a long overdue realignment of key welfare systems, involving: 'the practices of a group of people, at several hierarchical levels and in different places, functioning as a whole instead of going in different directions' (Briar-Lawson et al., 2001: 209). The chapter concludes with a view that in the expanding arena of family support work, new intervention strategies have the potential to create more integrated practice frameworks.

## SOCIAL CARE AND SOCIAL WORK: HELPING PEOPLE LIVE THEIR LIVES

Hermansen (1993: 3) has defined *social work* as 'the professional activity of helping individuals, families, groups, organisations or communities to enhance or restore their capacity of social functioning and creating societal conditions favourable to this goal'. According to Hermansen, social work methods and means are targeted towards four different levels of intervention:

- Individuals/families
- Groups/networks
- Organisations
- Communities.

Hermansen attaches the following social work method and means to the different levels:

- Counselling/family work
- Social group work/networking
- Social administration
- Community work.

*Social care work* is a generic term that covers a range of professional activities in the helping services. It reflects an amalgam of different enabling functions, performed by:

- Substitute carers of children in need of care and protection and children with special needs
- Substitute carers of adults with special needs/behavioural difficulties
- Community care workers engaged in providing outreach/family support services for children and adults living at home.

Social care practice is directed towards helping people in difficulty to live their lives. Social care practitioners may be said to operate at three levels:

- At the *primary* level, social care is concerned with promoting participation, autonomy, involvement and empowerment. At this level, social care work is characterised by its community focus. Family support activities typify the social care practitioner's remit at this level;
- At the *secondary* level, work is geared towards helping those whose circumstances have alienated them, whether by loss, deviant behaviour, disability or inability to manage crucial social roles. Here, social care practitioners engage in direct work with the elderly and those with learning difficulties, mental health problems, disabilities and criminal behaviour. This work (with individuals or groups) is undertaken in a range of settings, such as residential units and daycare centres;
- Work at the *tertiary* level is directed towards meeting the needs of children or adults who for various reasons of vulnerability, handicap or disturbance need 24-hour coverage. This is the more traditional domain of social care agencies such as residential services.

Social work and social care may therefore be regarded as professionally cognate but with distinct pedigrees. Best practice in social work and social care challenges practitioners to hone and develop their skills base and to set higher standards irrespective of the organisational configurations that may divide them.

## THE RELATIONSHIP BETWEEN SOCIAL CARE AND SOCIAL WORK

It is essential to establish the relationship between social care and social work as a precursor to assessing what might constitute best practice in these two branches of the caring profession. Lorenz, in mapping the contours of the profession of social educators in Europe, draws attention to: 'a perceived lack of academic respectability, familiar to a group of practitioners in the "caring field" who mostly develop their concepts out of and around their practice setting' (1994: 97).

In the European tradition, the influence of practice contexts has contributed to the evolution of different professional approaches within the 'caring field'. *Social pedagogy* originated in Germany, with an emphasis on self-directed learning processes. It has cross-fertilised with similar traditions in France and Italy and produced 'social educators' and *animateurs*. Social educators practise within the realms of daycare and residential services and 'practice and develop their skills very much by "living with people" in everyday situations' (Lorenz 1994: 97).

Social work in France is heavily influenced by a sociological perspective that emphasises the importance of conviviality and social cohesion in promoting the social welfare of children, youth and families:

> [S]ocial work has [had] to move from being a crutch (as it was in assistance mode) to being a form of social advice, and animateurs move from being providers of activities in a structured setting to something much more open and experimental. What is common is that the people themselves take charge of their affairs and try to negotiate in their own way — which is local social development or *animation locale*. (Cannan, 1997: 97)

For both Cannan and Lorenz, the locus of social work tends to be social services and agency settings, whereas the broad and multifaceted activities of those engaged in social pedagogy, education and care require 'theoretical positions beyond any distinct institutional setting and instrumental interest' (Lorenz, 1994: 96). Such theoretical insulation safeguards the autonomy of the social care profession and 'appeals to the reflective and communicative abilities of the worker as the key to competence' (Lorenz, 1994: 96).

Harris and Lavan (1992) examine key issues related to the mobility of professional social workers in Europe. They draw attention to the fact that social work is not a freestanding professional activity, but is bound up with socio-legal institutions in each member state. In this regard, social work in Ireland has become more closely identified with statutory tasks, while social care has increasingly come to resemble its European counterparts. Social workers are viewed as 'bureau-professionals' who strive to retain some principled professional autonomy in a climate of organisational imperatives and instrumental targets. The resulting tendency is towards a type of defensive practice that requires professionals to reframe their knowledge, skills and practices into new combinations and categories to suit internal and external audiences. Meanwhile, social care is downplaying its institutional nexus and is busily redefining its mission within a new dynamic social action framework.

## PRACTICE TRENDS IN SOCIAL CARE AND SOCIAL WORK

Before arriving at a 'one size fits all' model of best practice, it is necessary to reflect on the variety of settings and contexts that circumscribe the professional activities of social workers and social care practitioners. Skehill (1999) argues that, in order to achieve professional status, social work in Ireland needed state support. The expansion of social work that resulted from its identification with the area of childcare and welfare reflected a: 'concern to fit appropriate professionals into niches, in order to complete the predominantly medical and health-orientated nature of statutory social and health services' (Skehill, 1999: 168).

As social work developed in Ireland, it colonised some of the space opened up for professional development by the new structures established under the 1970 Health Act. Within the fledgling Community Care programme, considerable emphasis was placed on social work as a regulatory process. The National Social Work Qualifications Board survey of social work posts in Ireland, undertaken in 1999, revealed that the majority of social work posts in Ireland (83 per cent) fall under the auspices of the Department of Health and Children and that, within this group, the Health Boards dominate. Out of some 815 posts located in the Health Boards, 515 are primarily concerned with childcare and family work (NSWQB, 2000). Social work practice in the Health Boards is largely determined by the statutory framework governing the care of children.

In the field of social care, the statutory framework has arguably less direct influence on practice. National frameworks, filtered through Health Board and non-statutory social work practice, indirectly frame the day-to-day activities of social care practitioners. Thus, social care practice is at some remove from over-regulated systems that 'can lose the individual discretion and therapeutic skill of professionals in favour of administrative management and regulations' (Buckley, 1996: 53). Buckley suggests that, in social work, the resultant defensive practice is directed at securing the agency's integrity above the needs of the children and families it serves. Skehill (1999) ranges social work endeavour along a continuum between the polar functions of regulation and enablement. Social work is located near the regulation end of the continuum, and 'community care workers' at the enabling end of the continuum.

The continuing advancement of social care as a coherent and unified caring profession can be directly attributed to the expansion of personal/community social services in the statutory sector and the increasing demand for professionally trained workers in the voluntary sector. Social work practice has been overtaken by events such as the well-documented child-abuse controversies. An indirect consequence of the resulting public scepticism about the integrity of the childcare system has been that social workers have devolved responsibility for the day-to-day provision of family support work to volunteers and social care practitioners, whilst retaining responsibility for managing the connection between child protection and child welfare work. Thus, the types of practical linkages between child protection and family support include:

• Family Support and Community Childcare Workers who work with children and families as part of Community Care Teams
• Family Support Services in the community — provided by voluntary and state agencies — which link through referrals from Community Care
• Family Support Services in the community which accept referrals from the wider community as well (or even instead of) from Community Care. (Ferguson, 1997: 5)

Social care practice, therefore, is now a fulcrum for social action/social education, whereas social work as practised in the Health Boards is more closely identified with case management.

As this emerging practice is formalised and institutionalised, the way is open for Health Boards to integrate creatively social care and social work. For example, in the Mid-Western Health Board [MWHB], family support is part of a generic social work service that operates within a case management structure:

> whose primary concern is childcare. While direct concerns about children are referred to social workers they work with childcare workers [social care practitioners] providing direct services to lone parents and they work with children identified as being vulnerable. They work through after-school groups, youth work, parent support, child/family holidays and they also operate a home-maker service. (Interview with Childcare Manager, MWHB, 2000)

## IMPROVING SOCIAL WORK AND SOCIAL CARE PRACTICE

There are several issues of direct or indirect relevance to the development of quality standards of practice in social work and social care. One of these is the changing nature of families. Family life as upheld by our culture, and the actual experience of contemporary family life, is coming to terms with the reality of the 'postmodern family'. While myth-making served to obscure public awareness of the doctrinal nature of social policymaking until the closing years of the twentieth century, one of the dominant myths — that of 'happy families' — was shattered and the public was confronted with 'the dark side of family life', through a raft of child-abuse scandals, such as the Kilkenny Incest; the Kelly Fitzgerald and the McColgan cases.

A second dominant myth, that children incarcerated within the discredited industrial schools system 'were objects of charity, cared for by the religious of Ireland when no one else would do so' (Raftery and O'Sullivan, 1999: 11) has been exploded by the broadcasting of the *States of Fear* television series in 1999 and again in 2003.

The growing array of family forms and options contributes to a society characterised by co-existing sets of evolving family cultures. A changing family landscape invalidates the 'one norm fits all' assumptions that informed social policymaking since the foundation of the state. Sustained by a false dichotomy between individualism and 'familism', the pre-modern family, which endured as the dominant family form until the late 1960s, was essentially a corporate entity where individual wellbeing was subordinated to the collective functioning of the economic, social and political unit. The reification of this family form led to the decanting of large populations of children into institutional containers.

Contemporary service provision still does not fully acknowledge the ground between 'familism' and individualism. As a consequence, adults and children may still be defined solely as family appendages, rather than being seen as both family members and as individuals. Practice-led initiatives that reconcile the individual's membership of a family form with their own unique service needs can help to create an organisational or agency environment that is sympathetic to the idea of a continuum of care for adults, children and families.

## CRISIS IN THE RESIDENTIAL CARE SERVICES FOR CHILDREN

The current crisis (and its origin) that faces residential care services for children is well documented (Gilligan, 1999; Richardson, 1999; Raftery and O'Sullivan, 1999). First the *Kennedy Report* (1970) and then the *Task Force on Childcare Services* (1981) recommended changes in the organisation and delivery of substitute care services for children. The recommendations pointed in the direction of:

- 'Normalising' the experience through the setting up of small group homes and the development of fostering services
- Professionalising the service by upgrading the salaries, training and career prospects of those wishing to work in the service.

Both reports contained a rider that 'residential care should be considered only where there is no satisfactory alternative'. These recommendations underpinned a policy trend towards the development of fostering services at the expense of the residential sector. Fostering came to be seen as a panacea. But fostering may not meet the needs of older children, homeless children and certain children with behavioural difficulties. In relegating residential care to a secondary position, the Health Boards effectively downgraded its status and value. Downgrading the service over the past two decades has led to a serious shortfall in the provision of high-quality residential care for particular categories of children in need. Similar crisis tendencies are manifest in Britain.

In many respects, residential services for children and young people continue to be seen as an inferior alternative to foster care for those unable to live within their own families. This legacy relates to an association with the negative images of large-scale institutions, as well as more recent disturbing incidents of abuse and neglect. Added to this is a belief in 'family life' and a view that the contemporary (Eurocentric and heterosexual) nuclear family unit is the preferred and most effective location for child rearing, although the relative effectiveness of foster care vis-à-vis residential care is not unequivocal (Horrocks and Karban, 1999: 163).

Plans are afoot to address the serious shortfall in residential provision for certain categories of children. Several 'high support' centres are being established around the country, intended for children deemed to require secure care or protection.

## BEST PRACTICE IN SOCIAL CARE AND SOCIAL WORK

Social care practitioners and social workers need to develop practice interventions that can assist in the creation of supportive environments for individuals, families and communities, and thereby reduce the risk of children or adults being placed in residential or foster care. Social care practitioners are increasingly concerned with developing and establishing family support practices within a community development framework. Many of the important tasks in which social care practitioners are involved lie well outside the direct concerns of social work.

Social care practice has embraced a new social action paradigm that tackles the connected issues of citizenship, employment, exclusion, the quality of neighbourhood life and the changing structures and ties of family. Within this paradigm, youth centres and centres for families and children become the focal points for the development of social ties and the promotion of cultural identities and senses of belonging in a multicultural society. 'Joined-up services' that emphasise welfare as a decentralised process, rather than professionally determined services, are intended to narrow the divide between provision for adults and provision for children. Residential care work now constitutes but one element of the social care practice portfolio.

Despite their differing orientations, there needs to be a unified approach to standards across social care and social work. It makes no sense to address either in isolation, especially as there is increasing emphasis on partnerships and links between the two. Each attempts to reduce levels of social exclusion that negatively affect marginalised individuals and communities. Social work is, in the Irish context, mainly focused on childcare service provision, while social care practice aims to maximise the wellbeing of both children and adults who face adversity, disability and/or major life changes.

In social work practice, action related to the coordination of services is prioritised above all other direct practice approaches. Service delivery is equated with case management, networking and coordination activities. In social care practice, the emphasis is now on simultaneously providing effective services and generating social capital. A valid model of best practice recognises the complementary relationship that now exists between the two fields. The way ahead lies not in the further separation of these two cognate areas but through the development of local integrated strategies to promote the welfare of adults and children residing at or away from home.

## A MODEL OF BEST PRACTICE

There are four essential component parts to a unified model of best practice as set out by the UK National Institute for Social Work (Harding and Beresford, 1996):

## 1. The Quality of Relationships

The nature of the relationships between caring professionals and the individuals or groups who require/use their services is central to people's perception of what constitutes quality.

- *Empowering Relationships*
  Treating others as individuals/real people and engaging with them as equals rather than dependants, while acknowledging that the circumstances in which people come into contact with social care/work staff influences the extent to which relationships can be empowering. In this regard, practitioners need to recognise the difference between the support and care role and the regulation and control role, and learn to adapt their behaviour accordingly. Issues relating to use and abuse of power must be recognised and understood.

- *Credibility*
  Social care/work staff-members are required to be credible in order to gain the confidence of the people they are supporting. Workers can more easily inspire confidence if they have relevant experiences themselves, but confidence can also be 'earned' if they can integrate and come to terms with their own history and use it to constructive ends (see Chapter 8).

- *Respect*
  Demonstrating respect for those you are working with can be achieved by taking their views seriously, recognising their right to be heard and acknowledging their expertise regarding their own needs. Respecting the right of individuals to control their own lives is more easily accomplished if the practitioner is adept at recognising what is important to them in terms of, for example, religion and culture.

- *Confidentiality and Privacy*
  Rights to privacy and confidentiality exist for all those who may come into contact with the 'helping professions'. Where children are concerned (particularly in residential settings), rights to privacy and confidentiality can easily be overlooked.

- *Courtesy and Empathy*
  People value basic courtesies, and practitioners must try to see things from the point of view of the person with whom they are working. It is all too easy to stereotype people on the basis of their age, ethnicity or gender and thereby fail to see their unique perspective on any given situation.

- *Honesty*
  Being honest means not hiding behind a mask of professionalism. It is about recognising your own shortcomings and acknowledging responsibility. Lack of honesty can be disempowering as it does not allow the person using the service to understand the real issues. If a person does not know what the issues are, they cannot address them or make sense of what is happening. People are aware that caring professionals do not always have all the answers and cannot always supply what is needed. It is important to record un-met need, as this will provide evidence that may assist service users to make valid complaints.

- *Reliability and Continuity*
  Caring professionals should keep to appointments and schedules and avoid letting vulnerable people down. Continuity is also of critical importance to individuals in receipt of social care or social work services. It takes time to develop a relationship and for trust to emerge. Having your favourite care practitioner in a residential home suddenly disappear, or a new family support worker turn up on your doorstep unannounced, means a loss of familiarity and trust, often the loss of a real friendship, and starting all over again with someone new: 'just as reliability is an important quality for individuals, so it is essential for services' (Harding and Beresford, 1996: 37).

- *Be Wary of Pet Theories*
  While theory undoubtedly has its place, people may be averse to an approach in which they and their circumstances are subordinated to theoretical interpretations, or in which predetermined or inappropriate theories are imposed. Ideally workers should be flexible and responsive to each individual's unique circumstances.

## 2. The Quality of Skills

- *Listening and Communicating*
  The first step in listening is to give people your full attention. Listening is a skill that requires cultural awareness and understanding. Cross-cultural

communication is enhanced when workers affirm the value of difference. Black and ethnic minority communities engage with staff-members who understand their religion and culture. Real communication commences when the importance of the perspective of the person being worked with is acknowledged:

> [E]ffectiveness in communication is affected by the credibility and honesty of the sender of the message. The receiver who has reason to trust the competence and reliability of the sender will tend to be receptive to the message and its expectations. Effective communicators tune into and are sensitive to the feelings and situations of those they are communicating with. They are assertive without being overly aggressive or confrontational. (Johnson, 1998: 178)

Before communicating in writing, workers should take into account the difficulties that some people may have with the written word. They may need to think again about how to communicate in circumstances where they would normally expect to use the written word. Use of videos, tapes, discs and simplified texts may allow for more effective communication in certain situations.

- *Counselling and Understanding*
  These skills are used to make people feel comfortable in circumstances that are new to them and beyond their experience. The broader experience and insights of professionals can be used to support people, in crisis intervention, in focusing the area of concern to ease a sense of being overwhelmed, and in constructing a comfortable physical and emotional climate.

  Knowledge about local and national services is power. Professionals should have up-to-date knowledge about services and resources that may be of benefit to the people with whom they are working.

- *Enabling and Negotiation*
  Practitioners in an enabling capacity develop the skills to help individuals to achieve their goals. The practitioner is oriented towards enhancing the ability of individuals, groups and communities to resolve their difficulties by providing information and negotiating access to resources.

- *Basic Practical Skills*
  Practical support, home-care skills and befriending are activities equally important as counselling, and in many cases form the basis on which later counselling takes place.

  It is important to recognise that social care practitioners and social workers often have difficult judgments to make, particularly when it comes to judging appropriate levels of risk. But the imposition of blanket regulations and an avoidance of risk for fear of criticism are unhelpful and serve to undermine autonomy and disempower people.

## 3. The Quality of Services

- *Information*
  Information-giving should be proactive. People want information about: services, rights to services, the standards they can expect, the powers of professionals and agencies, what their rights are, what the process is that they are involved in, and how to complain. This information should be available in writing and in any other form that is necessary.

- *Advocacy*
  Where the role of workers is dominated by their regulatory function — by its nature disempowering for those in receipt of services — this imbalance needs to be redressed by the agency or organisation making provision for empowering measures such as advocacy services and information. Advocacy serves a number of purposes. The main focus is to support activities that maximise the entitlement, service access and help available to those using the services:

  > [I]t helps people know what their rights are, and what they are entitled to expect, it supports people in what they want to say; it enables people who share common experiences to support each other, develop confidence, skills and ideas, and their own collective voice. (Harding and Beresford, 1996: 30)

- *Choice, Flexibility and Control*
  Being able to exercise choice and control over our lives is important to us all. For those who may not be able to reside in their own homes or who may need ongoing support in order to remain at home, it is essential to retain some say in how services operating on their behalf are delivered.

- *Culturally Appropriate Services*
  Social work and social care agencies have a responsibility to provide culturally appropriate services, sensitive to age, ethnicity, religious differences, gender, and all the many components of socially constructed difference. Services should be available in sufficient quality and at the right time. There may be a need for a particular service to be made available at weekends or in the evenings. Time in general is a critical component of quality services:

  > enough time for talking over options, for making decisions properly, in an informed and considered way, and enough time for the services them-selves to be delivered with thought, care and respect. People working to the clock does not result in a sensitive quality service. Lack of continuity and shift systems can mean that young people in care find that no-one has time to listen. (Harding and Beresford, 1996: 36)

- *Accessibility*
  At the very least, all buildings should be accessible to those who are using the service. Accessibility also means ensuring that barriers or potential barriers are not placed in front of those requiring a particular service.

- *Fairness*
  All services must be underpinned by principles of equity and fairness. Entitlement to services should not be determined by who you are or where you live.

- *Avoidance of Harm*
  Services should not exacerbate the difficulties that people face or create new ones.

## 4. Improving Quality

Quality can be improved by engaging users on equal terms in a partnership to set standards. User-led evaluation will help to ensure that quality and standards that have been agreed upon are maintained. In order to develop a model of best practice that can be applied across different agencies and organisations, it may be necessary to enforce certain quality standards on a national basis.

## CONCLUSION: AMBIVALENCE AND ADVANCEMENT

Both social workers and social care practitioners 'intervene in people's lives in a very personal and intimate way, sometimes at a point of crisis, sometimes to provide longer term support' (Harding and Beresford, 1996: 1). It can be said that while social care work mirrors social work practice, it is determined by a different set of circumstances. But there is a legitimate societal expectation that, despite their different organisational and administrative orientations, both caring professions will set high standards of practice in their different domains. In order to achieve this aspiration, in the turbulent environment within which they both operate, it is necessary that they share the common goal of promoting improved standards and professional excellence.

In moving towards a unified approach to standards, both professions will signal their support for a shift away from reductionist philosophies towards more holistic or integrative ways of thinking. It is already clear that practitioners in both fields are having to develop new languages and forms of organisation that are outside traditional agency structures and professional categories. Some of these new formations require social workers to manage the connections between clinical or forensic activities and family support work. The Social Services Inspectorate [SSI] has a critical role in the development of an overlapping model of best practice that can integrate social care and social work practice. Its overall aim is to:

inspect social services against agreed standards and support developments that will help these standards to be met. This is done by inspection, advice to the Minister, input to government developments of standards and child-care policy, contribution to practice guidelines, research and training and disseminating findings. (SSI, 2002: 4)

The alternative to joint ownership of best practice is a continuing 'turf war' with potentially disastrous consequences for the users of services. For example, where lines of responsibility and spheres of autonomy between residential workers and field social workers are not clearly drawn, disagreements about preferable courses of action will adversely influence the quality of practice. Disagreements can be exacerbated because residential workers, by dint of their lower status within the caring professions, usually have less say. Conversely, open and frequent discussion between residential staff and field social workers, clarity as to jurisdiction, and a sense of partnership and of working together can set the scene for joint ownership of good practice.

Applying Lewin's (1951: 226) 'force-field analysis schema' to practice as it occurs in Children's Homes, we can represent in diagrammatic form forces that help or hinder best practice (Figure 17.1).

**Figure 17.1. Forces that Help or Hinder Best Practice**

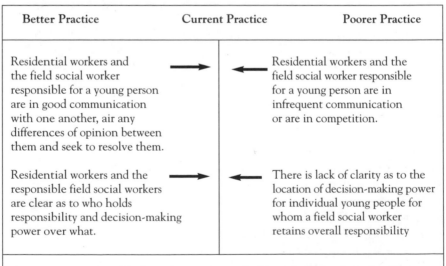

| Better Practice | Current Practice | Poorer Practice |
|---|---|---|
| Residential workers and the field social worker responsible for a young person are in good communication with one another, air any differences of opinion between them and seek to resolve them. | | Residential workers and the field social worker responsible for a young person are in infrequent communication or are in competition. |
| Residential workers and the responsible field social workers are clear as to who holds responsibility and decision-making power over what. | | There is lack of clarity as to the location of decision-making power for individual young people for whom a field social worker retains overall responsibility |

Arrows pointing towards the right press towards the goal of better practice. They are facilitating or supportive or helping factors. Arrows pointing towards the left work against movement towards the goal of better practice. They are hindering factors. Taken together, all of these factors keep practice in its current state. (Whitaker et al., 1998: 184)

Developing a unified model of best practice will require the establishment of closer structural links between the two professions. A common regulatory body is needed, together with some convergence in the training and educational routes open to those wishing to enter the caring professions (McElwee, 2000). The SSI is well placed to develop an overarching policy and practice framework that can orchestrate best practice in the two professions. While it is clearly unrealistic and naïve to place the entire responsibility for achieving higher standards on hard-pressed individuals working in a variety of different contexts, there is a need to reorient social care and social work. Agencies and organisations can facilitate and support best practice through joint training programmes. Attitudes within social work and social care toward common standards of professional excellence seem likely to remain ambivalent, while practice in both domains is in a constant state of flux. On the wider front, the reactive, ad-hoc nature of policymaking in the personal social services contributes to a professional culture that is over-committed to short-term practice responses. The time has come to replace this 'stop-gap' practice with a new approach that will advance and promote both inter-professional collaboration and partnership between service providers and service users.

# Part 4

## Social Care and Specific Population Groups

# 18

# Ask the Experts: Travellers in Ireland and Issues of Social Care

Ashling Jackson

## OVERVIEW

This chapter looks at social care issues relevant to the Traveller community in Ireland. The key issues are: Traveller children in care; Traveller perspectives on health; barriers to health services as identified by Travellers; and issues of access to education. These issues are examined in the context of racism and discrimination.

In order to gain an understanding of racism and discrimination as experienced by the Traveller community in Ireland, the origins of the community, key characteristics of the Traveller population, and Travellers' ethnic status are examined. This chapter is only an introduction to the Traveller community in Ireland and it is strongly recommended that social care students incorporate field-practice experience with Travellers or other minority groups as part of their social care studies. Consequently, the chapter concludes by looking at issues for consideration when working with Traveller groups.

The content of this chapter has been reviewed by Travellers and those working in the Tullamore Travellers' Movement, a local Traveller organisation established to respond to the needs of Travellers in the Tullamore region. Travellers training as Community Health Workers on the Primary Healthcare Project in Tullamore were also asked to comment. This consultation was considered essential in order that the information presented here would be endorsed by those working directly with the Traveller community, and Travellers themselves, as experts on their own lifestyle, culture and social experiences. All information contained herein is therefore deemed by 'the experts' (Figure 18.1) to be valid, and reflective of Traveller issues in Ireland.

**Figure 18.1. 'Ask the Experts'**

*Source*: Pavee Point (www.pavee.ie). Reproduced with kind permission.

## WHO ARE THE IRISH TRAVELLERS?

Irish Travellers are a distinct ethnic group that has existed for centuries. Ethnicity has been defined as: 'a shared cultural heritage. Members of an ethnic category have common ancestors, a language or a religion that, together, confer a distinctive social identity' (Macionis and Plummer, 2002: 324).

Travellers are often incorrectly considered part of the nomadic Romani, an ethnic group that originated in the region of India, now widespread throughout Europe. Irish Travellers are native to Ireland and their culture is not related to that of the Romani. While both are nomadic, Travellers are Roman Catholic and speak their own language. They boast their own culture, customs and traditions, as well as being noted for their musical and storytelling abilities.

The historical origins of Irish Travellers remain unclear, with a number of extant theories. Their language, Shelta, and various historical references, would seem to indicate that they are the remnants of an ancient class of wandering poets, joined by those driven off the land during different times of social and economic upheaval, such as Cromwell's campaign (1649–50), the Battle of the Boyne (1690) and the Battle of Aughrim (1691). Travellers have also been seen to be descendants of native chieftains, dispossessed during the English plantations of the seventeenth and eighteenth centuries. They may also be descendants of people left homeless as a result of the potato famines of the nineteenth century. Though the origins of the Traveller community in Ireland are uncertain, that they exist as a discrete group with a separate identity was recognised as far back as 1834, 'when the Travelling community was clearly distinguished from other poor who wandered the land in the report of the Royal Commission on the Poor Laws in that year' (Kedrick, 1998: 1).

## A CLOSER LOOK AT TRAVELLER CULTURE

> The Traveller community is the collective owner of Traveller culture and heritage. (culture at www.paveepoint.ie)

Pavee Point, an Irish national Traveller representative organisation, identifies language, nomadism, music, storytelling and the Traveller economy as among the important features of Traveller culture and heritage. These issues are especially important as they indicate considerable variation from the settled population in Ireland. Being a Traveller is an *ascribed* status: for an individual to be called a Traveller, it is assumed that that individual has at least one Traveller parent.

## Language

Travellers have their own language, known as Shelta, or by Travellers themselves as Gammon or Cant.

## Nomadism

The *Commission on Itinerancy* (DoSW, 1963) defined a Traveller as a person who habitually wanders from place to place and has no fixed abode. This narrow definition fails to include settled or partially settled Travellers who elect to live in houses as opposed to on campsites or halting sites. Nevertheless, nomadism remains a key component of Traveller culture. The importance of the freedom to travel as an essential part of Traveller identity cannot be emphasised strongly enough. The ill-effects that housing can have on Travellers are not well documented. For Duggan-Jackson (2000) it emerged very strongly in the Tullamore region as related to a range of unanticipated health problems, centred on depression, resulting from feeling confined and a perceived lack of mobility as a result of being housed:

> I get depression from being in the house all the time. I don't have the same freedom in the house. I'm on depression tablets from the doctor. I went to see the bishop to see if he could help and Fr. X in Athy he comes over to see me often. (Tullamore respondent, quoted in Duggan-Jackson, 2000: 65)

This reflects the observation made by McCann et al. (1994) that some Travellers become physically sick and depressed when they move into houses, and never adjust psychologically to living permanently in the one place. Many Travellers have left houses for these reasons. It was also pointed out by McCann et al. that just as settled people remain settled people when they travel, Travellers remain Travellers even when they are not travelling. Travellers who are not moving can, and do, retain the mindset of nomads (McCann et al., 1994: 96).

## Music and Storytelling

> Travelling singers, musicians and storytellers provided not only entertainment, but also served the useful social function of news bringer. (O'Reilly, 1993: 1)

The tradition of storytelling is used as a way to disseminate information among Travellers. Research into the health needs of Travellers in the Midland Health Board [MHB] region has shown that that Traveller group interaction is essentially based on storytelling (Duggan-Jackson, 2000: 37). Health information is disseminated through story-telling sessions, and health actions suggested. The validity of the health information given out depends on the person recounting the story. This in itself highlights the importance of generalised health awareness among all Travellers, in order to reduce information inconsistencies. Word of mouth is a strong and influential method of communication among the Traveller community in Ireland.

## The Traveller Economy

Today, Irish Travellers work mainly in recycling. This has replaced the traditional livelihoods of tinsmithing, horse-trading and peddling. Horses and wagons have given way to mobile homes pulled by motor vehicles. Of the 100 female research participants in a study conducted in the MHB region, some 26 per cent of the sample specified themselves as being employed outside the home (Duggan-Jackson, 2000). Interestingly, the Traveller self-definition of employment was not that traditionally considered as employment by the dominant population — structured work activities outside the home. In all cases where women attended a Training Centre, they specified themselves as being in employment (77 per cent of those who specified themselves as being in employment). Only four respondents had 'regular' work outside the Training Centre. These jobs took the following form (Duggan-Jackson, 2000: 48):

- self-employed — 1
- playschool on halting site — 1
- local Traveller organisation — 2.

## Travellers as a Distinct Ethnic Group

According to the previously cited definition of ethnicity, there can be no doubt that Travellers have a shared cultural heritage, characterised mainly by their tradition of travelling and resultant nomadic status. Given that this nomadic status is supplemented by a Traveller language and specific Traveller traditions with regard to economy and income generation, Travellers are deemed to be an ethnic group within Irish society. Travellers share many traits with the settled population: in looks, Travellers resemble the dominant culture; Travellers speak English; and

Travellers practise Catholicism. Their uniqueness tends to be more subtle than that of skin colour, religion or language, which may, ironically, place them at a disadvantage (McElwee, Jackson and Charles, 2003).

## KEY CHARACTERISTICS OF THE TRAVELLER POPULATION IN IRELAND

### Number of Travellers

According to the Central Statistics Office [CSO], close to 24,000 Irish Travellers, representing 0.6 per cent of the total population, were enumerated in the 2002 Census. Longford (1.8 per cent of the population) was the county with the highest proportion of Travellers, followed by Galway City (1.6 per cent), Galway County (1.4 per cent) and Offaly (1 per cent). Kildare, Cork county and Waterford county had the lowest proportions (0.3 per cent).

### Age Structure

The Traveller community in Ireland has an age structure very different from that of the settled population (Figure 18.2). In the 2002 Census, the average age for Travellers is 18 years, compared to a national figure of 32 years (Factsheet at www.paveepoint.ie).

**Figure 18.2. Percentage of Irish Travellers, and of the Total Population of the State at Each Age Group (Census, 2002)**

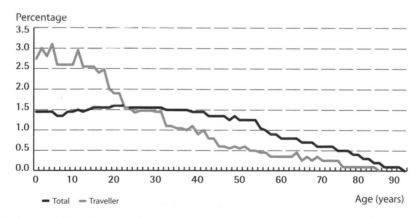

*Source*: Irish Travellers at www.cso.ie

Figure 18.2 indicates a significantly higher birth rate in the Traveller community than in the general population. There is also a notably higher percentage of children under 15 years in the Traveller population compared to the total population. And there is a noted difference in the percentages of those aged over

65 years compared to the total population. The proportion aged over 65 years is considerably lower than in the total population. This followed the trends in age structure noted in the 1996 Census:

> Fifty percent of the Travellers distinguished by enumerators were aged less than 15 years compared with slightly less than a quarter for the population in general. Older Travellers (those aged 65 years and over) accounted for just 1.43% of the total Traveller population while the corresponding proportion for the population in general was 11.4%. The distinctive age structure of the Traveller community resulted in a median age of 14 in 1996 compared with a national figure of 31. (*Central Statistics Office News*, 1996)

## Living Conditions

The 2002 Census showed that:

> [just over] 3% [of Travellers] were enumerated in communal establishments. Of the remaining 22,942, 59% lived in permanent accommodation (including permanent accommodation in Traveller encampments), 34% lived in cara-vans or mobile homes while 8% did not answer the relevant question. (Irish Travellers at www.cso.ie. Percentages rounded up)

The *Report of the Task Force on the Travelling Community* (1995) revealed the following statistics with regard to housing and facilities available to Travellers' families:

- 34% of respondents were in standard housing
- 20% had no toilet facilities
- 27% had only a shared cold water supply
- 32% had no electricity
- 40% had no bath or shower
- 18% had no refuse collection
- 47% had no access to a telephone.

It can be validly argued that health programmes will have a low priority among Travellers as long as more immediate requirements such as food, shelter and warmth are un-met. Mac Aongusa (1990) has pointed out that the harsh living conditions of Travellers have dictated that basic survival is their main focus of life. In their study of Travellers in England, Pahl and Vaile (1988) revealed that the concerns of many Travellers included dirt, fast traffic, rats, lack of safe play space, overcrowding, mud, dogs, cuts from broken glass, the site being filled up with toilet holes, noise from near-by factories, and smells from sewerage works.

# Health

The health status of the Traveller population in Ireland is considered to be very poor in comparison to the health status of the settled population (Barry and Daly, 1988; DoHC, 2002b). The 2002 Census found that only 3 per cent of all Travellers were aged over 65, as compared with 11 per cent for the population generally.

According to the only recent national Traveller health study, carried out by the Health Research Board in 1987 (Barry and Daly, 1988):

- The infant mortality rate for Travellers was 18.1/1000 live births compared to a national figure of 7.4;
- At birth, male Travellers can expect to live 9.9 years less than settled men;
- At birth, female Travellers can expect to live 11.9 years less than settled women;
- Male Travellers have over twice the risk of dying in a given year [as] settled males. For female Travellers the risk is more than 3 times.

Since most research in the area of Traveller health status tends to be of a regional nature, the proposed all-Ireland Traveller health status and needs assessment study as part of the *Traveller Health Strategy 2002–2005* (DoHC, 2002b) will be very important in terms of acquiring more up-to-date data.

Interestingly, a study (Feder, 1994) of Travellers' health in inner-city Hackney, East London, found that they prioritised environmental standards (the need for clean sites and running water) and control over mobility as aspects of prevention of ill-health. Travellers classified their health as 'very good' while 39 per cent thought they had 'good' health.

Research has indicated that children's health is given the highest priority in the Travelling community, with their illness prompting biomedical treatment much more often than adult illness. There is distinct evidence that children suffer from a higher incidence of illnesses (especially those of the upper respiratory and lower gastro-intestinal tracts) and of hospitalisations for at least some of those illnesses (Treadwell, 1998). Treadwell points out that there is a gradation in the seriousness of children's health and the necessity to seek biomedical care:

> This gradation is based on different stages of the life cycle. That is concern and care seeking strategies for illnesses are highest for young children and infants, slightly less for older children and generally fairly low for adults, and is explained by the concept that Traveller children become 'hardier' as they grow older. (Treadwell, 1998: 127)

Younger children who are considered more vulnerable, less capable of rational action and indeed less hardy are given much more personal, individual attention and care than older children. That is not to say that older children do not get any personal attention, but rather that the care and attention they receive is predicated upon the concept that they are more mature, more capable and hardier individuals. In this, Traveller parents are socialising their children to become independent adults — a gradual but constant process that begins in early childhood.

## Consanguinity

Consanguinity (the relationship by blood or a common ancestor) has been frequently mentioned in studies of Traveller health status as being highly contributory towards the increase of metabolic and congenital disease. Information was sought on the consanguinity of children's parents in a study carried out to examine aspects of the health status of children from a group of Travellers in Northern Ireland (Gordon et al., 1991). A total of 350 children, aged under 16 years, were included in the study. Community health doctors and health visitors used a standardised questionnaire to gather data. The results are outlined in Table 18.1.

**Table 18.1. Consanguinity Amongst Travellers: Parental Relationship Prior to Marriage**

| Parental Relationship Prior to Marriage | n | % |
|---|---|---|
| Children whose parents were first cousins | 71 | 20 |
| Children whose parents were more distant cousins | 62 | 18 |
| Children whose parents were unrelated | 80 | 23 |
| Parental relationship unknown | 137 | 39 |
| Total | 350 | 100 |

*Source:* Gordon et al., 1991: 388. Percentages rounded.

Studies in the MHB region have confirmed a younger age of marriage for Travellers (Flynn, 1986; Flynn et al., 1989). Flynn (1986) contended that marriage between first cousins occurs in 39 per cent of all unions included in his study. This is a matter of concern, especially when consanguineous marriage is repeated in successive generations. Flynn's study also found the usual age of marriage for Travellers to be in the late teens. Marriage is mostly arranged by parents, even in settled families with children who attended school. Ó Nualláin and Forde (1994) also verified that Travellers married at a very early age, and that consanguineous marriage was common. In their study, some 17 couples (61 per cent) claimed that they were related to one another, while 11 couples claimed they were not directly related, though they would have had intermarriage in their families in previous generations.

## Racism: Travellers as a Target Group

Before looking at Travellers' experience of racism, it is important to look at exactly what racism is, and how dominant and minority groups can relate to each other in society in a way that may cause a situation of racism towards a minority group. On 19 December 1965, the United Nations General Assembly adopted the *International Convention on the Elimination of All Forms of Racial Discrimination*. This defined racism as:

> any distinction, exclusion, restriction or preference based on race, colour, descent or national or ethnic origin, which has the purpose or effect of nullifying or impairing the recognition, enjoyment or exercise, on an equal footing, of human rights and fundamental freedoms in the political, economic, social, cultural or any other field of public life. (cited in Stratton and McPartland, 2002: 2)

For sociologists, a *dominant group* is a group in society that has a disproportionate amount of power. Importantly a minority is not always a numerical minority: for example, the Black population of South Africa. Conversely, a *minority group* refers to a group that does not have proportionate access to power. Often, because of physical or cultural characteristics, a minority group is singled out from others for unequal treatment. This is the case for Travellers in Ireland.

The relationship between the dominant and minority groups in any society can take the following forms:

- *Segregation*: the practice of physically separating occupants of some social statuses from occupants of others — for example, the structure of apartheid that used to exist in South Africa;
- *Assimilation*: members of ethnic groups are expected to conform to the culture of the dominant group;
- *Amalgamation*: process by which two or more previous racial, ethnic or nationality-identified groups inter-marry and have children;
- *Genocide*: the systematic annihilation of one category of people by another (as in so-called 'ethnic cleansing' or the Holocaust);
- *Pluralism*: a state in which racial and ethnic minorities are distinct but have social parity.

Very often, the relationship between the dominant group in a society, and the minority group, is reflected in government policy, and may also indeed be a result of government policy. Recent government policy within Ireland can be said to be more inclusive of the views of Travellers, with increased importance being given to Traveller opinion in the drawing up and implementation of policy that responds to Traveller-identified needs. This would seem to indicate a move away from assimilation towards pluralism at an official government level. This process of change is documented in Table 18.2 below.

## Table 18.2. Legislation in Ireland that Affects the Traveller Community

| |
|---|
| 1963: *Commission on Itinerancy*<br>Recommended assimilation of Travellers into the settled community. |
| 1983: *Report of the Travelling People Review Body*<br>Promoted the integration of Travellers into mainstream society without adequately supporting and promoting their cultural identity. |
| 1988: *Housing Act*<br>Provided the first statutory (government) recognition of Traveller-specific accommodation. |
| 1992: *Housing (Miscellaneous Provisions) Act*<br>Section 10 of this act empowered local authorities to remove Travellers, who are camped unofficially, to an official site anywhere within a 5-mile radius of where they are. |
| 1994: *Shaping a Healthier Future: A Strategy for Effective Health-Care in the 1990s*<br>Contained a section on Traveller Health and pledged to address the particular health needs of the Traveller population. |
| 1995: *White Paper on Education: Charting our Education Future*<br>Called for full participation in school life by Traveller children, by means of integration, while at the same time respecting Traveller culture. |
| 1995: *Report of the Task Force on the Travelling Community*<br>Made many recommendations covering all aspects of Traveller life and Government policy relating to Travellers, and acknowledged the distinct culture and identity of the Traveller community. |
| 1998: *Housing (Traveller Accommodation) Act*<br>Obliged local authorities to meet the current and projected needs of the Traveller Community. Sections of the act gave increased powers of eviction to Local Authorities. |
| 1999: *Employment Equality Act*<br>Outlawed discrimination in the employment field on several grounds including membership of the Traveller community. |
| 2001: *Housing (Miscellaneous Provisions) Bill*<br>Introduced sanctions against trespassing, which were viewed very negatively by the Traveller community. Public protests took place to try to prevent this Bill proceeding through the Dáil. |
| 2002: *Housing (Miscellaneous Provisions) Act*<br>Made trespass, previously a civil offence, into a criminal offence. Currently, camping on private or public land is punishable by one month in jail, a €3,000 fine and the confiscation of property.<br>In answer to a Dáil Question, the Government stated that in 2002–3, 88 evictions of Travellers had taken place under this legislation. In 2003, this law went to judicial review and may also be in contravention of the European Convention on Human Rights. (Accommodation and living conditions at www.paveepoint.ie) |
| 2001/02: *Youth Work Act*<br>This covers the provision of youth services to Travellers and the Settled Community. It is the first-ever act regarding youth work. |
| 2002–2005: *Traveller Health: a National Strategy*<br>Recognition at official level that Travellers are a distinct minority with their own culture and beliefs and, most importantly, that they have a right to have their culture recognised in the planning and provision of services. |

## Is There Racism in Ireland towards Travellers?

McGréil (1996) has assessed the extent and depth of prejudice in Ireland towards Travellers in the periods 1972–3 and 1988–9. Using the concept of social distance (the degree of intimacy to which a person is willing to admit a member of a particular group to their family, neighbourhood and so on), he noted a substantial *increase* in the levels of prejudice towards Travellers between these two periods.

In 2000, a nationwide survey (BAI, 2000) examined attitudes to Travellers and minority groups. It indicated that 42 per cent of the population held negative attitudes towards Travellers. Those who were negatively disposed towards Travellers tended to be more prejudiced than the average person and their prejudice tended to be accentuated in the case of Travellers. Similarly, research commissioned by Amnesty International (LMR, 2001) shows that prejudice against minority groups focuses specifically on Travellers and that they are least likely to be viewed as a sector of society that is welcome either personally, or in the neighbourhood. This view seems to have changed little over time. A public-attitudes survey (Brown, 2004), published by the government's *Know Racism* campaign in February 2004, showed that 72 per cent of respondents agreed that the settled community did not want members of the Traveller community living amongst them, while 48 per cent disagreed that Travellers made a positive contribution to Irish society. This research also showed that there is a strong link between non-interaction and negative perceptions about minority ethnic groups in Ireland.

It must also be mentioned that research indicates that discrimination, prejudice and racism are also social realities for asylum seekers, refugees and ethnic minorities in Ireland (Mac Lachlan and O'Connell, 2000; LMR, 2001; Collins, A., 2001). What is perhaps distinctive about the perception of and attitudes towards Travellers in Ireland is that Travellers are native to Ireland, and have a heritage intertwined with Irish history, but yet as a social group remain separate and marginalised from mainstream society (McElwee, Jackson and Charles, 2003).

It is also important to note that Irish children most likely to experience social intolerance are those of the Travelling community. Here there are similarities with native peoples outside Ireland. Gilligan (1991) likens the fate of Travellers to that of native peoples of North America. Both cultures are alike, for example, in their story-telling and word-of-mouth histories.

## SOCIAL CARE AND THE TRAVELLER COMMUNITY

### Traveller Children in Care

Traveller children are more likely to experience poverty and may also encounter issues associated with poor living conditions, such as alcohol abuse or begging. As a consequence, they are likely to be identified as being at risk, and in need of intervention measures such as community care services.

Traveller children, like settled children, may be taken into care for a variety of reasons. Sometimes a family is unable to look after a child because of problems in the home, or a child may be abandoned in a hospital or a police station. In situations where a child needs to be placed into care, the responsibility lies with the local Health Board to provide suitable accommodation. Children can be placed in care for short or long periods of time. A major issue for Travellers has been the placement of Traveller children in the care and culture of settled people. This can influence the child and may often cause feelings of displacement and isolation.

The *Report of the Travelling People Review Body* recognised the specific needs of Traveller children. It stated (1983: 131) that 'a small minority of Traveller families have multiple social problems . . . Many children of alcoholic parents lack adequate care and supervision'. As early as 1983, it was noted that residential childcare in the Dublin area was unsuitable for Travellers. The Travelling People Review Body recommended that Travellers should be provided with an opportunity to train to work with Travellers.

In response to the particular needs of Traveller children, the childcare service, which has developed a system of fostering for children who need either temporary or long-term care, provides culture-specific options for Traveller children. These may be offered after an assessment of the child's situation and needs has been carried out by a social worker and other professionals involved with the child's family. Supporting the cultural identity of the child can be difficult if they are placed without any contact with other Travellers in a residential setting, or with a settled foster family. As a result of growing concern, Travellers' Family Care was set up in the Eastern Regional Health Authority. This introduced an alternative option for Traveller children taken into care. It is called Shared Rearing (established in 1991) and ensures that the child maintains contact with the Traveller community by being placed with a Traveller family.

Services provide by Travellers' Family Care also include provision of an Emergency and Assessment Unit in Dublin. This short-term unit offers emergency residential care for young Travellers and support for their families. An assessment service examines how their needs can be best met, and an outreach service to the Travelling community is provided where necessary. Medium-stay residential care for young Travellers and a support service for their families were established in Co. Wicklow in 1986. A community-based service established in Dublin in 1989 provides support for Traveller families where they live, and provides help for young people leaving care to make the transition back to the Traveller community.

## Health Priorities for Travellers

Pavee Point has identified that Travellers are a distinct cultural group with different perceptions of health, disease and healthcare needs, requiring special consideration in the health service. Duggan-Jackson (2000) suggests that Traveller cognitive processes (ways of thinking and understanding) are based on a visual assimilation of facts and an ability to demonstrate awareness visually and verbally, rather then in a textual way. This extends to expressing health concerns and discussing health issues.

The patchwork quilt (Figure 18.3) created by the Primary Health Care Project trainees (Tullamore) epitomises a Traveller definition of health, and what key components of primary health care should be. This project was set up as a collaborative initiative between the Midland Health Board, Tullamore Travellers' Movement and FÁS. Primary health care for Travellers means that they are trained to work within the Traveller community as healthcare workers, to provide healthcare advice and to act as an intermediary between Travellers and medical/allied health professionals.

A Traveller definition of health can be seen to include female health issues, hygienic living conditions, dental health, nutrition, exercise, immunisation, and adequate child/general medical care; it also encompasses the importance of not smoking. Travellers also included depression as something to be overcome if full health status is to be achieved. A Traveller perception of health also included the issue of non-feminisation of illness. This implies that female health needs, namely those of the mother, are relegated behind the day-to-day needs of the family. This can lead to utilisation of health services in order to receive medical care for children, but under-utilisation of medical services in order to receive help for self (Duggan-Jackson, 2000).

**Figure 18.3. Traveller Definition of Health, and What Key Components of Primary Health Care Should Be**

## Barriers to Health Services for Travellers

In order to help the Task Force to make recommendations in relation to the use of, and access to, health services by the Traveller community, consultants were commissioned to carry out an assessment of how public health services relate to the needs of Travellers. Responses to survey questions in relation to women's health revealed a low uptake of postnatal services, with a very low rate of breast-feeding and a low rate of family planning. It was reported by all the Health Boards that the general hospital services most used by the Traveller community are accident and emergency, obstetrics and paediatric services. There was a low uptake of outpatient services and of utilisation of special hospital services, including psychiatric services.

Additional information to come out of the survey included that:

- 83% of Travellers held a medical card for a doctor in their locality;
- 17% had experienced difficulties in getting doctors to accept them on their lists;
- there was a low rate of Public Health Nurse intervention with most visits taking place at home as opposed to Clinics;
- there was a low rate of immunisation, for example 52% for Mumps, Measles, Rubella and 46% for HIB (vaccination for meningitis);
- 36% had used outpatient services and 33% had used in-patient services in the past year. (*Report of the Task Force on the Travelling Community*, 1995)

Three main obstacles for Travellers in accessing health services were also identified: illiteracy; failure to transfer records of Travellers who are mobile; and prejudice on the part of the general public and service providers (*Report of the Task Force on the Travelling Community*, 1995).

Treadwell (1998) has outlined that, for Travellers, once the healthcare system is accessed, generally through local family doctors and their practice(s), there are several things that Travellers expect. First, they expect to be seen immediately. If the illness episode has been determined to be serious enough to warrant medical attention, that attention should, they believe, be forthcoming.

Travellers expect to attend services when it is convenient for them. Unfortunately, the services are not structured accordingly. Likewise, many Travellers feel that even when appointments are made ahead of time, there is always going to be a queue, and many will go in up to an hour after their appointment. While it may not be unusual to have to wait to see the doctor, even when an appointment is made, doctors have the expectation that patients will arrive on time. As Travellers have different expectations around time, and around waiting, serious conflicts can arise, and doctors can get very frustrated. This can affect the services Travellers get and make them frustrated — a situation very often unsatisfactory for both parties (Treadwell, 1998: 115).

This issue of Travellers' perception of time as a contributory factor towards missing appointments or being late was also identified in Bonnar's study (1996) on family planning needs of Travelling women in the MHB region. She emphasised that barriers exist to good healthcare for Travellers. These barriers are a result of the mobility of Travellers, different cultural perceptions of illness and time-keeping, illiteracy, lack of postal services, and absence of continuity of care, and medical records. Mac Aongusa (1990) has also suggested that Travellers have a strong present-time orientation, because of their everyday struggle for survival. This leaves little energy for long-range planning.

## EDUCATION

A key function of education is the socialisation of children into mainstream society through the inculcation and acquisition of personal, social and moral values. A description of Travellers in Ireland often includes reference to their low educational attainment. The limited extent of Traveller participation in mainstream education has been well documented (Mac Aongusa, 1990; O'Reilly, 1993).

The National Traveller Education Officer (of the Department of Education and Science) estimates that in 2002/2003:

- 5,500 Traveller children attended primary schools;
- 1,608 Traveller children attend mainstream post-primary schools (40% of all Traveller children of post-primary age);
- the national retention rate to Junior Cert is 94.3%. For Traveller pupils the rate was only 51%;
- 62 Traveller children attended 6th year post-primary;
- visiting teachers estimate in 2002 that 16 Travellers attended third level education. (Education and Cultural Rights Factsheet www.paveepoint.ie)

Localised research in Co. Wexford shows exceptionally low participation by Travellers in education, training and employment. Only 2.9 per cent of secondary-age Traveller children were attending school in 1997 (Wexford Area Partnership, 2000). O'Reilly (1993) has pointed out that some aspects of Traveller culture make it difficult to do well in school compared with settled children. For example, Travellers perceive the family to be more important than the individual. Mac Aongusa (1990) explained that Traveller children will help a family member or friend with difficult schoolwork rather than compete for their own recognition. This may slow down the children, making them appear to be slow learners.

Mac Aongusa (1990) also argued that Travellers have witnessed few of their group obtaining employment after education. Since they are not accepted into the host society anyway, education does not seem necessary to many Travellers. Success at school does not enhance a Traveller's image amongst their people although it is understood that literacy is useful. Noonan (1994) concluded that many Traveller parents doubt the relevance of what their children learn in settled schools, and parents fear that their children will become alienated from the Traveller culture.

## CONCLUSION: ISSUES FOR CONSIDERATION WHEN WORKING WITH TRAVELLERS

This chapter has emphasised that Travellers, though severely marginalised and discriminated against in Irish society, remain 'the experts' on their own culture and on what constitutes acceptable care for them. This may range from family care to residential care to healthcare to educational care. These areas all involve social care practitioners to a greater or lesser degree. Consultation with Travellers, as with any group, is essential if a productive relationship for both the practitioner, as the caregiver/service provider, and the Traveller, as the care recipient/service user, is to be ensured.

Consultation can be defined as a process of engaging with a group (Travellers or otherwise) in order to determine the group's needs from the perspective of the members of that group. This can be done informally or through the use of standard research techniques. It also implies regular reassessment of the needs of the group, and inclusion of its views in all stages of programme design, delivery, and implementation. A case study that reflects an excellent model of consultation is outlined below. Here the principles of collaborating together on a formal and informal basis resulted in a process whereby Travellers were enabled to become advocates of their own and their community's healthcare.

Social care students should start the process of becoming aware of what consultation is, and how it should be engaged in. This process can be started by not assuming one knows what the Traveller experience in Ireland is, or has been, thereby allowing Travellers to be 'the experts' on themselves. Exposure to the Traveller community, and a willingness to get to know the Traveller individual, will dispel many preconceptions one may hold. Facilitating Travellers in identifying their own needs, and responding to those needs, will be an instrumental way of working in partnership and collaboration for the better good.

The effect of this open-minded approach cannot be overemphasised. Better acceptance of ethnic and cultural differences will lead to a more multicultural and eventually pluralistic Irish society:

> Change has a considerable psychological impact on the human mind. To the fearful, it is threatening because it means that things may get worse. To the hopeful, it is encouraging because things may get better. To the confident, it is inspiring because the challenge exists to make things better. (King Whitney Jr)

## CASE STUDY: PRIMARY HEALTHCARE PROJECT FOR TRAVELLERS (TULLAMORE) AS A MODEL OF CONSULTATION

Primary healthcare can be defined as the first level of contact people have with the health services.

*Aims of Project*
- Development in consultation with Travellers, FÁS, the Midland Health Board [MHB] and Tullamore Travellers' Movement of a Primary Healthcare Project aimed specifically at Travellers
- Training of Traveller women to work as Community Health Workers among Travellers in their locality.

*Background to Project*
- The Primary Healthcare Project in Dublin (partnership between Eastern Regional Health Authority and Pavee Point, 1994) was used as a model to design the project in the Tullamore region.
- A health needs assessment was carried out to determine the health needs of Travellers according to Travellers in the region (Duggan-Jackson, 2000).
- A partnership was established between Tullamore Travellers' Movement, the MHB and FÁS. Local Travellers were consulted regarding their own health needs. Trainees (Traveller women) were consulted about the design of the project and cultural appropriateness (mainly achieved through evaluation of project and inclusion of Travellers in that evaluation). Trainees were included at Steering Group meetings, which organised the running of the project.

*Structure of Project*

Stage 1: Capacity Building
Definition: Increasing the capacity (ability) of a community or organisation
Aim: to enable Travellers to begin to think about gaining greater control over social, political, economic, and environmental factors affecting their health.

Stage 2: Pre-Training Phase, 1999–2001
Aim: To assist Traveller participants to develop an understanding of health in conjunction with community development and personal development. The focus was on building ability; team-building; communication; identifying what primary healthcare is, and how Community Health workers could provide a primary healthcare service. There was an emphasis on responding to needs in an area, and developing a sense of community.

→

Stage 3: Health Intervention Phase, 2001–3

Trainees were given specific training in particular aspects of health identified as being important for Traveller health, such as immunisation, dental health and children's health. Training involved being able to give and have appropriate information, knowing where to refer people for further advice/ assessment, etc.

*Consultation Process*

1.  Local Travellers consulted with each other regarding their own health needs and understanding of health. This is demonstrated in the patchwork quilt (Figure 18.3). Community consultation was engaged in through research with the local Traveller community to identify local needs and key health needs/ concerns.
2.  Trainees (Traveller women) were consulted about the design of the project and cultural appropriateness. This was mainly achieved through evaluation of the project and inclusion of Travellers in that evaluation.
3.  The inclusion of trainees at Steering Group meetings to organise the running of the project was of paramount importance. The views of the trainees were welcomed and participation encouraged. Trainees were given training prior to meetings, with regard to capacity building and having the confidence to participate on an equal footing at meetings.

19

# Social Care and Disability

Karen Finnerty & Brendan Collins

## OVERVIEW

This chapter introduces current issues and thinking in relation to the provision of
services to people with disabilities (particularly learning disability). It aims to provide
an understanding and appreciation of the key issues. You may find some of the
content challenging and contrary to what you have previously learned or experienced
about disability. It is hoped that this chapter will promote discussion and debate and
help to contribute to the delivery of high-quality, person-centred services.

The chapter briefly sketches the historical development of services for people
with disability, particularly in the Irish context, showing how societal influences
impacted on how such services emerged. Terminology and definitions used to label
people with disability are outlined and discussed. An understanding of the issues
arising from such definitions is important as they continue to influence, directly or
indirectly, attitudes and decisions made in relation to people with disability and
the design and delivery of services.

Two models of service provision, the medical/traditional model and the social
model, are outlined in detail. The services you encounter as a practitioner will
most likely be influenced by one or both of these models. It is safe to assume that
many of the debates you will encounter will relate to the tension that arises where
they interface. Social policy and legislation as they relate to disability are
introduced, though space limits an extensive discussion of this highly complex
area. The chapter concludes with a discussion of the role of the social care
practitioner in the context of disability.

## INTRODUCTION

The good news is that disability is in the public consciousness and
increasingly on the political agenda. The bad news is that with all of this
exposure, we do not necessarily know what disability is, what it implies or
what to expect for ourselves, others, society or our environment. (Bowker
and Star, 1999, cited in Albrecht et al., 2001: 1)

In the context of social care provision in Ireland, disability is a major but often under-recognised component. Social care is more closely associated with provision of services to children in care or to marginalised groups than with people with disability. Partly this is accounted for by the fact that historically social care provision to children and marginalised groups was funded directly by government, whereas services for people with disability were developed and funded by voluntary and religious organisations.

Until relatively recently, we had no precise statistics on the number of people with disabilities receiving a service from relevant organisations. In 1996, the Commission on the Status of People with Disabilities estimated the number of people with disability at 360,000 — 10 per cent of the then population. The Commission reported that one of the most telling indications of the neglect of people with disabilities was the lack of such official statistics (A *Strategy for Equality*, 1996: 7).

This situation is beginning to change but statistical information is still limited and difficult to access. In 2000, the Health Research Board [HRB] completed an *Assessment of Need for People with Intellectual Disabilities*. The resulting National Intellectual Disability Database provides comprehensive information in respect to a number of important factors in the lives of people with learning disabilities. A corresponding database, the Physical and Sensory Database, is currently in development.

In 2003, 25,557 people with learning difficulties were listed on the database. Of this number, 23,464 people were in receipt of services (day service and/or full-time residential service) from agencies (including those in psychiatric hospitals). Currently 356 people are receiving no service and a further 1,737 have no current service requirements (Barron and Mulvany, 2003: 10). Gallagher (2001) suggests that the Physical and Sensory Database could include up to 38,190 people. Statistics from the Department of Health and Children indicate non-capital expenditure on the Disability Programme (intellectual and physical) increased from just under €200 million in 1990 to over €1,000 million (estimated) in 2003 (DoHC, 2004a).

In addition to the difficulty of establishing numbers of service users, equally complex is ascertaining the number of people who work in the disability area. According to the Department of Health and Children, 10,160 people were employed in Intellectual Disability Services in 2002. But a further 86,654 were employed in the public health service, and a significant number of these are involved in provision of service to people with disability (DoHC, 2004b). Furthermore, disability organisations often access other funding routes and engage in fundraising activities to sustain their activities. There is no breakdown available on the numbers of staff supported in such ways.

Despite the fact that statistics are difficult to establish, it is clear that services to people with disability are a significant and growing aspect of health and social service provision. As you will learn from this chapter, such provision has its own unique requirements and context.

## SERVICES FOR PEOPLE WITH DISABILITIES IN IRELAND

Prior to the industrial revolution, people with disabilities lived their lives in the context of the community into which they were born. The onset of the new industrial order laid the foundations for the institutions of the late nineteenth and early twentieth century, which evolved into the services we know today. Prosperity and urbanisation of the eighteenth century attracted people from rural areas to centres of high population. As the population grew, so too did the number of 'vagabonds' and 'beggars', giving rise for concern among citizens.

In Dublin, in 1773, the authorities responded to this concern by opening the Dublin House of Industry, where those regarded as social 'undesirables' were incarcerated. Such people were also occasionally sent to prisons and poorhouses. These institutions (generally known as workhouses) catered for many social problems but, within a very short space of time, the House of Industry had allo·cated separate space for those with mental health difficulties, then termed 'lunatics' and 'idiots'. This system continued to expand over the next number of decades and, by the time of the Famine, 163 workhouses had been built in Ireland (McCormack, 1997: 14). Here, the destitute received meagre food and lodging in return for work done. Rather than provide relief in or near people's homes, the authorities provided help, of sorts, only in the workhouses.

The idea of difference and practices of segregation continued to grow during the 1850s so that by the close of the nineteenth century, there were 22 district 'lunatic asylums', each with a catchment area of one or two counties. As these institutions expanded, further differences between people regarded as 'lunatics', 'imbeciles' and 'idiots' were identified. Some of these institutions were the fore-runners of today's services for people with mental health difficulties — St Patrick's Hospital, Dublin, for example.

In 1869, the Stewart Institution for Idiotic and Imbecile Children was opened in Dublin as a result of the work of a number of leading citizens. Its original aim was to train children with learning disabilities so that by the time they reached 18, they would be able to return to their homes and families. But the children did not return to their homes and, as numbers grew, few vacancies arose. Meanwhile, numbers in the district asylums had swollen, and a suggestion was made that auxiliary asylums be created for 'incurables' — primarily people with learning disabilities. This idea did not appear to be generally welcomed, as only two such institutions were opened, one in Youghal, Co. Cork, and the other in Portrane, Co. Dublin.

This situation persisted until the establishment of the Irish Free State. In 1926, a Catholic order of nuns, the Daughters of Charity, on the suggestion of the Archbishop of the time, agreed to turn the Workhouse School in Cabra into a home and school for children with learning disabilities. Over the next 30 years or so, religious orders opened at least ten similar types of institution around Ireland (McCormack, 1997: 21).

Post-Second World War Ireland shared the sense of optimism and the greater awareness of social issues that had begun to develop among the Allied nations during the last months of the conflict. This thinking and attitude was led principally by the United States, eventually influencing the culture and psyche of other western societies, including Ireland. The horrors of war and associated activities, as found in the Nazi concentration camps, created an appreciation of the wellbeing of the individual as paramount to the good of society. The effects of this change did not occur overnight but happened over a period of time. One consequence was a greater sense of social justice among individuals and groups. This gradual transformation also influenced service provision for people with disabilities (Collins, B., 2001: 57).

During the 1950s, several nondenominational organisations and agencies were founded in Ireland. In 1955, at the initiative of a mother with a son with a learning disability, a public meeting of parents and friends was held in Dublin's Mansion House and the first day-service for children with learning disabilities was founded. This association later became St Michael's House. Other organisations had their start in the pioneering work of individuals such as Valerie Goulding, responsible for the establishment of the Central Remedial Clinic in Dublin.

A major factor that influenced the structure of these agencies and organisations was the belief that children with disabilities should not have to be 'put away' but instead should receive specialist care and education in purpose-built centres during the day. This welcome progression did not mean that the large institutions were closed down. Rather, the introduction of new organisations and services influenced how institutional care was provided. Changes began to occur for the better within these settings, such as the building of group homes, albeit within the same grounds as the main building.

Many children and adults with disabilities now had opportunities to lead fuller lives and receive more humane services. But despite such improvements, the situation was far from perfect. In most cases, people had to attend centres away from their own neighbourhoods. Children at special schools were not expected to perform to the same level as children in ordinary national schools, limiting their later chances of interacting socially in adult life. Children and young adults were often collected from their homes by ambulance and brought to a centre that may have been known locally as the 'clinic', even though a school might also have been on site. Some agencies may even have incorporated the word 'clinic' into the official name of the organisation. Apart from attending class in the special or segregated school, children might also receive therapy. Many children might find that throughout the school day, they would receive more therapy — from a number of therapists — than they would education.

The public image projected by such organisations was that of a benign body that protected and cared for unwell and vulnerable children and adults. This image was promoted in order to raise funds for the organisation during 'flag day'. For many Irish people of a certain age, this approach would be similar to that of the penny appeal for African children, known as the 'black babies', organised through the national school system during the 1960s.

Not all organisations operated on the basis of presenting people with disabilities as being helpless victims in need of care. But while western societal attitudes to people with disabilities had generally improved, the overall response tended to be anything other than regarding these same people as complete human beings equal to the remainder of society.

Until relatively recently most services developed in such ways and operated on the basis of what is now known as the traditional model of service provision. The service is generally self-contained with little or no outside links. A hierarchical management system operates, with executive management at the top of the organisation (in control of funding and decision making) and people with disabilities (often referred to as clients, patients or service users) and their families at the bottom of the hierarchy, in receipt of services, but almost always without any influence in relation to real decision making (Figure 19.1)(Power, 1993: 31).

**Figure 19.1. The Traditional Service Model**

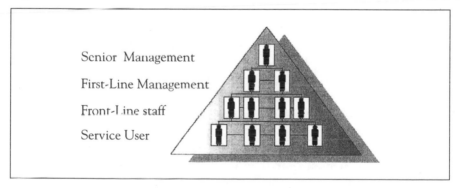

Senior Management

First-Line Management

Front-Line staff

Service User

*Source*: based on O'Brien & O'Brien, 1989.

Recent years have seen changes in the delivery of services for people with disabilities. One of the most significant changes has been a move away from the charity ethos of disability service provision to one grounded in rights. Evidence of this change was indicated in government policy documents published during the 1990s. The Department of Health's *Shaping a Healthier Future: A Strategy for Effective Healthcare in the 1990s* (DoH, 1994: 10) is underpinned by the principles of 'equity, quality and service accountability'. The Report of the Commission on the Status of People with Disabilities, *A Strategy for Equality* (1996: 5), advocated 'new structures for delivery of quality services within a framework of rights, not charity'. Subsequent policy documents such as *Enhancing the Partnership* (1997), *Toward Equal Citizenship* (1999) and *Quality and Fairness: A Health Strategy for You* (DoHC, 2001a) continued to build on this new approach and attitude, evidenced in the language of rights, equity, partnership and empowerment.

## THE MEDICAL INFLUENCE ON DISABILITY SERVICES

In addition to the charity ethos, another significant aspect of the development of services was the medical influence on service delivery approaches. People with disability were viewed as having a 'medical problem' that could only be assisted within a hospital or therapeutic setting. This thinking gave rise to what is now referred to as the *medical model* of service delivery.

What is significant about the medical model is that it operates from the belief that the condition (disability) can be restored or otherwise treated medically. It operates within the classic understanding of medicine — the science of diagnosing and treating illness and injury and the preservation of health. This approach is of course appropriate when the impairment can be fixed but inappropriate when applied in situations where the impairment cannot be helped by medical intervention. In addition, the medical approach also had the unfortunate tendency of not distinguishing the person from the disability. The person's right to be seen as a person first was lost in descriptions such as 'the cripple', 'an epileptic', 'the disabled'. A rejection of such terms has in recent times moved to acknowledging the person first and then the disability — for example, 'a person with disability'.

One of the consequences of the medical approach was that disability began to be defined in terms of an able-bodied 'norm'. If the person could not be defined as 'normal' then they were by definition 'abnormal'.

## DEFINITIONS OF DISABILITY

According to Costello and Webster (1997: 82) the words disability, impairment and handicap are often used interchangeably. They propose that it is important to understand the definition of each word and to use it accurately for three reasons:

- How we give meaning to something influences our behaviour in relation to it. If we define a disabled person as unable, an object of pity, we treat them as such, and eventually they react as such;
- We need to identify how many people belong to a certain category. While categorising people may seem unpalatable, it is difficult to budget for services when it is unclear how many people are affected or what we mean by the definitions we use;
- Most definitions have been worded by people who have not experienced disability and do not reflect the experiences of people with disabilities. Thus definitions usually compare disability to an able-bodied 'norm'.

The most commonly cited definition is that published by the World Health Organisation [WHO]. This three-tier definition draws a distinction between the concepts of impairment, disability and handicap:

> An *impairment* is any loss or abnormality of psychological, physiological or anatomical structure or function; a *disability* is any restriction or lack (resulting from an impairment) of ability to perform an activity in the manner or within the range considered normal for a human being; a *handicap* is a disadvantage for a given individual resulting from an impairment or a disability, that prevents the fulfilment of a role that is considered normal (depending on age, sex and social and cultural factors) for that individual. (WHO, 1980, s27.29.14. Italics added)

The language used in this definition places it clearly within the medical model focusing as it does on the cognitive, emotional and physical aspects of the person. It refers to concepts of abnormality and normality, concepts that are difficult to define definitively. The wide acceptance and usage of the WHO definition since 1980 served to reinforce the medical model and inhibit a move to a more socially focused approach.

While the WHO definition has wide acceptance amongst health bodies and governments in many countries, it is rejected by disability activists. They argue that disability is not caused by chance. It is a social construct, created through society's response to the disability and by its failure to put sufficient supports in place to ensure that the person with disability achieves the same quality of life as other members of society.

The Commission on the Status of People with Disabilities understood the term 'people with disabilities' to include 'children and adults who experience any restriction in their capacity to participate in economic, social or cultural life on account of a physical, sensory, learning, mental health or emotional impairment' (*A Strategy for Equality*, 1996: 11). The National Disability Authority Act (1999: 2) uses a similar definition:

> [D]isability, in relation to a person, means a substantial restriction in the capacity of a person to participate in economic, social or cultural life on account of an enduring physical, sensory, learning, mental health or emotional impairment.

In 2002, the WHO published the *International Classification of Functioning, Disability and Health* [ICF]. This document outlines a standard language and framework for the description of health and health-related states. It is a universal classification of disability and health. It is a significant development on the previous definition:

> [U]nlike the previous definitions ICF puts the notions of health and disability in a new light. It acknowledges that every human being can experience a decrement in health and thereby experience some disability. ICF mainstreams the experience of disability and recognises it as a universal human experience. (WHO, 2002: 3)

When a person has a disability, quality in life depends on a number of factors:

- The nature of the disability
- The person's adaptation to their disability
- The level of support from the immediate family
- How society views and responds to the disability.

In Ireland today, people with disability do not have the *right* to the services that would ensure their full participation and autonomy over their own life decisions. This situation has been successfully challenged in court on an ongoing basis as has been evidenced by particular cases. In 1993, Cork mother Marie O'Donaghue challenged the failure of the Department of Education to provide education to her child labelled 'profoundly mentally handicapped'. The judge in the case (Mr Justice O'Hanlon) held that the Constitution obliges the state to provide free, basic, elementary education for all children, including those with profound mental handicap (O'Hanlon 1993, quoted in Barr, 2000: 42). Despite this finding, little or nothing changed in the following years relating to state funding of educational services to those with severe or profound disability.

A further case (the Jamie Sinnott case) brought to public attention the hopelessly inadequate educational provision for people with autism. In his judgment on the case, Mr Justice Barr (2000) highlighted two fundamental weaknesses in government policy:

- An insufficient liaison between government departments. On this, he said, 'there is an urgent requirement for an integrated departmental approach to the fulfilment of the constitutional obligations of the State, to disabled sections of society';
- The 'Department of Finance appear to be insufficiently informed regarding the constitutional obligations of the State to the weak and deprived in society'.

Justice Barr listed a significant number of failings in the state's under-provision of education and treatment for Jamie Sinnott.

Many people with disabilities and their supporters believe that until there is a profound shift in societal attitudes, a radical change in the underlying paradigm of disability, and legislation governing the right to basic services, the situation will not change radically.

## THE SOCIAL MODEL OF DISABILITY SERVICE PROVISION

The social model of disability recognises that while people may have an 'impairment', they become 'disabled' by a society that actively or passively *excludes* them from full participation. It locates the cause of disability not in the person who experiences the impairment, but in society's response. The response is manifested in the language used to describe the person, the supports put in place to enable them to live a full and meaningful life, and how far they are empowered in relation to decisions governing their life.

This redefining of disability — in both a national and an international context — is a relatively new departure. In many ways, it reflects earlier experiences, particularly in America, of other marginalised groups, such as women and racial minorities. It was during the 1980s that disability as a human rights issue began to gather pace, and this can be seen in such actions as The International Year of the Disabled Persons (1981), The World Programme of Action Concerning Disabled Persons (1982) and The Decade of the Disabled Persons (1983–92). (It is worth noting that 2003 was also designated European Year of People with Disabilities.)

The changes of the 1980s and early 1990s culminated in the publication, in 1993, of *The United Nations Standard Rules on the Equalisation of Opportunities for Persons with Disabilities*. This document laid out a framework of 22 rules aimed at enabling people with disabilities to achieve full participation and equality in society. Although these rules are not a treaty, and therefore not binding, they were adopted unanimously by the United Nations General Assembly and have the support of European Union member states (Costello and Webster, 2003: 80).

Reflecting on the wider European influence in the 1990s, people with disabilities in Ireland began to re-frame their situation in terms of human rights. The Commission on the Status of People with Disabilities report, *A Strategy for Equality* (1996: 9), endorsed the UN approach on the change from a medical approach to a social approach:

> [A] given level of impairment or degree of restriction does not necessarily lead to disadvantage: It is the societal response (in terms of attitudes and expectations as well as the services and facilities made available) which has an important impact on the extent to which impairment or disability lead to disadvantage.

It went on to say:

> Disability . . . rather than being seen as a 'personal' or 'medical' problem which was the result of an individual's physiological, anatomical or psychological impairment and caused by disease, accidents or other 'personal tragedies', it is now seen as a 'social' problem whereby disability is caused by society's failure to adapt itself to the different ways in which those with disabilities accomplish activities.

In the late 1980s, John O'Brien, an American activist and writer on disability issues, developed an alternative model of service delivery that embodies the principles of moving from a traditional (medical) to a social model of disability. In his model, the service, rather than 'containing' individuals, acts as a facilitator to ensure that people are linked to and can participate within their own community.

The Basic Strategy (Figure 19.2) distinguishes between the person, the service and the community.

**Figure 19.2. O'Brien's Basic Strategy**

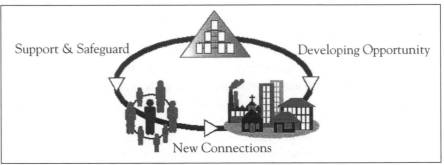

*Source*: adapted from O'Brien & O'Brien, 1989.

In this model, the person's network of friends and family is recognised as very important. The service is presented in the context of the individual and what the service offers them. The primary role of the service becomes one of support and safeguarding the individual within their own social network, and creating and developing new opportunities in the person's own community. The community is seen as a resource and as the place the person needs to be connected to, with the support of the service. This type of service has an individual focus, based on individual needs, as opposed to a mass management approach whereby groups of people engage in activities that should normally be undertaken on an individual basis (Power, 1993: 32).

As well as the promotion of equal rights, the aim of the individually focused service is to include people with disabilities within the community and society in general. The first stage in achieving this goal is *integration*. This concept has its roots in 'normalisation theory' which originated in Denmark in the early 1960s. The Danish Mental Retardation Act defined the aim of services as 'to create an existence for the mentally retarded as close to normal living conditions as possible' (Bank-Mikkelsen, 1980: 56). In Sweden, the concept was redefined as: 'making available to all mentally retarded people patterns of life and conditions of everyday living which are as close as possible to the regular circumstances and ways of living' (Nirje, 1980: 33).

The concept of normalisation evolved over the years to that of integration, but maintained at its core the notion of 'a doing onto them': the benevolent society allows the participation of those less fortunate. We have now moved a step further in the concept of *inclusion*, which recognises the right of people to belong in community — in short, putting into practice the principles of the social model.

Judith Snow (1989: 5–1), a leading activist in the disability movement, has described the absence of disabled people from community life as rendering communities incomplete. She has identified five clear losses to the community without the real presence of other excluded or marginalised groups:

- The community loses the underdeveloped contributions from isolated groups such as their work contribution;
- Other citizens lose the opportunity to relate to the excluded person and so lose opportunities to expand their giftedness and increase their contributions;
- The opportunities for citizens to solve problems, use their creativity and to care are diminished in number, kind and intensity;
- Ordinary citizens learn to fear any flaw or vulnerability that may be 'lurking' in their own minds or bodies;
- Ordinary citizens become more isolated in themselves, not sharing or caring in their attempt to become more independent.

For Snow, inclusion means 'people should be present in all community activities as participating active members such that it matters if he or she is not present'.

O'Brien and O'Brien (1989: 1–25) describe the 'five valued experiences' they consider all people seek out: relationships, choice, contributing, sharing ordinary places and dignity (Figure 19.3). They propose that all services for people with disability should be designed on these five valued experiences. When services operate in a way that ensures that service users experience the experiences, they achieve what the O'Briens refer to as the five service accomplishments: community participation, promoting choice, supporting contribution, community presence and encouraging valued social roles.

Figure 19.3. The Five Valued Experiences and Service Accomplishments

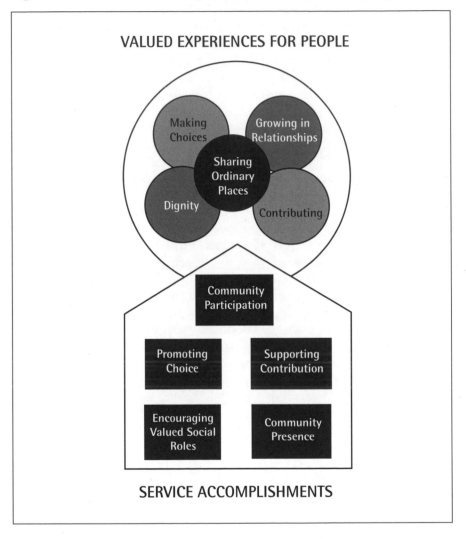

*Source*: adapted from O'Brien & O'Brien, 1989.

## SOCIAL POLICY, LEGISLATION AND DISABILITY IN IRELAND

The forerunner to all disability legislation worldwide is considered to be the Americans with Disabilities Act [ADA]. During the 1970s and 1980s, political pressure had been mounting in the United States for sweeping reform of all disability discrimination law, which was proving to be piecemeal, limited and inoperable in some cases. This culminated with the passing into law of the ADA, on 26 July 1990 (Quinn et al., 1993: 45). Reliance on established civil rights law was a major strength of the ADA: it pointed to disabled people's similarities with other marginalised groups and gave lawyers precedents on which to argue cases.

In subsequent years, several countries introduced antidiscrimination legislation to improve the position of people with disabilities; these countries included Australia, Canada and the United Kingdom. European countries have concentrated more on benefits than on formal rights but this is also beginning to change. Within the Irish context, there have been some recent significant developments in the area of policy and legislation. Earlier we mentioned some of the more recent and significant documents that reflect the policy shift in how disability is viewed in this country.

An outcome of the policy shift toward the social model was an attention to the inclusion of disability in legislation. The year 1998 saw the introduction in Ireland of the Employment Equality Act. This act describes discrimination as 'the treatment of one person in a less favourable way than another person is, has been or would be treated'. Discrimination is outlawed on nine distinct grounds — gender, marital status, family status, sexual orientation, religious belief, age, disability, race and membership of the Travelling community.

All aspects of employment are covered by the 1998 Act: equal pay, access to employment, vocational training, conditions of employment, work experience, and promotion or dismissal. The legislation applies to public- and private-sector employment, employment agencies, vocational training bodies, the publication of advertisements, trade unions, professional bodies, full-time and part-time workers and collective agreements.

Anyone wishing to challenge an employer on the grounds of the Employment Equality Act can get free advice from the Equality Authority, which has an inhouse legal service. The Equality Authority is an independent body set up under the Act. If an alleged act of discrimination becomes the subject of an investigation, and the case goes to court, the complainant may choose to represent himself or herself or may be represented by a trade union, solicitor or the Equality Authority. The Equal Status Act 2000 outlaws certain forms of non-employment-related discrimination — including access and public transport systems.

While the introduction of such legislation can improve the status of people with disabilities, the question arises as to whether it goes far enough. Woods suggests that:

> [N]ew laws cannot do away with years of inequality; anti-discrimination legislation cannot guarantee equality of participation nor can the rights approach kill off the spectre of charity overnight. The same and stronger could be said about the Employment Equality Act. All it can do is create a small patch of equal opportunities. (Woods, 2000: 14)

Many disability groups and/or their advocates do not accept this piecemeal approach to legislation. They called for a comprehensive piece of legislation specifically focused on disability and its related issues. Toolan (2001), commenting on these Acts and on the creation of the National Disability Authority (see below), questioned the effectiveness of the approach:

> Without the necessary power of a comprehensive Disability Rights Act creating such a culture will be somewhat stymied. But the State seems intent on restricting its capacity to really deliver a rights culture by not creating laws that categorically reference disabled people's rights.

In 2001, a Disability Commissioner Bill was put forward by the National Parents and Siblings Alliance. While that Bill was rejected by the government, a commitment was made to introduce a comprehensive Disability Bill. This was presented to the Dáil in December 2001. Disability groups took issue with the Bill because it was duty- rather than rights-based and ran contrary to the major changes that had developed in the field of disability policy since *A Strategy for Equality*. Furthermore, its terminology left much scope for those who would choose to find loopholes. As Woods argued (2002: 15): 'a major concern must be those weasel words which recurred throughout . . . These are "reasonable and practicable", "disproportionate" or "not justified on grounds of cost".' Following strong negative reaction, the government withdrew large parts of the Bill. A revised version was published in September 2004 along with a new National Disability Strategy. While the funding allocated for the strategy was welcomed, the details of the strategy and the bill itself have met with severe criticism from disability activists and organisations of and for people with disability. At time of writing, the matter is still far from resolved.

In addition to legislative initiatives, other changes have been implemented in how services are delivered to people with disability. From June 2000, the National Rehabilitation Board [NRB] ceased to exist. The NRB had been a specialist advice, information and monitoring body that specifically focused on disability. In line with broader policy changes, the services formerly provided by the NRB are now provided by mainstream organisations. This can be seen as an attempt to discontinue the practice of excluding people with disabilities through the provision of specialist services. For example:

- People with disabilities who want advice and guidance on vocational or employment skills and training are now dealt with by FÁS Employment Services, in line with the remainder of the population;
- Information and advice are provided by a new service, Comhairle, with a wider brief than disability;
- Health services are provided by the Department of Health and Children and a new body [NEPS] under the Department of Education deals with psychological services to children.

A new body, the National Disability Authority [NDA] set up under the National Disability Authority Act 1999, is an independent agency under the Department of Justice, Equality and Law Reform. It provides a key focal point for disability in the mainstream. Its principal functions are:

- To act as a central, national body to assist in the coordination and development of disability policy;
- To undertake research and develop statistical information for the planning, delivery and monitoring of disability programmes and services;
- To advise on the development of standards for programmes and services for people with disabilities;
- To monitor the implementation of standards and codes of practice in programmes and services for people with disabilities;
- To liaise with service-providers and other bodies to support the development and the implementation of appropriate standards for programmes and services for people with disabilities.

## DISABILITY AND THE SOCIAL CARE PRACTITIONER

Given the above changes in policy, legislation and service delivery, it is clear that new approaches are needed in the design and delivery of services to people with disability. It is worth examining as a fundamental principle whether disability is appropriately placed in the context of 'care' at all. The social model of disability, with its underlying ethos of empowerment, partnership and inclusion, suggests otherwise — particularly in relation to services for adults with disability. But given current structures and funding mechanisms it is unlikely that we will see substantive change in this area for many years. Thus it is best to focus on the design and delivery of services and on the professional training of those working in the area — including social care practitioners.

In the context of the social model, Hennessy (2002) outlines three primary principles governing service delivery in the field of disability:

- *Self-Determination*: a process that differs uniquely from person to person according to what each individual determines is necessary and desirable to create a satisfying and personally meaningful life. Self-determination is both person-centred and person-directed and acknowledges the rights of people with disabilities to take charge of and responsibility for their own lives.

- *Participation*: concerned with taking part in activities with other people. Community participation suggests active involvement with other community members, not only in ordinary activities but also in active decision making which directly affects people's own lives.

- *Empowerment*: power is given to people with disabilities so that they can directly control their own lives rather than other people fulfilling this role on their behalf. While the concept of empowerment has become quite popular within the human services in recent years, the reality of empowerment has yet to become the norm for the majority of people with disabilities.

Hennessy further outlines five key priorities of care as it applies to the role of the social care practitioner in disability:

- *Protection*: can be used in relation to those who might be perceived as being vulnerable or dependent upon others for their survival, safety or security. Social care practitioners assist in providing protection to people from the risks of ordinary life and also from particular risks a service user's present situation, current difficulties or life circumstances may create. In this protection role, we are also concerned with protection of the community from those whose behaviour may be dangerous and/or who cannot be responsible for their own behaviour.

- *Rehabilitation and Habilitation*: when the term rehabilitation is used, reference is often being made to people who have been incarcerated or institutionalised. In the rehabilitation role, you may be supporting a person or group of people who have suffered or are suffering breakdown, disablement, bereavement, loss, trauma and change through enforced circumstances, usually outside their own control. In rehabilitation work, the concern is with those who have lost a living environment of mutual supports, including family, friends and community.

    In habilitation work, the focus is less on the 're-teaching' of, or 'relearning' by, those who have lost skills, and more about enabling those who may never have had those skills before. For example, a social care practitioner may support someone to live independently for the first time in their life.

- *Prevention*: here the social care practitioner may work to prevent the often drastic and inappropriate reactions to a person's circumstances or condition by institutional responses to their needs, which can often be assessed inaccurately. Many social care practitioners in their professional service delivery seek to prevent the collapse of the person's capacity to cope with the normal stress of everyday life. The work concerned with prevention may also include designing strategies to prevent the collapse of normal supports in a person's family, friends and community. On a more global level, prevention relates to the avoidable risks posed to the community by poverty, ignorance or disease.

- *Care*: social care can be defined as care for those who cannot care for themselves by virtue of their circumstances and/or condition. Interestingly and increasingly, services are utilising social care practitioners to support people who cannot care wholly or any longer for their dependants, family, relatives or loved ones — in other words, people who are also carers themselves. Importantly, social care practice, particularly in the context of teamwork, can also mean caring for those who are employed to provide care and service in the first instance, so that they can be adequately supported in their caring tasks and not suffer breakdown, burnout or catastrophic loss of morale and motivation.

- *Quality of Life*: these issues are about the service response that enhances and improves the quality of a person's life by helping to provide services that are necessary, chosen, normal, continual and which can be evaluated in terms of the O'Briens' five service accomplishments.

## CONCLUSION

This chapter has aimed to introduce you to current thinking and approaches in relation to the delivery of services to people with disability. In one sense, the delivery of such services has come full circle. Prior to industrialisation, people with disabilities lived their lives in the context of the community into which they were born, although very often in poor and neglected circumstances. Having come through institutionalisation, normalisation, integration and inclusion, we are now moving toward the full inclusion of people with disabilities in all aspects of life, as equal rights-entitled citizens.

The most significant change in disability service provision in the past twenty years has been the move from the traditional or medical model of service delivery to the social model. The social model operates on the principle that people are disabled not by their impairments but by the failure of society to put supports in place to enable the full participation of all its members. Most organisations currently providing services are moving toward delivery of the social model, although some still struggle with the legacy of the structures and attitudes of the traditional approach.

The past ten years have seen major and significant policy changes in how people with disability are seen in Ireland. This change has been supported by important legislative changes but (at time of writing), we still await a fully comprehensive Disability Act that will encompass all areas pertaining to people with disabilities living full and equal lives. While the policy documents and reports of the 1990s were extremely valuable and have contributed to substantive change, many of their recommendations have still not been implemented.

You, as a potential future practitioner in the area, have an opportunity to contribute to this fundamental change in attitude and approach to how services work with people with disability, and their families and advocates. Rather than viewing people with disability as in 'need of care', you will be in prime position to work from the principles of empowerment, partnership and equal citizenship.

Note: Some material in this chapter was previously published by the Open Training College as part of its open learning course materials.

# 20

# Social Care Work and the Older Person

Carmel Gallagher

## OVERVIEW

This chapter examines issues related to social care work with older people. It outlines the principal policy developments in residential and daycare services for older people, with reference to key policy reports. It discusses the move from institutional care to community care and changes in philosophical approaches to care services for the older person. It describes the main sectors — public, voluntary and private — that provide all or part of the daily care of an older person where they experience some degree of incapacity or social isolation. Some examples of social care settings are described and an illustration given of daily activities. Examples are provided of good practice and innovative projects, analysed in relation to models of social care work with older persons. Finally some approaches to old age are considered, insofar as ideas and images of ageing influence our perception of the possibilities and opportunities for older people to achieve personally and socially fulfilling roles.

## INTRODUCTION

When social care work is discussed in relation to older people, we tend to associate it with meeting personal and social needs of frail, chronically ill or confused older people. Ageing or senescence is associated with a decline in physiological effectiveness that affects us all sooner or later and is an intrinsic part of growing old. While disease affects only certain members of the older population, many diseases are age-related. The combination of senescent changes, such as hearing loss or deteriorating eyesight, and a greater risk of illnesses such as stroke or heart disease, makes the older person more vulnerable and dependent.

The realities of old age have come to be seen by contemporary governments as presenting problems that require solutions. There has been an increase in the proportion of older people in the populations of many western countries. Ireland has been an exception to this trend as, while the absolute size of the elderly population has increased, its relative size has changed little since the early decades of the last century (Fahey 1994: 55). The 2002 Census showed that 11.1 per cent of the population was aged 65 or over (CSO, 2003). All the models of projected population trends predict a substantial increase in the percentage of people aged over 65 — to a level of 15 per cent of the total population in 2021 (NCAOP, 2004: 81).

This increase in the numbers of older people will give rise to additional demands for formal social care in both non-residential and residential institutions for the dependent elderly (Fahey and FitzGerald, 1997: 95). Traditionally many day services for older people were provided by voluntary organisations, with nuns from religious orders providing much of the expertise. With the decline in the number of religious, these services are increasingly coming under the remit of the Health Service. Given the preference of older people to be cared for at home, and the central role accorded to the family in the provision of day-to-day care, policy has been focused on support and advice for carers; the development of domiciliary services such as home help; and on improving the range of services and quality of care provided in day and residential centres, in partnership, where possible, with voluntary bodies. In residential care, the private sector has expanded within a framework of legislative regulations.

However, the services and supports necessary to give effect to such principles of 'ageing in place' have been slow to develop. Specific policy areas that have remained underdeveloped include the home-help service, rural public transport and sheltered housing for semi-dependent older people (Layte et al., 1999: 22). For example, a recent study of the use of health and social services by older adults in the community found that, among a sample of 937 older people in two health board areas, a substantial proportion (37 per cent) of those found to be severely impaired in carrying out activities of daily living had not received any home-based services in the previous year (Garavan et al., 2001: 23).

It is increasingly acknowledged that the older population is a more heterogeneous group than is often suggested. Most 'young elderly' are fit and active and the vast majority of older people live independent lives. Decline in physical function may be of little consequence to an older person until they cross some threshold that prevents them from carrying out necessary activities. Indeed, older people contribute to the quality of life of family and kin through being involved in a long-term chain of support, including emotional support and care for ill and dependent relatives. There is evidence of much practical and emotional support given in daily living, mainly to family but also to friends (Phillipson et al., 2001).

Chronological age has been institutionalised in public policies such as the institution of retirement. Sociologists have examined the interplay between institutions, beliefs about ageing and the lived experiences of older people themselves. Sociological critiques of the concepts of dependency and independency, and concepts such as the 'third age' of activity and leisure have helped to challenge the assumption that old age constitutes a social problem. They help to create a perception of ageing as a normal stage of the life course. Organisations that represent older people have been to the fore in projecting a more positive image of ageing and of the possibilities open to individuals in their latter years, to live full and interesting lives. One organisation that promotes a vision of such creative possibilities is Age and Opportunity. This is an autonomous, national agency set up in 1988, whose stated objectives are to challenge negative attitudes to ageing, to encourage the participation of older people in all areas of society, and to encourage understanding between the generations.

## POLICY DEVELOPMENT SINCE THE 1960S

Three government reports have shaped policy and services for older people in Ireland: the 1968 *Care of the Aged* report (Interdepartmental Committee on the Aged, 1968) was a seminal document that addressed in a coherent way the needs of older people as a distinct group. It shaped policy for twenty years. The 1988 report, *The Years Ahead: A Policy for the Elderly*, has been the subsequent basis of official policy for older people in Ireland. The 1994 report, *Shaping a Healthier Future: A Strategy for Effective Healthcare in the 1990s*, was concerned with the overall shape of the health services, but had particular relevance for services for ill and dependent older people. For today's older people, the range of services now provided — covering income maintenance, health care, domiciliary care and residential care — is wider than any previous generation of older people could have visualised.

Until the 1960s, social service provision for older people was limited to a number of core income maintenance schemes and a rather stigmatised system of residential care for infirm and chronically ill elderly people with limited means. The County Home had been endorsed by a White Paper in 1951 as the appropriate setting for the aged and chronic sick, and a programme of expansion and reconstruction was carried out that resulted in the creation of 2,195 new or replacement beds. The *Care of the Aged* report signalled a move away from institutionalised care to care in the community, based on the belief that 'it is better, and probably much cheaper, to help the aged to live in the community than to provide for them in hospitals or other institutions' (Interdepartmental Committee on the Aged, 1968: 13).

The County Home model of institutional care was to be replaced by a number of different types of geriatric/welfare facilities. Despite the trend for new facilities to be much smaller in size and part of a continuum of care, the legacy of the policies of the 1950s and 1960s — where all dependent older people were gathered together in one County Home — can still be seen in the high number of large, institutional geriatric hospitals and homes in all parts of the country.

The *Care of the Aged* report, while emphasising the dependency and vulner- ability of older people, saw the need for a comprehensive range of medical, nursing and social-support services that would enable people to be cared for in their own homes for a longer period of their lives. Its recommendations in relation to community-based health and welfare services were implemented through the new Health Boards set up in 1972.

Community care teams made up of medical, nursing, social care and para-medical staff were established in each Community Care Area to provide medical, nursing and social support to vulnerable groups, including older people. The voluntary sector was identified as having a key role to play in providing these services, in partnership with families and the state, particularly in personal care services and in organising social activities, including home visiting. The philosophy was one of encouraging a humane approach to older people with incapacities of one kind or another. It involved the development of community-based social services, more caring attitudes among the public, and encouragement of the unpaid work of voluntary groups and organisations.

While there is a strong sense in this approach of the dignity of each individual older person, there is little sense of older people having a contribution to make other than a suggestion that they could become involved as volunteers in social clubs. At the same time, the fact that housing continued to be the responsibility of local authorities meant that different bodies were now responsible for housing older people and for meeting their health and welfare needs. Voluntary organisations on behalf of older people grew significantly in the 1970s facilitated by grants provided by the Health Boards for the establishment of Social Service Councils and Care of the Aged committees.

The *Years Ahead* report was compiled by a Working Party on Services for the Elderly, appointed by the Minister for Health in 1986, and came to constitute official policy for the development of services for older people. Its terms of reference were:

- to enable the elderly person to live at home, where possible, at an optimum level of health and independence.
- to enable those who cannot live at home to receive treatment, rehabilitation and care in accommodation and in an environment as near as possible to home. (DoH, 1988: ix)

The four main principles of the report were:

- to maintain older people in dignity and independence at home in accordance with the wishes of older people as expressed in many research studies.
- to restore to independence at home those older people who become ill or dependent.
- to encourage and support the care of older people in their own community by family, neighbours and voluntary bodies in every way possible.
- to provide a high quality of hospital and residential care for older people when they can no longer be maintained in dignity and independence at home. (DoH, 1988: 38)

The *Years Ahead* report advocated a strong service-delivery model. There were over 120 recommendations relating to health and social care services for older people at home, in the community, in hospitals and in long-term care. The role of key health professionals and social care providers was emphasised, and considerable detail provided on staff levels, bed numbers and organisational structures. This focus reflects the growth in professional health and welfare services since the publication of the *Care of the Aged* report.

A challenge to this service-oriented approach came in the Health Strategy of 1994. It made two key points: first, one cannot assume that services have an inherent value — it is necessary to evaluate the health and social gain they produce; second, it is essential to have consumer participation in the planning of services and in ensuring the accountability of service providers.

Four years later, in 1998, the National Council on Ageing and Older People [NCAOP] in association with the Department of Health and Children launched a health promotion strategy for older people — *Adding Years to Life and Life to Years*. The strategy addresses health promotion for older people, in its broadest sense, acknowledging the impact of environmental and social factors on the quality of life of older people, and the contribution that many sectors outside the health sector make. The strategy aims to evaluate new initiatives designed to promote healthy ageing and to identify and promote models of good practice. An interesting initiative undertaken by the NCAOP in 2003 was the development of a Healthy Ageing Database.

## SERVICE DELIVERY

*The Years Ahead* had upheld the principles contained in the *Care of the Aged* in relation to caring for older people in their own homes and in the community. There was an emphasis on achieving 'dignity and independence' for older people through a service-delivery model that involved Health Board professionals in partnership with voluntary providers and families. In relation to meeting the needs of dependent older people, a flexible range of options was proposed involving sheltered housing, daycare, respite, convalescence and long-term care.

The community hospital was seen to have the potential to provide a range of interventions. The report saw merit in having a mix of public, private and voluntary beds for the care of the dependent older person, but there was little reflection on what type of life might be aspired to, particularly in private homes where statutory regulations are minimalist. The 1994 Health Strategy had emphasised consumer responsiveness, and Health Boards have taken various initiatives to empower older people to contribute to an improvement in services.

General initiatives include the introduction of complaints/appeals procedures, a Charter of Rights for residents of Health Board nursing homes, and the introduction of information handbooks in Health Board hospitals and residential homes. Individual Health Boards have also initiated research and pilot projects in relation to patient advocacy in hospitals and nursing homes and running leadership-skills training programmes in day centres and clubs.

## RESIDENTIAL CARE

Consideration of the provision of long-stay care for older people who can no longer be cared for at home for social and medical reasons gives insight into perceptions of the life course and, in particular, the needs of and possibilities for very frail and incapacitated older people. The term 'the fourth age' has been used in the literature to define an 'era of final dependence, decrepitude and death' (Laslett 1989: 77). This concept has been challenged as another form of the age stratification that the term 'the third age' had attempted to dismantle (Schuller and Young 1991: 181). Nonetheless, we must acknowledge a tendency to distance the very old, particularly where they have many infirmities; it has been suggested that it is a particular challenge to construct a positive image of deep old age that will help us to detach ourselves from the emotional response of aversion and disgust (Featherstone and Hepworth, 1990: 273). We will examine the different types of long-term care before considering the quality of care that infirm older people receive.

Care of the Aged had differentiated between four types of institutions providing extended care for older persons: general hospitals; geriatric assessment units; long-stay units; and welfare homes. Twenty years later, The Years Ahead recommended a wider range of facilities to meet the low- to medium-dependency needs of frail older people. These included sheltered housing with back-up daycare facilities; boarding out of older people under the supervision of the Health Boards; multi-purpose homes (as developed in Donegal); and community hospitals with a range of services to include assessment and rehabilitation, respite, daycare, short-term care and long-term care.

While The Years Ahead clearly recognised the role that private nursing homes play in caring for older people, and the right of older people to avail of such care as a matter of choice, its recommendations were confined to a licensing and inspection system as a safeguard for residents. It also recommended that Health Boards would provide subvention for patients assessed as being in need of continuing care. However, in reality, a lack of clarity on entitlement to a public long-stay place for older people too incapacitated to live at home, and the uneven provision of public extended-care facilities, has resulted in great inequalities between those allocated public beds and those who can pay for a private nursing home.

## LEGISLATION AND IMPROVED QUALITY OF CARE

Introduction of a regulation and inspection system under the Health (Nursing Homes) Act 1990 has improved the level of care provided in private nursing homes (EHB 1999b: 86). Since the introduction of this legislation, the role of the private sector in particular has been expanding; for example, in the Eastern Regional Health Authority [ERHA] area, private nursing-home beds are contracted by the Health Boards to meet demand. The care and welfare regulations are largely concerned with medical, nursing and health-and-safety standards, but there is no requirement in relation to social, recreational, creative or spiritual needs of older people, and no participative role envisaged for the residents themselves. Furthermore, the statutory sector is exempt from the quality controls and inspections that apply only to the private and voluntary sectors.

To overcome some of these criticisms, a voluntary *Code of Practice* was agreed by a group representing nursing homes, Health Boards, carers and others with experience in the care of older people, and published by the Department of Health (DoH, 1995a). It is designed to encourage nursing-home owners and staff to go beyond the minimum standards set by the Act and Regulations, with the aim of promoting a good quality of life for residents in nursing homes. The *Code* offers a set of principles and recommended practices, based on a holistic view of the person and the vision that life-enhancing possibilities can be created for a person at any age. While a study carried out on behalf of the NCAOP suggested that the code has received little attention (NCAOP 2000: 11), it does provide a blueprint for future policy initiatives. The NCAOP published a framework for fostering quality in long-term care, which recommended the introduction of national minimum quality standards (NCAOP, 2000). The achievement of such standards would have clear implications for the training of staff working in long-term care facilities.

## SOCIAL CARE SETTINGS

There are approximately 17,000 older people in long-term residential care in Ireland, representing about 5 per cent of the population of people over 65 (NCAOP, 2000). Private nursing homes are the most common long-stay settings, followed by Health Board geriatric homes and hospitals. Other settings are voluntary geriatric homes and hospitals, district or community hospitals and welfare homes (DoH 1997). The profile of residents in long-stay institutions shows that almost 70 per cent are aged 80 years or more, while almost 40 per cent are aged over 85 years (NCAOP, 2000).

Statistics from the Department of Health (DoH 1997) indicate that nursing-home residents are not as dependent as residents of long-stay geriatric hospitals and homes. Seventy-seven per cent of residents of old-style geriatric hospitals and homes were rated as having high or maximum dependency levels, compared with 60 per cent of voluntary and private nursing-home residents. Having high numbers of dependent residents together in large institutions poses particular challenges in providing a stimulating environment. Research carried out by the Dublin Institute of Technology (Gallagher and Kennedy, 2003) has shown the difficulty of providing any meaningful diversionary activity in large institutions, given existing staffing resources.

A research study (SHB, 1999) by the Southern Health Board of the attitudes, perceptions and preferences of older persons to their continuing care environments concluded that more activities needed to be provided for residents. Activities tended to be limited to television, radio and reading, and occupational therapy was not available at all in one institution. While residents were generally satisfied with their care environments, the study concluded that their expectations were often low on entering long-term care, and there was a certain passivity and forbearance in their acceptance of such a limited choice of recreational activities. These findings echoed those of O'Connor and Walsh (1986) who carried out a national survey of voluntary and private nursing homes. This study found that while residents expected their physical needs to be met, the majority had low expectations regarding their psycho-social needs.

Two models of public residential care that have become increasingly popular since *The Years Ahead* are community hospitals and community units. They provide a sharp contrast to the old-style geriatric hospital/home in size, range of services and emphasis on health and social gain. Community hospitals are designed to provide a broad range of services, including long-stay care; assessment and rehabilitation; convalescent care; day hospital and/or daycare services; respite care; and information, advice and support for those caring for older persons at home. The community unit is favoured by the ERHA to meet the non-acute medical and social needs of dependent older people. Community units are small nursing units catering for up to 50 persons, and they have a daycare centre attached. They differ from the traditional model in most respects, including: location (less isolated), architectural style, provision of individualised programmes of animation, a wider range of recreational activities on offer, and the sense of being part of the community. Of particular significance is the employment of a full-time Activities Nurse in each unit.

A proposal in the Eastern Health Board's 10-year action plan to phase out the old and outdated facilities and replace them with community units appears not to have been matched by political or public interest. There are only six community units in the ERHA, though the plan recommended the establishment of 29 by the year 2008. A review (Ruddle et al., 1997) of *The Years Ahead* reached a similar conclusion: the authors claimed that the development of community hospitals had been slow and uneven around the country because of totally inadequate funding. This indicates how aspirational many policy documents are.

Voluntary homes managed by religious orders and charitable groups tend to be smaller than Health Board geriatric institutions, but bigger than private nursing homes. On average, there are 134 beds in Health Board hospitals and homes, 44 beds in voluntary homes, and 25 beds in the private nursing homes (DoH, 1997). St Gabriel's is a voluntary nursing home in Raheny in Dublin. Purpose-built and opened in 1991 by a religious order of nuns, the Poor Servants of the Mother of God, it replaced an older residential home in the inner city. It does not have a specific catchment area, since admissions are determined by the management, but most residents come from the adjoining areas. It has 52 individual en-suite rooms on two storeys. Residents on the first floor are reasonably mobile, while those on the ground floor are more incapacitated. Each room is individually arranged by the resident with memorabilia, including photographs, pictures on the wall, and items of personal furniture. The day rooms are spacious and bright and there is a central conservatory. The use of glass creates a bright and sometimes sunny interior. In addition to a dining room, there are small kitchens attached to the sitting rooms, where residents may make a cup of tea. There is an Oratory where daily Mass is said and attended by both residents and daycare users. An activity programme, run by a part-time Activities Co-ordinator, is posted up each week. Activities include Sonas (a multi-sensorial programme of exercise to music), bingo, reminiscence programme, quizzes, pampering sessions and computers. St Gabriel's relies on volunteers to provide some of its activities, including reception staff, fundraising and visitation of residents who have limited mobility and few visitors.

## DAYCARE CENTRES

Daycare for older people is provided in daycare centres or day centres when a person needs support with daily living or is socially isolated. The main objectives of day centres, as set out in *The Years Ahead*, are:

- To provide a service such as a midday meal, a bath and a variety of other social services;
- To promote social contact among older people and prevent loneliness;
- To relieve caring relatives, particularly those who have to go to work, of the responsibility of caring for older people during the day;
- To provide social stimulation in a safe environment for older people.

Convery (1987), in a study of day centres in the Eastern Health Board area, found a lack of coherence in aims, structures, funding, range of services available and monitoring and evaluation criteria. She argued that day centres could accomplish much more with older people, and their social value could be greater. She specifically criticised existing services for:

- Supporting a dependent mentality
- Segregating elderly users
- Making little allowance for the needs of different client groups and individuals
- Scarcity of professional staff
- Absence of training for voluntary staff
- Lack of formalised funding procedures.

Gallagher and Kennedy (2003) indicate that a lack of consistency in daycare provision still existed over a decade after Convery's study.

Daycare centres provide a fuller range of therapeutic and social services, such as bathing, physiotherapy and chiropody, and are usually attached to Health Board geriatric hospitals, voluntary nursing homes or other long-stay facilities. They are staffed by paid staff, including nurse, care attendant and driver, and some have the part-time services of a social worker and physiotherapist. Day centres are managed mainly by locally based voluntary/parish groups and provide a meal and a more limited, mainly recreational, programme. They are often staffed exclusively by volunteers.

Healthy Ageing initiatives, that include an emphasis on physical fitness, are now being introduced to many day centres and daycare centres. The *Go for Life* campaign is a joint initiative of Age and Opportunity and the Irish Sports Council. It promotes physical exercise and sport activity to suit all ages and levels of fitness.

St Gabriel's Daycare Centre was opened in 1994 in the premises of St Gabriel's nursing home. It operates every weekday and offers a full programme of daycare one day a week to older people who live alone and are considered in need of social interaction, or whose carers need a break. Public health nurses are the principal source of referral. Some of the daycare users are in wheelchairs, some have had strokes, and some have a degree of senility, but most are able to look after their own daily care. Staff-members include a coordinator, care attendants and about ten volunteers. Bathing facilities are provided, together with a hot midday meal. Social activities include Sonas, bingo, reminiscence, quizzes and a sing-song. Staff-members make a special effort to mark the seasonal festivals of Christmas, Easter and Halloween. In 2003, there was a waiting list of 80 persons for this daycare centre.

An interesting initiative in daycare was the establishment of a daycare centre attached to a sheltered housing complex at Clareville Court in Glasnevin, Dublin, in 2000. This involved inter-agency cooperation between Dublin City Council, responsible for social housing for older people, and the Health Board. In addition to treatment and showering facilities, there is a full meals service and a wide range of activities to suit what residents themselves want. The ethos of the daycare centre is that the service users are encouraged to decide on a programme of activities and to be involved in decisions about the running of the centre.

In Co. Donegal, there are many examples of day centres attached to sheltered housing, which are models of good practice and reflect the input of committed volunteers and good cooperation between locally based volunteers and the local health board (the NWHB). For example, the St Colmcille Daycare Centre in Clonmanny, which covers a large catchment area, can cater for up to 50 people per day, and accommodate people on all five days of the working week if they choose to attend. In addition, there are 20 units of sheltered housing in the complex and, more recently, a 10-bed high-support unit was added. This offers a continuum of care and support. As well as provision of meals and a laundry service, there is an emphasis on purposive recreational activities, including art and craft work, cards and bingo.

## QUALITY INITIATIVES IN RESIDENTIAL CARE

The development of the community units in Dublin in the late 1990s provided management with an opportunity to develop a programme of recreational and social activities in consultation with staff and residents. Such discussions revealed many ideas and skills that could be used to help meet the needs and interests of residents, including aromatherapy, Sonas, gardening, art, dancing, local history and ideas about small tasks that the residents could do themselves, such as watering plants, bringing around a library trolley, and setting and clearing the table. Following consultation, several initiatives were taken, including a small gardening project, purchase of games, introduction of art sessions, membership of a local library for large-print and taped books, introduction of pets, playing taped music, and a tape recording of the rosary played in the Oratory. Considerable thought was given by management to ways to forge links between the Community Unit and the local community. The local Residents' Association and the Active Retirement group were invited to come and visit. An introductory letter was sent to local primary and secondary schools which were invited to come and visit, and perhaps undertake a project involving dance or music. Contact was also made with dance and music schools nearby (Hurson Kelly, 1998).

These ideas have influenced the whole approach to care in the six community units that have so far been opened in the Eastern Region. Cuan Ros Community Unit, Navan Road, was opened in 1996. It is a purpose-built unit with 36 long-stay beds, 6 respite beds and 6 convalescent beds. A full-time Activities Nurse facilitates a wide variety of activities including aromatherapy, quizzes, Sonas, massage, and celebration of birthdays and other festivals. Links with the community are maintained through visitation by local St Vincent de Paul volunteers, Legion of Mary and Transition Year students from local secondary schools. Residents recently participated in an Art in Health pilot project in conjunction with the Arts Council and the local health board.

Projects involving the introduction of Arts activities in care settings have been undertaken in recent years in order to enrich the care environment and provide opportunities for older people to develop their creativity and to learn different skills. An interesting training initiative, 'Arts for Older People in Care Settings', was undertaken by a partnership involving the Midland Health Board, Laois County Council and Age and Opportunity. The initiative was designed to enhance the quality of life of long-stay residents, by providing stimulation that was regular, reliable and part of the normal routine. This was to be achieved by developing the necessary facilitation skills in the staff-members themselves, to bring art and drama to residential care settings in the course of the daily routines.

A pilot training course commenced in October 2000 which was open to all the nursing and care staff of the Care Centres for older people in the Midland Health Board. In the first course, there were twenty-five participants drawn from eight Care Centres in the Midland Health Board. The staff participants learned practical skills by painting, making collages, working with clay, doing role plays and developing characters. They learned how to facilitate art and drama sessions, and then applied their skills by creating an activity with their resident group. One example was a dramatised wedding ceremony that involved dressing up, reminiscing and role play. Another project involved forming a céilí group for singing, dancing and music. An evaluation report (MHB, 2002) gave positive feedback from participants, facilitators, residents and Directors of Nursing. Among the benefits reported by the staff participants themselves were increased confidence, discovery of their own creativity, new ideas, greater empathy with residents, and raised awareness of the abilities and talents of the residents. Feedback from clients included an expanded range of activities open to them, an increase in communication and interaction with one another and with staff, discovery/rediscovery of their talents and skills, higher levels of morale, and a new sense of social inclusion/community. One of the challenges identified in the evaluation report was that of including the most dependent residents in arts activities, and this was a specific goal of the second level of training.

## SOCIAL CARE MODEL

There is a growing recognition that services for the dependent elderly should follow other services, such as those for people with intellectual and physical disabilities, in adopting a social care model in preference to a medical one in meeting their needs (see Chapter 19). Unlike other services, residential nursing homes and daycare centres for older people have developed and expanded in recent decades with little input from the emergent social care profession (Gallagher and Kennedy, 2003). The largest group of employees in residential care settings are nurses and care attendants. A medical model could be said to dominate, rather than a social care approach. The characteristics of a medical model are a focus on problems and deficits, institutional provision of care, with routines designed for efficiency and little attention to individuality, autonomy or normal daily living. In contrast, a social care model would aim to:

- Explore attitudes and expectations within a value framework which stresses individualisation and normalisation;
- Develop effective communication techniques and use of creative activities;
- Use space to bring life in from outside and bring residents out;
- Use older people themselves as a resource and involve them in decision making;
- See social emotional and spiritual needs as on a par with physical needs.

A social care model can be observed in the move away from large institutional settings with a hospital atmosphere to smaller homely units, and the increasing emphasis on purposive activity and links with the community. But the implications for training have not been worked out, given the traditional staffing structures of such services. Some tentative suggestions as to the way training could be developed for this sector have been put forward (Gallagher and Kennedy, 2003).

## PERSPECTIVES ON AGEING

A social care model needs to be underpinned by critical social thinking that challenges existing presumptions about what older people can expect from life, and that can imagine new possibilities for life-enhancing experiences in the older years. Age stratification can confine people to a straitjacket of narrow social and recreational activities resulting from presumptions about older people being slow, rigid, un-enterprising, incapable of innovation, and intellectually limited by reason of their age alone. Critical social gerontology has argued that there is no one way of ageing or one pace of ageing. The creation of new language such as the 'third age' can itself help to improve the social image and hence the self-image of 'the old' (Schuller and Young, 1991: 165). Research that examines the lived experiences of older adults can also contribute to the body of knowledge that informs social care perspectives.

Promotion of healthy ageing policies was recommended in the 1994 Health Strategy, and many health-promotion initiatives directed to the older person have been undertaken with the assistance of the NCAOP, Age and Opportunity and other voluntary bodies. In addition to a focus on the individual and their lifestyle, health-promotion programmes recognise the importance of the environment, both physical and social, as having a major impact on health status and quality of life:

> The physical environment is important, including housing, transport, clean air and access to sunlight, as well as freedom from threats of violence or other abuse. Access to an adequate income is fundamental to the mainte-nance of health. Social interaction and involvement of older people in their neighbourhoods and in voluntary groups can also add to the quality of life for older people as well as making an important contribution to the community. Support for carers who may themselves be old, can also improve the environment in which older dependent people live. (EHB, 1999b: 23)

It is clear that positive ageing is enhanced by attention to suitable housing, a safe environment and amenities and facilities for social and recreational activities. The contribution that older people make and can make in their own communities is increasingly being recognised. Traditional ideas about older people as 'good causes', while worthy and helpful in past decades in eliciting a humane response to deprivation, have been challenged by groups representing older people, who rightly aspire to a more participative role in society. In a recent report on volunteering in Ireland, a recommendation was that older people be targeted as recruits:

> There is great potential in older people given their accumulated skills and experience. They may benefit with a healthier lifestyle and more enjoyable life, while society benefits from greater social cohesion and intergenerational solidarity. (NCV, 2002: 72)

Services for dependent older people have developed from the institutional model of the County Home — still dominant up to the 1960s — to smaller more homely units where routines are designed to be more normal, where stimulating recreation is provided, and where links with the outside community are cultivated. Expectations in relation to what a dependent older person might expect in a residential unit have changed from an emphasis on physical care, to meeting psycho-social, spiritual and emotional needs. There are many innovative examples of good practice involving the arts in care settings; participation by service users themselves in the programmes provided in care centres; and more inter-agency cooperation in creating a better environment for older people in the community.

Underpinning all these developments must be a vision of what the possibilities are for living a full life during the latter stages of the life course, or of what constitutes good human functioning for the older person, whatever degree of dependency they may experience. Challenges remain in relation to how best practice can be introduced into private nursing homes and the old-style geriatric institutions, which are at opposite ends of the spectrum in terms of size and social background of residents. A key issue is that of education and training in relation to how best to promote a social care model in work with older people.

# 21

# Community Childcare

## Susan McKenna-McElwee & Teresa Brown

## OVERVIEW

It is a truism that when the child comes into contact with human services, the family does too. This chapter is written by two community childcare workers [CCWs], who now lecture on a social care programme. It traces the historical roots of the discipline of community childcare and comments critically on current practice. It examines the place of CCWs in multidisciplinary teams, particularly as they interact with social workers. It concludes with two case studies that describe the typical activities carried out by CCWs.

## INTRODUCTION

Community Childcare Workers are uniquely placed within the Irish social care system as they have a very specific remit to work within an ecological perspective with the entire family and the child or young person. CCWs adopt what Garfat and McElwee (2001) have referred to as a child and youth care approach to social care, by working and being directly alongside children in troubled and troubling times. Thus, the work of the CCW takes place in a variety of settings. The CCW could start work in the morning in a satellite centre, then drive to a family therapy centre, then on to a family visit and then on to a three-way meeting — and all with the same service user!

Community childcare is a career option much sought after by students, as it is seen to provide, perhaps, the greatest level of autonomy in social care practice. There are only 85 CCWs in Ireland, despite the fact that a quarter of our young people live in poverty. Although the profession is relatively new, it has responded to many changes, including changes in the social context of the work, in the legislative framework, and in working methods and conditions.

Community childcare workers are employed by Health Boards. The essential qualification for the post is a BA degree (formerly National Diploma) in Applied Social Studies. CCWs are directly responsible to the Senior Social Worker and must be no less than 21 years of age. Over 90 per cent of CCWs are female, 22 per cent hold honours degrees, 49 per cent hold ordinary degrees/diplomas and 34 per cent have been employed in their posts for more than five years (Ryan, 2000).

Community childcare, then, has the highest levels of qualification of any field of social care and is almost exclusively female dominated.

The South Eastern Health Board [SEHB] *Annual Review of Child Care Services* (1998) outlines the position of community childcare workers by noting that they:

> have become well established and valued members of the Community Care Service. Their particular professional training equips them to work directly with children and adolescents. Their remit includes providing therapeutic and developmental programmes to children identified as having particular needs, such as the need for regular and planned intellectual stimulation; the need for assistance in changing problematic behaviour; or the need for support in adjusting to significant family traumas. The Community Child Care Workers also provide encouragement and skills training to parents and to foster carers who are challenged by the demands of caring for children. They regularly arrange and assist with access visits between parents and their children in care. They help children who are planning to leave a care placement to prepare for their return home or for independent living. (SEHB, 1998)

As the job title suggests, most of the work conducted by the CCW is done in the community, be it in the client's home, a satellite health centre or other agreed venue. The CCW is normally assigned cases through the social work team leader; she then makes contact with the relevant professionals (if any) involved in the case and makes herself familiar with the history/background information of the case by reading files and relevant documentation. A meeting is established and, in some cases, other professionals who may be involved in the case, such as a psychologist or a social worker, accompany the CCW. The schedule of work to be engaged in is discussed and outlined and arrangements are made for future appointments.

Graham (2002) has identified nine key task areas for the Irish social care practitioner, including 'organiser, planner, team member, attachment builder, leader, liaison person, programmer, counsellor and therapeutic teacher'. The community childcare worker, at different times, plays all of these roles. She has to provide a network to statutory services, maintain the interests of the child and young person at all times and work across a number of professional interfaces. In all of this, she must win and keep the trust of the child and family for this is her key task in relationship construction. Table 21.1 indicates the types of work completed in one Health Board region.

**Table 21.1. Community Childcare Worker Areas and Tasks (SEHB area, 1997)**

| Total 1997 | Carlow / Kilkenny | Waterford | Wexford | South Tipperary | Total 1997 | Total 1996 | % change |
|---|---|---|---|---|---|---|---|
| New Families Referred | 32 | 54 | 18 | 22 | 123 | 124 | 1.61 |
| **Reason for Referral** | | | | | | | |
| Child at risk | 4 | 11 | 1 | 0 | 16 | 13 | 23.08 |
| Child abuse | | | | | | | |
| (a) Physical | 0 | 2 | 1 | 0 | 3 | 2 | 50.00 |
| (b) Neglect | 0 | 0 | 0 | 0 | 0 | 3 | – |
| (c) Sexual | 3 | 7 | 3 | 0 | 13 | 12 | 8.33 |
| Homeless/housing | 0 | 0 | 0 | 0 | 0 | 2 | – |
| Financial | 1 | 0 | 0 | 0 | 1 | 0 | – |
| Domestic violence | 2 | 0 | 2 | 0 | 4 | 4 | 0.00 |
| Single parent | 0 | 1 | 1 | 2 | 4 | 13 | (–69.23) |
| Parent not coping | 8 | 12 | 5 | 4 | 29 | 28 | 3.57 |
| Respite | 0 | 2 | 1 | 0 | 3 | 1 | 200.00 |
| Other | 14 | 19 | 4 | 16 | 53 | 46 | 15.22 |
| **Services Provided** | | | | | | | |
| Access visits | 48 | 286 | 37 | 38 | 409 | 445 | (–8.09) |
| Aftercare visits | 222 | 328 | 305 | 41 | 896 | 842 | 6.41 |
| Visits to family homes | 532 | 840 | 135 | 128 | 1,635 | 2,721 | (–39.91) |
| Direct work with children | 109 | 356 | 25 | 128 | 618 | – | |
| Protection work | 30 | 59 | 0 | 15 | 104 | – | |
| Parenting | 48 | 92 | 8 | 49 | 197 | – | |
| Other | 239 | 615 | 26 | 30 | 910 | 1,857 | (–51.00) |
| Case load @ end of month | 35 | 56 | 15 | 15 | 121 | 121 | 0.00 |
| No. families discharged | 43 | 33 | 4 | 31 | 111 | 103 | 7.77 |

*Source:* SEHB, 1998.

The community childcare profession has encountered and responded to many challenges over the past number of years (McElwee, 2003b). These challenges have often created situations where the practitioner felt undervalued and isolated. But it is clear that CCWs are in a much better place than they were at the end of the 1990s.

## THE JOURNEY OF THE COMMUNITY CHILDCARE WORKER

As far back as 1970, the stage was set for the introduction of the community childcare worker. The Kennedy Report emphasised that families should be supported and strategies and policies should facilitate this process. Ten years later, the *Task Force Report* identified how this process could be achieved, suggesting that: 'a specially trained worker could be instrumental in enabling some deprived children to continue living at home' (*Task Force Report*, 1981: 21).

This concept was further supported when, in 1985, the Task Force recommended that professional childcare services should be provided for children and families in their own homes. The Task Force also recommended specific professionals who could provide these services. It was the early 1990s before the above policy recommendations were executed, and CCWs commenced taking what we would suggest was their rightful place on the community care stage.

The 1990s was a decade marked by a number of developments that have proved hugely influential in creating and defining the role of the community childcare worker. The Child Care Act (1991) and the *Children First Guidelines* (DoHC, 1999) moved the child centre stage, and these were followed by the *National Children's Strategy* (2000) and the Children's Act (2001) at the start of this decade.

The early challenge facing the community childcare worker was to put into practice the 'working together' concept identified by the 1980 Task Force report and to create a role within a team that would reflect the principles and values of their own profession. This assumes that community childcare is a 'profession' in the true sense of that word — the issue of professionalism is explored in Chapter 4.

The 'working together' concept read well on paper, but when translated into practice proved somewhat difficult. A report by the IMPACT trade union (1998) noted that the rapid development of the position of CCWs was not preceded by any policy document, planning or forethought. This contributed to the role being allowed to develop in a haphazard and ad-hoc way that depended on the personality of the manager or practitioners rather than according to any clear definition or guidelines.

Although all the community childcare workers in the IMPACT survey reported that they received regular supervision and were relatively happy with it, all stated that they would prefer to be supervised by someone of the same profession.

Within the career structure area, there appear to be three issues:

- Many CCWs are employed in a temporary capacity: this can lead to lack of motivation and uncertainty, as they do not feel part of the team. This does not lend itself to comprehensive planning. Nor can such staff avail of the entitlements of permanency such as career breaks, holidays and better pay scales;
- Community childcare suffers in some respects from a lack of resources. The majority of practitioners felt that office space and equipment were not sufficient. They were content with the level of administrative support that they were receiving and that their budget was adequate;
- The majority of CCWs receive training based on individual needs and in-service training but reported that they did not have a high level of input into the type or content of the training received (Clarke and O'Carroll, 2001).

## SOCIAL WORKERS AND SOCIAL CARE PRACTITIONERS

The position of the community childcare worker on social work teams has not been without compromise. Various studies have endeavoured to examine the relationship between social workers and social care practitioners (see Chapters 1 and 17). Norton (1999) studied the working relationship between social workers and care practitioners and found that 56 per cent of social workers and 53 per cent of care practitioners did not have a good working relationship. Social workers suggested that the poor working relationship resulted from their lack of under-standing of the care worker role. This finding was further supported by Gallagher and O'Toole who found a lack of understanding between the two professions (1999). Corcoran sums up the relationship as follows:

> The resistance of the two professional groups vis à vis one another is usually related through anecdotal accounts of lack of understanding of each other's working conditions, inequalities of power and status as a result of the different styles of training between the professions. (Corcoran 1999: 14)

It is clear that particular structures and systems exist to facilitate and value the diversity of professions working in the community care area. But it is important to state that the current organisational structure of Childcare and Family Support Services is based on the Social Work Department model. This structure has essentially remained unchanged since the establishment of the Health Boards. As a consequence, community childcare incorporation into the community care team must be described as inadequate. This does not help to create an environment where social workers and childcare practitioners can work together effectively.

Coming from a practice background, we are aware that multidisciplinary work is complex (see Chapter 14). Charles and Stevenson (1990) outline some reasons for this complexity:

- Differences in background and training
- Differences within and between professionals
- Status and power
- Professional and organisational priorities
- Structures, systems and administration.

Understanding of the difficulties in working together was not enough. Community childcare workers did not want to be viewed simply as part of a problem — instead they worked on becoming part of the solution. Creating a voice was their first step towards being heard. They networked with colleagues across different Health Board areas and appointed a community childcare representative within the Irish Association of Social Workers. As well as having a belief in their own professional value, they were in a position to lobby and create some of the necessary conditions for working together between disciplines in human services (McElwee, 2003b).

Challenging the status quo has led to many positive changes for community childcare workers, though these are largely confined to attitudinal rather than structural changes. Community childcare workers and social workers now have a clearer understanding of each other's roles and realise that no single discipline or approach has all the answers. As Gilligan (1991: xiii) has noted: 'no professional grouping has a monopoly of knowledge or skill in relation to the needs of children'.

The first step in the process of working together was 'inclusion', as identified from the social work perspective by Powell:

> The big challenge that lies ahead is to be inclusive of cognate professional groups such as . . . social care workers. They have much to offer an evolving profession in terms of methodologies and traditions that offers hope as we look towards the challenge of the new millennium. (Powell, 1999: 4)

Structural changes have imposed many limits on certain areas of community childcare professional development.

Two areas that continue to cause some concern to CCWs are supervision and prevention. This concern was evident in findings of a study completed by Clarke and O'Carroll (2001) where a general lack of dissatisfaction was expressed with 'how' and 'who' delivered their supervision.

## PREVENTION

Clarke and O'Carroll's (2001) research with community child care workers found that an issue of concern for the CCW was the amount of time spent on preventative work. CCWs reported that only a quarter of their time was spent doing such work. In reality, community childcare workers spend much of their time responding to crises, leaving little time to formulate and establish prevention strategies for their clients.

Gilligan's (1991) view on prevention is that it is a concept that is widely supported but not so widely understood. Fifteen years after he made this remark, it is still felt by practitioners at the coalface. In the past, the Health Boards have been accused of providing a 'fire brigade' service to family issues: they arrive on the scene when the issue has escalated into a crisis.

Table 21.2 illustrates the four levels of prevention that CCWs are involved in on a daily basis. Limited resources and opportunities dictate that their intervention is less focused on the primary level than it ought to be. This is in spite of the fact that academics and practitioners have emphasised the value to the community and society of allocating resources to both the primary and secondary level of prevention. Community childcare workers are trying to move away from providing a sticking-plaster solution to case management and to focus on what is the rationale of the position — to work in a preventative manner with young people and families.

## Table 21.2. Four Levels of Prevention

| Key Characteristics | Primary | Secondary | Tertiary | Quaternary |
|---|---|---|---|---|
| Practice Ideology | Developmental Change system rather than people Empowerment | Welfare Help for the client Assessment of need | Judicial Rescue the victim Punish the villain | Judicial Maintenance Multi-agency involvement |
| Stage of Problem | Low or containable risk Problems common to many Citizens rather than clients | Low–medium risk but perceived need Acute crisis or early stage of problem Short-term client | Chronic, well-established problems High risks of harm to self or others High need for Protection of child Perceptions of parental need may be low | Acute risk of harm Acute need for protection of child |
| Major Unit of Need | Localities Vulnerable groups | Nuclear family | Individual family members perceived as a problematic or in need of rescue | Family — child |
| Principal Targets for Intervention | Welfare institutions Community networks Social policy | Family systems Support networks Welfare institutions | Personal change | Child |
| Objectives of Intervention | Reallocation of power Redistribution of power Increased rights for disadvantaged groups | Enhanced family functioning Enhanced support networks Family's increased awareness and motivation to make use of existing resources Welfare institutions more responsive to people's needs | Better adjusted, less deviant individuals Self-supporting families | To return the child home Family rehabilitation |
| Dominant Mode of Practice of CCW | Group work Parenting programmes Community networks Peer support groups for children Parent support groups After-school groups Women's support group Children's activity groups Teenage groups Developmental services aimed at children in the community | Parenting programmes Outreach work Contract work Group work with children Direct work with children, assessment of need Professional support for children and their families | Assessment of need Multidisciplinary work Co-work in child protection Court work – preparation of reports Therapeutic support Preparation for moves for children into and out of the system Court work Aftercare Conflict-resolution methods Supervision and observation of access | Short-term care Access Grief separation Personal identity Building and maintaining links with natural family Outreach Life-story book Work on self-esteem Community networking |

*Source*: IACW, 1996.

# CASE STUDIES

Two case studies illustrate the type of work CCWs typically engage in. Though based on real cases, the names and details have been changed to maintain confidentiality.

## CASE STUDY 1: THE CUMMINS FAMILY

| Family Relationship | Name | Age |
|---|---|---|
| Father | Pat | 45 |
| Mother | Bernadine | 44 |
| Children | Angela | 15 |
| | Matthew | 11 |
| | Mary | 5 |
| | Edel | 4 |
| | Janice | 18 months |

This family has been known to the Health Board Community Care Department since 1994. The family lives in a four-bedroom house in a large estate. The area social worker and family-support worker are in regular contact with the family. Concerns in relation to the mother's mental health have persisted since 1994. Pat has informed the social worker on frequent occasions that he finds it 'difficult to cope' with his wife's illness. Anonymous allegations have been made to the Health Board office referencing Pat's regular drinking patterns.

The children attend the local school and reports from the school are very positive, though it has come to light that Angela has been regularly absent from school.

In school, Angela has become withdrawn and, when confronted, has become very tearful and refuses to engage in discussion.

The social worker referred the above case to the community childcare worker. On reading the file, the CCW identified the issues that needed further exploration with Angela and her parents. The CCW and the social worker called to the Cummins home at a pre-arranged time and met with Angela and her parents. During this meeting, Angela appeared uneasy and responded to most questions with the reply, 'fine'. It was apparent at the meeting that Angela was not comfortable talking in the company of her parents, though she did agree to meeting with the CCW with a view to further involvement.

Mr and Mrs Cummins were very open to Angela's involvement with the services of the appointed community childcare worker, but were reluctant to have these sessions in the family home. It was agreed that the CCW would meet Angela in the health centre, in the short term.

→

The CCW's four sessions with Angela focused on the construction of a professional relationship. She appeared to have a difficulty with trust, citing examples of her home life. When the CCW explored with Angela her understanding of her involvement, she informed the CCW that it was 'to stop her going mad like her mother'. When absenteeism at school was explored, Angela informed the CCW that she missed school the days after her father had returned home intoxicated. Angela felt it was her 'job to sit with him when he was drunk so he would not drop his lit cigarette on the carpet'. Consequently, Angela was too tired to attend school on the days after these episodes

The following care plan was devised in consultation with Angela:

- Build relationship with Angela;
- Explore with Angela her understanding of mental illness;
- Identify programme that will focus on enhancing Angela's self-esteem;
- Meet social worker fortnightly to discuss case progress.

## CASE STUDY 2: MICHAEL

Michael (18) had been in care from the age of 12. His parents had separated when he was aged 10. His mother had a history of mental illness and had been hospitalised on several occasions. Michael's father had looked after him and his siblings. Both parents were unemployed. Social services became involved in the family when it was brought to their attention that the children were left in the house on numerous occasions without adult supervision.

When Michael's mother died, his family moved to a new area to make a 'fresh start'. They subsequently moved many times, never staying anywhere for any considerable period. When they did move back to their original address, social services were concerned with the level of care the children were receiving and it was decided that they should be taken into care. They were placed with two foster families.

Michael did not settle in his new environment and was moved to another foster family. At this point, Michael's behaviour was a cause for concern. It was believed that he had not dealt with the loss of his mother and felt very angry towards his father for 'abandoning him and his siblings'. These feelings manifested themselves in 'acting out' behaviour.

Michael was moved to residential care when he was 14. In retrospect, Michael has commented that he preferred residential care as he felt he didn't 'stick out', and 'wasn't the odd one out'. Staff in the unit had concerns about the way in which he dealt with anger. Michael engaged in the services that were provided for him; the staff had been working very closely with social services so as to aid Michael with his transition from care to independent living. Michael was looking forward to having 'his own place'.

→

A community childcare worker was assigned to Michael to support and assist him in his new environment. After a period, Michael started to have parties in his flat, and the landlord and neighbours voiced dissatisfaction with this. He started drinking and engaging in occasional drug-taking and, when provoked, he reacted by using force. The gardaí arrested him and he ended up before the courts.

The community childcare worker assigned to Michael started by 'befriending' him. Michael was aware of her role and the boundaries that accompanied it. At first, it was difficult to engage with Michael as he felt he did not need the support of any service. As his 'friends' came and went, an increase in his drink and alcohol intake was evident. Michael began to realise that there were unresolved issues that needed to be addressed.

As a community childcare worker, one must be aware of one's own limitations and the limitations of the role. In this case, Michael became, perhaps, over-reliant on the CCW. He would, for example, ring her daily, and was very distressed if she was unable to see him immediately. Meetings were arranged with various professionals, such as psychologists and addiction counsellors, which Michael did attend as the CCW provided transport. During this time, the CCW felt that she had developed a trusting relationship with Michael. He knew that the CCW would tell him the truth and would always maintain his best interests in any advocacy role.

In return, he engaged with the service and began to explore the issues that had lain dormant for many years. He felt angry at his mother for dying and leaving him, and he was angry at his father for abandoning him and not being there for him and his siblings. In dealing with such issues, Michael also had to take ownership of his own behaviour, his drug and alcohol misuse and violent outbursts when distressed. Utilising a therapeutic approach, he explored with the CCW issues such as anger management, separation and loss, self-esteem, relationships, sexuality and practical issues such as money management, finance, and how to manage as a homemaker.

With the CCW, Michael attended specific services for his addictions. The CCW maintained regular contact with the services so as to provide consistency for Michael. The various services provided different forums for discussion of Michael's case.

The CCW had succeeded in getting Michael a place on a computer course, and into independent accommodation. As he became more confident, he felt that he no longer needed the help of the addiction counsellors. He believed that he was at last able to make a fresh start and could move forward successfully. Michael and the CCW continued to meet regularly, as the CCW felt that she would be able to ascertain if he was in trouble, and also so that Michael felt that he was not entirely alone.

If you look again at Table 21.1 above, you can see that of seven 'services provided' by the community childcare team, the CCW in this case worked within four categories.

## CONCLUSION

This chapter has outlined and explored the development of the community childcare profession. There is no doubt that community childcare workers have made a valued contribution to service provision within Health Boards. This contribution can be attributed mainly to the skills and endeavours of the CCWs who have had to develop their roles in a very bureaucratic environment. It is also noteworthy that the Health Boards had to facilitate the development of these new positions by allowing the community childcare workers the space to be creative in their interventions.

The years ahead carry further challenges and opportunities. We would argue that the following three changes are essential if we are to respond to these in a way that ensures quality service provision:

- A career structure that will allow CCWs to manage the service
- Autonomy of practice
- The creation of additional community chidcare worker positions.

# 22

# Residential Childcare

John Byrne & John McHugh

## OVERVIEW

The aim of this chapter is twofold: first, to introduce the main influencing factors on the evolution of the childcare system in Ireland; second, to identify and discuss aspects of working in residential care settings (see Chapter 16 for a more extensive discussion of such work). The discussion is by no means exhaustive in either area; rather it is hoped that it will act as a stimulus towards further reading and research. Working with children in residential care is both challenging and rewarding. It may be beyond an individual, group, agency or government to provide perfect care in perfect settings, but all involved in residential care provision at whatever level must strive to develop and maintain the best possible care.

## TOWARDS AN UNDERSTANDING OF CHILDCARE

The Constitution of Ireland (Bunreacht na hÉireann) is the basis of Irish law. Article 42.5 clearly pledges the government to provide care for children who, for whatever reason, cannot be cared for by their parents:

> [I]n exceptional cases, where parents for physical or moral reasons fail in their duty towards their children, the state as guardian of the common good, by appropriate means shall endeavour to supply the place of the parents, but always with due regard for the natural and imprescriptible rights of the child.

This commitment has been elaborated on and further consolidated through the implementation of the Childcare Act of 1991 and the Irish government's ratification in 1989 of the United Nations Convention on the Rights of the Child. The government implements its commitment through the 'Children and Families Programme' of the Department of Health and Children.

Ferguson and O'Reilly (2001) state that social service intervention in a case of child protection is as a result of a concern being raised by an interested party. Upon notification to the Department of Health and Children, an investigation is carried out by a social worker in consultation with a social work team. Where further investigation and/or intervention is necessary, the focus is always on attempting to maintain children within their own family. The local Health Board may do this by providing a 'family support worker' to work with the family on issues of concern in their own home. The family-support worker is answerable to the social worker who maintains regular contact with the family (Ferguson and O'Reilly, 2001). Where it is deemed impossible to maintain the child in the family, the child may be taken into the care of the Health Board under the provisions of the Childcare Act 1991. A child taken into care may be placed either in foster care (possibly with the extended family) or in a residential childcare service.

The purpose of residential care is to provide a safe, nurturing environment for individual children and young people who cannot live at home or in an alternative family at that time. The environment aims to meet in a planned way, 'the physical, educational, spiritual and social needs of each child' (*Task Force on Childcare Services Report*, 1981: 8).

According to McKeon (2002), there were 126 residential children's homes across the ten Health Board regions in 2001. Seventy-four of these were in the former Eastern Health Board (now the Eastern Regional Health Authority) region, which consists of Counties Dublin, Wicklow and Kildare. This is an increase of 20 homes in that region since 1999 (EHB, 1999a). The number of children's homes nationally is difficult to ascertain given the short-term nature of some of the units. The Social Services Inspectorate [SSI] reported 176 children's homes nationally in 2002 (SSI, 2003) but not all these may be operational at any one time.

While all residential children's homes are funded by the Department of Health and Children, 74 of the 176 listed by the SSI were managed by the non-statutory sector. Twenty-nine of residential children's homes provide care for just one child (SSI, 2003); others have the facility to care for up to twenty-four children.

It is generally accepted that all children in care have experienced a degree of life trauma by nature of the fact that they have been separated from their birth

**Table 22.1. Reasons for Children Being in Residential Care**

| | | |
|---|---|---|
| Foster-care breakdown (n=20) | Abandoned/neglected (n=8) | Sexualised behaviour in child (n=6) |
| Sexual abuse by parents or foster parents (n=14) | Severe alcohol problems at home (n=8) | School exclusion (n=4) |
| Chaotic home environment, inability to cope (n=8) | Out-of-control behaviour (n=7) | Young people who have themselves been sexually abusive (n=4) |
| | Unintegrated children (n=7) | |
| Physical cruelty to child (n=6) | Psychological disturbance of child (n=6) | Suicidal tendencies (n=2) |

While the number of reasons for admission totals 100, the actual number of children in residential care for the period was 77, with some children being admitted for multiple reasons.

*Source*: Richards, 2003: 24.

families (Fahlberg, 1994; Kahan, 1994). Many have also experienced varying degrees of emotional and/or physical abuse or neglect. These findings have been reflected in an Irish context by Richards's (2003) study of residential childcare in the South Eastern Health Board region (Table 22.1).

The emotional impact of early life trauma on children is well documented (Pringle, 1998). Fahlberg (1994) suggests that children who have experienced early life trauma may present with particular emotional and/or behavioural difficulties. Often, children with such difficulties find it hard to cope with the necessary structures in place in residential services. The Eastern Health Board (EHB, 1998) found that some children may run away from residential care or be removed for presenting with chaotic violent behaviours and/or drug misuse. These children often end up homeless and are deemed to require a more secure form of accommodation. A number of cases have been before the courts in recent years, in relation to the lack of facilities available for such children (*F.N.* v. *The Minister for Education* (1995); *D.B.* v. *The Minister for Justice* (1999), *D.G.* v. *The Eastern Health Board*, (1998)).

The difficulties experienced by Health Boards in finding 'suitable' placements for homeless children with behavioural difficulties have led to the development of 'special-care' and 'high-support' services. While there is no accepted national definition of such services (SRSB, 2003), they generally consist of residential children's homes designed to meet the needs of children deemed to pose a danger to themselves or to someone else, or who may be frequent absconders from non-secure placements. According to McElwee (2000), while both special-care and high-support services work with similar types of children, there is a higher level of general security in special-care services; increased staff–child ratios are the main feature of high-support services.

Residential childcare services in Ireland are divided amongst three government departments. While overall responsibility for services rests with the Department of Health and Children, the Department of Education is responsible for the 'special school sector' which consists of five residential schools, which range from fully open facilities (Ferry House in Clonmel) to fully secure centres (Trinity House School, Dublin). The Department of Justice is responsible for St Patrick's Institution, the juvenile wing of Mountjoy Prison (situated in the same grounds). This caters for young people aged 16–18 years.

## WORKING IN RESIDENTIAL CHILDCARE SETTINGS

> The needs and problems of many children in care are complex and difficult to serve appropriately. Or more correctly, their needs are deceptively simple, but delivering the right response is deceptively complex. (Gilligan, 2001: 1)

This section will look at life and work across the range of residential care settings. Children and young people who live in residential care have faced, and bring with them, exceptional problems and difficulties. These may include neglect, abuse (physical, emotional, sexual), family breakdown, separation and loss, betrayal of trust. This may be their first care placement or they may have moved several times from one care setting to another. They may have a clear understanding and acceptance of what is happening in their life or may be confused, anxious or angry. The young person may be open to talk about their situation or may not yet be able to express what they are feeling. They may have an ability to form relationships quickly with new people or they may prefer to cut themselves off from any kind of relationship that involves trusting others. Their behaviour may be 'normal' and stable or unpredictable and even dangerous.

According to Chakrabarti and Hill (2000: 9), 'it is the responsibility of residential staff and carers, acting on behalf of society at large, to promote these children's well-being and to minimise the negative consequences of separation'. This overall aim is usually broken down into a number of professional tasks that permeate all aspects of life in residential care. They include:

- Developing and working with care plans and placement plan
- Relationship building
- Keyworking.

We will now expand on these key elements of residential care.

## Care Plan and Placement Plan

The Childcare (Placement of Children in Residential Care) Regulations, 1995, require that a written care plan is in place either before or immediately after a young person is placed in residential care. A distinction is made between the overall long-term plan for the care of the young person and the more immediate plan with regard to the time the young person is in the centre. The overall care plan takes account of the young person's educational, social, emotional, behavioural and health requirements. The placement plan focuses on how the residential care setting plans to meet these needs.

Childcare staff must have a clear understanding of the needs of young people generally. A knowledge of developmental psychology, attachment, behaviour management and health and safety will help in responding to the needs of particular children and young people. Care workers need to have:

> skills and knowledge . . . drawn from a number of different disciplines, ranging from the directly practical — nutrition, recreation and health care, for example — to personal, people centred skills — such as care and control, communicating with children, counselling and family work, backed by in-depth and detailed knowledge of child development. (Residential Forum, 1998: 11)

It should be noted that life in care for the young person may be far less clear than that reflected in the care or placement plan. Their unique story may have a lot of pain, hurt and confusion. Success of the placement depends much on the trusting relationships built with those with whom they share this part of their life. But the care plan can be a useful tool to assess progress and bring some overall clarity to the complex task of working with children in care.

## Relationship Building

The caring relationship is at the heart of good and effective professional social care. But relationships, in residential care settings or in life generally, are often complex. They change and develop over time and involve a sharing of ourselves with others at various levels — emotionally, physically, professionally. Relationships are entered into rather than created. While there is no easy formula for creating an effective relationship with positive outcomes, Rogers (cited in Murgatroyd 1996: 15) suggests that professional caring relationships have three basic qualities that the worker needs to be able to communicate if the relationship is to be successful. These are empathy, warmth and genuineness:

- *Empathy*: the ability to experience another person's world as if it were one's own without ever losing that 'as if' quality
- *Warmth*: accepting the person as they are, without conditions, and helping them to feel safe
- *Genuineness*: a way of being with other people built on open communication and respect.

In residential care settings, working with children and young people who have not experienced positive trusting relationships can make the task of relationship building even more challenging. Trying to define and analyse relationships may not be of much help in developing skills in relationship building. Think of important relationships in your own life: they are usually described in terms of actions and feelings rather than defined through words or terminology. Thus 'relationships are developed through the most mundane and routine of tasks from reading a story at bedtime, to repairing a puncture in a pushbike, or providing hugs or reassurance when a child falls over, as well as through sharing critical episodes and crises' (Residential Forum, 1998: 9).

Professional social care work in residential childcare settings is about creating and maintaining meaningful relationships through everyday activities. As Gilligan (2001: 56) suggests: 'it is often the little things that carers do that register with and reassure children. It seems that, through these little things, the carers somehow communicate interest and concern and help the child feel connected to the carer'.

The social care practitioner must be equipped for this kind of work. A thorough knowledge of the procedures, politics and legislation that provide the framework in which the caring agency operates is necessary. Practitioners also need to have a theory-base that gives them an understanding of people, systems and practices: 'the nature of relationship based work is that it gives rise to many questions. The purpose of theorising is to promote thinking so that practice is improved' (Residential Forum, 1998: 12). Perhaps the most challenging aspect of working with young people in residential care is sharing life — sharing experiences, sharing perspectives, sharing feelings, emotions, and beliefs. This aspect of professional practice demands a high level of self-knowledge through personal development.

## Keyworking

Keyworking is a system for providing individualised social care through named persons. The keyworker is the person who has responsibility and accountability for the care of the service user and for decisions relating to their situation.

Keyworking involves:

- Mutual trust and respect
- The social, physical, intellectual, cultural, emotional and spiritual aspects of the service user's development and wellbeing
- Creating a sense of purpose and change
- Partnership between the keyworker, other service providers and those who are the users of their services
- Planning (utilising the abilities of individuals and groups in the arena of problem solving)
- The changing of social environments (including, for example, the challenging of racist, sexist and ageist attitudes and behaviours) (SCA, 1991).

The residential care centre is a busy place. It has the busyness of daily living, breakfast, school, games, clubs, TV, homework, cleaning and cooking. There is the added complication that it is not a family unit. A team of social care practitioners takes on a parenting role. As Burton (1993: 48) puts it, 'I am not saying that the worker is a parent to the child . . . the worker remains a worker throughout, but we are using inner resources and knowledge — the most personal and tender and vulnerable areas of our inner selves — to do the work.' In the context of the residential care centre, the relationship between practitioner and young person is clearly of vital importance. But it can be difficult to develop and maintain significant relationships in an environment interrupted by shift-work patterns, or where high staff turnover puts an end to developing attachments and relationships.

Another factor that may impact negatively on quality personalised care and relationship building is the sheer amount of activity within and around the residential centre. This may include official business regarding the care and related issues of the children and young people; staff meetings; new admissions; aftercare; as well as daily living tasks and issues — school, hobbies and interests, shopping, eating, and so on. The primary role of the keyworker is to help make sense of this experience of living for the individual child or young person. Keyworking has been found to 'improve personalised care, relationships, the clarity of the residential tasks and helped to improve other aspects of life in the establishment . . . for the staff as well as for the resident' (Clarke, 1998: 31).

The keyworker is usually given particular responsibility in relation to a child — for example, accompanying the young person to appointments, to liaise with relevant professionals, agencies, school and family. For this to take place, emphasis is placed on developing a positive, professional caring relationship between the young person and the keyworker. The keyworker needs to have a clear under-standing of theory that underpins the work — for example, attachment theory, the hierarchy of need, developmental psychology, and so on. They must also develop competency in a range of skills, relating to communication, active listening, advocacy, boundary maintenance and confidentiality. Staff-members who take on a keyworker role should receive and use supervision and may need further training depending on the specific needs of the child. It is expected that the keyworker will attend reviews of children for whom they are responsible.

Times of transition or change in a young person's life often bring with them anxiety, insecurity and feelings of vulnerability. The keyworker can have an important role at these times. In preparing to leave a care setting, the young person may be supported, empowered and gain confidence through clear guidelines around moving on and outreach. The keyworker plays a vital role at this time and can provide further support through planned aftercare.

It is clear from this section that the role of keyworker within the residential care centre is central to the quality and effectiveness of care experienced by the young person: 'enduring relationships with committed people become very important for young people growing up in care. It is from these relationships that their "secure base" may emerge' (Gilligan, 2001). Enduring relationships are important in enabling any of us to negotiate our way through difficult periods of our lives. Young people in care have a special need to experience such relation-ships, as their home base is at best fragile and, perhaps, disintegrated. Developing a trusting, mutually respectful relationship with an adult can give the young person some of the tools to build that secure platform for future life experience.

## CONCLUSION

This short insight into the world of residential childcare has focused on structural and operational issues that ultimately affect the quality of service delivered to young people in care in Ireland. It may be easy to be intimidated by the raft of legislation, reports, reviews, guidelines and theories that informs practice in this area. But it is important to have an understanding of the context in which residential care takes place, in order to be able to focus on the quality of the professional caring relationship between practitioner and young people.

As we said at the outset, this chapter is by no means exhaustive. Indeed, the reports and legislation referred to may be superseded by amendments or further reviews. This reflects the nature of professional practice, with constant development, review and evaluation an ongoing element.

In using this chapter, you should try to relate the issues raised to your own practice experience and/or background reading, with a view to developing your own ability to work with children in residential care settings. The challenge must surely be to move from learning *about* to learning *with* children in care, in order that this sometimes necessary response can be of the best possible quality.

23

# Ethnicity and Social Care: An Irish Dilemma

Celesta McCann James

## OVERVIEW

For the first time in recent history, Ireland is a country of immigration, with movement, relocation and resettlement occurring for thousands of individuals and groups. Many come here from countries within the European Union [EU], while others are emigrating from different parts of the world. Though immigration to Ireland is not a new phenomenon, rapidly increasing numbers combined with a perception of 'difference' (for example, in relation to skin colour, clothing or religion) is unprecedented. Definitions and experiences of 'modern Irish society' are being challenged and changed. For many Irish citizens, who may previously have been accustomed to a single, dominant culture, exposure to different traditions, customs and routines is an unfamiliar reality. New faces, identities and practices appear in shops, local pubs, and the media; at recreational facilities, school, work and, sometimes, next door. Amongst the arrivals are those seeking asylum and refuge as they fear for their lives in their home countries. Ireland is legally and socially obliged to admit these immigrants as refugees, if and when their case is proven. It also has a political and, some would argue, a moral duty to ensure that immigrants have access to appropriate legal, social, health, and educational services.

Recognition of 'difference' raises ethical questions and has practical implications for the social care profession. This chapter focuses on three related aspects of social care work and ethnic diversity (it is acknowledged that any discussion on Ireland and ethnicity is incomplete without reference to Travellers. Their contribution to and participation in Irish society is discussed in Chapter 18). In order to put the discussion of care provision and ethnicity into an Irish perspective, recent trends in immigration will first be presented. This will include the identification of policy issues and current responses that support or neglect the care needs of immigrants. Having outlined social care provision for immigrants, the chapter will then contextualise key concepts related to ethnicity, racism and, in particular, institutional oppression. By recognising the effects of oppression upon social institutions, the chapter will clarify outstanding challenges that face the profession. Finally, a model for strategic change will be presented that offers an integrated approach to professional best practice for all those involved in social care.

# EMERGING TRENDS IN IMMIGRATION AND CARE PROVISION

Recent years have produced a growing body of research evidence and statistics on changing migration patterns in Ireland. In addition to migration between EU countries, there has been specific attention given to the upsurge of individuals and minority groups who enter Ireland either as refugees or as asylum seekers. In 1994, fewer than 400 individuals sought asylum in Ireland — by 2000, this number had risen to almost 11,000. According to statistics compiled by the Irish Refugee Council (IRC, 2004) from January to June 2003, 4,750 applications were made for asylum in Ireland; during the same period of 2004, 2,118 applications were submitted. The overall increase has been accompanied by serious economic and social challenges, particularly experienced in the eastern region of the country, as major responsibility for catering for the accommodation needs of asylum seekers falls to the Eastern Regional Health Authority [ERHA].

The need to provide services to a culturally diverse and ethnically heterogeneous population is unprecedented (Byrne, 1997; Cullen, 2000; Faughnan and Woods, 2000). Research has generated data in the areas of social services and inclusion, looking specifically at public awareness and social policy development (Begley et al., 1999; Faughnan, 1999; Fanning, 2001; Torode et al., 2001; Ward, 2001; Faughnan and O'Donovan, 2002; Feldman et al., 2002). More recently, studies have concentrated on the experiences of statutory service workers who respond to the reception needs of asylum seekers and refugees (Faughnan et al., 2002.)

## UNACCOMPANIED MINORS

Amongst the thousands of individuals, families and groups migrating to Ireland, many are children, accompanied or unaccompanied minors seeking refuge and/or asylum. The sudden growth in the numbers of refugee and asylum-seeking minors has been a focus of statutory and non-statutory bodies such as the Health Boards and the Irish Refugee Council. Such children are vulnerable individuals, dependent upon a humane and compassionate response from Ireland's social care services. This recognition has prompted research that explores procedures and working relationships between Irish social care professionals and unaccompanied children from ethnic minority backgrounds.

In 1999, the Irish Refugee Council published the report, *Separated Children Seeking Asylum in Ireland: A Report on Legal and Social Conditions*. At the time, there were thirty-two separated children seeking asylum in Ireland. By March 2003, the number of separated children entering Ireland and referred to the North Eastern Area Health Board was 2,717 (unpublished Health Board figures). Nearly half, or 1,113 children, were reunited with family members already in Ireland. A further 1,316 separated children, under the care of the Health Boards, made applications for asylum under the 1951 Geneva Convention on the Status of

Refugees. In response to this unforeseen increase, agencies have reacted by appropriating different aspects of existing community welfare services, such as dispersal and direct provision. Regrettably, proactive and strategic procedures had not been developed prior to the arrival of large numbers of immigrants, militating against effective provision of adequate services.

We know little about why separated children leave their country of origin. Research by Vekić (2003) cites factors such as escaping war and discrimination, parental detention or death, and poverty. Regardless of why children arrive, the UN Convention on the Rights of the Child states that:

> [P]arties shall take appropriate measures to ensure that a child who is seeking refugee status . . . shall, whether unaccompanied or accompanied by his or her parents or by any other person, receive appropriate protection and humanitarian assistance in the enjoyment of applicable rights set forth in the present Convention and in other international human rights or humanitarian instruments to which the said States are Parties. (Article 22 (1))

The Parties to this Convention also undertook in Article 22 (2) to cooperate with different organisations not only to protect and assist refugee children but to help trace family members in order to facilitate family reunification. Articles 19, 34, 37(a) and 37(c) of the Convention state that, if reunification with family is unsuccessful, the child shall be accorded the same protection as any other child permanently or temporarily deprived of his or her family environment. In Ireland, explicit provisions of the Child Care Act 1991 specify that unaccompanied minors are to be provided for. This includes an obligation under Article 3 (2)(a) on the part of the Health Boards to identify children who are not receiving adequate care and protection. In addition, it is the duty of the Health Board, under Article 4 (1) to take into care any child who is residing or located in the area of the Health Board and requiring care or protection.

Faughnan et al. (2002) have indicated that more than half of those surveyed from the community welfare service reported satisfaction with the assistance their young clients received — once referred. The remainder claimed that the Health Board service was generally under-resourced or offered little follow-up for minors. Two-thirds of respondents rated material services (medical services and material support) as effective, but other services such as mental health, childcare, interpretation, language tuition, legal aid and recreation were rated by half of the respondents as ineffective. An overriding recommendation from the study was for dedicated accommodation with increased input from social workers and support workers.

Significant concerns remain in relation to social care provision for children who are members of ethnic minority groups and separated from their families. According to the Irish Refugee Council (Veale et al., 2003), demand has exceeded the capacity of Health Boards to provide adequate resources such as professionally trained staff and childcare residential services. Interim care placements for unaccompanied children have consequently become a practice. In the East Coast Area Health Board, young people aged 15 years and upwards are generally placed in self-catering, privately managed hostel accommodation. Children aged 6–14 are placed in residential care, supportive lodgings, or in foster care, and attempts are made to place very young children in foster care. Despite all good intentions, limited resources make it necessary for some young people to rely on independent and unsupervised lodging.

As the Child Care Act (1991) does not refer to 'separated children', non-Irish unaccompanied children (unaccompanied minors seeking refuge or asylum) are treated as homeless Irish children for welfare purposes. For that reason, their care is often inappropriate and disordered. It has not been designed for specific circumstances, such as experience of recent trauma, coping with a new and unfamiliar culture, a different language, an unfamiliar educational system, or the absence of family and friends. Additionally, social care providers are constrained by lack of resources such as training in language and cultural diversity. Veale et al. (2003) have identified the following as immediate challenges that face both professionals and users of social care:

- Adolescent boys and girls are placed in unsupervised mixed-sex accommodation;
- Although there are some residential units with good care practice, other hostels catering for separated children accommodate more than eighty minors. They lack appropriate cooking, study, recreational and personal facilities;
- Regular monitoring of privately managed hostels is inadequate. This is the responsibility of individual Health Boards and should be carried out on an ongoing basis;
- There is a lack of individualised care plans for many minors who need supportive environments for their needs and maturity levels (e.g. pregnant girls and young parents). Plans should include long-term solutions to individual circumstances;
- Health Board staff should receive adequate resources and support for ongoing training regarding multicultural issues, policy and practice development;
- Separated children should receive psychosocial support that will promote and facilitate integration with asylum support organisations and national youth organisations;
- Professional carers and separated children should receive psychological support and education relevant to loss, grief and trauma.

## OTHER ISSUES RELATED TO CULTURAL DIVERSITY

As crucial as it is to implement practical and effective care for unaccompanied minors, we must not overlook the increasing challenge that faces the profession in providing care for other client groups. As in the 'Irish' community, ethnic minority groups have members who are, for example, disabled, elderly, homeless or socially troubled. Many refugees and asylum seekers enter Ireland as family groups and will present needs to professional care services that are broader than the requirement to assist unaccompanied minors. In many ways, care practitioners are already overstretched and under-resourced — how much more stretched will the profession be when caring for young and heavily pregnant women, or disabled or elderly immigrants, who have little English and unfamiliar cultural practices?

Practitioners and service users recognise that language and cultural barriers can limit the provision of effective and meaningful social care. When a client and worker do not speak the same language, we can expect that cultural understanding may also be absent or problematic. Multicultural practices are seldom part of care practitioners' backgrounds. The social care profession, therefore, is faced with the task of informing its practice with theoretical and skill-based experience in cultural diversity. This is not a challenge that will be easily met, but it can be addressed purposefully and systematically.

Fundamental instruction in language and cultural acquisition could be required as part of the curriculum offered to future care practitioners. O'Loingsigh (2001) maintains that although structural barriers inhibit the active or real participation by ethnic minorities in the educational system, intercultural education is an education for both the minorities and the majority community in Irish society. It is therefore important to create a curriculum that explores issues of tolerance, human rights, democracy and respect for difference, rather than concerning itself with integrating ethnic minorities into a social care system that makes them 'more Irish'. Academic care training might include regular exposure to, and experience with, diverse ethnic communities and practices throughout Irish society; it might also include modules taught by members of ethnic minorities, as well as programmes that facilitate exchanges with social care arrangements outside Ireland.

There is an increasing amount of information that can inform Health Boards and policymakers about the material and social needs of ethnic minority groups in Ireland. Statistics indicate the numbers of refugees and asylum seekers who enter the country on a monthly basis and we are now aware of how many of those entering are minors (unaccompanied or otherwise). As a result, social services are introducing measures that address the immediate and short-term needs of immigrants. But we have yet to determine — largely because of a lack of substantive research data — the longer-term challenges that face the social care profession. What are the models and procedures that we must implement for a 'charter of best practice' in Irish social care?

## CURRENT CHALLENGES FACING PROFESSIONAL SOCIAL CARE

As a profession, social care is faced with the challenge of providing adequate and appropriate care to vulnerable clients, such as minors, the disabled, older people and those outside of home. For some of these clients, their national and cultural characteristics may be different from those of the dominant Irish culture. Such distinctions do not make physical and social needs less legitimate, nor do they dilute the legal responsibility or social obligations to provide a fair and humane service to all those residing in the state.

There has been considerable media coverage of the welfare needs of selected groups of immigrants. It has been argued that such attention has helped to fuel hostility towards immigrants, who are seen by many as unworthy of social assistance (Pollack, 1999). Such individuals and groups are seen to be claiming that which is not rightfully theirs, thereby costing the Irish taxpayer unfairly and unjustly. According to Lorenz (1998), this perceived misappropriation of taxpayers' money is not limited to existing definitions commonly associated with commercial transactions (such as having paid into insurance funds as a precondition for getting benefits), but through cultural criteria such as not being 'of the same kind'.

Predominantly cultural factors rather than human rights are seen to define social relationships and subsequent social contracts in Irish society. As social care services, by definition, reflect more than physical or material support, we are drawn into an ethical and philosophical sphere where cultural uncertainties cause us to examine our beliefs and values. Therefore, the following questions deserve consideration by all social care practitioners:

- Do we, as a society, insist that care be provided on the basis of socially and culturally approved endorsement?
- Is social care afforded only to those in our society who are 'worthy' members of the dominant culture (such as Irish or EU citizens) or perhaps to those individuals who make 'genuine' contributions through voluntary or paid work?
- Is it time to query the social, economic, political, and ethical characteristics that define Irish social services?
- Are Irish social services provided or withheld on the basis of nationality or need, contribution or need, ethnic identity or need?
- Will we develop a strategic social care service that is capable of providing effective support for all residents in Ireland who need care?
- Whose interests are being served in the present provision of social care: state officials', administrators', the taxpayers', or the interests of those who are users of the care service?
- Will the Irish social care profession progress to ensure that ethnic and cultural differences are embraced thoughtfully and sensitively, guaranteeing a truly caring service that is inclusive of all those seeking or dependent on its provision?

Questions such as these are difficult to ask, but even more problematic to answer. Responses and solutions are dependent on complex systems that involve philosophies, politics and practices from a variety of perspectives. Inevitably they involve the use of contested concepts such as ethnicity, racism, and oppression. It is to a discussion of these terms that we now turn.

# ETHNICITY

The term *ethnicity* derives from the Greek *ethnos*, meaning people or tribe. The English word 'ethnic' was used from the mid-fourteenth to the nineteenth century to describe someone as heathen or pagan (Williams, 1976: 119). Simply defined, ethnicity describes the characteristics that relationally connect people together in a manner that negotiates a group identity, be it political, religious, cultural or social. The underlying beliefs and values that support such a bond offer solidarity and a 'sense of belonging', a collective membership, and shared experiences. Members of an ethnic group possess a cultural continuity that often extends from generation to generation, making them eligible to access the social, emotional and physical benefits of 'inclusion' within their community.

According to Smith (1991), ethnic groups may be defined both internally and externally, offering a way of distinguishing 'them' from 'us'. This is a two-way process where others, who separate cultural and historical groupings, identify a distinction between ethnic categories. At the same time, ethnic members themselves create an internal cohesion that defines and differentiates them from other ethnic groups. Unity is reinforced when an ethnic group sustains a collective sense of continuity by adopting a specific name, sharing historical memories and/or common ancestry, associating with a specific homeland, or differentiating elements of common culture, beliefs and boundaries (Glazer and Moynihan, 1975; Jenkins, 1996, 1997).

The issue of ethnicity is inevitably linked with questions of identity and difference. Ireland has until recently been categorised as a monocultural society with social institutions that reinforce sameness. As a result, Irish identity has exhibited specific forms of approved social practice, be they political, economic, religious, educational or familial. A consequence of Ireland's single cultural perspective has been a traditional and often restricted definition of society's values, beliefs, norms, knowledge and practices. This 'institutionalised culture' has informed and influenced individuals and group relationships and has defined the dominant values and patterns of behaviour exhibited in Ireland. As a result, ethnic and other minority communities have been socially stratified or ranked and organised in a subordinate fashion, being allowed at the very most to create Irish sub-cultures.

# RACISM AND INSTITUTIONAL OPPRESSION

*Racism* is a term used by sociologists to denote a belief (or an action based on belief) that one racial category is superior or inferior to another racial category. In early attempts to justify such beliefs, scientific claims advocated supposed innate differences, but these were later invalidated from evidence that showed no such biological distinctions. Racism may currently be defined as a pattern of thought or action that allows individuals or groups to be considered different, often with negative consequences for a specific racial group. Whether or not the thought or action *intends* to inspire discrimination is irrelevant as racism is seen to exist when a deliberate or unintentional attitude or behaviour disadvantages the social position of a specific group in society. Ireland has participated in the debate about racism and nationalism, seeking its own clarity as to the implications of 'Irishness' and citizenship. It has sought answers to rapid changes in a society where adjustments are occurring within the traditional cultural symbols of national identity, such as the economy, family structure, religion and language (Farrell and Watt, 2001; RIA, 2003; Lentin, 1998).

*Oppression* describes a complex condition that may result from many processes. It is a condition that is relatively stable and may be reflected in the education system, the legal system, the media and social customs. What separates it from other kinds of mistreatment is its systematic nature. By 'systematic', we mean that the mistreatment is part of the social system. It is a structure of inequality in which one group systematically dominates the other by means of interrelated social practices (Frye, 1983). Systematic domination is also present when hierarchical controls exist that are not consensual and that involve institutionalised inequality (Moane, 1994). Whenever there is systematic domination of the members of one group by the members of another group or by society as a whole, we call it oppression. The presence of racial discrimination in society is categorised as oppressive, then, when social structures are organised and operate in a way that maintains discriminating and unequal practices. For example, the social ranking or stratification of particular ethnic groups or communities may disadvantage their access to and equal participation in social services.

Oppression is not a random affair, but is predictable (Knoppers, 1993; Van Leeuwen, 1993). If we say that individuals or particular groups (such as refugees) are oppressed in Irish society, we should be able to predict the kinds of experiences they are likely to confront. These experiences will be encountered regardless of which individual member is involved. Although oppression can take the form of deliberate and premeditated abuse of vulnerable individuals or groups, it is described more often as camouflaged, operating within socially approved and authorised structures. Difficulty (or unwillingness) to discern the systematic nature of oppression facilitates its continuance and helps to maintain unequal power structures.

Knoppers (1993) claims that oppression is easily reproduced because its features become intertwined in society, where both dominants and subordinates fail to 'see' or 'feel' it in their lives. Moane (1994; 1999) maintains that although patterns of oppression are generally unrecognised, of those signs that are visible, most are viewed as unalterable. This helps to sustain long-standing hierarchical management and social systems. It is therefore understandable that institutional oppression, as encountered in the social care system, may be viewed as impenetrable. Although care practitioners may not consciously participate in oppressive behaviour, existing mechanisms that surround and support them facilitate the continuation of discriminating programmes and regimes.

Moane (1994) has identified psychological and social patterns associated with being dominant or subordinate in a hierarchical system. She emphasises the link between oppression and areas of psychological functioning that can be understood only by analysing the social context of individuals' lives. The central feature of this social context is that it is hierarchical, or stratified, so that a select number of people have access to power and resources, while other people are deprived of the same. Applying this framework, we now go on to explore the provision of social care services in Ireland and to draw parallels that reveal institutionalised patterns of control that legitimate the domination of dependent and vulnerable ethnic minority groups.

## THE NATURE OF OPPRESSION

Six indicators of oppression are listed below; each demonstrates the association between existing social care practice and the institutional oppression of ethnic minority groups in Ireland. Bear in mind that oppression is predictable and therefore experiences in any of the following categories are likely to apply to all members of discriminated groups, regardless of which individual encounters them.

1. *Physical control* is a primary mechanism of oppression and is reflected in punishment or the threat of it to ensure cooperation. It operates within a hierarchical system that depends on forms of coercion, intimidation, threats, imprisonment or beatings. Refugees and asylum seekers are physically controlled through the legal processes of immigration. The Refugee Act 1996, as amended by the Immigration Act 2003, incorporates provisions for asylum seekers under section 9(10)a. The Act states that the individual must be brought before a judge of the District Court 'as soon as is practicable'. In practice, this would normally be the next sitting of the court. An individual can be committed for ensuing periods of up to 21 days without charge by a judge pending the determination of their application under section 9(10)(b)(i). This is a recurring obligation if the judge orders the individual's continued detention. Refugees and asylum seekers are by definition subject to absolute physical control. They may additionally be referred to one or more agencies under the Department of Justice, Equality and Law Reform (such as the Asylum Policy Unit, Garda National Immigration Bureau, Office of the Refugee Applications Commissioner, Refugee Appeals Tribunal); the UN High Commissioner for Refugees; or non-statutory bodies. Noncompliance with any of these agencies may result in imprisonment.

2. *Economic control* reinforces physical control in that members of the oppressed group are kept powerless by locating them in low-paid, low-status jobs, or in unpaid work. Members of the oppressed group have far less wealth, earn considerably less, and are less secure in their jobs than members of other

groups. They regularly experience discrimination, lack of access to education and training and, therefore, a higher incidence of poverty. For refugees and asylum seekers, employment is prohibited while status decisions are pending. Health Boards provide accommodation and 'direct provision' plus €19 per week to adults. Fanning et al. (2000) indicate that when legally employed, refugees and asylum seekers encounter negative stereotypes and hostility in the workplace. Even with high levels of education and qualifications, many are relegated to low-paid, low-status employment. Furthermore, lack of state support, language skills and information regarding their entitlements increases the disadvantaged social status of, and economic control over, refugees and asylum seekers in Ireland.

3. *Sexual exploitation* is a further form of oppression, often operating through rape and prostitution. The Irish media has reported cases of young asylum seekers and refugees, often traumatised and vulnerable, left unsupervised while in the care of the Health Boards. Children as young as 13, and more often around 15 or 16, have been housed in mixed-sex hostels alongside adult asylum seekers (*Irish Times*, 27 October 2000). Even more worrying is the disappearance of minors who have fallen out of the welfare system. It has been reported that some minors are involved in trafficking or prostitution (*Irish Times*, 9 February 2001).

4. *Exclusion* is a further form of oppression that removes authority from the subordinate group by withholding power, either through restrictions or lack of representation. Exclusion can take on various forms, and when members of ethnic groups are demeaned through physical and economic controls (such as peripheral housing, language barriers, economic and employment restrictions), it is often the case that they are excluded and marginalised socially, emotionally and politically from mainstream Irish society. They are perceived as 'different' and often 'unworthy' of meaningful participation and decision making. The exclusion of ethnic minorities from the higher levels of social care structures renders them less influential over decisions that crucially affect their lives. This may apply to input regarding legislative change, care planning, cultural and religious practices, medical ethics, and educational practices.

5. *Psychological control* underlies most of the above forms of control. It is maintained by the dominant group controlling the definition of what is 'natural' or 'normal' for members of the oppressed group. Through its dominance of influential social systems such as education, the media, religion and language, 'Irish' ideology and culture are managed. As part of psychological control, there is a suppression (or erasure) of history and the propagation of stereotypes of inferiority, widely facilitated through prejudice, myths, misinformation and unawareness. As members of minority ethnic groups in

Ireland, individuals are subjected to an Irish society that has, until recently, been culturally restricted and purposefully isolated. Social care services reflect this background and consequently provide support (and expect cooperation from service users) that largely operates according to the customs and routines of the dominant culture.

6. *Fragmentation and tokenism* regularly occur in a system that promotes a select few of the subordinate group, thereby creating competition and envy among the subordinates — a situation of divide and conquer. In administrative departments in Irish social care, ethnic representation is minimal. Members from ethnic communities may be visible as interpreters or as volunteer workers, but as trained personnel with decision-making authority, they are all but absent.

In an analysis of oppression, Ruth (1988) examined problems in relationships and aspects that lead to a sense of inferiority. He suggests that the key to sustained oppression is internalised control. Internalised oppression is where people come to believe in their own inferiority and their powerlessness to change things. Members may typically have low self-esteem, disunity, fear and lack of information. The result is that a person essentially 'agrees' to be oppressed. Members of the oppressed group are commonly observed policing themselves while the dominant group takes a subtle or less visible role.

Irish legislation and social care practices operate to marginalise members of ethnic minority groups. They are physically and economically controlled, subjected to sexual exploitation, excluded from meaningful participation in Irish society, and psychologically dominated. Social care professionals and recipients may fail to 'see' or 'feel' oppressive features because a dominant hierarchy is systematically woven into the fabric of the social care system, camouflaging the mechanisms that enforce and reproduce power differentials.

As explained, 'systematic' implies that racism and oppression are part of a larger social system. This is marked by institutionalised inequality in which one group can dominate members of another by means of non-consensual, interrelated social practices. *Intent*, therefore, is not an essential factor, and well-meaning social care practitioners do not necessarily dominate users on purpose. While most care practitioners operate with transparency, it has been argued that existing structural forms (legislation, Health Board regimes) reinforce the preservation of hierarchical power, enforced authority and domination of service users. By internalising their oppression, ethnic minorities often believe in their own inferiority and powerlessness to change things. They comply with the status quo and therefore fail to confront the disadvantages and inequalities they are subjected to throughout the social care system. Consequently, their degraded social status pushes them further towards the most extreme margins of Irish society, leaving them vulnerable and more likely to remain dependent upon inadequate social services in the future.

## A MODEL FOR CHANGE

Irish social care is at a crossroads and must choose whether or not it will embrace diversity. It must choose between 'doing care unto them' in a patronising and oppressive manner or implementing care policies that are representative and inclusive. Ireland is still deciding if and when it will allow 'others' to use 'our' social services. Even though Irish legislation including the Refugee Act 1996 and the Child Care Act 1991 establish legal definitions and procedures for dealing with refugees and asylum seekers, the verdict is out as to whether Irish society will accept ethnic minorities as 'deserving' or 'worthy' social care service users and, if so, on what terms.

An equally demanding test for Irish society will be whether or not to facilitate institutional change at all levels, including the recruitment of ethnic minority group members as social care practitioners and Health Service administrators. In other words, the Irish social care profession is faced with a dilemma: is there to be a redefinition of care participation and delivery? The term *dilemma* is used deliberately here and implies a choice with no 'right answer'. While it does not necessarily presume that change will occur, it does describe a current difficulty or problem in our social care system that necessitates attention and action. In order to explain how social care might be understood in this context, four categories are proposed below which may help to resolve our present Irish 'dilemma'.

## The Identifier

The first category can be summarised as the 'identifier'. The identifier is best characterised by asking (and answering) the following questions:

- Who or what determines and/or defines a given problem?
- On what basis is it drawn into the public arena?
- Who or what sets the standards of what is worthy of disclosure, discussion, treatment, funding or change?

To some extent, membership of the EU has brought Irish social services to account for the management and treatment of ethnic minorities. In addition, the unexpected increase in immigrant numbers has prompted attention by the public, as well as by the Department of Justice, Equality and Law Reform. As a political institution, the Department is reinforced by the media and other state agencies, responsible for education, health, and welfare, in legitimating Irish social practices and cultural beliefs. As identifiers they are sanctioned to inform and direct the organisational structures of social care.

## The Identified

A second category is the 'identified'. The identified may be a situation, a problem, an individual, group, agency or institution. Relevant questions that may be asked regarding the identified include:

- What role, if any, do the identified have in naming a given problem or situation?
- What power relationships exist between the identifier and the identified?
- Are there social structures that serve to advantage, disadvantage or equalise all participants?
- Are all parties able to participate equally in the process of 'identifying the dilemma'?

Applying these questions to the present discussion, ethnic minorities have been identified as different, unworthy and not belonging in Ireland. Apart from a small number of token contributors, members from such communities are precluded from naming their care needs or solutions, thereby marginalising their participation in social care services. Their existence is acknowledged, but little if any attention is given to ethnic members' own analysis of their circumstances. There is a glaring absence of published work by or about refugees and/or asylum seekers, which would give first-hand accounts of their physical and social needs in Ireland. They remain as unequal subordinates in a hierarchical social system.

## The Movement

The third category is the 'movement'. Sometimes, movement occurs because the identifier changes; sometimes the identified changes; sometimes they both change; and sometimes neither changes. In order for movement to occur (or not occur), one must observe the following:

- Who or what changes?
- Does change occur as a result of pressure (or lack of pressure) from existing social structures and institutions?
- Does change come about as a result of public awareness, dissatisfaction, a sense of justice, or economic reality?
- How is change directed?
- What path does change take during the process of movement?
- When is change implemented and by whom or by what?

Although some movement is occurring in the provision of social care, to date it has been reactive rather than as a result of moral commitments or deliberate social policy. An awareness of 'foreigners' gaining access to 'our' social system has created public fear and dissatisfaction, based on a combination of prejudice, discrimination and socioeconomic reality. Up to now, attention has focused on exhausting Irish resources, the 'illegitimacy' of service users, the perceived abuse of lenient Irish citizenship laws (such as Irish citizenship acquired on the basis of birth rather than Irish parentage) and a 'dilution' of the Irish identity. Movement, therefore, has been directed at providing minimal services for clients who are believed to be draining our already limited social care resources. Unaccompanied children from ethnic minority groups are allowed to live in accommodation that would be considered unsuitable for Irish children in care. Language, dietary, religious and other cultural distinctions are less of a service priority for these clients than they might be for Irish clients. Care providers are largely from the dominant Irish culture and few are trained in ethnic or cultural diversity, leaving vulnerable clients reliant on an inadequate social service.

## The Beneficiary

Last is the 'beneficiary'. Clarification of this category requires answers to the following:

- Who or what benefits from any change or lack of change?
- If change occurs, who or what is advantaged or disadvantaged?
- Is there an economic, social or cultural cost to change or lack of change?
- If change does not occur, who benefits from the status quo?

If change does not occur, there may be some short-term savings for the exchequer, but there are no social beneficiaries. Ethnic minorities, the social service system, the Irish State, humanity — all lose. In order for the Irish social care system to benefit, there must be a radical shift in our perception of client worth and adequacy of provision. It is no longer enough to view 'deserving' clients as those whose surname is Finnegan, Murphy, or O'Malley. Nor is it satisfactory to supply care that lacks sensitivity and respect for cultural diversity. Inevitable benefits occur when changes focus upon empowerment and extend agency to ethnic minorities, as users and providers of care services. Only when a multiplicity of interests, cultures and belief systems inform our currently fatigued and disillusioned social care system will we have the potential for meaningful reform.

## CONCLUSION

If we seek to provide a care service based on best practice, it must have at the core of its policy strategy a regard for cultural diversity and a framework that incorporates into its development the inclusion of 'difference'. It must unite service providers, service users, a range of communities and traditional Irish society into an effective and transparent integrated whole. Integration within the social care profession will facilitate all participants with the ability to contribute fully without having to relinquish their cultural identity. According to the Department of Justice, Equality and Law Reform (DoJELR, 2000: 9), 'the emphasis of integration policy should be on supporting initiatives which enable the preservation of ethnic, cultural and religious identity of the individual.' Accepting this governmental assertion, it can be argued that an integration policy is not operating equitably if it requires cultural assimilation on the part of ethnic minorities.

Recipients of Irish social care services are, by definition, vulnerable and dependent clients who are linked to state care, protection, support, welfare and advocacy. They are entitled, as indicated by government policy, to benefit from 'initiatives which enable the preservation of [their] ethnic, cultural and religious identity.' They should not be required or expected to embrace a pre-defined form of Irishness, but should instead be provided with a service that respects and values diversity. In order for any such integration to operate effectively, strategic procedures must strengthen linguistic and cultural practices, as well as material, social and emotional supports.

This chapter has indicated that the rise in the numbers of immigrants entering Ireland has been paralleled by an increase in ethnic discrimination and unequal social services. While attempting to meet its legislative obligations, the Irish State has failed to engage with many of the moral and ethical challenges associated with models of best practice in social care. It is now time to reform current routines and procedures. We must organise our specialisations to present a service that not only considers the practical challenges of care that face an increasing number of individuals and groups from diverse backgrounds and experiences, but also philosophically embraces a multicultural Irish society. It is time to eliminate our prejudices and insecurities and replace them with an integrated service that provides support, equal access, and full participation in the identification and elimination of institutional oppression. It is our social moment to care!

# Reference List

*Bunreacht na hÉireann/Constitution of Ireland*. Dublin: Stationery Office.

*Child Care Act 1991*. Dublin: Stationery Office.

*Children's Act 2001*. Dublin: Stationery Office.

*DB (a minor suing by his mother and next friend SB)* v. *Minister for Justice, Minister for Health, Minister for Education, Ireland, The Attorney General and the Eastern Health Board*, High Court, [1999] 1 ILRM 93, 29 July 1998.

*DG (a minor suing by his guardian ad litem MR)* v. *Eastern Health Board, Ireland and the Attorney General, Supreme Court*, [1998] 1 ILRM 241, 16 July 1997.

*Employment Equality Act 1998*. Dublin: Stationery Office.

*Equal Status Act 2000*. Dublin: Stationery Office.

*Freedom of Information Act, 1997*. Dublin: Stationery Office.

*Health (Nursing Homes) Act, 1990*. Dublin: Stationery Office.

*National Disability Authority Act 1999*. Dublin: Stationery Office.

*Protection for persons reporting child abuse Act, 1998*. Dublin: Stationery Office.

*Safety, Health and Welfare at Work Act, 1989*. Dublin: Stationery Office.


Abbott, J. and T. Ryan (2001), *The Unfinished Revolution: Learning, Human Behaviour, Community and Political Paradox*, Stafford: Network Educational Press.

Ainsworth, M. (1973), 'The development of infant–mother attachment', in B. Caldwell and H. Riccuiti (eds), *Review of Child Development* (vol. 3). Chicago: University of Chicago Press.

Ainsworth, M., M. Blehar, E. Waters and S. Wall (1978), *Patterns of Attachment: A Psychological Study of the Strange Situation*, Hillsdale: Erlbaum.

Albrecht, G., K. Seelman and M. Bury (2001), 'The formation of disability studies', in G. Albrecht et al. (eds), *Handbook of Disability Studies*, Thousand Oaks (CA): Sage.

Aldridge, M. and J. Evetts, (2003), 'Rethinking the concept of professionalism: the case of journalism', *British Journal of Sociology* 54 (4). pp. 547–64.

Anglin, J. (1992), 'How staff develop', *FICE Bulletin* 6. pp. 18–24.

Anglin, J. (2001), 'Child and youth care: A unique profession', *CYC-Net* 35. pp. 1–3.

Anglin, J. (2002), 'Staffed group homes for children and youth: Constructing a theoretical framework for understanding'. Unpublished PhD thesis, School of Social Work, University of Leicester.

Arensberg, C. and S. Kimball (2001), *Family and Community in Ireland* (3rd ed), Ennis: CLASP.

Armstrong, M. and H. Murlis (1998), *Reward Management: A Handbook of Remuneration Strategy and Practice*, London: Kogan Page.

Askheim, O-P. (1998). *Omsorgspolitiske endringer*, Oslo: Ad Notam Gyldendal.

Atwool, N. (1999), 'Attachment and post-intervention decision-making for children in care', *Journal of Child Centred Practice* 6 (1). pp. 39–55.

Bacik, I., C. Costello and E. Drew (2003), *Gender Injustice: Feminising the Legal Professions?*, Dublin: Trinity College Dublin Law School.

BAI [Behaviour and Attitudes Ireland] (2000), *Attitudes to Travellers and Minority Groups*, Survey prepared for Citizen Traveller by Behaviour and Attitudes Ireland Ltd.

Baldry, A. (2003), 'Bullying in schools and exposure to domestic violence', *Child Abuse and Neglect* 27. pp. 713–32.

Bancroft, L. and J. Silverman (2002), *The Batterer as a Parent: Addressing the Impact of Domestic Violence on Family Dynamics*, London: Sage.

Bandler, R. and J. Grinder (1975), *The Structure of Magic*, I. Palo Alto: Science and Behaviour Books.

Bank-Mikklesen, N. (1980), 'Denmark', in R. Flynn and K. Nitch (eds), *Normalisation, Social Integration and Community Services*, Austin (TX): Pro-Ed.

BAP [Blanchardstown Area Partnership] (2001), *Action for Positive Change*, Blanchardstown: Blanchardstown Area Partnership.

BAP [Blanchardstown Area Partnership] (2002), *Social Inclusion Plan 2000–2006: A Social, Economic and Demographic Profile of the Blanchardstown Partnership Area*, Blanchardstown: Blanchardstown Area Partnership.

Barr, J. (2000), in *Sinnott v. Minister for Education, Ireland and the Attorney General*.

Barron, S. and F. Mulvany (2003), *Annual Report of the National Intellectual Disability Database Committee*, Dublin: Health Research Board.

Barry J. and L. Daly (1988), *The Travellers' Health Status Study*, Dublin: Health Research Board.

Battell, A. (2003), *Effective Support for Early School Leavers: An Integrated Pro-active Initiative Tracking and Mentoring Early School Leavers in Waterford City and County. Project Report*, Waterford: Waterford Regional Youth Service.

Batty, P. and N. Bailey (1985), *In Touch with Children*, London: British Association of Adoption and Fostering.

Beauchamp, T. and J. Childress (1994), *Principles of Biomedical Ethics*, New York: Oxford.

Begley, M., C. Garavan, M. Condon, I. Kelly, K. Holland and A. Staines (1999), *Asylum in Ireland: A Public Health Perspective*, Dublin: Department of Public Health and Epidemiology, University College Dublin and Congregation of the Holy Ghost.

Beker, J. (2001), 'Development of a professional identity for the childcare worker', *Child and Youth Care Forum* 30 (6). pp. 345–54.

Belbin, R. (1993), *Team Roles at Work*, Oxford: Butterworth Heinemann.

Belsky, J. (2001), 'Developmental risks (still) associated with early childcare', *Journal of Child Psychology and Psychiatry* 42. pp. 845–60.

Belsky, J. and M. Rovine (1988), 'Nonmaternal care in the first year of life and the security of infant-parent attachment', *Child Development* 59. pp. 157–67.

Bentovin, A. (2002), 'Preventing sexually abused young people from becoming abusers, and treating the victimization experiences of young people who offend sexually', *Child Abuse and Neglect* 26. pp. 661–78.

Berube, P. (1984), 'Professionalisation of childcare: A Canadian example', *Journal of Child and Youth Care* 2 (1). pp. 13–26.

Bessant, J. (2004), 'Risk technologies and youth work practice', *Youth and Policy* 83. pp. 60–77.

Bettelheim, B. (1950), *Love is Not Enough*, Glencoe: Free Press.

Blackburn, S. (2002), *Being Good: A Short Introduction to Ethics*, Oxford: Oxford University Press.

Bloomquist, M. and S. Schell (2002), *Helping Children with Aggression and Conduct Problems: Best Practices for Intervention*, London: Guilford.

Bonnar, C. (1996), *Family Planning Needs of Travelling Women in the Midland Health Board Region*, Athlone: Department of Public Health, Midland Health Board.

Bowlby, J. (1951), *Maternal Care and Mental Health*, Geneva: World Health Organisation.

Bowlby, J. (1953), *Childcare and the Growth of Love*, Harmondsworth: Penguin.

Bowlby, J. (1973), *Attachment and Loss, Vol. 2: Separation*, New York: Basic Books

Bowlby, J.(1978), 'Attachment theory and its therapeutic implications', in S. Feinstein and P. Giovacchini (eds), *Adolescent Psychiatry: Developmental and Clinical Studies*, New York: Aronson.

Bowlby, J. (1980), *Attachment and Loss, Vol. 3: Loss, Sadness and Depression*. New York: Basic Books.

Brezina, T. (1998), 'Adolescent maltreatment and delinquency: The question of intervening processes', *Journal of Crime and Delinquency* 35. pp. 71–99.

Briar-Lawson, K., H. Lawson, C. Hennon and A. Jones (2001), *Family Centered Policies and Practices: International Implications*, New York: Columbia University Press.

Briere, J. and M. Runtz (1990), 'Differential adult symptomatology associated with three types of child abuse histories', *Child Abuse and Neglect* 14. pp. 357–64.

Brown, M. (2004), IMS presentation of research findings on opinions on racism and attitudes to minority groups (www.knowracism.ie).

Brown, P. (1994), 'Toward a psychobiological model of dissociation and post-traumatic stress disorder',. in S. Lynn and J. Rhue (eds), *Dissociation: Clinical and Theoretical Perspectives*, London: Guilford.

Brown, W. and W. Rhodes (1991), 'Factors that promote invulnerability and resiliency in at-risk children', in W. Brown and W. Rhodes (eds), *Why Some Children Succeed Despite the Odds*, New York: Praeger.

Bruner, J. (2002), *Making Stories: Law, Literature, Life*, New York: Farrar, Straus and Giroux.

Brunner, R., P. Parzer, V. Shuld and F. Resch (2000), 'Dissociative symptomatology and traumatogenic factors in adolescent psychiatric patients', *The Journal of Nervous and Mental Disease* 188. pp. 71–7.

Bryman, A. (1986), *Leadership and Organisations*, London: Routledge and Kegan Paul.

Buckley, H. (1996), 'Child abuse guidelines in Ireland: for whose protection?' in H. Ferguson and T. McNamara (eds), *Protecting Irish Children: Investigation, Protection and Welfare* (*Administration* 44(2)).

Burton, J. (1993), *The Handbook of Residential Care*, London: Routledge.

Buss, A. and R. Plomin (1986), 'The EAS approach to temperament', in R. Plomin and J. Dunn (eds), *The Study of Temperament: Changes, Continuities and Challenges*, Hillsdale (NJ): Erlbaum.

Byrne, J. (2003), 'Professional social care representation in Ireland: A social care worker's perspective'. Unpublished MA thesis, Waterford Institute of Technology.

Byrne, R. (1997), 'On the sliding scales of justice: the status of asylum seekers and refugees in Ireland', in R. Byrne and W. Duncan (eds), *Developments in Discrimination Law in Ireland and Europe*, Dublin: Irish Centre for European Law, Trinity College Dublin.

Campbell, J. and L. Lewandowski (1997), 'Mental and physical health effects of intimate partner violence on women and children', *Psychiatric Clinics of North America* 20. pp. 353–74.

Canavan, J., P. Dolan and J. Pinkerton (2002), *Family Support: Direction from Diversity*, London: Jessica Kingsley.

Cannan, C. and C. Warren (eds) (1997), *Social Action with Children and Families*, London: Routledge.

Cavanagh, K. and V. Cree (eds) (1996), *Working with Men: Feminism and Social Work*, London: Routledge.

Chakrabarti, M. and M. Hill (2000), *Residential Child Care: International Perspectives on Links with Families and Peers*, London: Jessica Kingsley.

Charles, G. (1995), 'Dealing with allegations of childhood ritual abuse', in T. Nay (ed) *True and False Allegations in Child Sexual Abuse: Assessment and Case Management*, New York: Brunner/Mazel.

Charles, G. (1996), 'Experiences of extreme abuse'. Unpublished PhD thesis, University of Victoria, Canada.

Charles, G. and P. Gabor (1990), 'An historical perspective on residential services for troubled and troubling youth in Canada', in G. Charles and S. McIntyre (eds), *The Best in Care: Recommendations for the Future of Residential Services for Troubled and Troubling Young People in Canada*, Ottawa: Canadian Child Welfare Association.

Charles, G. and J. Matheson (2003), 'Self-mutilative behaviour among young people in residential settings'. Unpublished paper, Vancouver.

Charles, G. and M. McDonald (1996), 'Adolescent sexual offenders', *Journal of Child and Youth Care*, 11 (1). pp. 15–25.

Charles, G., H. Coleman and J. Matheson (1993), 'Staff reactions to people who have been sexually abused', in G. Northrup (ed), *The Management of Sexuality in Residential Treatment*. London: Haworth.

Chisholm, K. (1998), 'A three year follow-up of attachment and indiscriminate friendliness in children adopted from Romanian orphanages', *Child Development* 69. pp. 1092–106.

Chrisjohn, R. and S. Young (1997), *The Circle Game: Shadows and Substance in the Indian Residential School Experience in Canada*, Penticton: Theytus Books.

Christie, A. (1998), '"Balancing gender" as men social workers', *Irish Social Worker* 16 (3). pp. 4–6.

Christie, A. (ed) (2001), *Men and Social Work*, Basingstoke: Palgrave.

Clarke, F. and P. O'Carroll (2001), 'The role of the community child care worker'. Unpublished BA (Hons) thesis, Athlone Institute of Technology.

Clarke, A. and A. Clarke (1976), *Early Experience: Myth and Evidence*, London: Open Books.

Clarke, M. (1998), *Lives in Care: Issues for Policy and Practice in Irish Children's Homes*, Dublin: Mercy Congregation/Children's Research Centre, Trinity College Dublin.

Clarke, M. (2003), 'Fit to practise: the education of professionals'. Paper to third annual IASCE conference, Cork (www.itsligo.ie/staff/pshare/IASCE/Fit%20to%20Practice.doc).

Clarke-Stewart, A. (1988), 'The effects of infant daycare reconsidered: risks for parents, children and researchers', *Early Childhood Research Quarterly* 3. pp. 292–318.

Clough, R. (2000), *The Practice of Residential Work*, Basingstoke: Macmillan.

Collins, A. (2001), *Meeting the Needs of Asylum Seekers in Tralee*, Tralee: Kerry Action for Development Education.

Collins, B. (2001), *The Development of Services. Module 1: Introduction to Disability*, The National Diploma in Applied Social Studies (Disability). Dublin: The Open Training College.

Colton, M. (2002), 'Professionalization and institutional abuse in the United Kingdom', In E. Knorth et al. (eds), *Professionalization and Participation in Child and Youth Care*, Aldershot: Ashgate.

Commission on the Status of People with Disabilities (1996), *A Strategy for Equality. Report of the Commission on the Status of People with Disabilities*, Dublin: Stationery Office.

Commission on the Status of People with Disabilities (1999), *Towards Equal Citizenship: Progress Report on the Implementation of the Recommendations of the Commission on the Status of People with Disabilities*, Dublin: Stationery Office.

Condron, M. (1989), *The Serpent and the Goddess*, San Francisco: Harper Collins.

Connell, R. (1987), *Gender and Power*, Oxford: Blackwell.

Connell, R. (1995), *Masculinities*, Cambridge: Polity.

Connolly, L. (2002), *The Irish Women's Movement*, Basingstoke: Palgrave.

Convery, J. (1987), *Choices in Community Care — Day Centres for the Elderly in the Eastern Health Board*, Dublin: National Council for the Aged (Report no.17).

Corcoran, M. (1999), 'Standards and criteria for the inspection of children's residential homes: the challenge of interdisciplinary co-working', *Irish Social Worker* 17 Autumn/Winter. p. 10.

Costello, J. and B. Webster (2003), 'Concepts of disability', in *Module 1: Introduction to Disability*, The National Diploma in Applied Social Studies (Disability) Dublin: The Open Training College. (distance education package).

Courtney, D. (1998), 'Social care and the European dimension', *Irish Journal of Applied Social Studies* 1 (2). pp. 139–49.

Coyle, D. (1998), *Foyle Trust Leaving and Aftercare Project; Transition from Care Conference Proceedings*, Derry: Foyle Trust.

Craig, S., M. Donnellan, G. Graham and A. Warren (1998), *Learn to Listen*, Dublin: Centre for Social and Educational Research.

Cree, V. (2001), 'Men and masculinities in social work education', in A. Christie (ed) *Men and Social Work*, Basingstoke: Palgrave.

Crosson-Tower, C. (2002), *Understanding Child Abuse and Neglect*, London: Allyn and Bacon.

CSO [Central Statistics Office] (2000), *2002 Census: Principal Demographic Results* (www.cso.ie/census/pdr_comment.htm).

CSO [Central Statistics Office] (2003), *Population and Migration Estimates 2003*, Dublin: Central Statistics Office.

Cullen, P. (2000), *Refugees and Asylum Seekers in Ireland*, Cork: Cork University Press.

CYCAA [Child and Youth Care Association of Alberta] (2000), *Certification Manual*. Edmonton: Child and Youth Care Association of Alberta.

Dennis, M. and S. Stevens (2003), 'Maltreatment issues and outcomes of adolescents enrolled in substance abuse treatment', *Child Maltreatment* 8 (1). pp. 3–6.

Devlin, M. (2002), 'A new impetus? The EU white paper on youth', *Irish YouthWork Scene* 35. pp. 3–6.

De Wolff, M. and M. Ijzendoorn (1997), 'Sensitivity and attachment: a meta-analysis on parental antecedents of attachment', *Child Development* 68. pp. 571–91.

Dixon, N. (1994), *On the Psychology of Military Incompetence*, London: Pimlico.

DoE [Department of Education] (1970), *Reformatory and Industrial Schools Systems Report*, Dublin: Stationery Office (The Kennedy Report).

DoH [Department of Health] (1988), *The Years Ahead: A Policy for the Elderly*, Dublin: Stationery Office.

DoH [Department of Health] (1994), *Shaping a Healthier Future: A Strategy for Effective Healthcare in the Nineties*, Dublin: Stationery Office.

DoH [Department of Health] (1995), *Code of Practice for Nursing Homes*, Dublin: Stationery Office.

DoH [Department of Health] (1996a), *Childcare (standards in children's residential centres) Regulations, 1996*, Dublin: Stationery Office.

DoH [Department of Health] (1996b), *Report on the Inquiry into the Operation of Madonna House*, Dublin: Dublin: Stationery Office.

DoH [Department of Health] (1997), *Survey of Long-stay Units, 1995*, Dublin: Stationery Office.

DoHC [Department of Health and Children] (1999), *Children First: National Guidelines for the Protection and Welfare of Children*, Dublin: Stationery Office.

DoHC [Department of Health and Children] (2000), *Statutory Registration for Health and Social Professionals: Proposals for the Way Forward*, Dublin: Stationery Office (www.doh.ie/pdfdocs/statreg.pdf)

DoHC [Department of Health and Children] (2001a), *Quality and Fairness: A Health System for You*, Dublin: Stationery Office.

DoHC [Department of Health and Children] (2001b), *Youth Homelessness Strategy*, Dublin: Stationery Office.

DoHC [Department of Health and Children] (2001c), *National Standards for Children's Residential Centres*, Dublin: Stationery Office.

DoHC [Department of Health and Children] (2002a), *Action Plan for People Management in the Health Service*, Dublin: Department of Health and Children.

DoHC [Department of Health and Children] (2002b), *Traveller Health: A National Strategy*, Dublin: Stationery Office.

DoHC (2004a), Estimated Non-Capital Health Expenditure 1990 to 2003 Categorised by Programme and Service, Department of Health and Children statistics. Section L: Expenditure statistics (www.doh.ie/statistics/stats/sectionl.html).

DoHC (2004b), Department of Health and Children statistics. Health service employment statistics: Health service total employment (www.doh.ie/statistics/hses/2004_numbers_employed.html).

Doherty, D. (1998), 'Adapting health management structures to achieve health and social gains', in A. Leahy and M. Wiley (eds), *The Irish Health System in the 21st Century*, Dublin: Oak Tree Press.

DoJELR [Department of Justice, Equality and Law Reform] (2000), *Integration: A Two Way Process*, Dublin: Stationery Office.

Dolan, Y. (1991), *Resolving Sexual Abuse: Solution-focused Therapy and Ericksonian Hypnosis for Adult Survivors*, London: Norton.

Dominelli, L. (1997), *Sociology for Social Work*, Basingstoke: Macmillan.

Doolan R. (2002), 'Exploring the role of aftercare programmes in the lives of young people leaving residential care'. Unpublished MsocSc thesis, University College Dublin.

DoSW [Department of Social Welfare] (1963), *Report of the Commission on Itinerancy*, Dublin: Stationery Office.

Dozier, M., K. Case Stovall, K. Albus and B. Bates (2001), 'Attachment for infants in foster care: the role of caregiver state of mind', *Child Development* 72 (5). pp. 1467–77.

Draucker, C. (1995), 'A coping model: adult survivors of childhood sexual abuse', *Journal of Interpersonal Violence* 10 (2). pp. 159–75.

Driver, E. (1989), 'Introduction', in E. Driver and A. Droisen (eds), *Child Sexual Abuse: A Feminist Reader*, New York: New York University Press.

Duffy, J. (2002), 'An Irishman's diary'. *The Irish Times*, 2 December.

Duggan-Jackson, A. (2000), *The Voice of Traveller Women through Research: A Health Needs Assessment of Traveller Women by Traveller Women*, Athlone: Department of Public Health, Midland Health Board.

Eckenrode, J., M. Laird, M. and J. Doris (1993), 'School performance and disciplinary problems among abused and neglected children', *Developmental Psychology* 29. pp. 53–67.

EHB [Eastern Health Board] (1998), *Childcare and Family Support Service in 1998: Review of Adequacy*, Dublin: Eastern Health Board.

EHB [Eastern Health Board] (1999a), *Strategic Plan for Residential Care in the Eastern Health Board Region*, Dublin: Eastern Health Board.

EHB [Eastern Health Board] (1999b), *Ten Year Action Plan for Services for Older Persons, 1999–2008*, Dublin: Eastern Health Board.

Ehrenreich, B. and D. English (1974), *Witches, Midwives and Nurses: A History of Women Healers*, London: Compendium.

Elicker, J., M. Englund and L. Sroufe (1992), 'Predicting peer competence and peer relationships in childhood from early parent–child relationships', in R. Parke and G. Ladd (eds), *Family–Peer Relationships: Modes of Linkage*, Hillsdale (NJ): Erlbaum.

Elliot, G., R. Avery, E. Fishman and B. Hoshiko (2002), 'The encounter with family violence and risky sexual behaviour activity among young adolescent females', *Violence and Victims* 17 (5). pp. 569–92.

Elsdon, I. (1998), 'Educating toward awareness: Self-awareness in ethical decision making for child and youth care workers', *Journal of Child and Youth Care* 12 (3). pp. 55–67.

ERHA [Eastern Regional Health Authority] (2004), *Policy on Leaving Care*, Leaving Care Sub-group of the Youth Homeless Forum, Dublin: Eastern Region Health Authority.

Eriksson, L. and A-M. Markström (2003), 'Interpreting the concept of social pedagogy', in A. Gustavsson et al. (eds), *Perspective and Theories in Social Pedagogy*, Göteborg: Daidalos.

Esping-Andersen, G. (1990), *The Three Worlds of Welfare Capitalism*, New Jersey: Princeton University Press.

EUROARRCC [European Association for Research into Residential Childcare] (1998), *Care to Listen*, Dublin: European Association for Research into Residential Childcare, Dublin Institute of Technology.

Fahey, T. and J. FitzGerald (1997), *Welfare Implications of Demographic Trends*, Dublin: Oak Tree Press/Combat Poverty Agency.

Fahey, T. (1994), *Health and Autonomy Among the Over 65s in Ireland*, Dublin: National Council for the Elderly.

Fahlberg, V. (1994), *A Child's Journey Through Placement*, London: British Agencies for Adoption and Fostering.

Fanning, B. (2001), *Beyond the Pale: Asylum-Seeking Children and Social Exclusion in Ireland*, Dublin: Irish Refugee Council.

Fanning, B., S. Loyal and C. Staunton (2000), *Asylum Seekers and the Right to Work in Ireland*, Dublin: Irish Refugee Council and Combat Poverty Agency.

Farrell, F. and P. Watt (eds) (2001), *Responding to Racism in Ireland*, Dublin: Veritas.

Faughnan, P. (1999), *Refugees and Asylum Seekers in Ireland: Social Policy Dimensions*, Dublin: Social Science Research Centre, University College Dublin.

Faughnan, P. and A. O'Donovan (2002), *A Changing Voluntary Sector: Working with New Minority Communities in 2001*, Dublin: Social Science Research Centre, University College Dublin.

Faughnan, P. and M. Woods (2000), *Lives on Hold: Seeking Asylum in Ireland*, Dublin: Social Science Research Centre, University College Dublin.

Faughnan, P., N. Humphries and S. Whelan (2002), *Patching up the System: The Community Welfare Service and Asylum Seekers*, Dublin: Social Science Research Centre, University College Dublin.

Featherstone, M. and M. Hepworth (1993), 'Images of ageing', in J. Bond et al. (eds) *Ageing in Society*, London: Sage.

Feder, G. (1994), 'Traveller Gypsies and primary health care in East London'. Unpublished PhD thesis, St Thomas Hospital Medical School, University of London.

Feder Kittay, E. (1999), *Love's Labour*, New York: Routledge.

Feldman, A, C. Frese and T. Yousif (2002), *Research, Development and Critical Interculturalism: A Study on the Participation of Refugees and Asylum Seekers in Research and Development-Based Initiatives*, Dublin: Social Science Research Centre, University College Dublin (www.ucd.ie/ssrc/interculturalism.doc).

Ferguson, H. (1997), 'Child welfare and child protection in practice :are we getting the balance right?' Paper to 'The Childcare Act 1991. Promoting the welfare of children: Making it work in practice' Conference, Mullingar.

Ferguson, H. and M. O'Reilly (2001), *Keeping Children Safe: Child Abuse, Child Protection and the Promotion of Welfare*, Dublin: A & A Farmar.

Ferguson, H. and P. Kenny (1995), *On Behalf of the Child. Child Welfare, Child Protection and the Child Care Act, 1991*, Dublin: A & A Farmar.

Ferguson, R. (1993), 'Introduction: Child and youth care education: Approaching a new millennium', *Child and Youth Care Forum* 22 (4). pp. 251–61.

Fewster, G. (2001), 'Turning my self inside out: my personal theory of me', *Journal of Child and Youth Care* 15 (4). pp. 89—108.

Fielder, F. (1967), *A Theory of Leadership Effectiveness*, New York: McGraw Hill.

Finnegan, F. (2004), *Do Penance or Perish: Magdalen Asylums in Ireland*, Oxford: Oxford University Press.

Flannery, D., M. Singer and K. Wester (2003), 'Violence, coping, and mental health in a community sample of adolescents', *Violence and Victims* 18 (4). pp. 403–17.

Flew, A. (1984), *A Dictionary of Philosophy*, Basingstoke: Macmillan.

Flynn, M. (1986), 'Mortality, morbidity and marital features of Travellers in the Irish Midlands', *Irish Medical Journal* 70. pp. 308–10.

Flynn, M., M. Martin, P. Moore, J. Stafford, G. Fleming and J. Phang (1989), 'Type II hyperprolimaemia in a pedigree of Irish Travellers (nomads)', *Archives of Disease in Childhood* 64. pp. 1699–707.

Focus Ireland (1996), *Focus on Residential Child Care in Ireland: 25 Years Since the Kennedy Report*, Dublin: Focus Ireland.

Forkan, C. (2003), *Youth Perspectives*, Dublin: Foróige.

Foucault, M. (1980), *Power/Knowledge: Selected Interviews and Other Writings 1972–1977*, Brighton: Harvester.

Foucault, M. (1991), *Discipline and Punish. The Birth of the Prison*. Harmondsworth: Penguin.

Fournier, S. and E. Crey (1997), *Stolen from our Embrace: The Abduction of First Nations Children and the Restoration of Aboriginal Communities*, Toronto: Douglas and McIntyre.

Freidson, E. (1970), *Profession of Medicine: A Study of the Sociology of Applied Knowledge*, New York: Dodd, Mead.

Freidson, E. (1990), 'Professionalism, caring, and nursing'. Paper prepared for The Park Ridge Center, Park Ridge, Illinois (http://itsa.ucsf.edu/~eliotf/ Professionalism,_Caring,_a.html).

Freidson, E. (1994), *Professionalism Reborn: Theory, Prophecy and Policy*, Cambridge: Polity.

Freidson, E. (2001), *Professionalism: The Third Logic*. Cambridge: Polity.

Friedrich, W. (1993), 'Sexual behaviour in sexually abused children', *Violence Update* 3 (1). pp. 5–7.

Frye, M. (1983), *The Politics of Reality*, Freedom (CA): Crossing Press.

Furnell, J., S. Flett and D. Clark (1987), 'Multi-disciplinary clinical teams: some issues in establishment and function'. *Hospital and Health Services Review* 83(1). pp. 15–18.

Gaffney, M., S. Greene, D. Wieczorek-Deering and J. Nugent (2000), 'The concordance between mother–infant attachment at 18 months and maternal attachment 10 years later among married and single mothers', *Irish Journal of Psychology* 21 (3–4). pp. 54-170.

Gallagher, C. and K. Kennedy (2003), 'The training implications of a social care approach to working with older people', *Irish Journal of Applied Social Studies* 4 (1). pp. 21–35.

Gallagher, C. and J. O' Toole (1999), 'Towards a sociological understanding of care work in Ireland', *Irish Journal of Social Work Research* 2 (1). pp. 60–86.

Gallagher, P. (2001), *National Physical and Sensory Disability Database. Report of the National Physical and Sensory Disability Database Development Committee*, Dublin: Health Research Board.

Garavan, R., R. Winder and H. McGee (2001), *Health and Social Services for Older People (HeSSOP)*, Dublin: National Council on Ageing and Older People.

Garfat, T. (1988), 'The magic of children and youth: A participatory exercise', *Child and Youth Care Quarterly* 17 (2). pp. 70–85.

Garfat, T. (1993), 'On blind spots and blank spots', *Journal of Child and Youth Care* 8 (4). pp. iii–iv.

Garfat, T. (1994), 'Never alone: reflections on the presence of self and history on child and youth care', *Journal of Child and Youth Care Work* 9 (1). pp. 35–43.

Garfat, T. (1998), 'The effective child and youth care intervention', *Journal of Child and Youth Care* 12 (1–2). pp.1–168.

Garfat, T. (2001), 'Developmental stages of child and youth care workers'. *CYC-Net* 24. pp. 1–8.

Garfat, T. and McElwee, C. N. (2001), 'The changing role of family in child and youth care practice', *Journal of Child and Youth Care Work* 15–16. pp. 236–48.

Garnefski, N. and E. Arends (1998), 'Sexual abuse and adolescent maladjustment: Differences between male and female victims', *Journal of Adolescence* 21 (1). pp. 99–107.

Garnett, L. (1992), *Leaving Care and After*, London: National Children's Bureau.

Gaughan, P. and K. Gharabaghi (1999), 'The prospects and dilemmas of child and youth care as a professional discipline', *Journal of Child and Youth Care* 13 (1). pp.1–18.

Gerstel, N. and S. Gallagher (2001), 'Men's caregiving', *Gender and Society* 15 (2). pp. 197–217.

Gilligan, C. (1982), *In a Different Voice*, Cambridge (MA): Harvard University Press.

Gilligan, R. (1991), *Irish Child Care Services: Practice, Policy and Provision*, Dublin: Institute of Public Administration.

Gilligan, R. (1997), 'Beyond permanence? The importance of resilience in child placement practice and planning', *Adoption and Fostering* 21. pp. 12–20.

Gilligan, R. (1999), 'Child welfare review, 1998', *Administration* 47 (2). pp. 232–56.

Gilligan, R. (2000a), 'Developmental implications of life in public care', *Irish Journal of Psychology* 21 (3–4). pp. 138–53.

Gilligan, R. (2000b), 'Family support: issues and prospects', in J. Canavan, P. Dolan and J. Pinkerton (eds), *Family Support: Direction from Diversity*, London: Jessica Kingsley.

Gilligan, R. (2001), *Promoting Resilience: A Resource Guide on Working with Children in the Care System*, London: British Agencies for Adoption and Fostering.

Glazer, N. and D. Moynihan (1975), *Ethnicity: Theory and Experience*, Cambridge (MA): Harvard University Press.

Gleason, W. (1995), 'Children of battered women: Developmental delays and behavioural dysfunction', *Violence and Victims* 10 (2). pp. 153–60.

Global Youth Network (2002), *Good Practices. Alcohol Trends Among Youth in Europe* (www.undcp.org/youthnet).

Gogarty, H. (1995), 'The implications of the Childcare Act 1991 for working with children in care', in H. Ferguson and P. Kenny (eds), *On Behalf of the Child: Child Welfare, Child Protection and the Childcare Act 1991*, Dublin: A & A Farmar.

Goldfarb, W. (1947), 'Variations of adolescent adjustment of institutionally reared children', *American Journal of Orthopsychiatry* 17. pp. 449–57.

Goodin, R., B, Headey, R. Muffels and H-J. Dirven (1999), *The Real Worlds of Welfare Capitalism*, Cambridge: Cambridge University Press.

Gordon, M., D. Gorman, S. Hashem and D. Stewart (1991), 'The health of Travellers' children in Northern Ireland', *Public Health* 105. pp. 387–391.

Graham, G. (1995), 'The roles of the residential care worker'. *Journal of the European Association of Training Centres for Socio-educational Care Work*, 1. pp. 125–53.

Graham, G. (2002), 'A role matrix for the Irish social care worker'. Paper to Annual Conference of the Irish Association of Social Care Educators, Carlow.

Grupper, E. (2002), 'Child and youth care work at the cross-roads of the century', in E. Knorth et al. (eds), *Professionalization and Participation in Child and Youth Care*, Aldershot: Ashgate.

Guthrie, W. (1981), *A History of Greek Philosophy: Aristotle, an Encounter*, Cambridge: Cambridge University Press.

Hallstedt, P. and M. Högström (2004), *The Discourses of Social Pedagogy: Case Studies of Three Educational Programmes*, Department of Teacher Education, Malmö University.

Hamilton, C. (2000), 'Continuity and discontinuity of attachment from infancy through adulthood', *Child Development* 71 (3). pp. 690–94.

Hanmer, J. and D. Statham (eds) (1999), *Women and Social Work*, Basingstoke: Macmillan.

Harding,T. and P. Beresford (eds) (1996), *The Standards We Expect: What Service Users and Carers Want from Social Services Workers*, London: National Institute for Social Work.

Harker, L. (2004), 'What's social work'? *Community Care* 1–7 April. p. 22.

Harlow, H. and M. Harlow (1969), 'Effects of various mother–infant relationships on rhesus monkey behaviours', in B. Foss (ed), *Determinants of Infant Behaviour* (vol. 4), London: Methuen.

Harris, R. and A. Lavan (1992), 'Professional mobility in the new Europe: the case of social work'. *Journal of European Social Policy* 2 (1). pp. 1–15.

Hawke, J., N. Jainchill and G. de Leon (2003), 'Posttreatment victimization and violence among adolescents following residential drug treatment'. *Maltreatment* 8 (1). pp. 58–71.

Hawkins, P. and R. Shohet (1989), *Supervision in the Helping Professions*, Milton Keynes: Open University Press.

Hazan, C. and P. Shaver (1994), 'Attachment as an organisational framework for research on close relationships', *Psychological Inquiry* 5, pp. 1–22.

Hearn, J. (1999), 'A crisis in masculinity or new agendas for men', in S. Walby (ed), *New Agendas for Women*, Oxford: Polity.

Henderson, J. and D. Atkinson (2003), *Managing Care in Context*. London: Routledge.

Hennessy, S. (2002), 'Assessing work in the living environment', in: *Module 14: Creating Living Environments*, The National Diploma in Applied Social Studies (Disability). Dublin: The Open Training College.

Herd, P. and M. Meyer (2002), 'Care work: invisible civic engagement', *Gender and Society* 16 (5). pp. 665–88.

Hermansen, O. (1993), *Community Work: Working with Projects*, Aarhus: PEP.

Herrera, V. and L. McCloskey (2003), 'Sexual abuse, family violence and female delinquency: Findings from a longitudinal study', *Violence and Victims* 18 (3). pp. 319–34.

Hessle, S. (2002), 'What happens when social pedagogy becomes part of the academic higher social work education programme?' *European Journal of Social Education* 3. pp. 1–3.

Hilliard, B. (2002), 'The Catholic Church and married women's sexuality: habitus change in late 20th century Ireland', *Irish Journal of Sociology* 12 (2). pp. 28–49.

Hinman, L. (1997), *Ethics: A Pluralistic Approach to Moral Theory*, New York: Harcourt Brace.

Hirsch, P. (1998), *A Tribe Apart. A Journey into the Heart of American Adolescence*, New York: Fawcett Columbine.

Hobbes, T. (1965), *Leviathan*, London: Penguin.

Holmes, J. (1993), *John Bowlby and Attachment Theory*, London: Routledge.

Horrocks ,C. and K. Karban (1999), 'Being there: residential care of children and young people', in Violence Against Children Study Group, *Children, Child Abuse and Child Protection: Placing Children Centrally*, New York: Wiley.

Howe, D. (1995), *Attachment Theory for Social Work Practice*. Basingstoke: Macmillan.

Howes, C. and C. Hamilton (1992), 'Children's relationships with childcare teachers: stability and concordance with parental attachments', *Child Development* 63. pp. 867–78.

Huczynski, A. and D. Buchmanan (2001), *Organisational Behaviour: An Introductory Text*, Harlow: Financial Times/Prentice Hall.

Hug, C. (1999), *The Politics of Sexual Morality in Ireland*, Basingstoke: Macmillan.

Hurson Kelly, M. (1998), 'Recreational and entertainment needs and requirements of the elderly in a community unit'. Unpublished paper, Eastern Health Board, Dublin.

Hyman, S., S. Gold and M. Cott (2003), 'Forms of social support that moderate PTSD in childhood sexual assault survivors', *Journal of Family Violence* 18 (5). pp. 295–300.

IASCE [Irish Association of Social Care Educators] (2000), *Working Models. A Manual for Placement Supervision*, Carlow: St. Patrick's College.

IMPACT (1998), Submission to the Expert Review Group on behalf of care workers. Dublin: IMPACT.

Inglis, T. (1998a), 'Foucault, Bourdieu and the field of Irish sexuality', *Irish Journal of Sociology* 7. pp. 5–28.

Inglis, T. (1998b), *Lessons in Irish Sexuality*, Dublin: University College Dublin Press.

Inglis, T. (1998c), *Moral Monopoly: The Rise and Fall of the Catholic Church in Modern Ireland*, Dublin: University College Dublin Press.

Interdepartmental Committee on the Aged (1968), *Care of the Aged. Report of Interdepartmental Committee on the Aged*, Dublin: Stationery Office.

IRC [Irish Refugee Council] (1999), *Separated Children Seeking Asylum in Ireland: A Report on Legal and Social Conditions*, Dublin: Irish Refugee Council.

Jacobson, N. and J. Gottman (1998), *When Men Batter Women: New Insights into Ending Abusive Relationships*, New York: Simon and Schuster.

JCSCP [Joint Committee on Social Care Professionals] (nd), *Report of Joint Committee on Social Care Professionals*, No publisher given.

Jenkins, R. (1996), '"Us" and "them": ethnicity, racism and ideology', in R. Barot (ed) *The Racism Problematic: Contemporary Sociological Debates on Race and Ethnicity*, Lampeter: Mellen.

Jenkins, R. (1997), *Rethinking Ethnicity: Arguments and Explorations*, London: Sage.

Johnson, L. (1998), *Social Work Practice: A Generalist Approach*, London: Allyn and Bacon.

Jull, D. (2001), 'Is child and youth care a profession?' *Journal of Child and Youth Care* 14 (3). pp. 79–88.

Kahan, B. (1994), *Growing up in Groups*, London: HMSO.

Kant, I. (1959), *Groundwork of the Metaphysics of Morals* (trans. W Beck), New York: Bobs Merrill.

Karr-Morse, R. and M. Wiley (1997), *Ghosts from the Nursery: Tracing the Roots of Violence*, New York: Atlantic Monthly Press.

Kaukinen, C. (2002), 'Adolescent victimization and problem drinking', *Violence and Victims* 17 (6). pp. 669–689.

Kazenbuch, J. and D. Smith (1993), *The Discipline of Teams*, Cambridge (MA): Harvard Business Review Press.

Kearney, D. (2002), 'Youth participation: what makes it real?' *Irish YouthWork Scene* 36. pp. 10–11.

Kelleher, P., C. Kelleher and M. Corbett (2000), *Left Out on Their Own: Young People Leaving Care in Ireland*, Dublin: Oak Tree Press/Focus Ireland.

Kelly, M. (ed.) (1994), *Critique and Power: Recasting the Foucault/Habermas Debate*. Oxford: Blackwell.

Kenrick, P. (1998), *The Travellers of Ireland* (http://www.geocities.com/Paris/5121/ireland.htm).

Kennedy, K. and C. Gallagher (1997), 'Social pedagogy in Europe', *Irish Social Worker* 15 (1).

Kinard, E. (2001), 'Characteristics of maltreatment experience and academic functions among maltreated children', *Violence and Victims* 16 (3). pp. 323–37.

Knoppers, A. (1993), 'A critical theory of gender relations' in M. van Leeuwen (ed) *After Eden*, Grand Rapids (MI): Eerdmans.

Knorth, E., P. van den Bergh and F. Verheij (eds) (2002), *Professionalization and Participation in Child and Youth Care*, Aldershot: Ashgate.

Kochanska, G. (2001), 'Emotional development in children with different attachment histories: the first three years', *Child Development* 72 (2). pp. 474–90.

Korner, W. (1977), *Kant*, Harmondsworth: Penguin.

Kosonen, M. (1996), 'Siblings as providers of support and care during middle childhood: children's perceptions', *Children and Society* 10 (4). pp. 267–79.

Kotter, J. (1990), *A Force for Change: How Leadership Differs from Management*, New York: Free Press.

Kouzes, J. and B. Posner (1987), *The Leadership Challenge: How to Get Extraordinary Things Done in Organizations*, San Francisco: Jossey-Bass.

Kraemer, G. W. (1992), 'A psychological theory of attachment', *Behavioural and Brain Sciences* 15. pp. 493–541.

Krueger, M. (1998), *Interactive Youth Work Practice*, Washington (DC): Child Welfare League of America.

Krueger, M. (2002), 'A further review of the development of the child and youth care profession in the United States', *Child and Youth Care Forum* 31 (1). pp. 13–26.

Lakatos, K., I. Toth, Z. Nemoda, K. Ney, M. Sasvari-Szekely and J. Gervaj (2002), 'Dopamine D4 receptor (DRD4) gene polymorphism is associated with attachment disorganisation in infants', *Molecular Psychiatry* 5. pp. 633–7.

Laming, Lord (2003), *The Victoria Climbié Inquiry. Report of an Inquiry by Lord Laming Presented to Parliament by the Secretary of State for Health and the Secretary of State for the Home Department*, London: HMSO.

Laslett, P. (1989), *A Fresh Map of Life: The Emergence of the Third Age*, London: Weidenfeld and Nicholson.

Layte, R., T. Fahey and C. Whelan (1999), *Income, Deprivation and Well-being Among Older Irish People*, Dublin: National Council on Ageing and Older People.

Leavy, A. and B. Kahan (1991), *The Pindown Experience and the Protection of Children. The Report of the Staffordshire Child Care Enquiry*, Stafford: Staffordshire County Council.

Lees, S. (1993), *Sugar and Spice: Sexuality and Adolescent Girls*, Harmondsworth: Penguin.

Lentin, R. (1998), '"Irishness", the 1937 Constitution, and citizenship: a gender and ethnicity view', *Irish Journal of Sociology* 8. pp. 5–24.

Lewin, K. (1951), *Field Theory in Social Sciences*, New York: Harper.

Lewis, M., C. Feiring and S. Rosenthal (2000), 'Attachment over time', *Child Development* 71 (3). pp. 707–20.

Leyton, E. (1986), *Hunting Humans: The Rise of the Modern Multiple Murderer*, Toronto: McClelland and Stewart.

Likert, R. (1961), *New Patterns of Management*, New York: McGraw-Hill.

Lindsay, M. (2002), 'Building a professional identity: the challenge for residential child and youth care', in E. Knorth et al. (eds), *Professionalization and Participation in Child and Youth Care*, Aldershot: Ashgate.

Litrownik, A., R. Newton, W. Hunter, D. English and M. Everson (2003), 'Exposure to family violence in young at-risk children: A longitudinal look at the effects of victimization and witnessed physical and psychological aggression', *Journal of Family Violence* 18 (1). pp. 59–73.

LMR [Lansdowne Market Research] (2001), *Attitudes to Minorities*, Survey prepared for Amnesty International in association with Public Communications Centre.

Lorenz, K. (1952), *King Solomon's Ring*, London: Methuen.

Lorenz, W. (1994), *Social Work in a Changing Europe*, London: Routledge.

Lorenz, W. (1998), 'Cultural diversity as a challenge for social work', *Irish Social Worker* 16 (3). pp. 15–17.

Luft, J. (1969), *Of Human Interaction*, Palo Alto (CA): National Press.

Lynch, K. and E. McLaughlin (1995), 'Caring labour and love labour', in P. Clancy et al. (eds), *Irish Society: Sociological Perspectives*, Dublin: Institute of Public Administration.

Lyons-Ruth, K. and D. Jacobvitz (1999), 'Attachment disorganisation: unresolved loss, relational violence and lapses in behavioural and emotional strategies', in J. Cassidy and P. Shaver (eds), *Handbook of Attachment: Theory, Research and Clinical Applications*, New York: Guilford.

MacAongusa, M. (1990), *The Alienation of Travellers from the Educational System in Ireland*, Dublin: Sociological Association of Ireland.

Macionis, J. and K. Plummer (2002), *Sociology: A Global Introduction*, Upper Saddle River (NJ): Prentice Hall.

MacKenna, P. (1994), 'Ontario Association of Child and Youth Care Counsellors: Effectiveness and future directions', *Journal of Child and Youth Care* 9 (4). pp. 1–10.

MacLachlan, M. and M. O'Connell (2000), *Cultivating Pluralism: Psychological, Social and Cultural Perspectives on a Changing Ireland*, Dublin: Oak Tree Press.

Madsen, B. (1995), *Socialpedagogik og samfundsforvandling*, Copenhagen: Munksgaard, Socialpedagogisk Bibliotek.

Maier, H. (1963), 'Child care as a method of social work', in H. Hagan (ed), *Training for Child Care Staff*, New York: Child Welfare League of America.

Main, M. and R. Goldwyn (1984), 'Predicting rejection of her infant from mother's representation of her own experience: implications for the abused–abusing inter-generational cycle', *Child Abuse and Neglect* 8. pp. 203–17.

Main, M. and R. Goldwyn (1998), Adult attachments scoring and classification system (Version 6.3). Unpublished manuscript, Department of Psychology, University of California, Berkeley (CA).

Main, M. and E. Hesse (1990), 'Parents' unresolved traumatic experiences are related to infant disorganised attachment status: Is frightened and/or frightening parental behaviour the linking mechanism?' in M. Greenberg et al. (eds), *Attachment in the Preschool Years*, Chicago: University of Chicago Press.

Main, M. and J. Solomon (1986), 'Discovery of an insecure/disorganised attachment pattern', in T. Brazelton and M. Yogman (eds), *Affective Development in Infancy*, Norwood (NJ): Ablex.

Main, M. and J. Solomon (1990), 'Procedures for identifying infants as disorganised / disorientated during the Ainsworth strange situation', in M. Greenberg et al. (eds), *Attachments Across the Preschool Years*, Chicago: University of Chicago Press.

Malchiodi, C. (1997), *Breaking the Silence: Art Therapy with Children from Violent Homes*, Bristol (CT): Brunner/Mazel.

Mangelsdorf, S., J. McHale, M. Diener, L. Goldstein and L. Lehn (2000), 'Infant attachment: Contributions of infant temperament and maternal characteristics', *Infant Behaviour and Development* 23. pp. 175–96.

Mann-Feder, V. (2002), 'From the editor', *Journal of Child and Youth Care Work* 17, pp. 3–4.

Maslow, A. (1954), *Motivation and Personality*, New York: Harper.

Matas, L., R. Arend and L. Sroufe (1978), 'Continuity of adaptation in the second year: the relationship between quality of attachment and later competence', *Child Development* 47. pp. 511–14.

Mathews, F. (1996), 'The adolescent sex offender field in Canada: old problems, current issues, and emerging controversies', *Journal of Child and Youth Care* 11 (1). pp. 55–62.

Mathiesen, R. (2000), *Sosialpedagogisk perspektiv*, Hamar: Sokrates.

McCann, M. S. Ó Síocháin and J. Ruane (1994), *Irish Travellers: Culture and Ethnicity*, Belfast: Institute of Irish Studies, Queen's University.

McClellan, J., C. McCurry, M.Ronnei, J. Adams, A. Eisner and M. Storck (1996), 'Age of onset of sexual abuse: relationship to sexually inappropriate behaviours', *Journal of the American Academy of Child and Adolescence* 35. pp. 1375–83.

McCormack, B., (1997), 'Trends in the development of disability services', in: *Module 1: The Evolution and Development of Disability Services in Ireland*, The National Diploma in Vocational Rehabilitation, Dublin: The Open Training College.

McElwee, C. N. (1996), 'Issues of child care/social care policy and practice in the Republic of Ireland: The NCEA report on social and caring studies 1992 assessed', *Child Care in Practice* 3(1). pp. 94–104.

McElwee, C. N. (1998), 'The search for the holy grail in Ireland: Social care in perspective', *Irish Journal of Applied Social Studies* 1 (1). pp. 79–105.

McElwee, C. N. (2000), *To Travel Hopefully: Views from the Managers of Residential Childcare in Ireland*, Dublin: Resident Managers' Association.

McElwee, C. N. (2001a), 'Legislative and service initiatives: A personal perspective', in K. Lalor (ed), *The End of Innocence: Child Sexual Abuse in Ireland*, Dublin: Oak Tree Press.

McElwee, C. N. (2001b), 'Male practitioners in child and youth care: An endangered species?' (www.cyc-net.org/cyc-online/cycol-0401-irishideas.html).

McElwee, C. N. (2001c), 'Snowflake children: Aspects of risk, at risk and resiliency in the context of the youth encounter project system in Ireland. Unpublished PhD thesis, Waterford Institute of Technology.

McElwee, C. N. (2003a), 'Exploring the self: on being an effective child and youth care worker'. Paper to the Child and Youth Care Program at Grant MacEwan College, March.

McElwee, C. N. (2003b), 'Finding identity in family work: Community child care workers in Ireland', in T. Garfat (ed), *A Child and Youth Care Approach to Working with Families*, New York: Haworth.

McElwee, C. N. (2003c), 'Lead, follow or get out of the way', Paper to the Irish Resident Managers' Association Annual Conference, Dundalk, November.

McElwee, C. N. and T. Garfat (2003a), *Practicum Manual*, Limerick: EirCan Consulting and Training.

McElwee, C. N. and T. Garfat (2003b), 'What's in a name? Exploring title designations in child and youth care in Ireland', *Irish Journal of Applied Social Studies*, 4 (1). pp. 5–20.

McElwee, C. N., A. Jackson, A. and G. Charles (2003), 'Towards a sociological understanding of Irish Travellers: Introducing a people', *Irish Journal of Applied Social Studies* 4(1). pp. 103–19.

McElwee, C. N., A. Jackson, S. McKenna-McElwee and B. Cameron (2003), *Where Have All the Good Men Gone? Exploring Males in Social Care in Ireland*, Athlone: Centre for Child and Youth Care Learning, Athlone Institute of Technology.

McElwee, C. N., S. McKenna-McElwee and J. Phelan (2002), 'Living in the risk society: Some implications for child and youth care workers in relation to the touch and hugging debate', *Journal of Child and Youth Care Work* 17, pp. 118–29.

McGréil, M. (1996), *Prejudice and Tolerance in Ireland Revisited*, Survey and Research Unit, Department of Social Studies, St Patrick's College, Maynooth, Co. Kildare.

McKenna-McElwee, S. (1996), 'Children of St Augustine's'. Unpublished BA (Hons) thesis, Waterford Institute of Technology.

McKeon, O. (2002), *Findings of the National Childcare Worker Survey*, Dublin: Department of Health and Children.

McGuinness, C. (1993), *Kilkenny Incest Investigation*, Dublin: Stationery Office.

McLaughlin, E. (2001), 'From Catholic corporatism to social partnership', in A. Cochrane et al. (eds), *Comparing Welfare States*, London: Sage.

McMahan-True, M., L. Pisani and F. Oumar (2001), 'Infant-mother attachment among the Dogon of Mali', *Child Development* 72 (5). pp. 1451–66.

Mead. M. (1962), 'A cultural anthropologist's approach to maternal deprivation', in M. Ainsworth (ed), *Deprivation of Maternal Care: A Reassessment of its Effects*. Geneva: World Health Organisation.

Meenan, D. (2002), 'The phenomenology of career and personal development as perceived by residential child care workers in the North Western Health Board'. Unpublished MBA (Health Services Management) thesis, University College Dublin/Royal College of Surgeons in Ireland.

Merton, R. (1968), *Social Theory and Social Structure*, New York: Free Press.

MHB [Midland Health Board] (2002), *Tapping the Talent: A Report on the Arts in Care Settings for Older People Project*, Age and Opportunity, Midland Health Board and Laois County Council.

Mill, J. S. (1998), *On Liberty and Other Essays*, New York: Oxford.

Mintzberg, H. (1979), *The Structuring of Organizations*, Englewood Cliffs (NJ): Prentice Hall.

Moane, G. (1994), 'A psychological analysis of colonialism in an Irish context', *The Irish Journal of Psychology* 15 (2/3). pp. 250–65.

Moane, G. (1999), *Gender and Colonialism: A Psychological Analysis of Oppression and Liberation*, Basingstoke: Macmillan.

Morley, M., S. Moore, N. Heraty and P. Gunnigle (1998), *Principles of Organisational Behaviour: An Irish Text*, Dublin: Gill & Macmillan.

Morrell, P. (1999), British homeopathy during two centuries. M.Phil thesis, University of Staffordshire (www.homeoint.org/morrell/british/profession.htm #process).

Murgatroyd, S. (1996), *Counselling and Helping*, London: Routledge.

NACYCEP [North American Consortium of Child and Youth Care Education Programs] (1995), 'Special report: Curriculum content for child and youth care practice: Recommendations of the North American Consortium of Child and Youth Care Education Programs', *Child and Youth Care Forum* 23 (4). pp. 269–78.

NCAOP [National Council on Ageing and Older People] (1998), *Adding Years to Life and Life to Years: A Health Promotion Strategy for Older People*, Dublin: National Council on Ageing and Older People in association with the Department of Health and Children.

NCAOP [National Council on Ageing and Older People] (2000), *A Framework for Quality in Long-Term Residential Care for Older People in Ireland*, Dublin: National Council on Ageing and Older People (Report no. 62).

NCAOP (2004), *Population Ageing in Ireland: Projections 2002–2021*, Dublin: National Council on Ageing and Older People.

NCV [National Committee on Volunteering] (2002), *Tipping the Balance: Report and Recommendations to Government on Supporting and Developing Volunteering in Ireland*, Dublin: National Committee on Volunteering.

Nirje, B. (1980), 'The normalisation principle', in R. Flynn and K. Nitch (eds), *Normalisation, Integration and Community Services*, Baltimore: University Park Press.

Noonan, P. (1994), *Travelling People in West Belfast*, London: Save the Children.

Norton, F. (1999), *Social Care and Social Work: An Assessment of Student Attitudes*, Paper to FESET European Congress, Antwerp.

NSWQB [National Social Work Qualifications Board] (2000), *Social Work Posts in Ireland on 1 September 1999: A Survey Conducted by the National Social Work Qualifications Board*, Dublin: NSWQB.

NWHB [North Western Health Board] (2003), 'Optimising children's residential care provision within the continuum of care provision in the North Western Health Board'. Internal NWHB document, 10 June.

NYCI [National Youth Council of Ireland] (1994), *Towards the Development of a Comprehensive Youth Service*, Dublin: NYCI in association with the Task Force on Youth Policy.

O'Brien, J and L. O'Brien (1989), *Framework for Accomplishment*, Georgia: Responsive Systems Associates.

O'Carroll, I. and E. Collins (eds) (1995), *Lesbian and Gay Visions of Ireland*, London: Cassells.

O'Connor, J. and M. Walsh (1986), *It's Our Home: The Quality of Life in Private and Voluntary Nursing Homes*, Dublin: National Council for the Aged.

O'Connor, P. (1992), 'The professionalisation of childcare work in Ireland: An unlikely development', *Children and Society* 6 (3). pp. 250–66.

O'Connor, P. (1998), *Emerging Voices: Women in Irish Society*, Dublin: Institute of Public Administration.

O'Grady, M. (2001), *An Introduction to Behavioural Science*, Dublin: Gill & Macmillan.

O'Loingsigh, D. (2001), 'Intercultural education and the school ethos', in F. Farrell and P. Watt (eds), *Responding to Racism in Ireland*, Dublin: Veritas.

O Neill, E. (2000), *Professional Supervision in Social Care*, Dublin: Resident Managers' Association.

O'Neill, M. (2001), 'Utilitarianism and punishment' (www.people.fas.harvard.edu/~mponeill/law/utilitarianism.html).

O'Nualláin, S. and M. Forde (1992), *Changing Needs of Irish Travellers: Health Education and Social Issues*, Renmore, Galway: Woodland Centre.

O'Reilly, M. (1993), *With Travellers: A Handbook for Teachers*, Blackrock: Blackrock Teachers Centre.

O'Toole, J. (1998), 'Young women in rural Ireland'. Unpublished M.Soc.Sc thesis, Department of Sociology, University College Dublin.

Oakley, A. (1972), *Sex, Gender and Society*, London: Temple Smith.

Orme, J. (2001), *Gender and Community Care*, London: Palgrave.

Owens, G. and K. Chard (2003), 'Comorbidity and psychiatric diagnoses among women reporting child sexual abuse', *Child Abuse and Neglect* 27 (9). pp. 1075–82.

Pahl, J. and M. Vaile (1986), *Health and Healthcare Among Travellers*, Canterbury: University of Kent, Health Services Research Unit.

Parker, R. (1980), *Caring for Separated Children: Plans, Procedures and Priorities*, London: Macmillan.

Pearson, K. (1996), 'Care leavers and their babies', in D. Howe (ed), *Attachment and Loss in Child and Family Social Work*, Aldershot: Avebury.

Phelan, M. (1988), 'The certification of child and youth care workers', in G. Charles and P. Gabor (eds), *Issues in Child and Youth Care Practice*, Lethbridge: Lethbridge Community College.

Phillipson, C., M. Bernard, J. Phillips and J. Ogg (2001), *The Family and Community Life of Older People*, London: Routledge.

Pine, B., R. Warsh and A. Maluccio (2003), 'Participatory management in public child welfare agency: a key to effective change', in J. Reynolds et al. (eds), *The Managing Care Reader*, New York: Routledge.

Pinkerton, J. and R. McCrea (1999), *Meeting the Challenge: Young People Leaving Care in Northern Ireland*, Aldershot: Ashgate.

Pollack, A. (1999), 'An invitation to racism? Irish daily newspaper coverage of the refugee issue', in D. Kiberd (ed), *Media in Ireland: The Search for Ethical Journalism*, Dublin: Open Air.

Popkin, R. (1998), *The Columbia History of Western Philosophy*, New York: Columbia University Press.

Popkin, R. and A. Stroll (2000), *Philosophy*, Oxford: Butterworth Heinemann.

Powell, F. (1999), 'New millennium, new social work?', *Irish Social Worker* 17 (Autumn/Winter). p. 14.

Power, K. (1993), 'The basic strategy', in *Module 4: Focus on the Individual*, The National Certificate in Vocational Rehabilitation. Dublin: The Open Training College (distance education package).

Pringle, M. (1996), *The Needs of Children*. London: Routledge.

Putnam, R. (2000), *Bowling Alone: The Collapse and Revival of American Community*, New York: Simon and Schuster.

Quinn, G., M. McDonagh and C. Kimber (1993), *Disability Discrimination Law in the United States, Australia and Canada*, Dublin: Oak Tree Press/National Rehabilitation Board.

Raftery, M. and E. O'Sullivan (1999), *Suffer the Little Children: The Inside Story of Ireland's Industrial Schools*, Dublin: New Island.

RAPID (2002), *Blanchardstown RAPID Plan*, Dublin: RAPID.

Residential Forum (1998), *A Golden Opportunity. A Report on Training and Staff Development for People Working in Residential Services for Children and Young People*, London: National Institute for Social Work.

RIA [Royal Irish Academy] (2003), *Mosaic or Melting Pot? Living with Diversity*, Dublin: European Cultural Foundation and Royal Irish Academy.

Richards, J. (2003), Draft report of the review by Mr John Richards of Residential Care Services for children in the South Eastern Health Board. Internal South Eastern Health Board document.

Richardson ,V. (1999), 'Children and social policy', in S. Quin et al. (eds) *Contemporary Irish Social Policy*, Dublin: University College Dublin Press.

Ricks, F. (1989), 'Self-awareness model for training and application in child and youth care', *Journal of Child and Youth Care* 4 (1). pp. 33–41.

Ricks, F. (1992), 'Educating the enemy: A correspondence on feminist influences in child and youth care', *Journal of Child and Youth Care* 7 (2). pp. 75–94.

Ricks, F. (2001), 'Without the self there is no other'. *CYC-OnLine* 27 (www.cyc-net.org/cyc-online/cycol-0401-ricks.html).

Ricks, F., P. Laliberte, V. Savicki and F. Hare (1991), 'Child and Youth Care Education Consortium: Report on the consideration of accreditation for child and youth care education programmes', *Journal of Child and Youth Care* 7 (1). pp. 110–17.

Rogers, C. (1961), *On Becoming a Person: A Therapist's View of Psychotherapy*, Boston: Houghton Mifflin.

Rogers, S., S. Ozonoff and C. Maslin-Cole (1991), 'A comparative study of attachment behaviour in young children with autism or other psychiatric disorders', *Journal of the American Academy of Child and Adolescent Psychiatry* 30. pp. 483–8.

Roisman, G., E. Padron, L. Sroufe and B. Egeland (2002), 'Earned-secure attachment status in retrospect and prospect', *Child Development* 73 (4). pp. 1204–19.

Ruddle, H., F. Donoghue and R. Mulvihill (1997), *The Years Ahead Report: A Review of the Implementation of its Recommendations*, Dublin: National Council on Ageing and Older People.

Ruth, S. (1988), 'Understanding oppression and liberation', *Studies*, Winter, pp. 434–44.

Rutter, M. (1981), *Maternal Deprivation Reassessed*, Harmondsworth: Penguin.

Rutter, M. (1995), 'Clinical implications of attachment concepts: retrospect and prospect', *Journal of Child Psychology and Psychiatry* 36 (4). pp. 549–71.

Rutter, M. and M. Rutter (1993), *Developing Minds: Challenges and Continuities Across the Life-span*, Harmondsworth: Penguin.

Ryan, M. (2000), 'The community child care worker'. Unpublished BA(Hons) Dissertation, Athlone Institute of Technology.

Ryan, T. and K. Walker (1993), *Life Story Work*, London: Sage.

Sagi, A., N. Koren-Karie, M. Gini, Y. Ziv and T. Joels (2002), 'Shedding further light on the effects of various types and quality of early childcare on infant-mother attachment relationship: The Haifa study of early childcare', *Child Development* 73 (4). pp. 1166–86.

Sameroff, A. and B. Fiese (1990), 'Transactional regulation and early intervention', in S. Meisels and J. Shonkoff (eds), *Handbook of Early Childhood Intervention*, New York: Cambridge University Press.

Sanders, G. (1996), 'Recovering from paraphilia: An adolescent's journey from despair to hope', *Journal of Child and Youth Care* 11 (1). pp. 43–54.

Santrock, J. (1994), *Child Development*, New York: McGraw-Hill.

SCA [Social Care Association] (1991), *Keyworking in Social Care: An Introductory Guide*, London: Social Care Association.

Scher, A. and O. Mayseless (2000), 'Mothers of anxious/ambivalent infants: Maternal characteristics and childcare context', *Child Development* 71. pp. 1629–39.

Schore, A. (2000), 'The effects of early relational trauma on right brain development, affect regulation and infant mental health', *Infant Mental Health Journal* 22. pp. 201–69.

Schuller, T. and M. Young (1991), *Life After Work: The Arrival of the Ageless Society*, London: Harper Collins.

SEHB [South Eastern Health Board] (1998), *Annual Report 1997.*

SHB [Southern Health Board] 1999, *Ageing with Confidence: A Strategy for the People of Cork and Kerry*, Cork: Southern Health Board (www.shb.ie/content 1517140157_1.cfm).

Sheldon, E. and W. Moore (1968), 'Monitoring social change in American society', in E. Sheldon and W. Moore (eds), *Indicators of Social Change. Concepts and Measurements*, New York: Sage.

Shipman, K., J. Zeman, M. Fitzgerald and L. Swisher (2003), 'Regulating emotion in parent–child and peer relationships: A comparison of sexually maltreated and non-maltreated girls', *Child Maltreatment* 8 (3). pp. 163–72.

Sinclair, I. and I. Gibbs (1998), *Children's Homes: A Study in Diversity*, Chichester: Wiley.

Sipe, R. (1990), *A Secret World: Sexuality and the Search for Celibacy*, New York: Brunner/Mazel.

Skehill, C. (1999), *The Nature of Social Work in Ireland*, Lampeter: Mellen.

Skinner, A. (1992), *Another Kind of Home: A Review of Residential Child Care*, Edinburgh: Scottish Office.

Smiar, N. (1995), 'Respect in the face of violence: Keeping everybody safe', *Reclaiming Children and Youth* 4 (2). pp. 34–8.

Smith, A. (1991), *National Identity*, London: Penguin.

Smith, C. (1994), *Partnership in Action: Developing Effective Aftercare Projects*, Westerham: Royal Philanthropic Society.

Snow, J. (1989), 'The role of disability in shaping responsive community', in J. O'Brien and L. O'Brien (eds), *Framework for Accomplishment*, Georgia: Responsive Systems Associates.

Spieker, S. and L. Bensley (1994), 'Roles of living arrangements and grandmothers' social support in adolescent mothering and infant attachment development', *Psychology* 30. pp. 102–11.

SRSB [Special Residential Services Board] (2003), *Definition and Usage of High Support in Ireland*, Dublin: Special Residential Services Board.

SSI [Social Services Inspectorate] (2002), *Annual Report 2001*, Dublin: Stationery Office.

SSI [Social Services Inspectorate] (2003), *Annual Report 2002*, Dublin: Stationery Office.

Steele, H. (2002), 'Attachment theory', *The Psychologist* 15 (10). pp. 518–22.

Stein, M. (1992), *Leaving Care: From Research into Practice. The National Leaving Care Advisory Service*, London: First Key.

Stein, M. (1997), *What Works in Leaving Care*, Ilford: Barnardo's.

Stein, M. and K. Carey (1986), *Leaving Care*, Oxford: Blackwell.

Stratton, E. and B. McPartland (2002), *An Inquiry into Equal Opportunities of Employment for Non-EU Nationals in Ireland with an Examination of Practice in the Health Board*, Dublin: National College of Ireland. (www.ncirl.ie/Research/ working_papers/NCIRL-018-2002.doc).

Stuart, C. (2001), 'Professionalising child and youth care: Continuing the Canadian journey', *Journal of Child and Youth Care Work* 15/16. pp. 264–82.

Suomi, S. and H. Harlow (1972), 'Social rehabilitation of isolate reared monkeys', *Developmental Psychology* 6. pp. 487–96.

Takahasi, K. (1990), 'Are the key assumptions of the strange situation procedure universal? A view from Japanese research', *Human Development* 33, pp. 23–30.

Task Force on Child Care Services (1980), *Final Report to the Minister for Health: Task Force on Child Care Services*, Dublin: Stationery Office.

Task Force on the Travelling Community (1995), *Report of the Task Force on the Travelling Community*, Dublin: Stationery Office.

Terr, L. (1990), *Too Scared to Cry*, New York: Basic Books.

Thompson, N. (1997), *Anti-Discriminatory Practice*, Basingstoke: Macmillan.

Toolan, D. (2001), 'Considering a rights approach to disabled people's identity within Irish society', in: *Module 2: Key Issues*, Bachelor of Arts in Applied Social Studies (Disability), Dublin: The Open Training College (distance education package).

Torode, R., T. Walsh and M. Woods (2001), *Working With Refugees and Asylum-Seekers: A Social Work Resource Book*, Dublin: Department of Social Studies, Trinity College.

Tovey, H. and P. Share (2003), *A Sociology of Ireland*, Dublin: Gill & Macmillan.

Travelling People Review Body (1983), *Report of the Travelling People Review Body*, Dublin: Stationery Office.

Treadwell, K. (1998), 'Border crossings: negotiating marginalities and accommodating health issues among Irish Travellers'. Unpublished MA thesis, NUI Maynooth.

Tremblay, C., M. Hebert and C. Piche (1999), 'Coping strategies and social support as mediators of consequences in child sexual abuse victims', *Child Abuse and Neglect* 23. pp. 929–45.

Trieschman, A., J. Whittaker and L. Brendtro (1969), *The Other 23 Hours: Child Care Work With Emotionally Disturbed Children in a Therapeutic Milieu*, New York: Aldine de Gruyter.

Tuarim (1966), *Some of Our Children: A Report on the Residential Care of the Deprived Child in Ireland*, London: Tuarim.

van den Boom, D. (1995), 'Do first-year intervention effects endure? Follow-up during toddlerhood of a sample of Dutch irritable infants', *Child Development* 66. pp. 1798–816.

van Ijzendoorn, M. (1995), 'Adult attachment representation, parental responsiveness and infant attachment: A meta-analysis on the predictive validity of the adult attachment interview', *Psychological Bulletin* 117. pp. 387–403.

van Leeuwen, M. (ed) (1993), *After Eden*, Michigan: Eerdmans.

VanderVen, K. (1992), 'Developmental care: A proposal for a new profession whose time is coming', *Journal of Child and Youth Care* 7 (4). pp. 3–38.

Veale, A., L. Palaudaries and C. Gibbons (2003), *Separated Children Seeking Asylum in Ireland*, Dublin: Irish Refugee Council (www.irishrefugeecouncil.ie/pub03/sepchild-report.doc).

Vekić, K. (2003), *Unaccompanied Minors in Ireland: From Understanding to Response*, Dublin: Marino Institute.

Walby, S. (1990), *Theorising Patriarchy*, Oxford: Blackwell.

Waller, G. (1991), 'Sexual abuse as a factor in eating disorders', *British Journal of Psychiatry* 159. pp. 664–71.

Walmsley, J. (ed) (1993), *Health, Welfare and Practice*, London: Sage/Open University.

Ward, A. (1998), *Intuition is Not Enough: Matching Learning with Practice in Therapeutic Childcare*, New York: Routledge.

Ward, T. (2001), *Immigration and Residency in Ireland*, Dublin: City of Dublin Vocational Education Committee.

Waters, E., C. Hamilton and N. Weinfield (2000), 'The stability of attachment security from infancy to adolescence and early adulthood: General introduction', *Child Development* 71 (3). pp. 678–83.

Waters, E., G. Posada, J. Crowell and K. Lay (1993), 'Is attachment theory ready to contribute to our understanding of disruptive behaviour problems?' *Development and Psychopathology* 54. pp. 215–24.

Waters, E., N. Weinfield and C. Hamilton (2000), 'The stability of attachment security from infancy to adolescence and early adulthood: General discussion', *Child Development* 71 (3). pp. 703–6.

Weiss, R. (1991), 'The attachment bond in childhood and adulthood', in C. Parkes, J. Stevenson-Hinde and P. Marris (eds), *Attachment Across the Life Cycle*, London: Routledge.

Wekerle, C. and D. Wolfe (2003), 'Child maltreatment', in E. Mash and R. Barkley (eds), *Child Psychopathology*, London: Guilford.

Wexford Area Partnership (2000), *Social Inclusion Plan for the Wexford Area 2000–2006*, Wexford: Wexford Area Partnership.

Whitaker, D., J. Cook, C. Dunne and N. Redcliffe (1984), *The Experience of Residential Care from the Perspectives of Children, Parents and Care Givers*, University of York: SSRC Final Report.

Whitaker, D., L. Archer and L. Hicks (1998), *Working in Children's Homes: Challenges and Complexities*, Chichester: Wiley.

Whitfield, C., R. Anda, S. Dube and V. Felitta (2003), 'Violent childhood experiences and the risk of intimate partner violence in adults: Assessment in a large health maintenance organization', *Journal of Interpersonal Violence* 18 (2). pp. 166–85.

WHO [World Health Organisation] (1980), *International Classification of Impairments, Disabilities, and Handicaps: A Manual of Classification Relating to the Consequences of Disease*, Geneva: World Health Organisation

WHO [World Health Organisation] (2002), *Toward a Common Language for Functioning, Disability and Health*, Geneva: World Health Organisation.

Wieczorek-Deering, D., S. Greene, J. Nugent and R. Graham (1991), 'Classification of attachment and its determination in urban Irish infants', *Irish Journal of Psychology* 12. pp. 216–34.

Williams, D. and K. Lalor (2000), 'Obstacles to the professionalisation of residential care in Ireland', *Irish Journal of Applied Social Studies* 2 (3). pp. 73–90.

Williams, R. (1976), *Keywords*, London: Flamingo.

Wolfe, D., L. Sas and C. Wekerle (1994), 'Factors associated with the development of posttraumatic stress disorder among child victims of sexual abuse', *Child Abuse and Neglect* 18. pp. 37–50.

Wolfensberger, W. (1975), 'The evolution of the institutional model in the United States', in *The Origin and Nature of Our Institutional Models*, New York: Human Policy Press.

Woods, M. (2000), 'How far can law take us?', *Frontline of Learning Disability* 42. pp. 14–15.

Wyatt, G. and M. Newcombe (1990), 'Internal and external mediators of women's sexual abuse in childhood', *Journal of Consulting Psychology* 58. pp. 758–67.

# Index